STUDIES IN
WAR ECONOMICS

prepared at
THE OXFORD UNIVERSITY
INSTITUTE OF STATISTICS

A selection of articles, reprinted from the
BULLETIN OF THE INSTITUTE OF STATISTICS
and other periodicals

BASIL BLACKWELL
OXFORD
1947

6767

Printed in Great Britain for BASIL BLACKWELE & MOTT, LIMITED
by A. R. MOWBRAY & CO. LIMITED, London and Oxford

FOREWORD

FROM 1939 to 1945, the work of the Institute of Statistics centred mainly on the study of economic problems which were directly or indirectly connected with the war. The mobilization of manpower, the concentration of non-essential industries, the various techniques of economic control, the development of appropriate financial policies, the effects of the war on the welfare of different social classes—these were among the subjects which were periodically investigated. The results of most of the investigations were published, at the time, in the Institute's *Bulletin*; but the circulation of the *Bulletin* was necessarily limited and back numbers have long since been out of print.

As examples in the application of modern economic theory to contemporary problems, much of this work seemed to be of sufficient general interest to justify re-publication in a readily accessible form. Moreover, many of the problems connected with the present period of reconstruction, of which the world shortages of basic raw materials and foodstuffs are only the most obvious examples, are in some respects very similar to the problems which had to be tackled during the war; many of the changes which were brought about by the war may also be expected to have long-lasting effects on the national economy. A study of war-time experience may, therefore, be able to throw valuable light on some of our present-day problems. Accordingly, a selection has been made from articles which were prepared by members of the Institute on problems of war economics and these are now republished in the present volume.

In the rapidly changing circumstances of the war, it was frequently necessary to deal, at short notice, with urgent problems as they arose, and it was not generally possible—nor did it seem desirable— to present the implications of every argument with the fullness and rigour which would be appropriate in more leisured circumstances. Some of the articles are thus very topical in character but the attempt was made to consider the general principles involved in each particular problem, and its bearing on the system as a whole. No attempt has been made to cover all the problems of a war economy, or to link the different articles together.

War-time research was, of course, severely handicapped by the fact that publication of a great many statistics was discontinued. There was a notable advance, on the other hand, in the preparation of official estimates of the national income and expenditure, which were published in successive White Papers. The available figures on these and other subjects were naturally subject to continuous, and sometimes quite substantial, revision; and, since the end of the war, a great deal of new information has become available.

In those cases where the conclusions are materially affected, or where the substitution could be easily made, the articles included in this volume have been revised, on the basis of the most recent data available at the time of going to print. In other cases, it did not seem necessary to make changes in detail which would not affect the general outline. Various minor changes have also been introduced into the text of some of the articles; except in regard to the work of Mr. Kalecki, who was absent from the country, these changes have all been made by the respective authors. In a few cases, where direct information was lacking and figures therefore had to be estimated by indirect methods, the articles have been left in their original form, partly in order to illustrate the use of statistical methods which circumstances made necessary. By the time this book is published, new figures will probably again have become available; but, on matters of this kind, we can only ask for the reader's indulgence.

Acknowledgements are due to the Editors of *Economica, The Review of Economic Studies, The Banker,* and *Oxford Economic Papers* for kindly granting permission to republish articles which first appeared in these journals.

It is necessary to add, finally, that the ideas and recommendations put forward are those of the respective authors, and not necessarily those of the Institute of Statistics or of the Editor of the *Bulletin.*

July, 1946.

CONTENTS

STUDIES IN WAR ECONOMICS

I. ECONOMIC MOBILIZATION AND GENERAL CONTROLS

THE CONTROLS AND WAR FINANCE[1]

REPRINTED FROM *Oxford Economic Papers* BY THE COURTESY OF THE EDITORS

by Ian Bowen and G. D. N. Worswick

IF war has completely silenced the voice of the theoretical economist, it has brought the problems of practical economics nearer home. The man in the street is once more familiar with terms such as inflation, vicious spirals, rationing, and forced savings. The realities of the problems of allocating scarce supplies seem, moreover, to be easier *in principle* to grapple with intellectually than the problems of unemployment, of 'plenty', of advancing technique that paradoxically haunted mankind in the nightmare days of peace.

The problems of war economics are indeed not difficult to state. First, is the problem of organizing the full employment of all available national resources. Secondly, some criterion—not necessarily economic—has to be used in deciding the allocation of resources to various outputs. Thirdly, this criterion has to be applied in such a way that the output as a whole is suitably complementary—it is not enough merely to establish priorities; it is also necessary to see that tanks are not made without guns, aeroplanes without scientific instruments, and so on. Finally, there is the problem of financial and price policy which in war-time is used as an indirect means of attaining the rapid transfer of real resources to the war effort; finance is only one, and not necessarily the most important, of the methods to be used for this purpose.

Finance in war-time is thrust down into its proper place as hand-

---

[1] This article, written in June, 1940, and published in *Oxford Economic Papers*, No. 4, is reprinted without any amendment of substance.

The appendix of this article has been omitted, except for a brief excerpt which has here been incorporated in the text.

See also a further article on Raw Material Controls in *Oxford Economic Papers*, No. 6.

maiden to the real economic policies of the country; but even in war-time an ill-designed financial policy may hamper in some degree the efforts at solving the pressing economic problems of scarcity. If too much money is allowed to reach the pockets of the spending public—too much, that is, relative to the total consumption and investment goods which the War-Plan has allocated for private purchase in the period concerned—then there will be either a rise of prices or, worse still, an upsetting of the War-Plan, and the diversion of much-needed economic effort to satisfying private demands.

The part played by the raw material Controls in the finance of the war might easily be viewed as threefold: they can be used to cut down private investment to a minimum (the technique for this is simply to refuse licences for raw materials to any one who cannot produce a contract reference from a Government Department); the Controls can also be used as an indirect means of 'rationing' private consumption—but the word rationing here tends in practice to mean 'limiting the total supply available for'; and thirdly, the Controls are a handy instrument for regulating raw materials prices.

The purpose of the Controls may be stated quite generally; in war-time, when the national effort ought to be at its most intense, and when the use of material and man-power must put a strain on all available resources, real private investment and consumption must be cut down, so that the maximum proportion of our limited resources may be devoted to the war. There would be a scarcity of resources in relation to the national effort just as much if the country were self-supporting as if she were trading overseas. The special difficulty of shipping-space for certain—indeed, for all—of our vital imports is only an acute example of an ever-present difficulty; the scarcity is due not to our being an island—though that exacerbates it in certain directions—but to our limited man-power and limited purchasing-power.

The Timber, the Non-ferrous Metal, and the Iron and Steel Controls furnish ready examples of the effect on private real investment of the Controls' activities, and while timber is scarce chiefly in terms of shipping-space, and iron and steel in terms of plant and labour (and also, of course, shipping-space), non-ferrous metals fall somewhere between the two. The financial ban on new issues and on capital issues by local authorities[1] stopped virtually all new civil

[1] S. R. & O., 1939, No. 1620, dated November 23rd, p. 11.

building'.[1] Under section 6, sub-section (5) of the Finance Regulation[2] referred to, even mortgages, whether legal or equitable, were brought under the general treasury ban if issued by any local authority or by any person carrying on a business other than banking. These stringent and effective regulations were subject to a fierce attack in the press by architects and others interested in building, but the assault was resisted largely on the plea that the suspension of civil building activity was dictated by the shortage of the essential raw material, timber.[3]

All other building materials were in relatively plentiful supply, but 60 per cent of our normal imports of timber were cut off in the early months of the war (in terms of value). Under Order 5 of the Timber Control (dated September 30, 1939) it was decreed that no person should consume timber without a licence from the Minister of Supply, exemptions being granted only for very small quantities. The financial regulations, strict as they were, left open the possibility of individuals or firms with liquid resources embarking on new building; the Timber Control, by Orders No. 1 and 5 (dated September 1st and 30th), effectively blocked this and other loop-holes, although no doubt private finance has been responsible for such civil building as has escaped the double mesh. The 'rationing' imposed by the Timber Control has been strictly of the type of limiting the total amount released for civilian building purposes; this at least has been the general effect of the scheme, although its purpose has perhaps not been clearly realized in responsible quarters.

It is difficult, for instance, to fit into the general picture of the scheme the statement of Mr. Burgin to the Timber Trades Association. He said[4] that the 'national stocks bought by the Timber Controller would shortly be distributed. This, he assumed, would be done equitably on a quota basis having regard to past turnover and stocks.' But what significance have past turnover and stocks? Some firms may be well placed to do civilian work and hopelessly equipped for the receipt of a Government contract. Why should their past and peace-time activity be the test of their present capacity? It is fairly safe to conjecture that Mr. Burgin had in mind 'past turnover and stocks' as a rough basis for a 'fair' distribution of supplies,

---

[1] Letter to *The Times*, December 29, 1939, from E. Stanley Hall, President of the R.I.B.A.
[2] S. R. O & O., 1939, No. 1620.
[3] *Hansard*, April 4, 1940, Col. Llewellin: 'So far as the Ministry of Supply is concerned no ban has been placed on civil building, except in so far as arises out of the inability to release . . . more than a limited quantity of certain materials used in building which are in short supply.'
[4] *Financial Times*, April 13, 1940.

which would mitigate the criticisms of bias and favouritism so often levelled against the Controls. But the desire to preserve the *status quo ante bellum* may have influenced him, as it appears to have influenced so many administrators who were at heart opposed to a thorough-going planning in war conditions.[1]

The Iron and Steel Control presents the same picture of a clear purpose, in the main achieved, but partly yielding to the prejudice in favour of the principle of business as usual. In this industry there is little doubt that important persons in charge of the Control were at first inspired by the belief that 'Great Britain could produce as much iron and steel as she wants'. Overtime, increased numbers of employees, the bringing into production of idle furnaces, the building of new ones would, it was sometimes argued, result in an output at least equal to the armaments and civilian demands of 1939–40. With this strange view prevailing in high quarters it was not surprising that the Ministry of Supply, the Air Ministry, and the Admiralty (and the Home Departments) placed orders the satisfying of which would require an iron and steel consumption far in excess of the output capacity of the industry in this country. Thus, for the first seven months of the war orders were placed mainly by the Service departments with apparent disregard of total capacity, and the Iron and Steel Control confined its activities to orders that 'priorities' should in general be observed without noting that the demands of the first priorities were by themselves in excess of possible supply.

It was, indeed, the practice of prudent steel-consuming firms to quote Government contract numbers when ordering their requirements as evidence of how high up in the priority list their needs came, but there was no mechanism to ensure that the total amount of iron and steel ordered in a period should bear a strict relation to the supply available. It was thus inevitable that while order-books stayed filled, deliveries should fall into arrears.

The restriction on civil use of iron and steel is, and has been since the beginning of the war, almost absolute; but it was a result only in a confused way of deliberate planning. The Iron and Steel Control Orders gave early in the war a list of priorities in which civilian needs were given a very low place; but the effective prohibition of the use of iron and steel for other than direct military or Government needs

[1] Or cf. *The Times*, April 17, 1940: 'Members of the (shipbuilding) industry have derived some encouragement from the statement of Mr. R. S. Hudson, the new Minister of Shipping . . . that he was giving "the very difficult question of the shipbroking industry" his personal attention.'

came from the fact that the military departments—prudently in a sense—over-ordered and thus filled up the available capacity. On April 4th a complete scheme for the distribution of steel was announced in the form of Control of Iron and Steel (No. 8) Order.[1] The aim is to allocate every ton of steel to the best possible use and the Order is one of considerable complexity. The main outline is as follows:

The chief users of the main types of steel, which are listed in the Order, are grouped under twenty-six 'Departments'. Many of these 'Departments' correspond to actual Government departments, for example, Home Office, Air Ministry, and so on, but there are also some which have no such counterpart, for example, Electricity Commissioners. Finally, some Government departments cover two or more such 'Departments'; for example, Board of Trade (1), (2), (3), (4), and (5) are 'Departments'. The year is divided into four quarterly periods numbered I, II, III, and IV. Each 'Department' presents to the Joint Production and Materials Priority Sub-Committee its estimated requirements of finished steel in each period, and these estimates are related by the Sub-Committee, in conjunction with the Iron and Steel Control, to the total estimated capacity of the steel industry in that period. Allocations are then made to each 'Department' of 'global tonnages' of each type of steel required by it, and each 'Department' proceeds to allocate its tonnage among its main contractors and they among their sub-contractors.[2] In the case of building programmes of departments the Joint Production and Materials Priority Sub-Committee makes a special allocation to the Works and Building Priority Sub-Committee, who in turn allocate the tonnage among the various 'Departments', but each 'Department' will have the administration of its own quota in this connection.

In the case of contracts not placed by or for a 'Department' no licence is required under the scheme, but the purchase of the steel required for the contract must be approved, and in effect placed by one of the twenty-six 'Departments' named by the Order for that purpose. This rather obscure clause covers contracts for the delivery of steel for A.R.P., Schools, Health Services, Northern Ireland public services, railways, and agricultural machinery.

[1] S. R. & O., 1940, No. 496. The official circular from the Controller to Producers said: 'The Ministry of Supply felt it desirable that the requirements of Government Departments and Services . . . should be brought within the estimated capacity of the Industry to deliver. . . .'
[2] The allocations for certain steel users seem to be based upon the consumption for the corresponding quarter of 1939.

The new scheme is mainly intended to save from the allegedly rapacious maw of the Services some supplies for civil departments and for Board of Trade reservations for exports, or for the replacement of parts in factories privately or publicly owned; new civil investment involving the use of iron and steel is necessarily barred by the refusal which the Board of Trade would give to any request for a licence for such purpose. A survey in Birmingham[1] revealed that there was little question of leakage into undesirable civil investment; no maker of stoves or baths or piping—of any class of goods that might be for private or Government use—could obtain material to fulfil an order (or to replace his stocks) unless he was able to quote to the supplier a Government contract number. From the manufacturer's point of view this has been the situation since the beginning of the war.

The smaller engineering firms are engaged almost 100 per cent on war work, direct or indirect. Those whose products are not as much in demand by Government departments as by civilians, and who cannot turn their plant and skill to a new type of output, are being rapidly forced out of business; but it is a minority of them that are in this doubly unfortunate position. Most of them are either selling a product that is needed by the Government or are able to switch over their output quickly. The problem of diverting resources from civil to military (or Government) purposes is thus not so insoluble as might be thought in this trade; it presents much less difficulty than the problem presented, for instance, by surplus building labour. Engineers (especially in the small, individually highly skilled firms) are singularly adaptable although they are specialists; and the main problem in these trades is that of correct technical co-ordination rather than of adapting or absorbing resources.

Rationing of iron and steel to the engineering trades has inevitably, under the official schemes, devolved in practice partly upon the iron and steel manufacturers themselves. Since over-ordering was rife—and even now arrears so caused have not been worked off—the iron and steel manufacturers found the responsibility of deciding which consumers should finally receive their output devolving upon their own heads, and they naturally followed the principle of trying to satisfy as many of their old, or good, customers as they could; they even might have to decide from time to time whether an Air Ministry,

---

[1] A survey undertaken in the Spring of 1940 by the authors of this article of the effects of the Iron and Steel Control Orders on a representative sample of Birmingham engineering firms.

say, or an Admiralty contract should have precedence when immediate delivery was required.

That section of the Non-ferrous Metals Control that covers copper, lead, and zinc was forced to adopt a complete licensing system from the beginning of the war; the metals concerned were in too scarce a supply, coming mainly, in the case of copper and lead, from the overseas Empire, and necessary for the French as well as our own war industries, to allow for trifling with their allocation. From Control Order No. 1 (dated September 1, 1939)[1] all transactions in these metals were subject to the Ministry of Supply's approval and licence.

In non-ferrous metals, however, as in the case of timber, a kindly regard for the vested interests in the industry seems to have obscured the clear lines of policy that might otherwise have emerged. The immediate effect of the Control Orders was the closing of the London Metal Exchange, since middlemen and middlemen's profits were no longer required as all consumers could buy direct from the Ministry of Supply; the merchants of the Metal Exchange protested loudly, and to some extent effectively, for by Control Order No. 5 (dated December 16, 1939)[2] additions to maximum prices were allowed in certain circumstances 'in accordance with trade usage'; and representatives of the Metal Exchange were appointed to the Advisory Committee of the Control.

It is, however, fairly safe to assert that this compromise with the *status quo* principle affected price policy—if it affected policy at all— rather than rationing policy. The rationing policy of the Non-ferrous Metals Control has successfully diverted all supplies to firms working on Government orders or for the export trade. In the Birmingham survey it appeared that the Non-ferrous Metals Control was well organized, and business-like in its dealing even with small firms, in contrast with the delays sometimes met with among the other Controls. There was little sign among the Birmingham trades of a serious leakage to non-ferrous production for the civilian home market.

Controls and the distribution of raw material

Private consumption and private investment have undoubtedly been reduced at the 'production end' of the economic system by the action of the Controls. It remains to consider whether their rationing and distribution policy has been equally successful, and whether their

---

[1] S. R. & O., 1939, No. 997.   [2] S. R. & O., 1939, No. 1812.

policy in relation to prices has represented a happy compromise between *laissez faire* and complete control.

Rationing has varied considerably in scope and in purpose from one Control to another. Iron and steel are subject to restriction to the 'global' tonnages allotted to each department. Wool has been rationed for civilian purposes from November 1, 1939, the amount of an individual firm's civilian ration being controlled by a series of committees and a presiding council. Paper has been cut down since Feb. 12th, 1940, to 60 per cent of pre-war requirements; this percentage has since been reduced farther, and individual firms may receive only 30 per cent of their pre-war supplies. Cotton, rayon, and linen piece goods are rationed at the wholesale stage, sales being restricted to 75 per cent of pre-war production; in the case of linen alone the cut has been to 25 per cent.

Thus materials have sometimes been 'rationed' at the source, sometimes at a later stage. In some cases an attempt has been made to see that the allocation as between civilian firms should be equitable; in others, such as cotton, much power has been placed in the hands of wholesalers on whom the final allocation really devolves.

The allocation of raw materials in 'suitable' or 'correct' degrees of complementarity is difficult to assess; clearly the problem arises in its most acute form as a matter to be decided by the Ministry of Shipping. For unless shipping space is assigned appropriately as between one material and another, nothing that the Controls do at home can remedy the situation. Nor can the success of the Controls in releasing raw materials for civilian purposes be estimated solely in terms of correct complementarity, since, when the needs of the Forces have been provided for, it may well be that the residual materials do not dovetail with any easily foreseen precision.

It is well known that some firms have been held up for lack of, or delay in, the provision of one or other of the vital materials. Despite the general clauses in most of the Control Orders providing for emergency demands, it has often happened that a firm having dealings with several Controls found an essential material especially difficult to obtain, even though it needed only a small quantity. A cutting-tool might need repair, but the hard steel, although in plentiful supply near by, might not be obtainable by the firm without a Government permit; the permit would be written for; days later permit forms would arrive; they would be filled up and dispatched by return of post; a week later the permit itself might arrive. Meanwhile the cutting-tool, the machinery, and the arms output would be at a standstill.[1] Such delays as these are to be regarded, not as isolated incidents, but as examples of the failure of Government machinery to keep pace with a special problem—the issue of small quantities of scarce materials to vital strategic points in the industrial system.

It should perhaps be pointed out that while there is a local organization of the Ministry of Supply to deal with the contract-placing side of the Ministry's business,[2] the corresponding organization for the Controls does not seem to be so complete. These are all 'centralized' —if that term is not abused in describing Controls scattered over the country—and redress for delays is difficult to obtain.

Price policy of the Controls

The history of the Controls in the first nine months of the war does not suggest that a consistent price policy has been followed, or perhaps contemplated; this is a statement of fact and not necessarily a criticism, since a planned economy could hardly be introduced overnight. Raw material costs form a varying and usually relatively small percentage of the total costs of finished commodities; a rise in raw material costs is nevertheless not a negligible factor in the general movements towards higher prices. The policy of fixing raw material prices should therefore be fitted into the general financial plan of the Government, and must bear some relation to its monetary policy.

Freight costs of the neutral, and in less degree of the British, mercantile marine of course rose enormously during the period under consideration. The Controls, had they wished to stabilize raw material prices, would have had to accept or to subsidize a rising loss on the materials that they handled or controlled; their policy in general was to permit prices to follow the change in costs, but the Controls differed from each other in the degree to which they allowed this rise to act as a lever of rising commodity prices. The Iron and Steel Control followed the policy of raising the prices of finished and unfinished steel in due relation to each other. The Wool Control, on the other hand, kept the price of raw wool stable from the middle of October until the beginning of March, but allowed yarn prices to rise steadily. The Cotton Control left the price of raw cotton to the mercy of speculators, but finally agreed in January, 1940, to fix the 'spinners' margins'. The Jute Control, after the first three weeks of the war, made no attempt to fix prices.

---

[1] Some instances of this kind were quoted to us in our survey in Birmingham.
[2] But the Admiralty and the Air Ministry place contracts separately, and sometimes in keen competition with the Ministry of Supply.

B

Prices and a planned economy

A war economy is necessarily planned. How great a degree of planning is required is a problem that opens up a wide field of discussion; it is apparent, for instance, that any complete price policy would have to be discussed in connection with wages policy, and with the question of how far the powers of industrial conscription should be used. It is indeed one of the main conclusions emerging from any study of the Controls that *partial* price control is totally inadequate to solve, or even to help solve, the financial problems of the war. It is clear that *in so far* as wages and employment have been uncontrolled, then the rise of commodity prices must have tended to results that have been inflationary; and there is a strong case to be made for more rigid stabilization.

In a planned economy the State may either fix the level of costs by decree, or allow costs to have an 'objective' meaning. Under the former system costs are purely fiat costs, and the amount of production of all goods has to be determined by the State; under the second system, even though productive resources may be under State control or ownership, prices still have to be fixed so that on the one hand supply is forthcoming and on the other no surpluses of commodities occur. Under one version of the first system prices might be allowed to find their own level, but profits or losses made by the various industrial trusts under Government control would not be used as a guide to future output; there would be fiat production as well as fiat costs, and the criterion of consumer's demand as a guide to output would be wholly rejected. Under the second system the State, if it were not content with the distribution of incomes, could effect redistribution by taxation and direct or indirect 'transfer' payments to the poorer members of the community, but costs would nevertheless have an 'economic' meaning (be equal to some estimate of the marginal product), even though they were not the sole determinants of final distribution.

The degree of control that can be exercised in the immediate future is likely to be nearer the second of these theoretical systems than the first, although later it may approach more nearly to the first. But whether or not cost is to have some economic meaning, if the war plan is to be fulfilled, some *stability* of costs is essential. No system of Government auditing yet devised is likely to be able to keep the prices charged by private enterprise under control if the entrepreneurs have the constant excuse to offer that all their costs are rising.

For this reason the policy of fixing the costs of raw materials for a considerable period ahead might well prove to be fruitful. Before the war most of the important raw materials of the world had their prices fixed by international cartel agreements; during the war the Government is the agent most suited to carry out the task of stabilization. This means the acceptance of some financial losses on the account of the Controls, but the rise in the cost of the final commodities sold to the Government would be correspondingly reduced. The losses on 'fiat costs' would be book-keeping losses.

How could this policy be carried out? It may be safely asserted that the Wool Control has hitherto evolved the simplest mechanism —even if it has not pursued necessarily the ideal policy—by purchasing the entire stock of the raw material that it has to deal with. The question arises whether, in principle, the Controls, if they become the sole buyers in all cases, should charge one, two, or more discriminating prices on resale. This question can only be answered in conjunction with a discussion of the general finance of the war; some specific conclusions may, however, be listed.

Prerequisites of a successful policy

The buying of all raw material by the Government is one essential step that might be taken. Whether requisitioning, 'fiat' prices, and rationing were to be introduced, or some less drastic variant of a planned economy, a successful policy requires a stricter attention to the objectives of Control than has yet been achieved. Not only must the objectives be understood by officials; they need also to be *explained* to business men. The need for publicity on behalf of the Controls became apparent on our industrial survey; business men frequently claimed that they did not understand the purposes of regulations with which they were anxious to comply, and the machinery to find out what they wanted to know was sometimes laborious as well as uncertain.

It is quite clear that costs—but not necessarily prices—need to be kept down for purposes of export. The setting up of boards to encourage exports is of little avail if costs are rising, and if the temptation to produce for the home market is not offset at the beginning.

Secondly, it is clear that in the first nine months of the war the home market has not been adequately restricted. The export drive cannot be successful without the imposition of much heavier sacrifices on the domestic consumer than he has yet faced.[1] This is particularly

---

[1] This statement perhaps requires modification in view of the recent closing of important European markets to our exports.

true in the case of luxury articles, but also applies to cotton goods and other goods of widespread consumption.

Thirdly, the regard for vested interests that has so far been a persisting feature of our war effort has to be diminished; for whatever may be said in favour of such an attitude in peace-time, it cannot be consistent with an economizing of skill and resources to make maximum profit and not maximum output the criterion of successful industrial management. On this point innumerable examples could be quoted from the history of the Controls as well as from other sources.

An even stronger line might indeed be taken by the Government at this point than has yet been suggested. The Controls have so far, in dealing with business interests which they have inevitably injured, been inclined to apologize for their actions, and excuse themselves on the ground that temporary inconvenience was unavoidable. But it is perhaps unwise to present too optimistic a view to the interests affected; the holding out of false hopes delays adjustments that were better made rapidly and finally.[1] The planned economy, moreover, has probably come to stay; in whose interests the plans will be made is a political question of the post-war world, but however that is answered, much of the mechanism of centralized buying and selling is likely to be too useful to destroy.

---

[1] In connexion with the Contracts side of the Ministry, it has, for instance, been unwise of the Minister of Supply to buoy up the hopes of small firms, whose products cannot conceivably in fact be wanted by the Government, with the idea that better organization would secure Government work for them.

MONEY INCENTIVE AND THE PRODUCTION DRIVE

by T. Balogh

FROM BULLETIN, VOL. 3, NO. 14 (OCTOBER 11, 1941)

IN the present note we propose to restrict ourselves to a discussion of the problem of incentive. It seems, however, to be necessary to state emphatically that the extension of rationing to cover all necessities of life is a *condition sine qua non* of any attempt to deal with the problem of promoting efficiency and effort through the money incentive without having to fear inflation, and is increasingly necessary if we are to be able to secure a just distribution of available scarce supplies, which seems the only basis for an optimum cut of civilian consumption, hence also of maximum war effort.

The problem of incentive can be divided into that of economic and that of non-economic incentive. To the latter belongs the problem of creating an atmosphere in which each individual is determined to give his best effort. Comprehensive rationing and compensation—as methods to ensure equality of sacrifice—would seem to fall in a certain sense into this field. So do measures of welfare enabling workers to devote themselves fully and without injurious effect to their health to the war effort. Finally, to the sector of non-economic incentive belongs the establishment of whole-hearted and intelligent co-operation between managements and workers which is still lacking in many industrial undertakings. Complaints have been made that the lack of knowledge about the object of orders and the frequent transfer of workers is a serious source of discontent impinging on the war effort. It is not possible in this context to enlarge on this topic.

Incentive for Labour

Turning to the question of economic incentive for labour, we must distinguish between two problems. There is first the problem of giving an incentive to achieve the highest possible effort by all, both in the so-called non-essential and in the so-called essential trades.[1] Secondly, we have to solve the problem of transferring

---

[1] This problem is of some urgency even from the point of view of full mobilization of man-power. The higher the output per head in non-essential trades, the more workers can be released to the war sector.

labour from non-essential to essential industries, and that of employing the hitherto non-employed. The transfer problem is a temporary one because eventually all unnecessary output, except by persons who cannot be adapted to change of occupation, ought to disappear.

The solution of the first problem, of ensuring generally maximum effort, in so far as it can be solved by the operation of economic incentive, depends on maintaining marginal income on a high level. A low marginal income, such as is produced by the reduction of the income tax exemption limits and an increase in the rate of tax, results *ceteris paribus* in disinclination to work harder. Though the greater part of the increase in income tax is in the nature of 'forced saving', psychologically it has had identical results with increased taxation. In so far as comprehensive rationing would also result in 'forced saving' it might be argued that the incentive of higher earnings would vanish even if they were not taxed at the source. This argument fails to take into account the different impression created by not being able to spend money which is 'available' and not receiving the money at all. But, apart from this 'irrational' reaction, 'deferred payment' cannot *now* be used for discharging capital liabilities, purchasing capital assets, or in case of emergencies. Rationing would not prevent such 'innocuous' use of income. One expedient of solving the problem is to exempt overtime pay as well as efficiency and output bonuses from income tax.[1] (This method was adopted in Germany, after the scheme of abolishing overtime pay and other bonuses during the war had broken down.) Several difficulties must be mentioned in this connection. Working hours have been stretched too long in certain cases from the point of view of efficiency, because the basic wage rates (that is, average income) were too low. It is possible, on the other hand, that the grant of too steeply rising overtime—if maximum hours are not fixed—will in any case lead to a decrease in effort during 'ordinary' working time so as to conserve energy for overtime. Remuneration by result would tend to check this tendency, but it is difficult to administer, especially as 'idling' due to reasons unconnected with workers (air-raids, shortage of raw materials or of parts) is said to be prevalent. The establishment of harmonious collaboration between managements and workers, perhaps buttressed by mixed regional, local and workshop boards, or committees to administer working conditions, might be useful in solving these problems.

[1] It would also be possible to issue additional rations to workers who have performed heavy work. The Russians have extensively used the system of discriminatory rationing for marginal incentive.

The solution of the second problem, the transfer of workers into the war sector, could be facilitated by keeping the average level of wages higher in the war than in the 'unessential' sector.

The Profit Incentive

The institution of the 100 per cent Excess Profits Tax was the psychological measure which seemed necessary to obtain the whole-hearted co-operation of the Labour Party in war industrial effort and to secure their consent to the relaxation of Trade Union restrictions. We now need more sustained effort in production. Proposals to decrease Excess Profits Tax further and to effect other changes with a view to restoring the profit incentive, not accompanied by a readjustment of the productive system, giving adequate representation and safeguards to labour, might again raise labour resistance.

With the present rate of income tax it would require a very drastic reduction in Excess Profits Tax to act as an incentive, and if the alleged beneficial results of industrial self-financing out of free profits are to be realized, even a 50 per cent Excess Profits Tax might still be too high.[1]

Moreover, 100 per cent Excess Profits Tax need not necessarily restrict the income of the people who are actually in charge of production, whereas it ensures that higher money rewards are not paid to people (shareholders) who do not contribute (*qua* shareholders) to the increased war effort. It is not so much the shareholders that need be given money incentives as the actual managers of the firms who under the present system are free to receive higher incomes corresponding to higher effort and could, just as workers and salaried employees, be given efficiency and output bonuses. The interest of shareholders should be safeguarded and hardships should be avoided, but it is doubtful whether they should receive windfall gains, particularly as these windfalls would benefit mainly shareholders in war industries who are not adding as such to the war output, while those in contracting civilian industries would, as a group, suffer losses. A general reduction in Excess Profits Tax would therefore tend to discriminate against owners and shareholders in civilian industries which are unable to maintain profits without applying the incentive specifically to the productive agents in the war sector.

The failure to achieve optimum war production arises partly out

---

[1] Some of the proposals under discussion overlook the fact that Excess Profits Tax has already been reduced by 20 per cent—though, of course, only by way of giving 'deferred credits' for post-war use. It seems that Capital as much disregarded this forced saving—from the point of view of incentive—as Labour.

of the fact that industry is carried on by independent firms whose structure, organization, and personnel of their managements are not deliberately chosen in view of maximizing the war effort, but are the result of haphazard development in peace-time. These firms, moreover, are still expected to carry on their business at their own risk. It is understandable that they bear their economic future in mind when deciding on production policy. As long as this is not changed it will be impossible (1) to eliminate bad managements, (2) to pool technically small firms and thus enable them to apply modern technical principles and to work several shifts (which is difficult now in the case of the owner-manager), (3) to eliminate consideration of their position after the war, hence to obtain maximum expansion of war production.[1] The restoration of profits to individual firms cannot solve these difficulties.

Most of these problems could be solved ideally by the compulsory pooling of industries through the establishment of temporary war-time State financed holding operating companies, with full compensation to the owners, which has been advocated in this BULLETIN.[2]

Economic incentive has its important rôle to play in war economics. But the restoration of the peace-time incentives does not solve the whole problem of achieving maximum output.

---

[1] In so far as the Government provides capital equipment this obstacle has been weakened but not altogether eliminated.

[2] Cf. my note on 'Economic Mobilization', Bulletin, Vol. 2, No. 10. An overhauling of the regional organization of the Supply Departments, the clearing of orders and machinery and a strict supervision of labour-force would, of course, very much improve the present position.

THE PRODUCTION EXECUTIVE'S
REGIONAL BOARDS

by J. Steindl

FROM BULLETIN, VOL. 3, No. 12 (AUGUST 30, 1941)

1. The Priority System

THE recent reorganization of the Area Boards offers an opportunity to discuss the question of regional organization, as far as it is concerned with war production; the problem can, however, be considered only on the basis of a broad outline of the existing priority system.

The two chief aims of this system[1] are, first, to secure a balanced output, which implies that no particular part of production should be held up because other parts are behind schedule; and second, to secure that the available factors of production should be used for the most urgent purposes.

In contrast to the priority system in the last war, which worked with a grading according to products, the existing system is primarily one of rationing and allocating scarce raw materials. Its first task is to allocate the available industrial capacity, raw material, labour, and means of transport to the various supply departments. The need for an impartial authority to carry out this allocation and to eliminate competition between departments has led the priority organization through several stages, which are marked by the Ministerial Priority Committee (early stage of the war), the Production Council (from May, 1940), and the Production Executive (from January, 1941). What was originally a body co-ordinating the various Departments' priority organizations has retained many of its original characteristics; its authority in deciding between the claims of various departments was, however, apparently not strong enough, for in May, 1941, a new Minister of State was appointed as 'referee' in questions of priorities. This appointment has since been cancelled; according to a statement by the Prime Minister (July 16th) the Chairman of the Production Executive is now responsible for the settling of conflicting priorities and claims of the different departments.

Each department, having received its share of industrial capacity

[1] See Select Committee on National Expenditure, 1940, 10th Report.

and material, distributes it by means of its own priority organization between various uses. The individual manufacturer has his capacity allocated to one or several departments, and his activities are directed by a system of rationing and licensing of materials. Much more important than this, however, are the progressing organizations[1] of the departments, which are able to speed up, control, or shift production directly. They are the strongest instrument for overcoming bottlenecks.

Apart from the system of allocation there is a general priority direction issued by the Ministry of Supply, giving priority to certain specified classes of armaments.

2. *The Motives for Decentralization*

The demand for a certain degree of decentralization of the control of war industry arose directly from the requirements of the priority system itself. (1) The working of this system requires a knowledge of the available resources, especially of industrial capacity, and the survey of these resources must be kept up to date in view of changing circumstances (for example, destruction by enemy action). It is clear that this current survey can only be carried out by people on the spot who are acquainted with local conditions. Thus, the necessity of finding out the capacity of a multitude of smaller firms was the first reason for setting up the Area Boards. (2) The progressing organization, which is a most important part of the whole system,[2] also needs people on the spot who can ascertain at rather short intervals the shortcomings or difficulties experienced in carrying out the production programme, and who must be familiar with the particular plants in which they do progressing. (3) The same arguments which apply to progressing also apply to cost control; if it is to be achieved without delay it can only be carried out on the spot. (4) If production is held up on account of lack of raw materials the necessary speed in taking remedial action can be achieved only by a local organization which can quickly ascertain the facts, and possibly reallocate materials in the region. (5) If it becomes clear at any moment that one firm cannot carry out some orders with its own equipment whereas other firms, not far away, have equipment and labour available, the contracts should be redistributed;[3] it is claimed that this redistribution

---

[1] The duties of the progress officers are to ascertain at short intervals (say fortnightly) the state of fulfilment of the production programme, to report on it, to find out where production has to be speeded up and what reasons there are for any delay in a particular line.

[2] Compare Reports of the Select Committee, 1940, 10, p. 14.

[3] 'War Economy—the third Stage', *Banker*, September, 1940.

of contracts, which must be based on intimate knowledge of the productive equipment, efficiency, labour available, etc., can be effected with the necessary speed only if there is no need to refer back to a central authority.

3. Development of the Area Organization

The actual development of regional organization has passed through three stages since the beginning of the war. In the first stage, Area Boards consisting of departmental officials were set up in each of the Defence Regions. Their functions were not clearly defined and their staff was obviously inadequate for the achievement of any serious purpose.[1] In the summer of 1940 the Area Boards were reconstituted so as to include three representatives of the employers and three representatives of the trade unions in the Region, the representatives of the three supply Ministries, of the Board of Trade, and the Ministry of Labour, and a liaison officer between the Area Board and the Industrial Capacity Committees. The Area Boards in their corporate capacity were responsible to the Industrial Capacity Committee of the Production Council (now Production Executive). The official members of the Board, however, were responsible to their respective departments. The progressing organization remained outside the Area Boards; the production branches posted progress officers in the areas, who reported directly to their departments but were supposed to be in close touch with the Area officers.[2] The functions of the reconstituted Area Boards remained undefined.

An idea of the practical working of the reconstituted Area Boards is given in an article by the Chairman of the London and South-Eastern Board.[3] This Board had instituted nine capacity clearing centres (based on Ministry of Labour divisions) to keep the survey of capacity up to date and to effect the interchange of machine tool capacity between firms. At that time (last autumn) the Board was still mainly concerned only with big firms of the engineering industry, and many employers and workpeople were 'as yet imperfectly aware of the existence of the Board.'[4]

The main achievement of the reconstituted Area Boards was the survey of machine tool capacity which became available after about one year of war. They do not seem, however, to have overcome the difficulties which beset the working of the priority system 'at the

[1] Select Committee, 1940, 6th Report. See also Hansard, August 7, 1940.
[2] According to Select Committee, 11th Report, 1940, p. 22, there were 44 Progress officers, 20 Movement officers, and 7 Machine Control Progress Officers.
[3] *Board of Trade Journal*, November 21, 1940.   [4] Ibid., p. 315.

factory level' (see the 12th Report of the Select Committee, 1941, p. 3, referring to evidence received in March of this year). There are still the old complaints about idle capacity, work held up on account of delays in the allocation of raw material, delays in transport and conflicting instructions.[1]

The third stage in the development of decentralization was reached in June, 1941, when the Area Boards (in their corporate capacity) were made directly responsible to the Production Executive; they were renamed 'Regional Boards of the Production Executive'. At the same time a Central Joint Advisory Committee, consisting of twelve employers and twelve trade unionists, was set up to advise the Production Executive on all matters concerning the Regional Boards. The Boards include, as before, three representatives of employers and workers respectively, representatives of the three supply departments, of the Board of Trade and of the Ministry of Labour; in addition there is now a representative of the Ministry of Works and Buildings (Emergency Repair Organization), and one of the Raw-material Department of the Ministry of Supply as well as the Regional Transport Commissioner, and the Chairman of the Machine Tool Area Committee. The functions of the Boards have now been defined, but it appears from their enumeration as well as from an explicit statement in the House that they are merely advisory. They do not include progressing, so that the separate progressing organizations are maintained as before. Apparently, the official members of the Board continue to be individually responsible to their own departments.

Among the functions assigned to the Regional Boards, there is the maintenance of the register of capacity, the interchange of machine tool capacity, and advising on action to be taken to adapt the distribution of orders to the capacity of firms. Almost all of the remaining duties are to be undertaken in co-operation with other regional organizations which have not been embodied into the Regional Boards and lead a separate existence.[2] It thus appears that there is only a very small number of questions which the Regional Boards will be able to deal with by themselves, the majority of the questions being dealt with in collaboration with other bodies. This, and the fact that all its functions are only advisory, will certainly mean that

---

[1] See the article, 'Handcuffs for Industry', *Times*, May 21, 1941.

[2] The Emergency Service Organization of the Ministry of Aircraft Production, the emergency repairs department of the Ministry of Works and Buildings, the Regional Controller of factory and storage, the Railway officer, the Regional Transport Commissioner, the Control Organizations of the Ministry of Supply, etc.

the Regional Boards will fail to gain a predominant place as compared with the various other regional organizations.

While executive functions are at present withheld from the Boards they may be allocated to them in case of an emergency: the Boards are directed to establish contact with the Regional Commissioners in order to draw up plans to meet an emergency.

In order to see the recent changes in Area Organization in their proper perspective it may be useful to compare the present state with the recommendation put forward a year ago by the Select Committee:[1] 'That the whole Area Organization should be expanded and unified on an inter-departmental basis; that it should be fully responsible for all area work concerned with production, capacity, labour, and transport, and should co-ordinate and *translate into action* the decisions of the Government Priority Committees'. Up to date, neither has unification of the various area organizations been achieved, nor have powers been granted to them to translate central plans into action.

4. *Shortcomings and Remedies*

What are the reasons for these shortcomings? The first is the vested interest of the different Departments. Each Department tries to maintain its own organization under its own control, partly because of the system of departmental responsibility. To make decentralization effective, it is, however, necessary not only to unify all the departmental area organizations[2] into one body but also to pass all communications between this body and the Centre through *one channel*; at present there are channels of communication between Regional Boards and the Production Executive, between each official member and his respective department, and, in addition, between all the other area organizations (for example, progress and production) and their respective departments. An effective organization could be achieved only if *one* unified area organization, and each of its members, were exclusively responsible to one central authority: for example, the Production Executive. This, incidentally, would give to the Production Executive at once the necessary apparatus for planning, and controlling the execution of plans, which it so badly needs.

The second reason why decentralization so far has not been effectively carried through is that it would render superfluous the

[1] 10th Report, 1940, p. 20 (our emphasis).
[2] As far as they are concerned with production of war material.

present system of sub-contracting and therefore weaken the dominating position of the firms which act as main contractors. At first sight it seems that the system of sub-contracting was chosen because it seemed impossible for the departments to deal directly with a great number of small and middle-sized firms; an easy solution in peace time is to deal with a few big firms only, who redistribute the orders which they cannot carry out themselves. At present this system is not satisfactory, because, for many purposes, there must be (or at any rate there should be) direct contact between the department and the producing firms, for example, for the purposes of progressing, or of cost control. The big firms, however, are still retained in their function of relieving the administration of work with regard to contracting. The system of sub-contracting is open to serious objections; it often happens that the main contractor charges a profit on the sub-contracted work (in addition to the sub-contractor's profit) for which there is little justification. It leaves the main contractor the choice of his sub-contractors without, however, making him fully responsible for their shortcomings. Most important of all, it does not secure that idle capacity is used, that continuity of production is achieved, and that orders are distributed so as to secure the lowest possible cost. To secure a redistribution of orders so that available capacity is more fully utilized, it is proposed to extend the institution of 'capacity clearing centres'; this is an attempt to bring some organization into the system of sub-contracting, but it is far from being a satisfactory solution. The clearing centres act as official intermediaries between firms which want to pass on orders, and firms which have idle capacity. The firms may use this opportunity or they may not; the clearing centres have no power, and even less obligation to redistribute contracts, if they find that some firms cannot execute their orders in time, or are inefficient and wasteful, whereas others have idle capacity and lower costs of production. The functioning of the clearing centres must apparently rely again on the initiative of private entrepreneurs acting under the profit incentive, but it has been made abundantly clear that this mechanism does not work at present.[1]

---

[1] The conception of capacity clearing centres is influenced by the German model of the District Order Equalization Boards; these Boards have organized 'Order Bourses' which represent a kind of organized market for sub-contracts and are based on a high degree of standardization of certain orders; another necessary condition for the working of this system is the absence of cost-plus contracts. There is not enough evidence to judge the success or the shortcomings of this system, but it must be noted that in Germany the dispersion of orders over a large number of firms is due not so much to a search for idle capacity as to considerations of strategy, location of labour, transport, etc. It would therefore be wrong

The obvious solution to the problem of dealing with a great number of firms is that all the functions of the 'main contractor', instead of being left to a private firm, should be taken over by the Regional Boards; in this way, the great number of small firms would, as hitherto, be dealt with by an intermediary with the only difference that this intermediary would be part of the Government organization and that it would be a systematic and stable organization instead of a casual and changing one. The Regional Boards would do all the surveying, progressing, and distributing of orders within each Region, and the Centre—in the ideal case the Production Executive—would only be concerned with the summary figures for each Region. The Centre could draw up a production programme on the basis of summary figures of resources for each Region, distribute orders *en bloc* to the different Regions, and allocate raw materials in the same way, without concerning itself with the details of the distribution within each Region. As the Regions are very big, the system would probably have to be carried further by subdivision (the clearing centres have already involved sub-dividing the Regions).

As against the above proposal, it is often suggested that some functions, such as progressing and allocation of material, should be taken over by the Regional Boards while others, the distribution of orders, for example, should be exercised by the centre.[1] But the functions connected with the control of production (survey of capacity, contracting, allocation of material, progressing, cost control, to mention the most important) are all closely connected. The placing of contracts must be based on the survey of capacity, the most recent progress reports, and the results of cost control; if contracts are placed at the Centre it means in practice that the distribution of all the sub-contracts is left to private firms, and is only loosely, if at all, connected with the work of the official progress organization, capacity survey, and cost control. An equally close connection exists between contracting and allocation of material; this connection becomes particularly important in case of a redistribution of contracts, as materials have to be re-allocated as well.

to expect much from an imitation of the German organization in this respect, the more so since the latter has largely resulted from a conflict between the interests of planning and the interests of the big concerns which dominate the German economy. This is not to deny that the regional organization in Germany has, in many respects, reached a more advanced state of development than in this country. The 'District Economic Boards' (which correspond to the 'Regional Boards') represent a complete unification of all regional organizations; they are directly responsible to the War Economic Staff and they are executive organs of the latter.

[1] A *Times* leader (June 12, 1941) advocating 'regionalism' at the same time stresses that 'contracts will continue, of course, to be placed at the centre'.

The close connection between allocation of materials and progressing need not be stressed.

It thus appears that the five functions mentioned could be carried out effectively only by specialized departments of one and the same area organization, dealing all with the same firms, and keeping in closest touch with each other. The interconnection of these functions, incidentally, also shows that it is not economical to divide executive and advisory functions by vesting the former in a central authority and the latter in a regional organization. The decisions reached at the Centre must be based on the detailed information collected locally, and this means that all the detailed problems dealt with by the area organizations have to be considered over again by the Centre. This implies a great amount of duplication, and considerable delay. The two factors, amount of administrative work and delay involved in making decisions, are indeed decisive for the functioning of control, for, if the administrative machinery is overstrained, and if the delay threatens to do too much damage, things tend to be left, as in the times of peace, to the discretion of private industry. The conclusion is, therefore, that the control of the war economy could only be carried through with full effectiveness if sub-contracting were abolished, and all the functions ordinarily performed by the main contractors were taken over by regional and sub-regional bodies, which would then serve as executive organs of the central authority, while the latter would be free to devote itself to the control of the broad outlines of the production programme.

OUTPUT AND EMPLOYMENT POLICY

by F. A. Burchardt

FROM BULLETIN, VOL. 4, No. 2 (JANUARY 31, 1942)

THE Government's policy of harnessing industry to the war effort moved ahead in various directions during 1941. At the beginning of the year the original priority organization was overhauled and transformed into a Production Executive. This body, on which all the Supply Departments are represented, attempted to square departmental requirements with existing resources by allocating priorities *en bloc* to the various departments. This bulk distribution of priorities was a step forward, but little else was done to close the gap between the planning centre and the producing units, apart from the improved working of the Regional Boards acting in an advisory capacity. Nor has there been any decisive progress in the organization of industry, although the exchange scheme for machine tool capacity, the Government pool of road transport, and similar measures have gone some way to remedy specific weaknesses.

Greater progress has been made in the reorganization of the non-essential industries. Although the Government's method of voluntary concentration has been criticized on various grounds and the release of man-power and factory space did not quite come up to expectations, there can be little doubt that, in spite of leakages, substantial resources were shifted from the civilian to the war sector; additional man-power was freed from the shrinking export trades and by combing-out other industries.

The instrument of the Essential Work Order tied workers in important industries or firms to their job, thus preventing a reflux of labour to more remunerative but less essential jobs, competitive enticing of skilled labour by manufacturers, and an uncontrolled movement of labour within the essential sector. These measures were supplemented by a drive to enlist into industry reserves which were hitherto not gainfully employed. The Government relied on the voluntary method, and although the drive had some success its results fell appreciably short of needs. As the Forces, particularly the A.T.S., were short of women volunteers too, the Government decided in December to introduce conscription for certain age groups of single women. The provisions of the National Service Act signify a substantial increase in the demand for man-power of the Forces, to be obtained by combing-out men from all industries and by drafting in single women, and an attempt to replace withdrawals from industry and to satisfy the demands of the new factories partly by transfers from less essential occupations, partly by conscription of single women desiring to do munitions work rather than to join the Forces, and partly by inducing married women to take on industrial work.

TARGETS FOR 1942

The debate on the Bill showed fairly general agreement between members of different parties and Government spokesmen as to the problems which await solution in 1942, but considerable disagreement about the ways and means of tackling them. Admittedly there is room for considerable improvements and Mr. Bevin's call for a 30 to 40 per cent increase in output has set the target. However, the optimum use of resources cannot be obtained by one bold stroke of policy. It depends on the appropriate interlocking of many agencies and on psychological, social, and political factors, the relative importance of which cannot easily be ascertained in a quantitative way. To state the difficulties and to summarize the remedies which have been suggested may nevertheless be useful.

Improvements are demanded in three directions: steadying the flow of orders and supplies, fuller and more even use of existing resources, and bringing in of additional resources. This threefold nature of a production and employment policy has been very much stressed in recent debates. For our purpose the following classification of more concrete targets seems to be preferable.

1. *Dovetailing of Governmental and Industrial Organization*

According to the Chairman of the Select Committee on National Expenditure (*Hansard*, December 2, 1941, col. 1081) the system of the Production Executive seems to work in the following way:

'The Cabinet decide the weapons required by the country and order the priorities for the production of them. The Production Executive . . . translates that decision into a general line of policy and lays down the limits for each purchasing Department. At that point the system ceases to function. For every Department goes throughout the country to get, as is natural, the utmost possible to fulfil their quotas.' 'The confusion comes not . . . from the control at the centre but lower down when the orders are translated to production itself. . . . Why should there be this competition between Departments? It is the system which is to blame not the Departments' (Ibid., 1082).

If these observations describe the situation correctly there seems to be a case for extending the organs of the Production Executive so as to direct the flow of orders from the centre via intermediate agencies to the producing units in a non-competitive, planned way. To this end the Regional Boards, which have at present mainly advisory functions, should, it has been suggested, be given executive authority to allocate regional block orders to firms within the region and to act as clearing centres for the exchange of capacities.[1] Such reconstituted Regional Boards would, it is argued, eliminate departmental competition in the placing of contracts, decentralize the bureaucratic machinery sufficiently to keep producing units and placing units in close touch, distribute orders to the main contractors and take a hand in the distribution of sub-contracts by bringing in the smaller firms. They might also be the appropriate body to introduce an exchange of technical and social manufacturing experiences and to tackle the thorny question of trade secrets and patents which industries or firms would hardly do. Such an exchange would be of great value in spreading the knowledge of successful methods and particularly in bringing less efficient firms on to a higher level. As regional organizations the Boards would be within easy reach of the firms and factories and at the same time be in a better position to investigate and remedy frictions and hold-ups in production.

Even if this decentralized planning for war were carried out, its successful operation would not be a matter of easy routine. The argument that regional executives would multiply in each region the rivalries between the supply departments at the top need perhaps not be taken too seriously, but it is clear that the Production Executive would have to be transformed from a joint meeting of departmental chiefs into a properly staffed department if it is to allocate orders to the regions broadly according to their specific production facilities. Many of the products are specialized and can be produced only by certain firms in certain regions. Sub-contracting as well may have to be undertaken on an intra-regional basis as well as within the region, and Regional Boards might interfere with traditional business relations and customary trade channels, which may mean greater efficiency in the end but cause temporary disturbances in the beginning.

[1] J. Steindl, 'The Production Executive's Regional Boards,' see p. 17.

Moreover, the necessity of intra-regional planning, the industrial density of some of the regions and the myriad of products required for modern warfare make it doubtful whether Regional Boards can effectively deal with individual producing units. In order to do so they would have to be staffed by civil servants, with power to act quickly and independently within well-defined limits, and with considerable experience in handling technical and manufacturing problems. The British pre-war system did not provide much chance for the formation of this type of civil servant. Under the impact of war there may grow up this new type, familiar with the work of industrial planning (needed also for the reconstruction period). In the meantime a better organization of industry may ease the task of the Regional Boards. About the appropriate forms of organization opinions will differ, and the methods may differ for various industries. Where efficiency would be substantially increased, nationalization, pooling, the formation of public corporations and similar methods may be used; in other cases, or where the former method is rejected on political and other grounds, comprehensive organization of an industry with regional and sectional subdivisions could be adopted. Such industrial groups should be represented by works managers, technical experts and workers in the industry, strengthened by civil servants. This form of organization would give responsible civil servants a chance to meet the men toiling in the industry, to see all sides of a case and many related cases by immediate experience and to decide on this basis what is needed and practicable to maximize the war effort. Industrial groups of this type could act as advisory panels to the Central and Regional Production Executives and as intermediaries for the collection of information and for carrying out their policy. The admixture of civil servants and workers' representatives may also partly offset monopolistic tendencies of such organizations, tendencies which would clearly be strong if existing cartels and industrial associations were entrusted with this task.

2. *Checks and Controls*

Directing output from the centre down to the producing unit requires some organization, but the first condition of effectual planning for war (and also for reconstruction) is an accurate knowledge of the facts. If the Production Executive or Regional Boards are to function properly they must have an up-to-date record of the use and location of existing resources in the various firms, sections, and districts. Without such a current census there can be no control of efficiency, costs, or wastages, no advance planning and no intelligent discussion of policy. Government and critics alike may be aware of certain deficiencies but have no quantitative idea of their extent and no machinery to discover it. As to costs, we have the statement of the Select Committee that the situation is even worse.

A current collection of data on the composition and use of the labour force, on hours worked, on ouput per man, dispersion of costs, etc., would enable Regional Boards to investigate the reason for sub-average results, to redistribute orders with a view to preventing idleness, to discover slackness and other frictions. To get correct information will not always be easy when presumed or real interests pull in the opposite direction, and some positive measures will be required to induce both managers and workers to reveal things rather than to veil them. It seems probable that a regional organization would be in a better position than centralized departments to collect and handle this information with good effect, and the cost in man-power to work these controls is likely to be negligible compared with the gains from better utilization of all industrial man-power.

However, the need for better information and better controls may be generally recognized while methods of getting them may be disputed. Some improvement may be obtained from unified costing, or from a scale of standard costs for certain manufactured goods, or from a more automatic control on efficiency such as that discussed in another part of this book by Mr. Kalecki,[1] or by a system of efficiency bonuses to managers.

3. *Higher Output per head*

Better organization and closer scrutiny of results may go some way towards increasing the output of the employed resources. But this action from above will hardly give the optimum effort if it is not accompanied by a drive from below to maximize output with the minimum of real costs. What stimuli can be applied to get managers and workers interested to get the job done as quickly and as cheaply in real resources as possible?

The choice of potential stimuli is very wide indeed. It ranges from appeals to duty and patriotism and calls for the defence of democracy and freedom to Aid for Russia appeals; from creating hopes or fears to establishing a self-interest or imposing penalties; from promises of a better world in the future to present improvements in social and

---

[1] See 'Excess Profits Tax and Government Contracts,' p. 386.

material conditions.[1] We are not concerned here with this important aspect of the problem, and confine ourselves to the so-called economic incentives. It would be equally wrong to under-estimate *their* importance and/or the interrelation of economic and psychological incentives.

Our question is, then: what economic measures can be taken to increase output per head? Broadly speaking, improvements may be sought for in three main directions: (*a*) rationalization, (*b*) adjustment of methods of pay and working conditions, (*c*) efficiency inducements to managers and entrepreneurs.

(*a*) Rationalization is taken here in the wider sense and includes not only technical improvements in plant and equipment but also better organization, selection of the most efficient producers, limitation of types of products and standardization of parts. Comparatively little has transpired of the technical progress in manufacturing processes, and Company Reports are for obvious reasons silent about it. Clearly it is more difficult to get new machinery in war-time when just these resources are needed for the production of weapons; though public policy should weigh up the labour or material saving of improved techniques against the initial costs in real resources. It may be presumed that technical improvements in the war industries proper are considerable as the new factories are built on modern lines. In other fields less attention seems to be paid to this form of saving in man-power. Moreover, it is well known that very substantial savings in resources can be obtained even without very great investment in new equipment by concentrating output in the most efficient units, by limiting the number of types of products and by standardizing parts. Wherever concentration of output in the most efficient units is practicable, or telescoping of industries is contemplated, or man-power can be freed from trades with a low output per head (non-food retail trade), it will be a gain for the economy as a whole and benefit the war sector. The same applies to limitation of product types and standardization of parts. There again not all the facts are known and efforts have been made in numerous industries ranging from ship-building (ugly duckling) and bricks to clothing (utility clothing), but there are indications and statements of manufacturers and others which seem to show that post-war considerations are frequently

[1] It would be unwise to underrate the power of the psychological incentives: the anxieties after the collapse of France and the Aid to Russia Campaign gave a great impetus to production; co-operation of management and workers in Works Councils has in many cases improved output; the collectivization of the mines may increase the coal output although it may not alter the material conditions of the miners.

acting as a brake on a more forward policy. These considerations may be justifiable but there can be little doubt that more standardization in the war sector as well as in the civilian sector would free resources for an increased war effort, and through greater interchangeability of parts[1] speed up manufacturing and, what is becoming more and more important, the repair process.[2]

Such technical rationalization is sometimes made easier by administrative rationalization. In many cases the need for such reorganization had been recognized in peace-time by special Commissions and expert Committees (coal mining, milk distribution, electricity distribution); economy standards in war-time will necessarily be stricter and rationalization, through better organization, may be profitably extended over other fields (wholesale trade, banking, transport, etc.). Admittedly it is easier to demand a rational organization or to prepare a blue-print of a scheme than to reconcile the conflicting interests and views which determine actual policy. To recognize the existence of these difficulties could, however, hardly justify disregarding this important factor in output strategy.

(b) Given adequate organization and technical efficiency, actual output will depend on the efforts of workers and managers. Now, these questions of wages and productivity, Excess Profit Tax reductions and efficiency, working hours and absenteeism, works' committees and women's work, have been constantly under public review. Numerous explanations have been given for existing deficiencies and suggested remedies are even more plentiful. And this, in turn, explains partly the groping and hesitant way in which policy has proceeded in this field. Let us make the following assumptions (admitting that the absolute and relative importance of the different elements is not known): Men are working sixty hours a week and more, very often a seven-day week. They are interested in working overtime to increase their earnings. This attitude is somewhat modified (at least for the higher wage groups) by the extension of income tax to these income groups, which reduces the incentive of, or the benefit from, overtime. Partly for this reason, partly because of the irregular flow of work, workers do not always produce with a view to getting the job done in the shortest possible time and to the

---

[1] The British Standards Institution has done valuable work in the past and undoubtedly during the war may tender advice to the Government on many of these questions. A general survey of its work during the war would be of great interest.

[2] Standardization is also of great importance for the operation and control of rationing schemes.

optimum of their capacity. These 'facts' are interrelated and can, I believe, be considered as one complex problem.

The aim is to maximize output with a given number of workers.[1] That requires that each job is done with optimal intensity and speed and that the length of the working week is adjusted to the intensity of the work so as to enable workers to operate at the optimal speed for longer periods.

Many statements from workers' representatives and employers confirm that a speed-up is possible and practicable.[2] Workers demand adequate pay for greater effort and better co-operation of managers and workers.[3] The latter demand, recently re-emphasized by Sir Walter Citrine, has been met in many workshops and factories, and the Government, in understanding with the Trade Unions, may encourage the extension of these schemes, which, according to the Select Committee on National Expenditure, have an important bearing on absenteeism, strikes, bottlenecks, and on the intensity of work in general. The real stumbling-block remains, however, the establishment of a proper relation between pay and effort. Putting aside the problem of inflation as irrelevant in this context,[4] the question boils down to this: what method or methods of payment by result will guarantee an increase in pay proportionate to the increase in output per unit of time? If this principle could be translated into practical policy, aggregate output would increase without increasing costs per unit of output. Its application is difficult. A great variety of methods of payment by result is in operation; the standard output per unit of time differs greatly from one factory to another; the output of a reference period on which to base the proportionate increase may not be a representative period for all factories or industries; improved equipment and technique may lead to higher output without greater effort on the part of workers; frequently output depends on team work rather than on individual effort, and so forth. To admit these difficulties does not prove the impossibility of such a policy. It shows that Trade Unions and employers, with the assistance of the Government, must tackle the problem industry by industry, or product by

---

[1] The question of increasing the total labour force will be discussed later.

[2] The Aid to Russia weeks (providing temporary stimuli) tend to show that even some bottlenecks disappear, when workers are intensifying their effort.

[3] Certain improvements in working and living conditions: better transport, billeting, day nurseries, shopping facilities, etc., must be tackled locally and are disregarded here.

[4] The dangers lie not in higher incomes but in increased consumer spending. The appropriate anti-inflationary instrument is rationing, not restrictions on incomes generating higher output. See p. 147.

product, and, if necessary, factory by factory and by way of successive approximation.

If the income tax (including post-war credits) on lower incomes proves to be an obstacle to an intensified production effort, the choice would seem to lie between accepting the men's sub-potential effort, and sacrificing what was regarded as just taxation and wise fiscal policy to the superior aim of increasing output.[1] From the point of view of fiscal policy the Chancellor of the Exchequer should gain in the form of savings what he loses on taxation, provided that the greater disposable income cannot be spent on consumers' goods. If rationing equates supply of consumers' goods at current prices with demand, wage claims cannot be based on the cost of living argument and hence cannot lead into a vicious spiral. This is in a sense a restrictive wage policy, eliminating certain 'harmful' types of wage claims. A positive policy, though preserving these restrictions, would link increases in earnings to increases in output.

A similar scheme of positive inducement might be elaborated for managers and firms. Efficiency bonuses based on the average efficiency of the industry with a betterment bonus for increased production would be one possibility. Bonuses to firms may be made attractive by permitting their use for purchasing certain materials at present prices for post-war use, or by guaranteeing them a certain sum of post-war contracts. Such opportunities of 'deferred investment' in tangible objects or contract promises may be a greater inducement than money bonuses which inevitably go into Excess Profits Tax.

A concerted policy to increase output per head, proceeding on these various lines, might well result in, say, a 5 per cent increase of output per industrial worker. That would be equivalent to, say, one half to one million men-years at present productivity rates. In other words, a better use of employed man-power might very well equal or surpass in quantitative importance the reserves of woman-power which the Government hopes to bring into industrial employment.

RAISING THE LABOUR FORCE

To operate the newly-equipped factories and to fill the gaps arising from new call-ups, the Government decided in December last to conscript single women, aged 20 to 30, mainly for the Auxiliary Services and civil defence but with a choice to take on specified munitions work. How many of the conscripts will decide for factory

---

[1] The Nazis had to retract some steps of war-time taxation on wages and overtime pay and have recently offered tax exemptions for voluntarily blocked savings.

work cannot be estimated, but the Prime Minister's statement gave the impression that after satisfying the demand of the Services not more than 250,000 additional women would be available for industrial work. It is clear, however, that a considerable number of these single and hence relatively mobile and adaptable women will be needed to fill places for which married women are not available because of the location of the factory or other reasons. The manpower shortage requires that Service demands and industrial demands will be adjusted and timed very carefully. In working out such a policy the Government will have to assess the numerous factors which affect women's employment and part-time schemes in big and small businesses and in various industries, and therefore not a linear but a multilinear policy must be developed requiring the co-operation of the Ministry of Food with respect to shopping hours and un-rationed foods, the Ministry of Health (day nurseries and sanitary conditions), the Ministry of Labour (employment exchanges placing), the Supply Ministries and the Board of Trade (to contact the industrial organizations), the Trade Unions (to discover women's grievances in questions of pay and working conditions), and the Social Services (to experiment, say, with the 'Box and Cox' method of householding which the Prime Minister has mentioned). Here, as in other cases, it is the interdependence of the various factors in reality confronted by departmental specialization which makes concerted action on various lines so difficult.

CONCLUSION

The main conclusions which emerge from this survey are simple. The different aspects of production policy must be seen as a whole. Individuals in the production process cannot be expected to see much more than their particular sector, and they have no control over the many factors which must be harmonized for a smooth flow of output. It is, therefore, up to the Government to establish conditions in which the individual's effort produces maximum results. No single measure (nor a single Minister) will achieve the optimum combination of all the social, technical, administrative, and economic factors bearing on production. A method of systematic 'infiltration' proceeding on many lines and converging on the strategic object is likely to give better results than a frontal attack at one point. Furthermore, a co-ordinated policy which assigns to each Department the part it has to play in the drive for greater output would seem to have better chances of success than piecemeal and independent departmental actions which often counteract each other.

LABOUR IN THE WAR INDUSTRIES OF BRITAIN AND U.S.A.

From Bulletin, Vol. 5, No. 11 (August 7, 1943)

A. SOURCES OF MAN-POWER IN THE BRITISH WAR SECTOR

by M. Kalecki

The 'Real Sources of War Finance'

THE analysis of the sources of war finance consists mainly in showing how public expenditure on goods and services is covered by the excess of national income over personal consumption, disinvestment at home and abroad, and indirect taxation (see, for instance, the White Paper Cmd. 6347, Table I). By comparing these items in a given war year with their pre-war level it is possible to say how much changes in the national income, personal consumption, investment at home and abroad, and indirect taxation contributed to the increase in public expenditure on goods and services. All these changes, however, are expressed in money terms; as prices usually increase considerably in war time, there arises the problem of the 'real sources of war finance'. This may, I think, be best stated as follows. Let us assume that we are able to construct appropriate price indices for deflating personal consumption, home investment, and exports and imports (visible and invisible). We can then find the value of these items in a given war year at pre-war prices. Adding these 'real values' of personal consumption, public expenditure on goods and services, home investment, and exports and subtracting the 'real value' of imports, we obtain what may be called 'real' national output. It is then possible, by comparison with pre-war data, to establish to what extent the increase in 'real' public expenditure is covered by the increase in 'real' national output, the fall in 'real' personal consumption, the fall in 'real' home investment and the rise in the excess of 'real' imports over 'real' exports.

This procedure is, however, by no means easy in practice since the calculation of 'appropriate price indices' usually presents formidable difficulties, in particular with regard to Government expenditure. Apart from this, however, there arises the more fundamental question of the actual significance of the analysis of the 'real sources of war finance'. It is often implied that such an analysis gives a picture of the mobilization of resources for war purposes either by increasing their utilization or by shifting them from peace to war uses. But a simple example will show that this is not the case.

Imagine that labour and raw materials are shifted from private investment to armaments. If the percentage profit margin is lower in Government contracts the value of goods produced by the same factors will fall. As a result private investment will be reduced by a greater amount than that by which Government expenditure will rise, and the 'national output' will decline although the utilization of resources is not diminished.

A similar 'loss in value' occurs when raw materials and labour are shifted from consumption to armaments. For the value of consumption goods is inflated by the retailer's margin, and there-fore the value of armaments increases by a smaller amount than that by which consumption is cut down, and as a result the national output falls. It may be argued in this case that the fall reflects a smaller utilization of the retailer's resources (premises, management, etc.), but the picture given by the analysis may be misleading because it may wrongly suggest a diminished utilization of the factors in which we are primarily interested, as for instance man-power. It seems that a more satisfactory approach to the analysis of the real sources of the war effort may be achieved by considering this problem for various factors of production. We can try to estimate, for instance, how the increase in total employment and the reduction in consumption, investment, and exports contributed to the rise in the volume of man-power applied to war production. And analogous 'balance sheets' could be set up—if adequate data were available—for ship-ping space or foreign exchange.

The Sources of Increase in Labour in the Government Sector

The purpose of this article is to estimate roughly the sources of the increase in insured labour embodied in the Government purchases between 1938 and 1941 and 1942. Before we proceed, however, to the actual estimates a few definitions must be given.

We may distinguish in the output of an economy four sectors according to the ultimate use of the product: private investment in fixed capital (for the sake of replacement or expansion), personal consumption, exports, and Government purchases. It is possible to calculate how much direct and indirect home labour (measured in worker-hours) is contained in these four categories of products. For instance, for a building one might calculate the direct labour of building workers, the labour used in producing building materials, the labour of miners producing coal for the manufacture of building materials, etc. (The foreign labour embodied in imported timber must not be, of course, included). However, the total volume of labour of all four sectors thus evaluated will not agree in general with the actual volume of labour because of changes in inventories, that is, working capital and stocks. If these increase [decrease] the actual volume of labour exceeds [falls short of] that embodied in investment in fixed capital, consumption, exports, and Government purchases by an amount which is equal to labour contained in the increase [decrease] in inventories. We shall add [subtract] this difference resulting from changes in inventories to the labour contained in the investment in fixed capital. In this way the *actual* volume of labour will be divided in four parts corresponding to the following categories: (1) gross private investment, including changes in inventories; (2) personal consumption; (3) exports; (4) Government purchases.

With regard to Government purchases of goods and services the following points should be made clear. (*a*) The Government expenditure includes purchases 'of fixed capital assets (such as sites, buildings and stocks of goods) previously owned privately'[1] which are nothing more than financial transactions; we do not include them in our Government purchases. (*b*) Government means Central and Local Government; but it is convenient for our purpose to include all investment of Local Government (except that connected with Civil Defence) and of the Post Office in private investment. (*c*) As we are dealing here only with *insured* labour the services 'produced' by soldiers do not come into the picture. (*d*) Food and uniforms purchased by the Government for the soldiers are included not in personal consumption but in Government purchases.

By considering only labour insured under the General Scheme, aged 16–64, we leave out of account changes in the number of agricultural workers and domestic servants. Thus, for instance, domestic servants going into munition factories will be reflected in our calculation as an increase in the volume of insured labour.

More complicated is the situation with regard to certain categories of railwaymen and employees of the Central and Local Government excepted from unemployment insurance. These exceptions did not apply to *new entrants* since the beginning of the war into these occupa-

---

[1] Cf. Cmd. 6347, p. 3.

tions. Such new entries *will* thus be reflected in the increase of insured labour in the Government sector.[1]

It remains to be added that in the period 1938–41 there were two changes in the scope of unemployment insurance: in the Spring of 1938 domestic workers in businesses not carried on for gain and chauffeurs were included, and in the Autumn of 1940 salary earners between £250 and £420 p.a. To eliminate the resulting increases in the volume of insured labour the scope of insurance has been assumed throughout the same as in 1941.

Changes in the Volume of Employment

Our task is now to estimate to what extent the war-time increase in insured labour embodied in the Government purchases of goods and services as defined above is covered (*a*) by a net increase in the volume of insured employment, both in numbers and in working time, (*b*) by reduction of private investment, civil consumption, and exports respectively.

It has been estimated that the number of insured persons in employment increased from 1938 to 1941 by 5 per cent.[2] The rise in average working time in this period was seven per cent. Thus, the total increase in the volume of insured labour would be 12 per cent. The number of insured in employment in 1938, at the scope of insurance in 1941, may be estimated at 13·1 million.[3] It follows that the total increase in the volume of insured amounted in round figures to 1·6 million of '1938 workers', that is, persons working the average time of 1938.

According to the estimates quoted, the number of insured persons in employment increased from 1938 to 1942 by something like 8 per cent. The increase in working time from 1938 to 1942 amounted to 9 per cent. We may thus assume that the total percentage increase in the volume of labour between 1938 and 1942 was 17½ per cent. Since employment was 13·1 million workers in 1938 this amounts to an absolute increase of about 2·3 million '1938 workers'.

---

[1] If the new entrants *replace* people exempted from insurance the increase in insured employment is higher than the increase in actual employment. The resulting error is unlikely to be significant.

[2] See page 204.

[3] The number of insured in full and part time employment in 1938 (at the scope of insurance in the middle of that year) was 12·7 millions. (This includes only labour insured under the General Scheme, aged 16–64, and does not include agricultural workers). If we add to this salary earners between £250 and £420 p.a., the number of which is about 0·4 millions, we obtain for the 1941 scope of insurance 13·1 millions as the number employed in 1938.

The Release of Labour from the Non-Armament Sector

We shall now estimate the release of insured labour by the reduction of civilian consumption, private investment and exports, between 1938 and 1941. As we shall see below, it was chiefly labour in mining, manufacturing and building industries which was released by these reductions, and our first step will be to find out how much of this type of labour (measured throughout in '1938 workers') corresponds to the reduction of the three items in question. Thus, out of civilian consumption of goods and services we shall first take into account only that of goods, that is, retail sales. Further, the insured employment in the manufacturing of food, drink, and tobacco industries are not important in our considerations and we may confine our argument to the fall of retail sales other than food, drink, and tobacco.

Our procedure will now be as follows: we shall estimate the wholesale value of the retail sales other than food, drink, and tobacco, of investment, and of exports in 1938 and 1941; we shall estimate the 1938 insured employment in mining, manufacturing, and building corresponding to these items; we shall roughly deflate their 1941 values so as to reduce them to 1938 prices; and on the basis of the results of this calculation we shall be able to get a rough estimate of the labour in mining, manufacturing, and building released by their curtailment.

1. Retail sales other than those of food, drink, and tobacco may be obtained from the data on personal expenditure on consumption in the White Paper (Cmd. 6623). They amounted to £960 million in 1938. To this we add the expenditure on household fuel and lighting (coal, gas, electricity) and the estimated expenditure on private motor cars. We obtain, then, an approximate figure of £1,200 million for retail sales in 1938 (including household fuel).

The retailers' gross margin, evaluated for a sample of department stores for the last pre-war years by Grant and Fowler, was about 30 per cent of the retail sales.[1] As Department Stores deal chiefly in goods in which we are here interested we may use this margin to obtain the wholesale value of the sales. For 1938 we thus obtain about £840 million.

The *real value* of the retail sales considered (including household fuel) was reduced in 1941 to 68 per cent, and in 1942 to 62 per cent of the 1938 value (this calculation is based on the White Paper, Cmd. 6623, Table 22). If we apply these figures to the wholesale value in

---

[1] Manchester Statistical Society, *The Analysis of Costs of Retail Distribution*, December, 1938.

1938, we get an estimated wholesale value at 1938 prices of £570 million in 1941 and of £520 million in 1942.

2. We shall now estimate the reduction in private investment (to which is to be added non-war investment of public authorities) in 1941 and 1942 as compared with 1938.

The net private investment plus non-war investment of public authorities in 1938 has been estimated in the White Paper (Cmd. 6623) at £345 million. This figure does not allow for the changes in the value of stocks resulting from the valuation at lower prices at the end than at the beginning of the year. Mr. Barna has estimated the adjustment for this factor at £95 million,[1] which, added to £345 million, gives £440 million. The relevant figure of sinking funds, depreciation, etc., according to the White Paper (Cmd 6623), is £440 million. Thus, private gross investment and non-war investment of public authorities may be taken as about £880 million.

The net investment in 1941 is estimated in the White Paper at — £230 million.[2] No allowance has been made in this figure for the fact that the stocks at the end of year have been valued at higher prices than at the beginning. Mr. Barna has estimated the necessary adjustment at £150 million[3] and this amount must be subtracted from the above value of investment to eliminate the changes in the basis of valuation of stocks. We thus arrive at — £380 million. With sinking funds, depreciation, etc., of £475 million this gives for gross investment £95 million. As the White Paper figure of investment accounts for the sales of fixed assets to the Government by persons and firms, we have to make a positive correction which is probably appreciably lower than £100 million. This correction will raise the figure of gross private investment plus non-war public investment to probably something like £150 to £180 million.

For the prices of investment goods, we have an indication in the cost of building. The increase in cost of building between the outbreak of war and 1943 has been estimated at about 70 per cent.[4] In 1941 the increase must have been less. Other types of fixed investment have probably not increased as much in price. We assume a price index of investment goods of about 150 for 1941. Deflating the estimate of investment in 1941 with this index, we obtain, in round figures, £100 millions in 1938 prices.

The calculation for 1942 can be carried out similarly. The only important difference is that the White Paper figure for investment in

---

[1] *Economica*, May, 1941.   [2] Including expenditure in making good war damage.
[3] Ibid.   [4] See S. Moos, 'The Cost of Building Materials,' p. 313.

1942 is — £150 million as compared with — £230 million in 1941. Further, the adjustment for the change in the basis of valuation of stocks at the beginning and at the end of the year is something like £50 million as compared with £150 million in 1941, or £100 million less. This raises the money value of gross investment in 1942 by £180 million as compared with 1941, provided that other elements of the calculation are unchanged. We thus obtain £330 to £360 million. We shall deflate it in the same way as in 1941 with a slightly higher price index. This gives us a figure of the order of £200 million.

It is hardly necessary to add that our estimates of investment in 1941 and 1942 are nothing but mere guesses. Fortunately, however, this is of no great importance for the results of our calculation; a change in our figures of investment in 1941 and 1942 by £100 million corresponds to 0·35 million workers, while our results are rounded off to the last 0·5 million (cf. Table II).

3. The exports of U.K. produce and manufactures, except food, drink, and tobacco, amounted in 1938 to £430 million. The index of export volume (1938 = 100) was 56 in 1941 and 36 in 1942. We may, therefore, estimate the exports exclusive of food, etc., at £250 million in 1941 and £150 million in 1942.

4. The results obtained above are put together in Table I.

TABLE I

CIVILIAN OUTLAY IN 1938, 1941, 1942

	1938	1941	1942
	at 1938 Prices		£ million
Retail sales other than of food, drink, and tobacco, at wholesale prices	840	570	520
Gross private investment (inclusive of Local Government)	880	100	200
Exports of U.K. Produce and Manufactures (except food, drink, and tobacco)	430	250	150
	2,150	920	870

It follows from this Table that the total 'civilian outlay' was reduced in real terms as compared with 1938 by 57·5 per cent in 1941 and by 59·5 per cent in 1942. It is plausible to assume that labour employed in mining, manufacturing, and building, which was embodied in the three items considered, fell approximately by the same percentage. It may be estimated that mining, manufacturing, and building labour corresponding to the three items considered was 7·1 million '1938 workers'.[1] On the above assumption this amounts to a 'release' of

[1] The total number of insured workers fully or partly employed in mining, manufacturing (except that of food, drink, and tobacco), and building in 1938 was 7·5 million. This figure

D

4·1 million '1938 workers' in 1941 and 4·2 million '1938 workers' in 1942.

In order to have a rough idea about the distribution of the 'labour release' between civilian consumption of goods other than food, drink, and tobacco, gross private investment and exports, we subtract the respective 'real' values in 1941 from the corresponding 1938 figures and divide the labour release proportionately to these reductions.

TABLE II

LABOUR RELEASE 1941 AND 1942

	Reduction as compared with 1938 at 1938 prices £ million		Labour release million workers	
	1941	1942	1941	1942
Retail sales other than of food, drink, and tobacco at wholesale prices	270	320	0·9	1·1
Gross private investment	780	680	2·6	2·2
Exports of U.K. produce and manufacturers	180	280	0·6	0·9
	1,230	1,280	4·1	4·2

5. In addition to this release of labour there is still to be considered the labour released from manufacturing of food, drink, and tobacco, and from services (inclusive of those in transport, wholesale, and retail distribution, and Central and Local Government officials in so far as they are insured). Workers employed in manufacturing of food, drink, and tobacco in 1938 numbered 0·5 million, and labour released from these industries was insignificant. Services in the above sense employed in 1938 4·9 million. It may be assumed that the labour release from this source was in 1941 of the order of 0·5 million workers, mainly as a result of reduction of civilian consumption. This raises the total labour released by the reduction of civilian consumption to 1·5 million '1938 workers' (cf. Table II). For 1942 the labour release from services must be assumed to be higher, so that it will bring the figure of labour release resulting from the cut in consumption to something like two million '1938 workers'.

is exclusive of salary earners between £250 and £420 p.a. A correction proportionate to that introduced for the total number of insured raises insured employment in mining, manufacturing, and building in 1938 to 7·7 million workers. This figure corresponds to the three items in question plus Central Government investment. This was almost fully for defence purposes and amounted to about £190 million. The three items considered above *plus* this amount make £2,370 million, out of which Central Government investment accounts for about 8 per cent. By deducting this percentage from the total employment in mining, manufacturing, and building, which gives 7·1 million, we obtain the approximate labour equivalent of our three items.

Summary of Results

The results of the above calculation are summed up in the Table below (in round figures).

TABLE III

INSURED LABOUR EMBODIED IN GOVERNMENT PURCHASES

The Sources of Increase from 1938 to 1941 and 1942

	1941	1942
	Million workers	
Increase in the volume of labour as a result of increase in the number employed and in working time	1·6	2·3
Reduction in civilian consumption	1·5	2
Reduction in private investment (inclusive of Local Government)	2·5	2
Reduction in exports	0·5	1
	4·5	5
Increase in Government purchases	6·1	7·3

The total increase in the number of '1938 workers' from 1938 to 1941 is 6·1 million. The corresponding figure for 1942 is 7·3 million. It should, however, be emphatically stressed that because of crudeness of the estimates and rounding off of figures no conclusions can be drawn from the comparison of 1941 and 1942 figure, except that the volume of labour in the Government sector increased from 1941 to 1942 and that the rate of increase was very much lower than in the first two years of the war. (This does not mean that the rate of increase in output was relatively small as productivity of labour might have increased considerably).

Local Government investment[1] has been included in our inquiry in private investment. Central Government investment, except that of Defence Services, was negligible before the war. If we assume in addition that there were no important changes in the personnel devoted to 'normal' functions of Central and Local Administration, the increase in labour in the Government sector, calculated above, coincides roughly with the increase of labour in the war sector (provided that we include in it such activities as building of merchant ships on Government account). As we estimated the insured labour employed directly and indirectly in armaments in 1938 at 0·6 million, the total volume of insured labour employed in the war sector in 1941 may be estimated at about 7 million and in 1942 at about 8 million '1938 workers'.

The number of insured workers in employment in 1938 was given

[1] Except that connected with Civil Defence.

above as 13·1 million, and the increase in the volume of insured labour up to 1941 has been estimated at 1·6 million, and up to 1942 at 2·3 million '1938 workers'. The total volume of insured labour in 1941 may be thus estimated at about 14·7 million, and in 1942 at 15·4 million '1938 workers'. It follows that the war sector absorbed in 1941 about 45 per cent and in 1942 a little more than 50 per cent of insured labour. The percentage would not be significantly changed if we added to the total volume of insured labour workers excepted from employment insurance. It may thus be said that 45 per cent in 1941 and a half or a little more in 1942 of all manual workers (except those in agriculture and domestic service) and lower grade salary earners (below £420 p.a.) were employed in the war sector.

B. THE U.S. WAR EFFORT IN TERMS OF MAN-POWER[1]

by J. Steindl

The following is an attempt to estimate the employment in the war sector in the United States so as to enable us to draw a rough comparison with the figures produced in the preceding article for Great Britain. It is possible, in the case of the United States, to choose

TABLE I

NON-AGRICULTURAL EMPLOYMENT IN U.S. IN '000 OF EMPLOYEES

	1939	1941	1942	1943
1. Manufacturing	10·080	12·970	15·050	16·920
Index of Working Time	*100*	*108·*	*114*	*119*
Equivalent at 1939 hours	*10·080*	*14·000*	*17·200*	*20·200*
2. Mining	850	950	970	890
Index of Working Time	*100*	*108*	*114*	*123*
Equivalent at 1939 hours	*850*	*1020*	*1100*	*1100*
3. Construction	1750	2240	2080	1260
Index of Working time	*100*	*106*	*112*	*118*
Equivalent at 1939 hours	*1750*	*2370*	*2330*	*1490*
4. Transport and public utilities	2910	3250	3430	3619
Index of Working Time	*100*	*101*	*105*	*108*
Equivalent at 1939 hours	*2910*	*3280*	*3600*	*3910*
5. Trade	6620	7380	7260	7030
Index of Working Time	*100*	*100*	*100*	*100*
Equivalent at 1939 hours	*6620*	*7380*	*7260*	*7030*
6. Finance, Services	4160	4440	4450	4120
Index of Working Time	*100*	*100*	*100*	*100*
Equivalent at 1939 hours	*4160*	*4440*	*4450*	*4120*
7. Government	3990	4450	5200	5890
Index of Working Time	*100*	*100*	*105*	*110*
Equivalent at 1939 hours	*3990*	*4450*	*5500*	*6500*
Total Employment	30·350	35·670	38·450	39·730
Equivalent Employment at 1939 hours	*30·350*	*36·940*	*41·440*	*44·350*
Implicit Index of working time	*100*	*104*	*108*	*112*

[1] Revised in January, 1946.

a more direct approach, and estimate employment in the war sector on the basis of data relating to the distribution of output between war and non-war uses. Employment in the civilian sector is then obtained as a residual. All the following estimates are necessarily rough, and significant only to the nearest million.

The total employment considered is the non-agricultural employment given by the Department of Labour.[1] It excludes all self-employed persons, employers, and domestic servants; apart from these categories it includes all employees (salary and wage earners) outside agriculture. To obtain the contribution which the increased use of the labour force has made to the war effort, we have to form an approximate estimate of the increase in weekly working time. For some industries (manufacturing) this is available directly, for others we have to use scattered data (transport and general utilities) and for still others we can form a guess on the basis of the estimated overtime paid.[2]

TABLE II

PROPORTION OF WAR PRODUCTION IN INDUSTRIAL OUTPUT IN PER CENT

	1941	1942	1943
Manufacturing	22	56	66
Manufacturing, durable goods	30	74	81
Manufacturing, non-durable goods	9	30	43
Minerals	20	40	50
Industrial production (Manufacturing and minerals) ..	22	55	66

Source: *Survey of Current Business,* January, 1944

TABLE III

EMPLOYMENT IN THE WAR SECTOR IN U.S. IN 'OOO OF EMPLOYEES

	1941	1942	1943
1. Manufacturing: durable goods	2000	6160	8160
Equivalent at 1939 hours	*2220*	*7340*	*10000*
2. Manufacturing: non-durable goods ..	570	2020	2940
Equivalent at 1939 hours	*600*	*2180*	*3350*
3. Mineral production	190	390	450
Equivalent at 1939 hours	*200*	*450*	*550*
4. Construction	690	1350	780
Equivalent at 1939 hours	*730*	*1510*	*920*
5. Transport and utilities	300	1100	1450
Equivalent at 1939 hours	*300*	*1150*	*1570*
6. Federal War agencies	350	1000	1600
Equivalent at 1939 hours	*350*	*1050*	*1760*
Total War Sector	4·100	12·020	15·380
Equivalent at 139 hours	*4·400*	*13·680*	*18·150*
Implicit Index of working time (1939 = 100) ..	*107*	*114*	*118*

[1] *Monthly Labour Review,* September, 1944.   [2] *Survey of Current Business,* July, 1944.

TABLE IV

EMPLOYMENT IN WAR SECTOR AND CIVILIAN SECTOR IN U.S. IN MILLIONS OF EMPLOYEES
(Equivalent of Employment at working hours of 1939)

	1939	1941	1942	1943
1. Total Non-agricultural Employment	30·4	36·9	41·4	44·4
2. Employment in War Sector	—	4·4	13·7	18·2
3. Employment in Civilian Sector	30·4	32·5	27·7	26·2
4. Increase in total employment	—	+6·5	+11·0	+14·0
5. Change in civilian employment since 1939	—	+2·1	−2·7	−4·2
6. Ratio of employment in War Sector to total employment	—	12%	33%	41%

Multiplying the employment in each industrial division with the index of working time on the basis of 1939, we obtain the equivalent of employment in terms of 1939 working hours (see Table I). The sum of equivalent employments in all divisions gives us the total employment equivalent at 1939 hours. The implicit index of working time derived from a comparison of total employment, and total employment equivalent at 1939 hours, is shown in Table I. Up to 1943 working hours in all industries, according to this estimate, have increased by about 12 per cent. The actual employment up to 1943 has increased by 28 per cent, and the equivalent employment at 1939 hours by 42 per cent.

The number of employees in the war sector will now be estimated for various industrial divisions. The *Federal Reserve Board* has estimated the proportion of total output which is going into munitions and other war supplies (construction of war plant, clothing for the forces, food for lend-lease and forces, etc.), in manufacturing industry and mineral production (Table II). On the basis of the proportions given for durable goods manufacturing, non-durable goods manufacturing, and mineral production separately, we estimate the number of employees in the war sector in these industries. (This assumes that differences in productivity as between war and civilian sectors can be neglected; as we calculate the proportions for durable and non-durable goods separately, the error involved should be small). The resulting figures for the war sector are given in Table III.

It remains to consider war employment in construction, transport, and public utilities and in government agencies. The last of these items—the war-time civil service—has been given directly for various dates,[1] and the annual averages are estimated by interpolation. Employment in war construction has been roughly estimated by dividing the construction employment in the proportion of the value

---

[1] *Survey of Current Business*, January, 1944, p. 2.

of war construction to the value of total construction. For transport the measure to be adopted must necessarily be a little arbitrary. We might divide the employment in transportation in the same proportion as the industrial output is divided between war and non-war. But a large amount of transport is used for carrying agricultural goods which are largely for consumption. We therefore reduce the 'war proportion' in transport somewhat below that in industry. To this we have, finally, to add an allowance for electric power production in war industry (all other public utilities we regard as non-war).

The resulting figures for actual employment in the war sector are again inflated by the respective indices of working time (Table III), so as to give equivalent of war employment in terms of 1939 hours.

We are now in a position to find how much of the war employment has been made possible by a reduction in civilian employment and how much was accounted for by increase in total employment and working time. For this purpose war employment is subtracted from total employment (both in terms of 1939 hours). We obtain the equivalent civilian employment in 1939 hours (Table IV, line 3). This rose up to 1941 by 2 millions, and began to decline in 1942 only. Of the total war employment equivalent of 18 millions in 1943, only 4 millions were provided by a reduction in civilian employment and the remaining 14 million by increase in employment and hours.

The increase in use of idle reserves has thus played a much larger rôle in the United States than in Britain, whereas the rôle of the cut-down of civilian production was much smaller in the former than in the latter country. It may be said, on the basis of other information, that the release of labour has come mainly from private investment, as consumption as a whole has not been reduced but rather increased since 1939.

Table IV gives also the proportion of employment in the war sector to total employment. (This is again calculated on the basis of equivalent employment in 1939 hours; in 1939 weekly hours as between industries, differed less than later. By taking the equivalent we take into account the greater input of hours in the war sector.) The proportion of labour in the war sector was 12 per cent in 1941, 33 per cent in 1942, and 41 per cent in 1943. The corresponding proportion for Great Britain, as calculated in the preceding article, was about 45 per cent in 1941 and 50 per cent in 1942.

Another comparison made possible by the preceding calculations is that between the absolute amounts of labour in the war sector in Britain and the United States. The input of labour in the war sector in Britain has been calculated by Mr. Kalecki in terms of '1938 workers', that is, on the basis of the average working week in 1938. According to the White Paper on War Finance (1938–1944, Cmd. 6623) average hours worked in the principal industries in Britain in 1938 were 46½. We must therefore express the American figures of war employment in terms of a working week of corresponding length to make them comparable. We can assume, very roughly, that in the U.S. War sector the working time was little over 40 hours in 1941, about 44 hours in 1942, and about 46 hours in 1943. On the basis of this assumption, war employment in U.S. in terms of a working week of 46½ hours (comparable to Mr. Kalecki's figures) would be 3½ millions in 1941, 11½ millions in 1942, and 15½ millions in 1943. This compares with about 7 millions in 1941 and about 8 millions in 1942 in Great Britain (in terms of '1938 workers').

It is probable that war employment in Great Britain has not increased *appreciably* above the level reached in 1942. On the other hand, employment in the war sector in U.S. reached its peak in 1943. We can therefore say that *at the peak* the war employment in U.S. and Britain was in the relation of 2 to 1 (or somewhat less than 2 to 1).

No conclusions can be drawn from these figures as to the proportion of the output of war supplies in the two countries. Not enough is known about relative productivity, and moreover, the composition of the output is so different as to make comparison highly problematic. The figures, therefore, merely indicate the proportion of man-hours put into the war effort in the two countries.

THE DRIFT TOWARDS A RATIONAL
FOREIGN EXCHANGE POLICY

REPRINTED FROM *Economica* (August, 1940) BY COURTESY OF THE EDITORS

by T. Balogh

'The horror of that . . .', the King went on, 'I shall never, *never* forget'. 'You will, though', the Queen said, 'if you don't make a memorandum of it'.—*Through the Looking Glass.*

THE Order in Council of July 17, 1940,[1] represents the institution of a system of almost comprehensive exchange control based on bilateralism. With this step the Authorities themselves have condemned their previous attempts at maintaining a sham-freedom in foreign exchanges. They have eventually, if grudgingly, accepted the main contentions of those who were not prepared to wait complacently until the force of foreseeable developments should hound them into conclusions which a study of the basic character of the war economic problem and of the experiences of other countries could have furnished much earlier.[2]

The battle between dilettante empericism and logical thinking in this—alas too restricted—field is over. And the canons of the well-bred would now impose silence. 'I told you so' is never more resented than when it is patently true. If, then, I take up the cudgels once more and seem to belabour a dead mule it is for two reasons. First, because the history of exchange control shows more abundantly than any other aspect of war-economic organization the pernicious consequences of what Professor Toynbee has so aptly termed 'adulation of ephemeral methods'. Secondly, because even in their retreat from *laissez-faire* the Authorities succeeded in destroying most of the possible gains which might have resulted from the new methods of planned compulsion. A survey of this problem may, therefore, demonstrate that the lack of central war economic planning based on logical reasoning must reduce the efficiency of our war effort; and

---

[1] S. R. & O. 1940. No. 1254.

[2] The first proposals for a comprehensive system of exchange control were made in a memorandum prepared for the Institute of Statistics by the present writer in November, 1939, and published in the *Economic Journal*, March, 1940. (The haphazard groping after a coherent and rational policy, which this article illustrates, and which has since been almost wholly forgotten, explains the tardiness of the war-mobilization in Britain. It also helps to explain the length of the war.)

at the same time shed some light on the nature of the deficiencies in our governmental machinery responsible for the origination of policies, deficiences which prevent and will continue to prevent the adoption of a rational war economic system, essential to victory.

PART I

PRINCIPLES OF A RATIONAL FOREIGN ECONOMIC WAR POLICY

'In this country we distrust those who predict developments and advocate policies for their mitigation.'—*Lord Halifax.*

The task of economic policy in war is to mobilize fully all available productive capacity and the accumulated real wealth of the country for the two basic purposes of (1) maintaining the supply of goods (and services) for consumption by the fighting forces, and by the civilian population, at the minimum level compatible with effectively sustaining the war effort, and (2) using all other productive factors for war purposes. The latter implies not only the establishment and maintenance of the maximum of striking force but also the accumulation and safe storage of maximum reserves—with due consideration to the factor of durability—of all the essentials in view of a probable enemy interference with production.

From this, the most general view of the tasks of economic war policy, certain axioms follow automatically:

1. The individualist competitive economic system—even in the rather corrupted form in which it existed before the war—cannot, without radical reforms and modifications, provide a basis for war economics. This system is based on satisfying actual (or expected) effective demand by way of an interplay of the price-mechanism and the profit motive.

2. The price-mechanism (that is, the relative price system) as a criterion for the most efficient satisfaction of demand becomes inoperative if the demand of one buyer (the State) rises to a considerable proportion of total demand and is not limited by economic considerations (for example, previous income or size of liquidable capital assets).

3. Price movements cannot be relied upon to limit the civilian demand in war-time because with full employment, lag of taxation, etc., private money demand increases *pari passu* with the increased money demand of the State. The imposition of priorities (and rationing) is the only remedy against the development of a vicious inflationary spiral.

4. The production for current home consumption of all goods which are not essential and which are either exportable or absorb an appreciable quantity of productive factors which could be used in essential production (civilian and military), must be prohibited.

5. The production of essential products above the minimum for current needs must be stocked until sufficient reserves are accumulated for any future contingency. Even *after* such reserves have been established there should be no question of permission to increase consumption so long as there remain the alternatives of increasing exports or diversion of the 'surplus' factors to other (defence) needs.

6. The production of goods or services which, though not essential, cannot be exported and which do not absorb an appreciable amount of productive factors readily usable for essential or export production should not be disturbed, since any interference would cause an unnecessary diminution of the real income of the population.

7. Increased income taxes[1] cannot solve the problem of repressing consumption. This is not merely because of the inevitable lag between the increase in incomes and the payment of taxes but also because those who possess capital assets can always maintain their consumption by drawing on them. As, moreover, the individuals' scales of preferences in consumption are unlikely to coincide inversely with the need of the State for certain products (or rather for the productive factors absorbed by their production), the extent to which income would have to be suppressed by direct taxation in order to free a certain amount of productive factors is greater (that is, a certain—possibly considerable—amount of unnecessary sacrifice has to be imposed) than if indirect taxes are imposed on the products needed. Even less sacrifice would have to be exacted and social justice could be better safeguarded if consumption were to be directly regulated by rationing and prohibition of production for civilian purposes needed for defence.[2]

[1] Excess income taxes could only be considered as just if the distribution of income prior to the outbreak could be taken as a 'norm', as is clearly not the case.

[2] Indirect taxes would still be open to the objection at the beginning of this paragraph. The argument—in war time—against income tax is at an interesting variance with the doctrine that income tax reduces consumers' surplus less than an equivalent direct tax (cf. Hicks, *Value and Capital*). This variance can, of course, be explained by the fact that the task of peace economics is the provision of maximum satisfaction of effective demand of the individuals and that of war economics the provision of maximum striking power for the nation.

8. Such planning of production cannot be worked by private firms.

    The haphazard reduction of home consumption by taxation or other global measures causes unnecessary hardships and unemployment both for labour and employers, results in a chance (and probably unjust) distribution of available supplies and does not, necessarily, free the specific resources required. It also reduces efficiency in production as the reduction is not—for a long time—effected by closing whole factories but by reducing the scale of operations. This increases overhead cost per unit of output. In real terms this means that the labour and other resources represented by overhead cast are not released. Nor does this method guarantee that the resources freed will be used for increasing stocks or for exports if they are not required directly for defence purposes, and will not remain unemployed.

9. The solution lies in a compulsory pooling of firms by industries into holding companies under State control; these should have the right to borrow without interest from the Treasury so as to be able to finance the holding of stocks (and, as we shall see below, to execute export orders). The reduction of output can then be effected in such a way as to release more labour or equipment according to need. Certain factories could be taken over for essential production. Others could be held in reserve against air raid damage, or cleared of equipment to house essential works in case their buildings became damaged.[1]

    The financial pooling would permit a just distribution of the sacrifices which are unavoidable if resources are to be diverted, thereby removing a serious obstacle to the war effort.

    Increased efficiency, of course, also demands the standardization over a large field of (both military and civilian) products. This should also facilitate the introduction of rationing.

10. The scheme implies a complete change of attitude and policy towards 'unemployment'. Men compulsorily displaced must be given their standard wages no matter what employment is given to them (including retraining). In Germany even soldiers' dependants are given compensation in accordance with the peace-time earning of their mobilized men.

[1] Such Government-financed pooling would have permitted the establishment in peace-time of the necessary war industries without fear of competition, which has done much in retarding preparations.

These axioms can suitably be applied to the field of international economic policy in war-time:[1]

1. All productive factors which cannot be *usefully* employed on essential defence tasks (including the provision for civilian minimum consumption) and whose products can be exported should be fully and continuously employed for export. The interpretation of the word 'usefully' will depend on various considerations:

   (a) The urgency of defence demand.
   (b) The relative speed at which it can be satisfied at home and abroad; the difficulties in the way of diverting labour from export to defence industries.
   (c) The size of foreign reserves.
   (d) The difficulty of procuring credits.
   (e) The strategic factor (shipping, air raid risks).
   (f) The terms on which essential products can be purchased in exchange for exports abroad as compared with their relative cost at home.

The importance of safeguarding our foreign markets is very great. The risk of the establishment of protected domestic industries in countries formerly customers was substantial even before the war. If supplies cannot be maintained it will become a certainty. Experience shows that once secondary industries are established the vested interests created will be protected even if they are inefficient. Hence the loss of foreign markets is likely to be permanent or at any rate can be reversed only at the cost of a serious worsening of the terms of trade. If, therefore, defence demand is not extremely urgent (that is, there is no extreme labour shortage) and the shipping position is not unfavourable, some sacrifice should be incurred (that is, the peace-time export production continued and armaments obtained from abroad even at a somewhat more unfavourable price) so as to obviate the social cost involved in retraining and diverting the labour force and undertaking the new investment in defence industries.

All *stocks* of exportable non-essential products available at the outbreak of the war should have been exported.

---

[1] For a more detailed demonstration of these axioms I have to refer to 'How shall we pay for the war?', *Round Table Pamphlet No. 1*; and 'Foreign Exchange and Export Trade Policy', *Economic Journal*, March, 1940.

2. Measures must be taken to prevent a drain on the foreign reserves of the country:

    (a) All unnecessary imports must be prohibited and other imports directly rationed because, in war conditions, price and exchange movements lose their efficacy. Some expedient must be found to permit the stocking of essential imports irrespective of the (permitted) level of current demand.

    (b) Capital exports by residents and the withdrawal of capital by foreign creditors must be prohibited.

3. The war-time policy must ensure that whatever is exported secures the best possible terms relative to the imports which have to be bought.

These principles suffice to determine the character of war foreign trade policy.

As has been demonstrated elsewhere,[1] 'individualist' methods of readjusting the foreign balance are, if not wholly impracticable, like deflation, incapable of fulfilling these requirements. In a situation where productive factors tend to be fully employed, and relative prices are strictly controlled for internal reasons, the free exchange market mechanism would not reflect the true comparative cost position of a country and therefore could not be relied upon to guide exports.[2]

Currency depreciation, unless so extreme as to lead to serious internal repercussions, is unlikely to achieve the full employment of all specific factors which could potentially be used to increase exports. The increased risks involved in foreign, in contradistinction to home, trade during hostilities, the low price-elasticity of home-demand in war-time, and uncertainty concerning the future, reduce the effectiveness of the price-mechanism through which depreciation tends in peace-time to increase exports (and to reduce imports or replace them by home products). Depreciation is, moreover, likely to worsen the terms of trade in commodities in which international trade continues because of the inevitable frictions in the adaptation of home to foreign prices. Finally it would tend to dissipate rather than to increase stocks pending the opening of new foreign markets.

It has become accepted in the past few years that a country could improve its trading position if it succeeded in exploiting the imper-

---

[1] Cf. footnote, p. 53.

[2] But even if it did, the very fact that labour shortage is threatening should discourage the Authorities from depreciating the currency, as in those circumstances only products in which the country possesses the highest comparative advantage should be exported.

fections of foreign markets and establishing a monopoly buying or selling position. Except for products of which the country in question has a monopoly control and which moreover are produced under monopoly conditions, this is only possible where measures are taken to prevent the supplying country from using the proceeds of its exports to the controlling country to buy in the cheapest market, or where foreign trade is either put under State control or is taken over by the State altogether. The maximum benefit from foreign trade can, therefore, be reaped only if exchange control is instituted on a strictly bilateral basis, that is, if clearing agreements are negotiated. Where the whole of the foreign trade of the controlling country is conducted exclusively as a State monopoly—as in Russia—it does not much matter internally what rate of exchange is fixed. The 'sterling' price of exports could then be adjusted suitably for each deal, with respect to each country, so as to reap the maximum advantage according to the urgency of that country's demand for our products and the strength of our bargaining power with respect to its exports. The same applies to imports.

If, however, it is desired to maintain at least part of the foreign trade of the controlling country on a more or less free basis—though controlled through licences—then the fixing of the rates of exchange becomes important. If, then, the clearing rate of exchange is so fixed as to overvalue the controlled currency in terms of the currency of its clearing partner a maximum benefit from the clearing agreement would automatically be obtained. Nor would this benefit be restricted to the present. The overvaluation of the currency of a strong buying country would be tantamount to a subsidy for the producers of the goods it needs at the expense of the consumers of the goods it exports to that country. This will mobilize a powerful vested interest in favour of the continuation of this state and lessen the dangers of the establishment of secondary industries.[1]

---

[1] This procedure has a drawback: the urgencies of foreign countries' demands for our produce (partly caused by their necessity to sell to us—not having other foreign customers) are widely different. Some countries might possess alternative markets and suppliers. Others will have no possibility to replace us. To achieve maximum benefit we must fix rates of their currencies in terms of sterling proportionate to these differences in their 'elasticities' (urgency) of demand. But the resultant cross-rates (that is to say the price of currency, for example, of Brazil in terms of the currency of, say, Greece, reckoned over sterling,

$$\frac{milreis}{pound} : \frac{drachma}{pound} = \text{(theoretically)} \frac{milreis}{drachma},$$ may be different from the rates

quoted in either of the countries on each other. We might, of course, be able to prevail on them to change the structure of their rates to suit ourselves. This is the more unlikely as their commercial and financial transactions with one another will in all probability be governed by different factors from those which render the sterling rates on each of these

In order to lessen the frictions arising from this 'bludgeoning' of the clearing partners several steps are necessary. First, in commodities in which the price, reckoned at the clearing rate of exchange, which overvalues sterling, is so high as to prevent the export of British goods in spite of the pressure exerted on the Central Bank of the clearing partner by the ever-increasing clearing credit[1] in its favour, a method must be found by which the 'sterling' price of exports can be suitably lowered. This can be accomplished either by subsidies or by interpolating a State-financed agency or company between the home manufacturer (or the private export merchant) and the foreign buyer, an agency which would be empowered to sell at a (nominal) sterling loss abroad.[2] The resistance against straight subsidies by foreign countries renders the first method less attractive. There is, moreover, a danger that subsidies may involve financial irregularities and be used to bolster inefficient factories. The second method would eliminate these dangers as competition at home need not be affected, though for other reasons a pooling of industry would seem a more appropriate policy. Where such pooling has taken

countries advantageous for us. Thus, if we wish to preserve the advantage implicit in these rates we must prevent them from selling pounds to each other—for otherwise we lose these advantages: the rate at which they sell pounds would be different from the rates we impose on them. This was the main argument in favour of bilateral clearing agreements. But there would be some advantage also in being able to preserve (at least partially) a solution which permits multilateralism, provided it did not lose us the benefits of bilateralism.

In the case of countries which produce only a limited number of staple commodities—and most countries with which we still have commerical relations would fall into this category—a solution can be found which gives us both benefits. The rate of general clearing should, in these cases, be established on the basis of the official rate in New York and the cross-rates there ruling. This would enable us to conform, in such parts of our foreign trade as are not under direct Government control, to the U.S. exchange position and the relative exchange rates ruling there, which determine, for example, the rates of South American countries among themselves. Those commodities, however, which are purchased in bulk, should be dealt with on the basis of differential rates of exchange expressing our bargaining power. It may be asked why this complicated solution should be adopted when these commodities are, in any case, purchased by the State under monopoly conditions; so long as we pay *low sterling prices* it might seem that the rate of exchange is of no importance. This objection overlooks the fact that it is of the utmost interest to us not only that we should pay low sterling prices but that the producers of the commodities we need *should receive high prices in their own* currency so as to render the production of these commodities in those countries relatively more advantageous than other production (for otherwise they will tend to increase their secondary industries). (The fact that we can, under these circumstances, conclude long-term production contracts, which eliminate the risk of price fluctuations, enables them to plan their production and obtain capital for its execution. This renders production of these commodities relatively favourable, even at 'low' prices.)

As soon as the proceeds of the sales to us are credited in sterling (at a different rate from the general clearing rate) they would be amalgamated with the general clearing account.

[1] Incidentally the existence of such clearing credits in favour of our purchases eliminates the risk of a global default on exports, a risk which is in war-time far greater than the risk of the bankruptcy of individual clients abroad.

[2] That is, buy from the home producer at 'cost' price and sell at a competitive sterling price abroad.

place the War-Holding-Companies or the subsidiaries organized in each industry could properly take over the functions of such export companies.

Subsidies, or the losses incurred by export companies, can be financed either by a levy on the industry itself[1] or by a charge on the general Budget. The first method would seem to be rather un-economic, under certain circumstances anti-social, and in any case an inefficient solution of the problem. An adequate amount could be levied only on commodities which have a large internal market. But in war-time these ought to be exclusively essential commodities. Hence the levy would amount to nothing more than a regressive method of extrabudgetary taxation, so much in vogue lately.[2]

Priorities for export production will, of course, be a necessary element in all these schemes, for otherwise the pressure of home demand would stultify the policy. It would, however, be foolish to rely on export priorities alone for stimulating exports. Even if the exchange rate policy actually adopted is not the correct one—that is, even if sterling is not overvalued in terms of other currencies—it is very doubtful whether a continuous full employment of all *potential* export industries could be achieved by such *negative* measures. The differences in comparative advantage of industries is very great, especially if *potential* export industries are included, as they should be in war-time, even though in peace-time they may have served the home market exclusively. If a policy of export priorities is coupled with measures to stabilize raw-material prices at a low level, then it is likely to result in an unnecessary worsening of the terms of trade (being the equivalent of a policy of depreciation varying in propor-tion not to the elasticity of demand abroad—which would maximize our gain—but according to the quota of these raw materials used in export industries, a wholly irrelevant basis). A policy based on export priorities or subsidies, or a combination of the two, cannot solve the problem of stocking exportable goods pending the development of the new export market, which always takes some time. (Much the same problem arises, of course, in connection with essential goods for the home market.) The same War-Holding-Companies could be used for that purpose and also effect bulk imports at monopoly buying prices.

---

[1] In Germany certain industries were subsidized by a levy on another industry.
[2] Very much the same objection can be raised against currency depreciation as a method of export stimulation. It means nothing more than a flat subsidy financed by a flat 'levy' on imports: a haphazard method of distributing the burden.

E

These considerations show that only a policy based on—

1. bilateral exchange clearing agreements which tend to over-value sterling and which are discriminating (either by import commodities or by countries),
2. coupled with the establishment of export companies capable of organizing the sale of export goods at competitive prices irrespective of sterling cost and the stocking of exportable goods pending sale,

can vouchsafe a continuous full employment of potential export industries and maximize the benefit from trade.

The character of exchange policy cannot, however, be determined solely by reference to current commercial transactions. A country such as Britain possesses an accumulated wealth in gold, foreign balances and assets, whose liquidation would permit imports without countervailing exports. It has also been the depository of foreign balances and a considerable foreign investment in British securities has taken place in the last two decades.

As far as the preservation of the value of our foreign assets is concerned the policy determined by considering current commercial transactions alone would seem to meet the requirements fully. It is obvious that, as the larger part of our foreign assets is in terms of sterling, as high a rate of exchange as can be obtained is desirable. It is obvious, also, that bilateralism would meet our war-time requirements much better than methods which in effect prevent us from bargaining separately with each country. Fortified by clearing agreements, the liquidation of our loans and other assets can be regulated. This would enable us to end the impossible situation which results from the practice of many debtors of first defaulting on their obligations and then using the accruing foreign exchange, not for resuming the debt service, but to repurchase at low prices securities depreciated by their own default.

The existence of foreign balances and assets in the country, on the contrary, does somewhat modify and complicate the solution. If the volume of these balances and assets is considerable and the rate of exchange is favourable to sterling (that is, the terms on which we buy imports in terms of sterling are favourable, and therefore the internal price is, relatively, low) the liquidation of these balances will be very costly. If, however, the rate of exchange is allowed to depreciate and nothing is done to delimit the use of these balances (that is, if they can freely be used in payment for British exports) then all the unfavourable consequences of a depreciation will ensue (except that that part of the worsening of the *terms of trade* which is due to the *cheapening of exports* is borne by the creditor, but the *country* will lose the proceeds of the exports). If, moreover, these balances can be transferred internationally by holders, bilateralism will break down, even if the country from which Britain imports has an exchange control: for the exporter, instead of invoicing in his own currency, will try to invoice in sterling, which can be sold against 'free currencies', and will base his sterling price on that rate of exchange at which he can obtain 'free currency' against sterling, that is, the lowest ruling rate of exchange for sterling in a free market. This will tend, therefore, to depreciate sterling further. The prices of these imports will rise against us.

Hence a segregation of 'commercial' sterling—that is, sterling originating in current commercial transactions—from 'financial' sterling is necessary if a rational exchange policy is to be followed. At a later date or in exceptional circumstances alleviations could be granted from these restrictions. There must, however, be a further segregation—according to countries. If the nationals of one country could transfer their balances or assets to the nationals of other countries, then (even though the segregation of financial and commercial sterling had taken place and therefore their multilateralism could not interfere with the bilateralism of the clearing agreements and thus eliminate the possibility of discrimination) there is a grave danger that nationals of countries with which Britain has a relatively strong bargaining position will transfer their balances and assets to countries whose relative position is stronger. This may well prejudice the success of any clearing negotiations. Hence there must be a segregation, both according to origin (commercial and financial) and according to ownership, of all foreign balances and securities in this country. The several policies can be listed and graded according to severity towards the foreign owners (several of which can be applied simultaneously if the segregation according to the nationality of the owner has been carried out).

The possible policies can be listed according to severity of restriction on foreign-owned sterling balances:[1]

(*a*) Foreign-owned sterling of whatever origin could be converted into foreign exchange at the official rate by the Control.

(*b*) The conversion of foreign-owned sterling into foreign exchange

---

[1] The investment in British assets and securities should be encouraged. (All these suggestions were subsequently adopted by the Control).

would not be allowed, but the balances could be used freely for payments in Britain and also be sold to foreigners of *whatever* nationality (except in the case of nationals of those countries with which we have clearing or payments agreements).

(*c*) The conversion of foreign-owned sterling of whatever origin would be guaranteed at a *fixed* rate different from the official rate.

(*d*) The conversion of foreign-owned sterling into foreign exchange would not be guaranteed at a fixed rate and it could only be used—

   (*i*) for paying for certain exports and debts as well as investment in Britain;
   (*ii*) for paying for 'additional' exports and other specified purposes:

but could still freely be sold to foreigners of any nationality.

(*e*) The conversion of sterling owned by foreigners could be guaranteed at the official rate *if* originating from current transaction (*i*) into a free currency, (*ii*) into the currency of the foreign country with which the transaction had been concluded which gave rise to the transfer of sterling to the foreigner.[1] Those balances which originated from past transactions are treated separately and differently either by ($\propto$) giving foreign exchange for them at a fixed but lower rate, or (β) refusing to guarantee their conversion into foreign exchange and dealing with them as under either (*b*) or (*d*).

(*f*) Strict bilateral clearing agreements are concluded at fixed and discriminating rates and 'financial' balances are separately dealt with. These measures can be varied.

Discrimination does not mean outright 'blocking'. 'Blocking' arrangements should be negotiated separately: in case of certain commodities where our bargaining position is strong we could pay in block sterling, that is, we could arrange for a credit under favourable conditions. In those cases we should be willing to give exchange guarantees.

The foregoing seem to demonstrate that both the aim of securing maximum benefit from current transactions and the task of conserving as much as possible the foreign reserves of the country, demand the imposition of strict exchange control and bilateralism,

---

[1] If that currency is 'controlled' this means in effect that clearing takes place. Otherwise there is no difference between (*e*) (*i*) and (*e*) (*ii*). There would be no sense in quoting differential lower rates.

combined with such reorganization of foreign trading as would permit the introduction of a collective element into the individualist competitive system of trading. As soon as these measures are completed and the position is under control, a policy of liberalization, of increasing but controlled multilateralism can be begun. As the control would be continuous no unexpected reverse need be feared.

It is true that the 'international' character of sterling would be abandoned and a series of 'special' sterling species would be established, varying in value according to the uses permitted. But the very fact that the control is so strict would enable the Authorities to permit the establishment of free sectors very much like 'free ports' in relation to customs. Hence, as the possibility of leakage would be all but excluded, very much more liberal policies could be followed in isolated sectors and thus the invisible exports of the country maintained.[1]

PART II

THE METHOD OF CONTROL

Prior to the war, in private and in public, assurances were profuse that the preparations for the immediate establishment of a comprehensive system of war economics were complete, that once the day of need arrived the mobilization of the whole economic potential would be immediate. Quite apart from the fact—the discussion of which does not fall within the compass of a review of economic measures—that legitimate doubt might be entertained as to the date when such mobilization should have been regarded as necessary, these assurances now seem to have been somewhat rash.

In fact—at least as far as opinions can be formed on the basis of published material, which is necessarily incomplete and may to a certain extent be misleading—it would hardly be an exaggeration to maintain that most of the measures taken were implicitly acknowledged by succeeding regulations to have been incomplete, some inappropriate, and some, not the least important, inimical to the interests of the country. This is all the harder to justify as the problems facing this country in the late summer of 1939 closely resembled those which had faced Germany at certain earlier stages of her race for arms. Even if the Authorities mistrusted deductive reasoning, they were in a position to learn from the

---

[1] The establishment of bilateral controls in conjunction with centrally controlled export companies would also permit of the maintenance of the control over commodity markets even if the transhipment through Britain had to be discontinued.

experience of Germany, especially as the Nazis and Dr. Schacht did not operate from á theoretical base but 'solved problems as they arose'.

There was a prelude to the establishment of control. And in the first ten months of war not less than four sharply delimited phases can be distinguished. Each of these shows an increase in the degree of control, a fact strongly suggesting that the Authorities had either failed to recognize the gravity of the situation at the outset of the war, or at least had shown themselves incapable of devising satisfactory measures to safeguard the foreign reserves of the country. Finance—even external finance—is rapidly losing its importance in these days of more acute preoccupations, of the growing completeness of controls and of increasing sympathy and willingness to participate in sacrifice in those countries on which, in the main, we have to rely economically. It is rather as a symptom of a far deeper-seated malaise that this dogged resistance to the reconsideration of past policies and methods is remarkable and disquieting. It is customary to argue that the stricter measures could not have been applied for (mainly international) psychological and practical reasons. This line of argument is not convincing. The bargaining power of the Allies was far greater at the outbreak of hostilities than it is now. And a strict control would not have excluded liberal exemptions in cases where it appeared opportune.

I. PRELUDE

'If it were done when 'tis done then 'twere well it were
done quickly.'—Macbeth.

The dollar exchange rate fell from roughly $5 to the £ in the beginning of 1938 to below $4·70 after the Munich crisis had made the dangers of the European situation manifest. This fall was caused and accompanied by a very large export of capital. At the same time the slowly increasing rate of rearmament resulted in a direct increase of imports and tended by its general effects to worsen our balance of trade. The Tripartite Agreement expressly provided for such contingencies. The successive French devaluations were undertaken with the full consent of the American Authorities. The British Treasury did not avail itself of this opportunity.

From March, 1939, onwards the Exchange Equalization Account set itself to resist any further depreciation of the pound. The $ rate in London was held rigidly at 4·68¼. When speculation in the forward market forced up the three-months rate from $1\frac{3}{4}$ per cent at the beginning of August to $2\frac{1}{4}$ per cent on the 18th, the Account extended its operations to the forward market and stabilized, at further considerable losses, the forward premium on dollars. The disintegration of the so-called sterling block could not be prevented by these efforts to stem the depreciation of the pound. The Scandinavian countries deserted first, taking with them most of their reserves at the high rate of exchange. The Argentine peso followed suit. Japan and Portugal and the Empire remained attached to the pound. The intervention was suspended only on August 25, 1939. Sterling thereupon fell to $4.10. In the last week prior to the declaration of war violent and unnecessary fluctuations occurred between $4·25 and $4·40 to the pound. The Chancellor of the Exchequer subsequently[1] defended the depreciation of the pound to 4·04 middle (and its further reduction to 4·03 middle on September 14, 1939) as a carefully conceived readjustment of the external value to the 'true' value of the pound. It is difficult to see what the Treasury affected to mean by that expression. Did they wish to exclude or include capital export? It would, in any case, be interesting to know how they arrived at an assessment of this level, especially in war-time, when the 'normal' price mechanism is completely paralyzed by rationing. But whatever they meant it is obvious that *if* the depreciation of the pound was justified at any time *after* the institution of exchange control it was much more justified *prior to* the, at first somewhat ineffectual, prohibition of the export of capital. Then it would have at least tended to safeguard the foreign exchange holdings of the country.[2] But the level chosen was *below* the level to which the flight of capital had reduced sterling. How it could have been justified by any appeal to any sort of 'norm' passes rational comprehension. The whole incident is the more amusing —intellectually—as such utter silence accompanied the announcement on June 8, 1940, of the appreciation of the pound from somewhere below $3·25 to $4·03 to the pound, as far as exports other than those already specified in April, 1940, were concerned. In the meantime our unfavourable monthly balance had increased from an average of £36 Mn. early in 1939 to over £60 Mn. in 1940, wages had increased by some 10 per cent, and the discrepancy between dollar and sterling prices by some 25 per cent. No one except the Government would, under present conditions, refer to the un-

[1] *The Times*, April 10, 1940.
[2] Once depreciation was decided upon the rebound which caused an appreciation from 4·10 to 4·40 ought to have been used to recoup some of the losses in reserve.

fortunate purchasing power parity. But, as the Government did, how can this reversal of its policy be justified? How can the 4·03 parity, if it was a 'true' value in September, 1939, remain so in June, 1940? But perhaps the 'practical' and 'psychological' considerations had changed. Or, having paid a stiff price, the Treasury had begun to learn its lesson.[1]

II. THE FIRST MONTHS OF CONTROL

'He rode off in all directions at once.'—Grimm's Fairy Tales.

Democratic countries are supposed to suffer from the excessive slowness of Parliament to face up to problems. No such handicap was experienced in Britain. The required empowering bills were passed in hours rather than days. The Emergency Powers (Defence) Act, the Import, Export and Customs Powers (Defence) Act, and the Currency Powers (Defence) Act are so generously drawn that no Authoritarian Regime could boast of wider discretionary powers.

The theoretical considerations in the first part of this paper show abundantly (what simple common sense would also have suggested) that a very strong central executive organ possessed of a large and practically experienced, as well as theoretically well trained, planning secretariat would be essential if the transition from the hybrid *laissez faire* system, in which we lived, into a full war economy was to be achieved without immense frictions, loss of efficiency and weakening of the war effort. The comparative lack of secrecy which the Nazis thought themselves able to afford after 1937, that is, as soon as they had reached the stage of minimum armaments required in a war with first-class powers, and had freed themselves from the weakness imposed on them through the demilitarization of the Rhineland, should have enabled the Treasury to make a tolerably accurate estimate of the task we were confronted with. Mr. Churchill, long before he joined the Chamberlain Government, and others, had had no illusions on that score. Even then an estimate based on the most optimistic hypothesis for us ought to have suggested that, whatever superiority in long-run economic potential the Allies possessed, only a determined use of all available resources—including foreign reserves enabling us to draw upon American productive capacity—could equalize in the short run the considerable advantage in actual striking power

[1] It seems questionable whether the magnanimity shown to the international bear speculation against sterling, which reaped considerable profits at the expense of the Treasury, made the requisitioning of foreign balances and securities easier.

which the Nazis gained by having mobilized their inferior productive power for the provision of armaments fully four years before the declaration of war.

The control of foreign economic relations was entrusted to a host of Departments, some newly-organized or so hurriedly expanded as to be as good as new. The Board of Trade organized Import and Licence Departments, the latter to work in close co-operation with the Ministry of Economic Warfare so as to prevent any essential materials from reaching Germany. The Board of Trade in conjunction with the Ministry of Supply was to control (or at least watch over) prices. The Ministry of Supply was given, together with the Ministry of Food, control over specified products, the import and export of which they had to regulate (or undertake themselves). The Bank of England was entrusted with the working of the Exchange Control and remained a powerful factor in determining financial and monetary policy. Co-ordination among these multifarious organs—some of which, as we shall see presently, were inextricably mixed up with private interests and could hardly be expected to work smoothly without supervision—was supposed to be provided by the Treasury. But the Treasury was understaffed —and therefore overworked—even in peace-time. And such expansion of its staff as was hesitatingly permitted was not allowed to extend to the heights where policy originates.

The consequences were probably inevitable. (1) As far as exports were concerned the difficulties of clearance were immense, and the delays and uncertainties discouraged both the foreign clients and the exporters. This tendency was aggravated by the failure either to introduce rationing or to restrict home demand by adequate tax measures (though, as we have seen above, even drastic taxation could not have accomplished a real reduction in home demand without rationing). Many of the home trades, after the setback due to evacuation, black-out, etc., began to expand, or rather, failed to shrink sufficiently to promote exports except for those branches, such as building, where direct prohibitions caused unemployment. Such unemployment as was caused was not accompanied by adequate measures for diversion into defence production. Excessive home consumption and the dissipation of stocks which ought to have been requisitioned or exported were further stimulated by the sudden reversion of the Bank of England to *laissez faire* methods of 'deflationary' readjustment in the midst of controls and budgetary inflation. The bank rate was raised to 4 per cent on

August 24th. On the outbreak of war, moreover, an indiscriminate flat war risk premium was put on stocks, which raised the effective rate of interest to over 10 per cent. A rise in the bank rate could not be expected to attract foreign lenders. Domestic lenders to foreigners were forced to call in their credits by the Defence Regulations (September 3rd). Thus the general effect on demand of a rise of the rate of interest once capital issues were controlled was negligible. The only appreciable result of this measure was a pressure on stocks. But stocks should have been preserved at all cost.

It was, presumably, the fear of inflation which dictated this policy. But, unaccompanied by more direct controls, the measure was calculated to promote excessive inflation *later* at the cost of using existing stocks. The same urge must have been responsible for the price-policy in this period, which also worked in the direction of dissipation of stocks not only at home but also in the export trade. Instead of controlling inflation at its source or canalizing it in innocuous channels through a direct regulation of consumption and investment, resort was had to the old game of altering the temperature by changing the thermometer. Prices were to be maintained at all costs. Such exports as remained were thus thrown away at below replacement cost by this combination of exchange depreciation and price stabilization. Exactly the opposite policy would have commended itself.

(2) The *import* policy was hardly happier. Its execution was entrusted to:

(*a*) The raw material controllers under the Ministry of Supply.

(*b*) The Ministry of Food.

(*c*) The Board of Trade Import Licence Department.

Owing to the peculiar constitution of the Ministry of Supply Controls[1] adequate restriction of imports could hardly be looked for. The continued adherence of the Board of Trade to its tradition of trying to increase exports by permitting imports, also militated against a proper handling of the problem. Finally, the system was based on the principle of permitting all imports unless prohibited, instead of the reverse. Such restriction of imports as was practised caused in many instances a violent rise of prices. As import licences were not sold by the Government at competitive prices, this meant in the case of consignments that the loss of foreign exchange was greater than if full imports had been permitted, or, in the case of

[1] *The Economist*, February 17, 1940.

purchases abroad by residents, and as a lesser evil, unjustifiable profits. Shipping space was of course saved. The loss of foreign exchange due to the failure to control imports effectively in the first six months of the war has been put by one of the foremost financial experts at not less than £50 million. There are reasons to suspect that even this is an underestimate. How much exchange was lost by the failure to increase exports and obtain satisfactory prices is impossible to estimate. If the possible requisitioning and export of stocks of luxuries is taken into account it could hardly be much less. It is melancholy to reflect that the preservation of our foreign exchange reserves was mainly practised, first, by a strict control over pre-emption of products useful to the enemy in countries contiguous to Germany; and secondly, over the assembly of adequate stocks of essential raw materials (which had been previously made difficult in many instances—rubber, copper—by restriction schemes to which yet another Government Department was in effect a party). This control seems to have been effective because it was exercised not over 'outside' interests but over Government expenditure. Another field in which control seems to have been strict appears, according to American figures, to have been the orders for arms and machines in the United States, then not encumbered by their own rearmament plants.

(3) Exchange Control. The control over foreign payments was instituted on September 3, 1939.[1]

The official rates of exchange were fixed by the Bank of England on September 5, 1939, on the basis of a dollar parity of 4·04 middle, that is, appreciably below the last 'free' quotation. This was subsequently reduced to 4·03 middle. The order required private holders of gold and foreign exchange to surrender it to the Treasury at the official rates.[2] The currencies concerned were designated by the Treasury in a Minute dated September 4, 1939. The implications of this depreciation of the official sterling rate have already been discussed.

Even more important, however, were the consequences of the failure to tighten immediately the rules concerning the transfer of s erling to foreign accounts and those concerning the transfer of securities to and from foreigners. These loopholes, together with

---

[1] The registration of foreign assets in specified foreign currencies was ordered as early as August 26, 1939. No registration of sterling loans was ordered and foreigners could continue to repurchase them at current prices, depressed as they were by the financial measures.

[2] The penalty for evasion does not appear to have been sufficiently promptly applied. The first prosecution started only after some time.

the absence of any regulations permitting a check on export and import[1] prices, gave a free rein to the export of capital by residents. The whole process was much aggravated by the decision of the Authorities not to interfere with the sale of sterling balances or assets owned by foreigners to other foreigners of any nationality, or with their use for fulfilling obligations in Britain. The international and unitarian character of sterling was to be maintained at all cost. The word 'blocking' assumed an evil, almost obscene, connotation and all suggestions for a stricter control seemed to consist of 'blocking'.

The non-enemy alien therefore was allowed to remit out of the country by sales abroad:

(1) Sterling balances which were in his possession at the outbreak of the war.

(2) Sterling balances which he acquired by—

    (a) exports to this country;

    (b) liquidation of his securities and other capital assets, and profits and reserves of his direct investments and any other income (interest, royalties, etc.);

    (c) any loans granted to him by a bank or private individuals.

As foreign holders were not given foreign exchange by the Control, there was a steady supply of 'free' sterling on the overseas markets. Since foreigners could sell to one another irrespective of nationality the rate of 'free' sterling was uniform in all foreign countries possessing exchange markets. The steady flow of liquidations depressed the 'free' rate below the official rate. The discount at one time in October was as high as 7 per cent. The 'international' character of sterling was being maintained—at a cost. The cost consisted in the fact that British exports tended to be invoiced in sterling even more regularly than before; exporters could thus quote higher sterling prices or rather could undersell in terms of foreign exchange those of their competitors who invoiced in foreign exchange and therefore had to deliver the proceeds of their exports to the Control, in accordance with the Defence Regulations, at the higher, official value of sterling. But by invoicing in sterling to foreigners who obtained from other foreigners the funds necessary for paying for British exports, the control obviously lost the proceeds of British exports. British importers, on the other hand,

---

[1] The empowering regulation was issued only on September 21, 1939 (S. R. & O., No. 1251 of 1939). It was not enforced effectively for some time. Even now doubts may be raised on its efficacy.

tended to buy in terms of foreign exchange, thereby obtaining
the necessary funds from the Control at a better rate than they
would have been forced to pay in sterling which foreigners could
only sell abroad at a discount. This meant that there was a tendency
for the Control to lose foreign exchange for imports without gaining
the proceeds of exports.[1] But, in many trades, sterling invoicing was
customary. Moreover, all exporters with currencies that were
controlled—and there were few currencies which were not controlled—preferred payment in sterling which they could sell against
dollars. Hence, in spite of the contrary interest of the British importer
there was an additional fairly heavy supply of sterling originating
from British imports. This supply was increased by the failure of
the Authorities to perceive that as long as sterling remained an
'international' currency, the permission to transfer sterling to foreign
accounts was indentical with permission to buy foreign exchange
from the Control—except that it tended to depreciate the 'free'
quotation. It was not at that time conceded that such depreciation,
especially as it was coupled with a policy of keeping sterling prices
as stable as possible, had unfavourable repercussions on our balance
of foreign payments. Permission for nationals to transfer to foreign
accounts was very much easier to obtain than foreign exchange
because the ultimate decision was left to the so-called Authorized
Dealers. The form E.1, which was necessary before doing so, was
much less detailed, not numbered and did not require to be made
out in duplicate. It was mainly devised to guard against transfers
to enemy nationals. Thus, even though the Treasury strenuously
denied any discrimination against the invoicing of imports in foreign
exchange such discrimination did persist. In this way the loss of
exchange to the Control due to the first reason was aggravated by
the unfavourable internal consequences of depreciation to the
economic system as a whole.

The loopholes in the Exchange Control in the first two or three
months after the outbreak of hostilities were made even wider by
the peculiar policy followed with respect to the personnel appointed
to manage this, one of the most central and at the same time most
complicated pieces of the control machinery. The Exchange brokers,
having lost their livelihood, were chosen to supplement the staff
of the Bank of England in fulfilling its new duties. They had
previously been acting mainly as automatic telephone centres. The
actual execution of control was entrusted to so-called Authorized

[1] The foreigner would undoubtedly have charged higher prices in terms of sterling.

Dealers. All joint-stock banks in Great Britain were given this character, and 'oversea' joint-stock banks were entrusted to deal with the currencies of the countries with which they had connections. The greater proportion of these banks and most of the branches of all of them had never dealt in foreign exchange before. The private bankers who had in the main specialized in this business were excluded from their number. They were later given powers to deal with applications for sterling transfers (E.1). The intricate arrangements about commissions[1] on the one hand, and the fact that control was left in the hands of competing banks interested in the volume of their business on the other, resulted in a further weakening of the control[2] and also tended to increase the importance of sterling invoicing of imports, thus exerting a further depressing influence on the 'free sterling' rate.

Finally, no effective control was exercised on payments to countries which were members of the sterling block. As the strictness of the regulations and administrative ability in these countries (including not only the Dominions but also Iraq and Egypt) was rather varied, further not negligible loopholes were opened in the exchange control. Expert opinion puts the loss in foreign exchange on this score at another £50 million in the first six months of the war. This estimate in all probability errs on the low side.

III. THE STRATEGIC RETREAT FROM THE 'INTERNATIONAL' STERLING

(a) *The attempt at a compromise solution*

'I know what you are thinking about, said Tweedledum, but it isn't so, nohow.'—*Through the Looking Glass.*

The process of tightening the foreign exchange control and solving the foreign trade problem began almost immediately after the first regulations had been issued. On September 14th an attempt was made to solve unilaterally the problem of payments to France. No unification of the Allied Controls and establishment of a com-

---

[1] Authorized and other bankers were allowed to charge $\frac{1}{8}$ per cent commission to the public. Authorized dealers handling the order of a non-authorized banker were given $\frac{1}{32}$ per cent commission by the Bank of England, but could not charge anything to the non-authorized bank, thus losing $\frac{1}{16}$ per cent.

[2] The exemption of 'pre-hostility' contracts from control or rather the lack of regulation about proof concerning such transactions has a similar effect. There were violent denials that capital export had taken place. The rate at which privately-owned foreign securities were taken over (the first, very haphazard, list was published in February, the second, and more comprehensive, in April), does not bear out these denials.

mon policy took place. On September 21st powers were taken to control the proceeds of exports without attempting to deal with the problem of prices. On October 4th a circular was sent to authorized dealers requesting them to discourage the invoicing in U.S. dollars of imports from other countries. Imports from countries with restricted currencies were to be invoiced either in sterling or in the currency of the exporter. This attempt at bilateralism was repeated by a further exhortation on December 14th to the British Chambers of Commerce. It was rendered completely nugatory by the continued permission to foreigners to sell sterling balances to aliens of any nationality.

A beginning was made with the control of credits in sterling to the account of foreigners by requiring the production of documents prior to effecting the transfer (November 23rd). But the procedure was still not made identical with, nor as severe as, the applications for foreign exchange. Some beginning was also made at least in the collection of statistics of dealings in non-'specified' currencies. The new regulation also gave power to the Treasury to buy foreign exchange and gold holdings by compulsion. Two further amendments were made in the regulations governing security transactions between residents and foreigners.

This phase of the Control closes with the batch of regulations, amendments and instructions issued on December 22nd, 1939, and January 3th, 1940, to come into effect on January 8th, 1940. These regulations at last made the requirements to be fulfilled in the case of transfers of sterling to the account of foreigners identical with applications for foreign exchange. Once the foreigner obtained sterling, he continued to enjoy the freedom outlined above. At the same time credits to foreigners were made more difficult to obtain. Finally, a strict clearing agreement was announced between this country and France. But no attempt was made to arrive at a unified policy or full agreement over the principles of war controls. Nothing was heard about agreements with other sterling countries concerning the establishment of a joint control through clearing agreements, though articles in the *Economist* suggest that some agreement was arrived at in respect of the sterling balances of these countries. And the control exercised in these countries, payments to which from this country were completely exempt from restriction, showed considerable differences in strictness. The Canadian measures passed in October surpassed in strictness the contemporaneous British regulations. For example, they prohibited the sale of commodities on long credits or at below fair price. No such provision was enacted in Britain.

The system thus established remained in force until the 'freedom' of sterling was made increasingly unreal by measures prohibiting its use for the purchase of a growing number of British products. This represented a compromise between control and bilateralism and the wish to avoid what was still erroneously regarded as 'blocking'. The consequences of this failure to deal with the basic problem continued to weaken the reserves of the country, though the semi-official statements issued from time to time were finally strenuously re-emphasized in Parliament by the Chancellor,[1] who maintained that the turnover of the free market was trivial and that no export of capital had taken place. The subsequent complete change of policy throws in this connection an interesting light on the effectiveness of Parliamentary control by questions.

More fundamental were the changes in import and export policy during this period. The control over all foodstuff imports was assigned to the Ministry of Food. The import of a growing number of articles was controlled and the quotas were slowly though not sufficiently reduced. Finally, the outcry caused by the very sharp slump of British exports led to a growing agitation for remedial measures. The procedure necessary for obtaining export licences was speeded up. The Board of Trade and the Ministry of Supply attempted to encourage exports by giving raw material priorities to firms which maintained their foreign trade. As this did not seem to produce adequate results the new President of the Board of Trade formed an Export Council.[2] Apart from representatives of all Ministries concerned, prominent business men were invited to participate, a few of whom were to give their full time services. A statement issued[3] announced that the Government would not hesitate to apply the most unorthodox methods in order to expand exports. The first months of the Council were taken up by the formation of Export Groups—with no powers except persuasion. The priorities for exports, however, were made more effective. Some recovery of exports did in fact take place. The problem of pricing and of stocking was not touched.[4]

---

[1] *The Economist*, April 13, 1940, p. 692. (Subsequently statements made to the U.S Treasury in connection with Lend Lease indicated a loss of about £200 million: hardly a 'trivial' sum.)

[2] *The Economist*, February 10, 1940, p. 244; March 1, 1940, p. 410; March 16, 1940, p. 453.

[3] Cmd. No. 6183, 1940.

[4] The formation of the U.K. Trading Corporation cannot be regarded as an effort to solve the general trade problem. It was a belated attempt to deal with the problem of competing with totalitarian trade methods in the Balkans.

(b) *The Road to Bilateralism*

'Contrariwise, continued Tweedledee, if it was so it might be; and if it were so,
it would; but as it isn't it aint.'

The first step in the enforcement of strict bilateralism was taken in March, 1940. A new regulation[1] was issued prohibiting the export of certain important commodities to free exchange countries except against payment either in the currency of the country to which the goods were exported or in sterling obtained from an authorized dealer (if the export was effected against sterling bills the Authorities had to be satisfied that the payment would eventually be effected by these methods). In May diamonds were added to the list of 'specified' products.

In so far as the commodities 'specified' were products of a colonial and luxury type, the price elasticity for which is low, this measure (which represented an appreciation of sterling by roughly 2 per cent —'free sterling' was then quoted at 3·94)—was a step in the right direction even from the point of view of exchange *rate* policy. Prohibition of the use of British exports to enable foreigners to withdraw their capital was obviously a step essential for the preservation of our foreign resources.

But the Authorities did not take any further steps. Hence the anomaly that foreigners could sell their 'free' sterling to each other continued. As a large part of the demand for free sterling was cut off the rate slumped first, to roughly 3·70, afterwards moving around 3·50, and fell eventually, after the Norwegian war, to below 3·20 to the dollar. This slump aroused criticism. The Authorities once more maintained that the free rate had no importance and that capital export was not taking place.[2]

But with free sterling quoted at almost 25 per cent discount the interest for British exporters to invoice in sterling goods other than those specified was overwhelming. Quite apart from its internal repercussions on prices, this depreciation affected our economic system in two ways: certain imports, especially from countries which had introduced exchange control, were still invoiced in sterling at higher prices than would correspond to the official rate (for example, leather) and the non-specified currencies—that is, currencies for which the Bank of England did not quote official

[1] S. R. & O., 1940, No. 291.
[2] 'Further light was thrown on the topic of the importance of the free sterling market by the prohibition by the Argentine of the use of free sterling for payments in Great Britain.'— *Times*, April 11, 1940. Unnecessary and harmful delays occurred in incorporating the Belgian and Dutch Colonial Empires into the sterling-franc bloc.

F

prices—were moving with the free sterling rate. But in the case of most of these countries—and more especially Italy—depreciation was contrary to all sense, as we had a favourable balance with them, and we ought to have appreciated, not depreciated, sterling against them to help to liquidate the balance. This irrational position could not be expected to last.[1]

In the field of foreign trade policy, Hitler's extension of enemy controlled territory (which, apart from its direct effects, meant a welcome lessening of the pressure for imports by the Foreign Office and the Board of Trade) and apprehensions about port facilities at last led to a sounder policy with respect to imports. All imports were now required to be licensed.[2] If licences, especially general open licences, are still granted somewhat freely, if some essential imports are still not under sufficient control, it is to be expected that with the reorganization of the Ministry of Supply the import position will be brought on to a war basis.

In the field of export policy the Board of Trade decided to promote exports not by reorganizing the export trade, or by restricting home demand, but by restricting home supplies. A restriction scheme was promulgated by the Restriction of Supplies (Miscellaneous) Order[3]. It was decided to apply it at the stage of deliveries from the wholesalers to retailers. As the Chancellor of the Exchequer failed even to approach a solution of the budgetary problem, quite apart from the fact that not even a solution of that problem could—as we have seen above—have provided a solution for the problem of limiting home demand, and as, on the other hand, no direct measures were taken to limit home demand, this policy would not seem calculated to provide a socially equitable solution. In fact retail sales remain high. Stocks are being exhausted. People with adequate capital reserves are providing for the future. When the full rigour of restriction really makes itself felt, the poorer classes will be further hit, as there is no safeguard that future supplies will be distributed according to need.

As, moreover, the restriction scheme was operated in the distribution sphere and merchants were allowed to cancel orders, while the manufacturers were unable to cancel their supplies, while trades

---

[1] The Authorities themselves evolved a distinction between 'soft' and 'hard' currencies. They took no steps, however, to ensure that arbitrage operations in free sterling between these countries should not render this distinction in effect farcical. In the meantime the distinction was operative only in so far as it complicated and slowed down direct purchases by Government Departments from certain countries. The old position by which control was made ineffective except in slowing down the war effort continued.

[2] S. R. & O., No. 873 of 1940.   [3] S. R. & O., No. 874 of 1940.

were thrown into utter confusion (especially cotton). No parallel planning in the production of raw material spheres having taken place, the reduction of output was left to chance. Hence financial rather than efficiency considerations decide if and what factories should close down. In the main, as was to be expected, the reduction was effected by a general reduction of the scale of operations. In many instances Government orders were forthcoming to fill part of the gap. But as they, also, were unplanned, the method was calculated to maximize hardship for both employers and workers. The release of productive factors per unit of reduction of civilian supplies was reduced far below the level which could have been attained by a more careful planning and less reliance on bastard *laissez faire* methods. As cost per unit of both production and distribution must under these circumstances rise, 'even' the Price of Goods Act does not seem an adequate safeguard against a further rise in prices.

In the case of cotton the Government at last perceived that the restriction of home supply and consumption could not automatically increase exports. A company, the first export company, was formed in July, the eleventh month of the war. Instead, however, of spreading the cost incidental to financing exports over the whole community according to capacity to pay, it now seems clear that a levy on the industry is planned. In so far as the Government is a large customer of the industry this will cause no damage. But, so far as civilian supplies are concerned, cotton is still bought mainly by the poorer classes. Hence we are confronted with one more of the fashionable regressive extra-budgetary taxes.[1]

(c) *The Present Position.*

In the beginning of June the free sterling rate moved to below 3·20 to the dollar.

At that moment the Treasury suddenly decided drastically to reverse its policy. The new regulations were passed with such speed that their operation had to be postponed for a few days after their passing because of the repercussion on exports. Foreign securities

---

[1] Some of the export groups now seem to operate as export cartels. In so far as internal competition is avoided this is all to the good. But it does not solve the problem of subsidization. It is not clear whether these export groups have been assessing levies or not. In August the export insurance schemes were further extended to cover normally uninsurable risks. This amounts to a subsidy, but as it is haphazard in its operation it can only palliate the problem and not solve it. The time still does not seem to have arrived when a systematic scheme will replace piecemeal messing about.

were completely blocked—presumably because there were no means at hand for distinguishing between 'financial' and 'commercial' sterling, a distinction so contemptuously rejected before, and which would have served its purposes so well. Hence extreme measures had to be taken to shut off this source of free sterling.[1]

The new order (S. R. & O., 1940, No. 892), followed by a more comprehensive one (S. R. & O., 1940, No. 1254), finally ended the 'international' status of the pound, so heroically defended for almost a year. The first order provided that all exports from Britain to 'specified' countries were to be paid for in sterling obtained from the Control or from 'special' accounts (the rate for which is the official rate and which can be credited only for specified reasons and with the permission of the Bank of England) or in foreign exchange. It was announced that payments agreements were to be negotiated with all neutral countries. The second order also regularized the position with respect to the United States and Switzerland, the only two 'free currency' countries, and systematized the position with other countries.

The scheme as now in force amounts to a modified form of clearing agreement. The rates of exchange are fixed. 'Special' or 'registered' accounts as the case may be are used exclusively for current transactions. In the case of a few favoured countries 'sterling area' accounts have also been created into which the interest and other income due to foreigners from sources other than current transactions may be paid (and amounts can also be transferred from registered or special accounts of the same nationality). These accounts can be used only for specified purposes inside the sterling area. Balances cannot be transferred from one nationality to another. The 'free' sterling balances which remain can be used, in the main, only for transfer to foreigners of the same nationality or for payment for purposes other than those in respect of which 'registered' or 'special' accounts sterling must be used. As the volume of these balances cannot increase they represent no further problem. As 'arbitrage' is prohibited, the 'free' rates will of course be different in different countries.

With this measure full bilateralism was established in principle. Payments agreements were negotiated with speed, and at the moment of writing include all important countries. The loopholes

---

[1] The enabling regulation was issued on May 12 (S. R. & O., 1940, No. 708). The last links in the exchange control were also tightened up (bearer bonds, etc.). Curiously enough no stamping of home-owned securities was ordered, which would have rendered the execution of this order much easier.

in our exchange control have been stopped except perhaps as far as price control over exports is concerned.

Yet the reversal of the declared policy of the Treasury has not resulted in such reorganization of our foreign economic policy as would be necessary to secure the maximum gain from our exports:

(a) We have now the possibility for discrimination. But all agreements have been negotiated either on the basis of the 'official' rate or the last 'free' quotation. The latter basis (Portugal) is especially reprehensible. No attempt seems to have been made even to establish 'special' accounts with a high rate for sterling for the purchase of specific commodities (wine, etc.) in which we have a strong bargaining position.

(b) No attempt has been made (except in the case of films) to use the device of blocking for the purposes of obtaining credits (especially in the case of agricultural products).

(c) The absence of 'financial' or 'security' sterling inflicts unnecessary hardship on foreign owners of British securities. There is no sense in completely blocking these securities. What ought to be forbidden is the use of their proceeds for other than 'capital' purposes. If there were more sub-division of sterling a much more elastic policy would be followed.

(d) Budgetary, exchange rate, internal production, and export price policies still lack co-ordination. It is foolish to inflict hardship without purpose on employers and labour. The new measures imply an appreciation of sterling by almost 33 per cent for most of our exports to U.S. Does the Treasury think that a policy of penalization and exhortation will, under present conditions, result in increased exports?

(e) The all-important problem of stocking has not been even tackled (except in a very half-hearted way in the case of coal).

(f) By a continued lack of inter-Imperial co-ordination and supervision one of the most important sources of leakage and divergence still persists.

(g) The method of payment of balances accumulating in the new special and registered accounts has not been published, except in the case of America, where gold or dollar payment is stipulated. It is to be hoped that a growing proportion of exports will be paid for in some kind of blocked sterling and that the question of the liquidation of our foreign assets and repayment of our loans will be regulated. No indication has been forthcoming that new methods are being followed in these directions.

(*h*) It is very much to be hoped that the statement alleged to have been made by Sir F. Phillips in Washington that it is proposed to abandon the system of controls and return to *laissez faire* after the war is not a considered expression of Government policy. The reconstitution of our markets and of our foreign reserves is an essential problem of demobilization and would hardly be possible without strong controls.

These are specific points arising out of the export problem. But behind it all remains the unsolved question of total-war organization. As a sample of the whole war-economic organization, the history of our foreign economic war policy presents a melancholy picture of delay, lack of imagination and lack of initiative. The Government (and in this very complicated field, as in others, this exclusively means the Civil Service) were unable to free themselves of their peace-time prejudices, were unable to analyse afresh the new problems which were thrust on them by the war and which they could not escape. They resisted all change. They denied that problems existed. They countered criticism by statements as complacent as they were misleading. Finally, when they were driven in a sector to accept their critics' policy, in their fundamental resistance to that very policy they robbed it of most of its merits by a continued lack of imagination and planning.

The outworn divisions between the functions of Departments clearly demand an early review. It seems hardly tolerable that matters which are inherently interconnected and which demand unified decision and specialized expert knowledge, imagination and initiative, should be dealt with by two or more Departments, the permanent staffs of which, and more especially their Senior Officials, are overburdened by other tasks and, owing to their peace-time traditions, have divergent outlooks and methods of approach, and that an uneasy compromise should then be laboriously worked out. It is useless to blame Ministers who cannot, in the nature of things, be expected to know the background of the problems or to form an opinion on the soundness of the solution. There is a basic conflict to-day between the facts of the position and the constitutional fiction of Ministerial Responsibility for which a solution must be found.

A system in which the concept 'administration' is separated from, and in most cases opposed to, 'theory', in which 'intelligence' is not equivalent to 'action', seems to suffer from grave handicaps when confronted with a system in which central planning is made elastic by decentralized execution.

II. WAR FINANCE

WHAT IS INFLATION?

by M. Kalecki

FROM BULLETIN, VOL. 3, No. 8 (JUNE 7, 1941)

ALTHOUGH the fundamental problem of war finance is: 'How to avoid inflation?' no generally accepted definition of inflation actually exists. Even less is known about how to measure the extent of inflation. In this paper we review briefly the most important current definitions of inflation and then try to elaborate a concept of inflation which gives a basis for its measurement.

Budget Deficit Theories of Inflation

Inflation is sometimes identified with the existence of a large Budget deficit. It is not difficult to prove that this definition is not satisfactory. It is now more or less generally recognized that with considerable unused plant capacity, unemployed labour and adequate raw material imports, even a big rise in the Budget deficit may not have any appreciable influence upon prices, and results merely in an increase of employment and output.

Thus, a Budget deficit does not necessarily involve inflation. On the other hand, it may be shown that a balanced budget is not a safeguard against it. Imagine that income tax on higher income groups has been raised so much that the Budget deficit disappears, but that the rich people concerned do not curtail consumption but merely reduce their saving. Nothing happens, then, except that the amounts in question are taxed away instead of being borrowed.[1] The conditions of demand for and supply of goods remain unaffected: if there was already 'inflation' it has not been stopped by balancing the Budget. In actual fact the rise in income tax *is* likely to press down consumption of the taxpayers to a certain extent and affect the general economic situation through this channel. However, the extreme case considered above is not at all excluded.

Since identifying the existence of a large Budget deficit with

---

[1] We ignore the influence of income tax on investment in fixed capital which in war-time is anyhow severely restricted by direct controls.

inflation proves to be obviously unsatisfactory, an attempt is often made to determine inflation as the amount by which the deficit is 'too great' in relation to available 'savings'. But here also a fundamental difficulty at once arises. In fact, a Budget deficit always creates automatically just enough savings to finance iteslf. If, for instance, Government expenditure increases by an amount d without an increase in tax revenue, and private consumption increases by c, while private investment (that is, increase or decrease in fixed and working capital, in stocks, or in gold and foreign assets) remains constant, the total value of current production and thus current incomes increases by $d + c$. Since private consumption has increased by c, the excess of private incomes over private expenditure, or saving, increases by the amount d by which the deficit has risen.

Since the deficit always provides automatically just enough saving to finance itself, the theory in question has tried to distinguish between 'genuine' and 'non-genuine' savings. The argument runs usually as follows. To the extent to which the deficit is financed by long-term securities it is assumed to be covered by 'genuine' savings as opposed to its financing by floating debt. In particular, if Treasury bills are sold to banks and a corresponding amount of deposits accumulates, the Budget deficit is said to be financed by 'credit creation' not by 'genuine savings', and it is this way of Government borrowing which is held responsible for the evils of inflation.

It is evident, however, that the accumulation of bank deposits corresponding to the accumulation of Treasury bills in banks means an increase of the claims of the public against the Government. Thus it is just as true saving as the accumulation of long-term securities in the hands of the public, in the sense that both mean an increase in the assets owned by individuals and institutions. Further, savings are 'invested' in deposits either because more of them are needed as cash balances for transactions, or because this type of reserves seems, for various reasons, more attractive than the holding of bonds. In the first case, deposits accumulating on current account are 'tied up' in settling transactions (chiefly by firms) and are not available for spending on consumption. The second case, the accumulation of deposits mainly on deposit account, does not differ fundamentally from investment in long-term securities. It is sometimes said that it is easier to liquidate deposits than bonds and to use the proceeds for consumption. This, however, is relevant only when actual dissaving takes place: as long as consumption is below current income the form in which past savings are held is of no importance. And even in the case of dissaving, the obstacles in parting with a bond as compared with withdrawing a deposit seem to have been rather exaggerated. It follows clearly that the way of financing the Budget deficit cannot be considered the essence of inflation.

The 'Vicious Spiral'

Inflation is sometimes defined as a state in which a rising effective (money) demand for goods is not met by a similar increase in supply. In its crudest form this theory identifies any rise in the general price level with inflation. This is obviously confusing the issue. For there are many causes making for a higher price level, which are not 'inflationary' in the proper sense. A rise in the price level due to devaluation of the currency, or an increase in wage rates followed by a rise in prices in an economy with unemployed resources, will not start the type of self-generating spiral process for which the term inflation is generally reserved.

However, if the above definition of inflation is understood in the sense that a growing demand for goods *cannot* be met by their growing supply owing to scarcity of plants, labour or raw materials, it comes very near to the truth. But even in this modified form the definition is too general. In particular it does not indicate how to measure the extent of inflation. Since prices may, and do, usually rise not only owing to the scarcity of the factors of production but also to the subsequent rise in wages, the increase in prices cannot be considered such a measure.

These shortcomings may be remedied if we focus our attention on the fact that the 'vicious spiral' arises because, after a fall in real wage rates, money wages cannot 'catch up' with prices and restore the real wage rates to the previous level. This is caused by the fact that in the periods in question the supply of consumption goods is for one reason or another inelastic.

If, for instance, employment and consequently the wage-bill in the war industries rises, and it is impossible to increase the production of consumption goods, the prices of these must rise even if the costs of labour and raw materials remain unaltered. For, unless purchasing power is cut by taxation or rationing, the increasing demand is confronted with a constant supply and it is the rise in price which brings them into equilibrium. The rise in money wage rates cannot restore the previous level of real wage rates, and only produces a new rise in prices. For the root of the problem is the increase of the total employment not accompanied by the rise in the supply of consumption goods. Thus, if the consumption of non-wage-earners is not reduced correspondingly the average remuneration for an hour's work in terms of consumption goods must fall. This is the actual cause of the 'vicious spiral'.

It must be noticed that not every fall in real wages leads to a vicious spiral. If it is a result of the adverse terms of trade (for instance of the increase in the prices of imported raw materials) it may always be made good by a sufficient rise in money wages.

Size and Structure of Inflation

It follows that the characteristic of inflation will be the rise in price of consumers' goods in relation to the relevant costs of labour and raw materials. In 'normal times' when factors of production of a certain consumption good (say, cotton piece-goods) are in ample supply, there will be a more or less close correlation between its price on the one hand and the costs of labour and war material (say, cotton)[1] on the other. The supply curves are then, on the whole, horizontal or slightly rising over the relevant range of output and therefore an increase in employment need not be accompanied by a significant fall in real wages. During inflation the steeply rising part of the supply curve comes into the picture. Prices jump significantly above the value corresponding to the 'normal relation' between price and prime costs. Imagine that this discrepancy is 10 per cent of the price. We may then say that 10 per cent of the total sales of the goods in question constitute inflationary profits. And the sum of all such profits, wherever they exist, may be taken as the measure of inflation.

This approach has the advantage of not only measuring the global phenomenon, but showing in what sections of the community it really exists. This is very important from the point of view of remedies. It follows directly that to prevent 'inflation in general' one must deal with 'inflations' in particular groups of commodities, and this may be done only by rationing: to avoid inflation it is necessary to cut purchasing power in those sectors of the economy where it is directed on goods in short supply.

It is, of course, necessary to take into account the fact that rationing of certain commodities will increase expenditure on others, the supply of which might have been previously adequate to meet demand and thus may create inflation in new sections. Rationing, therefore, should be sufficiently comprehensive to make impossible such 'shifting' of inflation from one section of the economy to another.

---

[1] And excise or duty if any.

The above theory permits us to put into the true perspective the rôle of the Budget deficit in developing inflation. If Government expenditure is very large and taxation relatively low, there will be a considerable increase in spendable incomes. Moreover, Government expenditure absorbs man-power into the armed forces and war industries on a large scale. In such a situation bottlenecks are likely to develop in various sectors of consumption goods industries, and this leads to inflation in the above sense. However, the connection between the Budget deficit and inflation is not at all close. First, as emphasized in the first paragraph, a balanced Budget does not mean necessarily that expenditure on consumption has been restricted sufficiently to prevent inflation, because increased taxation may reduce chiefly, not personal expenditure, but saving. We may add now that even if taxation does press down expenditure on consumption it may do so just with respect to goods which are not in short supply, and thus it does not relieve the pressure on 'inflationary sectors' of the economy. Secondly, shortages in supply do not necessarily arise as a result of absorption of factors of production by Government expenditure, but for quite different reasons, as for instance curtailment of imports as a result of enemy action. Indeed, such shortages are very often more acute than those caused by the scarcity of labour.

Two Forms of Hidden Inflation

It is not difficult to see that running down of stocks may delay for a certain time the actual inflation. If demand for a certain commodity increases while the factors required for its production are in short supply, its price may not rise if the deficiency in output is supplemented out of stocks. Such a state of affairs is, however, clearly temporary: after exhaustion of stocks the inflationary rise in prices must set in. It is therefore reasonable to consider the running down of stocks of consumption goods a *latent inflation* which may be measured by the rate at which stocks are being exhausted. Here again, although the global amount of 'latent inflation' may be easily calculated by adding the value of particular items, the latter have a great significance for locating in what sectors of the economy the latent inflation takes place. And the remedy against exhaustion of stocks will be exactly the same as against the inflation proper: rationing of expenditure on goods in short supply. 'Latent inflation' may, of course, and often does, go hand in hand with inflation proper: running down of stocks is accomplished by inflationary price increases.

What happens if stocks of some commodities are exhausted, no rationing is introduced, but prices are kept from rising by a rigid control? There arises then what may be called haphazard distribution. It is not a state of inflation proper because prices do not rise. But bidding for goods concerned goes on. It takes the form of customers trying in as many shops as possible, illegal additions to the official price, etc. One can say that is a state of *repressed inflation*. It is not measurable, but it has this in common with inflation proper, that it causes an inequitable distribution of scarce goods. It discriminates against people having no spare time or servants for 'thorough' shopping, being not *persona grata* with a shopkeeper, etc. In addition, it creates temporary shortages and queues which complicate enormously housekeeping and shopping.

Inflation cannot thus be considered overcome by mere control of prices. The only radical, fair, and efficient way of dealing with it is rationing.

THE BUDGET AND INFLATION

by M. Kalecki

From Bulletin, Vol. 3, No. 6 (April 26, 1941)

THE new budget proposals are based entirely on an increase in income tax. The standard rate is raised from 8s. 6d. to 10s. and the 'reduced rate' from 5s. to 6s. 6d. in the pound. This will add about £125 millions to revenue. At the same time allowances and relief for earned income are substantially reduced and are estimated to yield also £125 millions. This measure cuts deeply into the lower income groups, and is expected to bring in 2,000,000 new taxpayers at the lower end of the scale. The revenue from reduced allowances and relief is to be put to the credit of the taxpayer 'to be made available to him after the war in such manner as Parliament may determine'; but this future advantage is likely to be heavily discounted by the taxpayers. The level of tax-free income for a childless couple is now fixed at £3 a week.

It should be noticed that the new tax will practically cancel out the extra rate of over-time over normal time work and will also diminish the financial inducement for married women to enter industry.

Is the Budget 'realistic'? Does it really solve the problem of inflation?

The Chancellor assumes that without the new tax and Government expenditure 'at home'[1] of £3,700 millions the 'inflationary gap' would be of the order of £500 millions. Out of this £250 millions he considers covered by the new tax while for the other half he relies on an increase in personal savings.

The Chancellor of the Exchequer calculates the inflationary gap as the difference between the future Government expenditure 'at home' of £3,700 and the sum of the tax revenue expected at 'old' rates (about £1,600 millions), *plus*, what he calls, the present level of savings (also about £1,600 millions). On closer examination, however, these 'savings' appear to be the total sum available for Government borrowing from domestic sources; it thus includes the considerable amounts (perhaps about £400 millions per annum) released by running down of stocks or provided by 'inflationary

---

[1] By this is meant the expenditure exclusive of Lease and Lend aid and after deduction of net overseas payments of U.K.

savings'—i.e. by savings out of profits due to rises in prices disproportionate to costs. Even if it is assumed that the 'new' £500 million gap will be wiped out by the new tax and the increase in 'non-inflationary saving', there remains still the gap which exists at present.

It must be noticed, however, that for the financial year 1941–42 the actual yield of the new tax is estimated at £150 millions. And it is this amount which should be compared with the 'inflationary' gap. True, in the 'full year' this yield is £250 millions, but this rate of revenue will be actually achieved only in the period autumn 1941–autumn 1942, when the 'inflationary gap' may well be altogether different. Moreover, the estimate of the future increase in 'non-inflationary' savings is rather optimistic especially if considered in conjunction with the increased taxation.

Thus a sober view upon the situation is that the new Budget will not prevent inflation, that running down of stocks of consumption goods which takes place now will go on and will be followed by strong rises in prices in relation to costs. The symptoms of the latter process are already in sight.

The Chancellor of the Exchequer promised to stabilize the cost of living approximately at the present level by means of subsidies. The subsidies are a very valuable instrument to keep down prices of certain consumption goods in spite of increases in cost of raw materials used for their manufacture (due, for instance, to the rise in freights) and may be so in the future. But this will not be the case if prices of consumption goods rise, not owing to their cost but to their shortage. Subsidies cannot produce goods. If supply is short of demand, prices tend to rise to adjust the former to the latter and subsidies cannot remedy the situation.

The only way to prevent the rise of prices of goods in short supply is rationing. And it is important to have it introduced *before* stocks are exhausted and this for two reasons. Firstly, a higher uniform ration is secured for a longer period, the alternative being unnecessarily high and unfairly distributed consumption until stocks are exhausted, followed by a very low ration afterwards. Secondly, low stocks mean always serious disturbances in the process of distribution such as temporary shortages and queues.

The present budget, which imposes a heavy burden upon low and medium income groups, cannot be considered a safeguard against inflation. The only fair and efficient way to stop the inflationary tendencies is some type of comprehensive rationing which should be organized before stocks will fall to a dangerously low level.

THE BUDGET (1942–1943)

by M. Kalecki

FROM BULLETIN, VOL. 4, No. 6 (April 25, 1942)

No Inflation?

IN the part of the Budget Speech dealing with the review of the developments in the last financial year, Sir Kingsley Wood stated, rather confidently, 'that during the last year we have definitely held our own against the onset of inflation. The enemy is still at our gates. Our vigilance must not be relaxed for a moment, but we can at least claim that as yet he has not established a bridgehead against our financial defences'. This statement seems to be a little too optimistic. The Chancellor of the Exchequer rightly pointed out that the prices of controlled goods, especially of those entering into the cost of living index, have been kept nearly stable since April of last year. There has, however, been a violent increase of prices in the uncontrolled sector both in food and in household goods. In these sectors a typical inflationary development has taken place.

However, price increases out of proportion with costs are not the only symptom of an inflationary stituation. Another indication of divergency between demand and supply is the depletion of stocks. Now, what is called home disinvestment amounted in 1941, according to the White Paper, to about £360 million, and its rate in the last quarter of 1941 was probably substantially higher. Depletion of private stocks is certainly an important item in home disinvestment. Sir Kingsley Wood said on the subject: 'I can say with some confidence that there has been no dangerous inroad into private stocks, although the supply of non-essential goods no longer currently produced is naturally and properly gradually drying up'. It is rather difficult to imagine that there are sufficient statistical sources to show that the 'drying up' was chiefly in goods no longer currently produced, and, indeed, the White Paper[1] formulates this rather more cautiously, saying that depletion of stocks 'mainly affected finished products and non-necessary materials'. Now, there are two aspects of this process. First, it indicates that there was a discrepancy between actual consumption and the supply of consumption goods as determined by

---

[1] Cmd. 6347, page 4.

imports, home production, and the Government's policy of increasing or reducing their stocks, and as long as consumption is not diminished or supply, as ruled by the above three factors, is not increased, the reduction of private stocks will continue at the same rate. Secondly, the inroad into the stocks of 'unessential' goods is by no means without danger. Among these 'unessential' goods there are, for instance, household goods, the supply of which may be very important if the bombing of this country is renewed.

Sir Kingsley Wood stressed, with satisfaction, the rise in personal saving from 1940 to 1941. It should be noticed, however, that in this item there is a part which has not been saved voluntarily or as a result of orderly rationing, but was enforced by the difficulty of buying goods owing to shortages and queues, which are a symptom of *sui generis* inflation.

As one of the tools which greatly contributed to preventing inflation, the Chancellor of the Exchequer mentioned rationing. That was undoubtedly so, but rationing was rather a windfall to the Treasury. We found no mention of its being planned in the Chancellor's speech last year. And, indeed, it was introduced last year rather under the pressure of events than as part of a comprehensive plan to prevent a divergency between demand and supply from arising. This time the position is different because Sir Kingsley Wood explicitly relies, in his speech, on an extension of rationing in the next year to fight the 'enemy round the corner'. Let us hope that the extension will be this time introduced *before* the urgent necessity arises.

Direct Taxation

Although direct taxation plays but a small part in the Budget proposals, the problems connected with it were prominent in the Budget speech. The spreading of income tax to wage earners in the Budget of last year is generally known to have created severe difficulties. As was anticipated in this Bulletin[1] it tended to hinder the war effort by taxing overtime pay severely and, to a lesser degree, but still very strongly, the wages of married women. The other problem was the formidable difficulty encountered in the collection of income tax—which was originally designed for taxing the high and middle incomes—from wage earners. One of the problems involved was tackled radically by the Chancellor by increasing the allowance to married women in employment from £45 to £80. There was, however, no mention of the problem of overtime although, for

[1] 'The Budget and Inflation', p. 86.

G

instance, the representatives of the shipyard workers stressed a few months ago the urgency of the problem. A small improvement in the technique of the collection of the tax has been introduced, but it can hardly be considered as satisfactory. Whether it would not be better to increase the earned income allowance and exempt thereby a great part of the wage earners from income tax altogether is an open question. The essential accompaniment of such a step, which would increase purchasing power and so be a weakening factor in the fight against inflation, is the greatest possible extension of rationing.

Sir Kingsley Wood tried to show also that the taxation of the rich as a serious contribution to revenue is out of the question. 'If we were', he said, 'to take away every penny of income above £2,000 from those whose incomes at present exceed £2,000, the gain to the Exchequer and the decrease in current purchasing power would be about £30 million.' However, an estimate by Mr. Nicholson[1] shows that the excess of net incomes of those who at present earn more than £1,200 after taxation is about £80 million and therefore it remains an important source of revenue. It is quite true that this 'taxing of the rich' cannot be expected to contribute much towards fighting inflation, because they will be able to maintain their consumption by dissaving or to cut such expenditure, for instance on rent, which does not help in reducing the danger of inflation. But if taxation is considered not only as a weapon to cut consumption but is also imposed to reduce the future Government debt, this source of revenue should not be neglected. Another source of revenue for this purpose may be an annual capital tax.

Indirect Taxation

The indirect taxation on which the current Budget relies may have two purposes: (1) to bring in more revenue and thus to reduce the future indebtedness of the Government, or (2) to curtail consumption and thus to prevent inflation. The first purpose is definitely the less important one, and might be best achieved by taxation of high incomes and/or an annual capital tax. Total consumption will probably be curtailed by indirect taxation, because it will be a serious new burden on low incomes and the people concerned will be compelled to cut the consumption either of the goods affected (tobacco, beer, and entertainment) or, while maintaining their present consumption of these goods, to reduce their expenditure on other goods

[1] See page 237.

nd services. It is, however, paradoxical to maintain that such type of curtailment of consumption is a fight against inflation. To fight inflation by increasing prices is indeed self-contradictory. True, there s a difference between the price rises caused by indirect taxation and by *laisser-faire* inflation, because the first is planned by the Government and thus affects only certain commodities. However, beer and obacco are commodities of mass consumption quite comparable s necessities with certain types of food, and even in the luxury group which the new Budget proposals subject to double Purchase Tax are ome which are commonly used by large masses of the population, s for instance cosmetics. One might argue, of course, that in the present emergency the use of cosmetics could be abolished altogether, out it is no proper solution of this problem to make them so expensive hat they will be accessible only to the relatively well-to-do.

The tax on entertainment suffers from the general disadvantages of indirect taxation, and in addition it is likely to curtail consumption n a quite unhelpful way: the reduction in frequenting picture theatres loes not release any raw material and hardly any labour for the war effort.

Conclusions

The danger of inflation in one form or another seems in the light of the above much graver than was depicted in the Budget speech; he more so that further cuts in supplies must now be expected. At he same time no satisfactory remedy against inflation is proposed. As pointed out above, indirect taxation does not in fact differ substantially from *laisser-faire* inflation in its incidence upon consumers.

It is significant that the best parts of the present Budget are the amendments to last year's and this year's Budget proposals: the increase in the allowance to married women in employment, the exemption of men in the Forces from tobacco tax, the exemption of utility clothing from purchase tax. This is not accidental. Neither direct nor indirect taxation are satisfactory weapons to cope with the problem of inflation, which consists in cutting consumption in an equitable way. This function may be performed only by a scheme of comprehensive rationing.

THE BUDGET (1943–1944)

by M. Kalecki

FROM BULLETIN, VOL. 5, NO. 6 (APRIL 24, 1943)

1. In the present Budget, as in the last, the Chancellor relies fo. the increase in revenue on indirect taxation. The new taxes are expected to yield about £100 million in a full year, and the leading rôles are played again by Beer and Tobacco.

There may be two reasons for imposing indirect taxes. One is that, like any tax, they reduce the Budget deficit and thus ease the future burden of the National Debt. The second is that they pres down consumption of either the article taxed or of other good and services and thus are supposed to counteract the danger o inflation.

With regard to the 'revenue aspect' it has been argued in thi *Bulletin* that it is not of primary importance.[1] The increase in the National Debt does not constitute any burden for the econom' as a whole, because the payment of the interest on it represents : mere transfer problem. It is only necessary to arrange a transfe in such a way that it should not disturb output and employment This may be achieved by financing the interest on National Deb by an annual capital tax or a modified income tax.[1] For such . financing of the interest on National Debt does not affect significantl' the total volume of investment and consumption and thus is more o less neutral with regard to output and employment.

2. Even though many people may disagree with this argumen most of them will probably accept the view that in the presen emergency considerations of the future burden of the Nationa Debt are of secondary importance. However, for people concernec with the 'revenue aspect' (or with the prices of tobacco shares) i may be of interest that the prospects of tobacco consumption ar now rather worse than a year ago. The heavy increase of tobacc duty in the last Budget caused only a slight reduction of its con sumption in 1942–43 as compared with 1941–42. It must be taken into account, however, that almost throughout 1941–42 there was (sometimes acute) scarcity of tobacco which resulted frequentl in rationing of customers by shopkeepers. The rise in tobacc

---

[1] M. Kalecki, 'The Burden of the National Debt,' see p. 124.

prices 1942-43 cut out the weaker consumer, reduced the pressure of demand and thus enabled quite a number of people to *increase* their consumption. As tobacco is now plentiful, however, this process of compensation will not happen again, and although the price increase is this time less, the fall in consumption may be much heavier than in the last financial year. It may be seen, however, from the Budget estimates of the revenue from tobacco duties that only a slight fall in the consumption of tobacco has been assumed.

3. We shall now consider in turn the 'curtailing-of-consumption aspect' of indirect taxation. An increase in indirect taxes will normally reduce both consumption of the article taxed or of other goods, and savings. In the case of beer and tobacco, which are consumed by poor and rich alike, the effects are roughly as follows. The poor man saves rather little and his saving is of what may be called an inelastic type (insurance, etc.), he must therefore cut either his consumption of beer and tobacco or the expenditure on clothing, household goods and entertainment. The more well-to-do are able to reduce their saving and thus to evade the pressure on consumption. Thus, even if expenditure on beer and tobacco took the same percentage of lower and higher incomes the consumption of the poor would be likely to be curtailed more than that of the rich. However, above a certain income limit the expenditure on beer and tobacco in relation to income is the lower, the higher the income. Thus there are three reasons for the poor being penalized by beer and tobacco taxes: (1) the same percentage cut in consumption means greater hardship on the poor than on the rich; (2) the same percentage cut in the real income of the poor means usually a higher percentage cut in their consumption than in that of the rich because of their inability to reduce savings; (3) the percentage cut in real income of the higher grades as a result of increase in prices of beer and tobacco is smaller than in that of the lower grades.

It is precisely for these reasons that curtailing consumption by a general price increase, i.e. by inflation, is considered undesirable. It is therefore paradoxical to fight inflation by taxation of semi-necessities which has similar repercussions. Indeed, indirect taxation is nothing else but a Government controlled inflation. Also its repercussions with regard to the 'vicious spiral' are much the same. The workers asking for wage increases as a result of the rise in cost of living are not interested in what way this rise has been brought about. The only important 'advantage' of taxation of tobacco and beer in this context consists in the fact that tobacco is heavily under-weighted in the cost of living index of the Ministry of Labour, and beer is not represented in it at all. But if an index deviates too much from the actual state of affairs it gradually loses its significance.

But then, what taxes should have been introduced by the present Budget? None at all? That perhaps would be the most reasonable course to take. At the present juncture the fight against inflation is being actually waged not by the Treasury but by the Ministry of Food and the Board of Trade. For they have at their disposal the most effective weapon: the ration book.

THE BUDGET (1944-1945)

by M. Kalecki

FROM BULLETIN, VOL. 6, No. 7 (MAY 20, 1944)

No New Taxes

THE present Budget is the first of the war-time budgets that does not introduce any new taxation. In a fairly fully controlled economy like that of Great Britain, the importance of taxation as a means of curtailing consumption is in general very much reduced. Some sectors of the economy, however, remain still free. If the supply of goods and services in these sectors falls while incomes are still on the increase, direct taxation provides a useful weapon in the fight against inflation alongside with rationing and price control. Such is not, however, the situation at present. The rise in Government expenditure anticipated in the new Budget is small compared with the previous year. The transfer of workers from the civilian to the war sector of industry has more or less ended. Nor does there seem to be any danger of a drastic reduction in imports which would necessitate cutting down rations and thus increase the pressure on the uncontrolled sector. In these circumstances a Budget without new taxes is even more natural than it would have been last year. For then the non-imposition of new taxes, though quite 'safe', might have required some additional rationing and price control.

It should be added that the introduction of the pay-as-you-earn system, which in periods of rising incomes increases revenue as compared with lagging taxation, also exerts some pressure on consumption. For many people are likely to budget their consumption on the basis of their income net of the income tax *paid* in a given period.

On closer examination of the Budget Speech, however, it becomes a little doubtful whether no measures equivalent to new taxation are involved in the present Budget. The statement of the Chancellor of the Exchequer that he may not use to the full the weapon of subsidies to keep the cost of living at the present level, if it does not imply the cutting down of present subsidies, it means at least that in budgeting subsidies no sufficient provisions have been made for preventing a rise in the cost of living as a result of the possible future rise in the production costs of the respective goods. Now, an actual or potential cut in subsidies is equivalent to an increase in indirect taxes. In fact it is even more harmful than an increase in duties on beer, tobacco, etc., because it causes a rise in the price of necessities.

Prices and Wages

The Chancellor of the Exchequer stated that in present circumstances he cannot consider the cost of living (as measured by the index of the Ministry of Labour) at the level of 25 to 30 per cent above pre-war as sacrosanct and that for the next year he guarantees only a level of 30 to 35 per cent above pre-war. The reason given for this change of policy is as follows. The cost of living index of the Ministry of Labour is now 28 per cent over the 1938 level. However, the index of retail prices of all consumption goods and services after eliminating the influence both of subsidies and indirect taxes was, in 1943, according to the new White Paper (Cmd. 6623), 43 per cent over the 1938 level. This discrepancy between the 'natural' and artificial price level is considered dangerous by the Chancellor of the Exchequer.

If, however, we use the information contained in the White Paper a very different picture emerges. We find, on the basis of these data, that the index of *market* retail prices (that is, prices actually paid by consumers) was 51 per cent higher than before the war. This is the 'artificial' price level, in the sense that it is influenced both by subsidies and indirect taxes. When indirect taxes are subtracted and subsidies added we obtain the figure of 43 per cent for the increase in the 'natural' price level over pre-war which the Chancellor mentioned. Now, the divergence between these two indices is in the opposite direction to that stressed by the Chancellor[1] who used as a measure of the 'artificial' price level the Cost of Living Index and *not* the figure which measures the overall increase in prices to consumers.

How is it explained, however, that the cost of living index is so much below the index of retail market prices calculated from the White Paper? This may first be due to the fact that prices relevant to working-class budgets increased less than those relevant to the overall consumption of goods and services. (To the extent to which this is the case the figure for the increase in the retail prices net of subsidies and taxes which is relevant for comparison with the cost of living index will be below 43 per cent mentioned above). But a far more important reason for the discrepancy in question is that subsidized necessities are heavily overweighted and goods subject to

[1] Because indirect taxes, in fact, heavily outweighed subsidies.

indirect taxation heavily under-weighted in the Ministry of Labour cost of living index. If the necessary corrections were introduced it is likely that the cost of living index would show a rise as compared with the pre-war level of 48 per cent or more.[1] If this is taken into account the rise in money wage rates by about 40 per cent as compared with pre-war is likely to represent some fall in real wage rates. The results of the above discussion are shown in the following table.

Increases in Price and Wage Indices as Compared with 1938

Retail market prices of consumption goods and services in 1943 (White Paper)	51 per cent
The same prices after subtracting taxes and adding subsidies in 1943 (White Paper)	43 ,, ,,
Ministry of Labour Cost of Living Index, March, 1944	28 ,, ,,
Probable increase in price index of working-class consumption ..	48 ,, ,,
Index of money wage rates (Ministry of Labour Index), January, 1944	40 ,, ,,

Now, quite apart from the validity of the above argument, let us consider what would be the result of an increase in retail prices relevant to working-class consumption. First of all, the wages of several millions of workers will rise *immediately*, because of existing agreements linking wages to the cost of living. Other workers are likely to press for corresponding increases and it is difficult to see on what grounds these claims can be rejected if some millions have already obtained a rise. This rise in wages will lead to further price increases. But, even provided that the policy were successful in reducing the relation of wages to prices (that is, real wages) by increasing the cost of living without this having a proportionate effect upon money wage rates, what would be the implications of such a policy? The Chancellor of the Exchequer, quite rightly, considered that this would make it possible to abolish controls earlier without causing an inflationary rise in prices thereafter. But the inflationary pressure *after* decontrol will be reduced only to the extent to which prices have risen in relation to wages *before it*. In short, this method amounts to preventing price increases after decontrol by making prices rise in the same proportion earlier. Just like indirect taxation, it consists in replacing spontaneous inflation by a planned increase in prices.

The Price Level and Foreign Trade

The Chancellor of the Exchequer also mentioned that the subsidies to keep down the cost of living are necessitated not only by the rise in cost of production due to wage increases, but also by increases in prices of foreign raw materials. He considered it dangerous to in-

---

[1] Cf. J. L. Nicholson, 'Employment and National Income during the War,' p. 202.

crease beyond a certain limit the gap between home and world market prices. The dangers involved in such a situation are not very clear. The relatively low level of home retail prices cannot in any way impair the position of exports. It is true that to the extent to which it increases the purchasing power of the population it raises the demand for imports. The Chancellor of the Exchequer indicated, however, at the beginning of his speech that the Government is committed to a full employment policy. Under *laisser-faire*, higher prices in relation to wages would depress effective demand and employment and thus reduce the demand for imports. In the regime of full employment, however, the deficiency in effective demand would be made good by counter-measures and thus the demand for imports would be roughly maintained.

It is true that in particularly unfavourable conditions for exports, full employment may lead to difficulties in equilibrating the balance of foreign trade and thus cause bottlenecks in the supply of imported goods. The problem arising out of this situation would have to be solved by rationing and controls.

The above analysis shows that it is difficult to find any advantages in the abolition of the price stabilization policy. The upward revision of the cost of living will contribute nothing to the solution either of home or foreign problems, but will stimulate a rise in wages and as a result lead to further price increases.

THE WHITE PAPER ON THE NATIONAL INCOME AND EXPENDITURE IN THE YEARS 1938–1943[1]

by M. Kalecki

From Bulletin, Vol. 6, No. 9 (July 1, 1944)

IN the following pages a number of problems connected with war finance are discussed on the basis of the information given in the White Paper.

The Relative Share of Wages in the Product of Industry

Before analysing the data concerning the relative share of wages and other incomes in the distribution of the product, we must discuss a theoretical question relevant to this problem. As is well known, the magnitude of profits depends on the *valuation of stocks*. In the White Paper (Cmd. 6623) no attempt is made to eliminate the change in the basis of valuation of stocks from the beginning to the end of the year. This actually amounts to the valuation of stocks being made on a cost basis throughout, for in the period of continuously rising prices (1940–1943) firms preferred (for tax purposes) to value their inventories at cost rather than at current prices; and for 1938 the valuation at cost and at current price would have given similar results.

If we want to obtain a figure for disinvestment in stocks, that is, a measure of their *quantitative* reduction, we have therefore to correct the White Paper figures for the changing basis of valuation of inventories, and we obtain correspondingly a corrected figure of profits. It can be shown, however, that for the present purpose of analysing the distribution of the national income such a correction is probably not necessary, and that the uncorrected figures of profits given by the White Paper are more adequate for this purpose. With the valuation of inventories at cost, profits in a given year are equal to sales *minus* the factors of production *purchased* during the year *plus* inventories at the end of the year at cost *minus* inventories at the beginning of the year at cost. This means that profits

---

[1] Revised on the basis of Cmd. 6623.

are equal to sales *minus* the cost of factors actually *used* in the production of goods sold during the year. If a is the value of sales, $b =$ the value of the factors of production *purchased* during the year, $b' =$ the value of the factors *used* in manufacture of the goods sold during the year, $c_1 =$ inventories at the beginning of the year and $c_2 =$ inventories at the end of the year, profits are equal to $a - b + c_2 - c_1$ or $a - (b + c_1 - c_2)$. But $b' = b + c_1 - c_2$ and thus profits $= a - b'$. Now if entrepreneurs, as seems usually to be the case, do their pricing on the basis of purchase cost, then profits, as defined above, *plus* overheads correspond to gross margins assumed in pricing. It is this figure, therefore, which must probably be taken into account in the analysis of the distribution of the national income.

We shall calculate first the relative share of wages in the national income, not including in either the remuneration of soldiers. As in the White Paper wages in the strict sense are shown separately from the pay and allowances of H.M. Forces and Auxiliary Services we obtain directly:

		1938	*1939*	*1940*	*1941*	*1942*	*1943*
National income	.. ..£m.	4,619	4,970	5,913	6,877	7,554	8,079
Pay and allowances in cash and kind of H.M. Forces and Auxiliary Services	.. ..£m.	78	124	386	622	805	999
National income less soldiers' remuneration	.. ..£m.	4,541	4,846	5,527	6,255	6,749	7,080
Wages	.. ..£m.	1,735	1,835	2,115	2,419	2,708	2,916
Relative share of wages	.. %	38·2	37·9	38·2	38·6	40·2	41·1

The relative share of wages in the national income, less soldiers' remuneration, was more or less stable at the pre-war level up to 1941; in 1942 and 1943 it was significantly higher than in 1938. As we shall see, however, this is due to the relative fall in the income of 'non-wage industries', namely of real estate and retail trade (the latter employs shop assistants, but they are classified in the White Paper as salary earners) and to the fall of overseas incomes. To eliminate these factors we subtract rents, gross income of the retail trade and (very roughly) overseas incomes from the national income before calculating the relative share of wages.

The sum of rents (only residential, because rents on factory buildings, etc., which are mostly imputed, must be considered rather a part of the income of the respective business) and the gross income of the retail trade has been estimated for the years 1938 to 1943. We now subtract the respective figures from the national income and calculate the relative share of wages on a new basis:

		1938	*1939*	*1940*	*1941*	*1942*	*1943*
National income less soldiers' remuneration .. .. £m.		4,541	4,846	5,527	6,255	6,749	7,080
Estimate of residental rents and gross income of retail trade £m.		960	970	970	950	970	950
National income less soldier's remuneration, residential rents, and inc. of retail trade £m.		3,581	3,876	4,557	5,305	5,779	6,130
Wages .. .. £m.		1,735	1,835	2,115	2,419	2,708	2,916
Relative share of wages .. %		48·5	47·5	46·5	45·7	46·8	47·5

We must still deduct from the national income the income from overseas, which has no counterpart in wages. In 1938 the income from overseas was £235 million; the deduction of this amount from the national income raises the relative share of wages from 48·5 to 51·9 per cent. In the war years the income from overseas has considerably diminished; according to Cmd. 6707[1] it fell to £97 million in 1945. The net share of wages may be estimated now (in round figures) as follows:

Hypothetical relative share of wages in the national income after deduction of soldiers' remuneration, residential rents, gross income of retail trade and overseas income

	1938	*1939*	*1940*	*1941*	*1942*	*1943*
Per cent ..	51·9	50·0	48·0	47·0	48·0	48·5

This series gives us some idea of the movement of the relative share of wages in the national income after eliminating the influence upon it of the relative decline of important 'non-wage industries' in war-time. We shall now try to interpret this movement.

We see that the relative share of wages shows a continuous fall from 1938 to 1941 and a rise in 1942 and 1943. However, the level reached in 1943 is lower than in 1938 (and 1939).

It is interesting to notice that already in 1939 a significant fall as compared with 1938 is noticeable. Part of the decrease may be perhaps explained by high profit margins in armament contracts. (As an instance of these may be mentioned contracts for the construction of warships ordered from 1936 to 1939 described in the report of the Committee of Public Accounts issued in 1943.) In 1940 this factor must have been of much smaller importance; although some contracts concluded in previous years were still running, they were swamped by new ones in which profit margins were much lower. There is, however, another factor which would

[1] Statistical material presented during the Washington Negotiations.

account for a lower relative share of wages in the latter year as compared with 1938 (and 1939). The rise in the prices of raw materials in 1940 as compared with 1938 was much steeper than that in wage costs. If, as is plausible to assume, firms fix their prices normally by 'marking up' prime costs, that is, costs of materials and wages, overheads *plus* profits increase roughly in the same proportion as prime costs. Thus, if raw material prices rise more than wages, overheads *plus* profits also increase more than wages.

The further fall in the relative share of wages from 1940 to 1941 cannot be attributed to this factor as there was no important change in the ratio of prices of raw materials to wage costs. But, in this period there was an inflationary rise in prices in certain consumption goods, that is, price increases out of proportion to prime costs, due to demand outrunning supply. (A further reduction in profit margins in Government contracts probably offset partly the effect of this inflationary factor upon the relative share of wages). In 1942 and 1943 the more rigid handling of contract prices and price control over consumption goods, while wage rates were still increasing, succeeded in reversing the movement of the relative share of wages, although there might have been still inflationary price increases in some sectors.[1]

Disinvestment

According to the White Paper the total amount of private disinvestment at home in the four years 1940–43 is £770 million. We shall try to estimate this item in another way; in doing so we may also shed some light upon its components. They are: (*a*) the reduction in the value of inventories except that caused by war damage and disregarding the increase in work in progress on Government account financed privately; (*b*) the excess of maintenance and depreciation allowances over expenditure in new fixed capital, except that on making good war damage to buildings; (*c*) sales to public authorities of fixed assets previously owned privately.

We shall try first to make a reasonable guess for item (*a*): Let us start from the data on retail trade given in the Bank of England Statistical Summary. In 1943 the value of non-food sales was 93 per cent of the 1939 level, and the value of non-food stocks at the end of 1943 was 98 per cent of that at the end of 1939. Non-food retail

---

[1] The movement of the relative share of wages was of course affected by many factors not taken into account in the above interpretation. We have picked out only what seemed to us the most important determinants.

sales at 1938 prices have been estimated to have fallen from 1938 to 1942 by about 40 per cent, and from 1938 to 1943 by about 45 per cent. Judging from the Bank of England data just quoted stocks must have fallen a little less, and thus we can take 40 per cent as an estimate of the fall in non-food retail stocks up to 1943. The value of the relevant retail sales in 1938 may be estimated at about £1,1000 million which, assuming a period of turnover of three months, amounts to a level of stocks of £275 million at the end of 1938. The reduction of 40 per cent in this is about £110 million (at 1938 prices).

We have seen that the non-food retail stocks have fallen more or less proportionately to the volume of sales. If we assume the same to be true with regard to manufacturing of non-food goods for home consumption and of goods produced for export, the resulting reduction of stocks and working capital may be estimated at £300 million at 1938 prices.[1] Together with the reduction in retail non-food stocks this amounts to £410 million (at 1938 prices). To this should still be added the reduction in the stocks of wholesalers, but there is also an offsetting factor, namely the reduction in stocks caused by war damage which must *not* be accounted for in our estimate. These two items may be well of the same order and we shall take £410 million at 1938 prices as the total disinvestment in stocks and working capital in production and distribution of non-food goods for home consumption and of goods in the period 1940–43 for export. This probably gives an approximation to the *total* disinvestment in stocks and working capital. The reduction in stocks of food, drink, and tobacco was probably a small item. (The reduction in fixed capital under construction is assumed to be accounted for in disinvestment in fixed capital.) At current prices this disinvestment may be estimated on the basis of available wholesale and retail price indices at something like £650 million.

It is not, however, this figure which is the component of the White Paper figure of total disinvestment. Indeed, the White Paper figure includes the change in the value of inventories, while what we have calculated is the value of the quantitative reduction of inventories.

[1] It may be roughly estimated that the value of non-food home consumption at wholesale prices plus exports was in 1938 about £1,270 million. In 1942 the value of these two items at 1938 prices fell to approximately £670 million (cf. *Sources of Man-power in the War Sector*). It may be concluded that exports and non-food home consumption fell by something like £600 millions at 1938 prices. We may further estimate that working capital and stocks in the manufacture of those products amounted to something like six months' value of exports plus home consumption of non-food goods. Thus, if inventories have fallen proportionately to the output of finished goods in question, the resulting reduction in stocks and working capital would amount to £300 million at 1938 prices.

Owing to the considerable appreciation of inventories in war years (in particular 1940 and 1941) the former figure is much smaller than the latter: the fall in the *volume* of stocks was partly offset by the rise in the *value per unit*. According to Mr. Barna[1] the total appreciation is of the order of £500 million. Thus, out of £650 million, which is the value of the quantitative reduction, only £150 million will be left as a measure of the reduction in the value of inventories (exclusive of the value of the quantitative change of fixed capital under construction).

We shall now examine the items (*b*) and (*c*), that is, disinvestment in fixed capital and sales of fixed assets to public authorities. Our starting point is the White Paper disinvestment figure for 1943, which is given as £220 million. The reduction in stocks in that year must be assumed rather small, as the fall in output and consumption of non-food goods and probably in exports had more or less ceased. We may suppose that the current value of the quantitative reduction in that year was something of the order of £50 million. There was, judging from the price indices, no significant appreciation or depreciation of stocks, so that we assume the fall in the value of inventories at £50 million, which leaves us with £170 million for disinvestment in fixed capital and sales of fixed assets to public authorities. The allowances for maintenance and depreciation are estimated in the White Paper at £475 million.[2] Deducting £170 million, we obtain £305 million as a measure of gross investment minus sales of fixed assets to public authorities. What about the previous war-years? The *volume* of gross investment was probably higher, especially in 1940 and possibly also in 1941. The *prices* of investment goods were, however, lower and the sale of fixed assets probably higher than in 1943. On balance the average rate of excess of depreciation allowances over gross investment *plus* sales of fixed assets to public authorities might be not very different from that in 1943, that is, £170 million, and for the four years 1940 to 1943 this would make about £700 million. This, together with the decrease in the value of inventories estimated above at £150 million would amount to £850 million. It is this figure that is comparable with the total war-time disinvestment given in the White Paper at £770 million. The difference is considerable, but this is not surprising in view of the extremely shaky basis of our estimates and of possible considerable errors in the White Paper figures which are obtained as relatively

[1] *Economic Journal*, June–September, 1943, p. 264.
[2] Exclusive of the greater part of the outlay on repairs except on those to buildings.

small balancing items of two large amounts and therefore are considerably influenced even by small relative changes in these amounts.

It is fairly likely on the basis of the above discussion, that our estimate of £850 million as the total disinvestment during the war is too great, so that we may take it as the upper limit. What is the *real* disinvestment corresponding to this figure? We have assumed that stocks and working capital in the 'civilian sector' fell proportionately to output. With regard to disinvestment in fixed capital, it has been assumed that the rate of gross investment, *minus* sales of fixed assets to the Government, was at the rate of £305 million p.a. at current prices, which makes something like £200 million at 1938 prices. Depreciation in war-time, based on purchase cost of equipment was taken as £475 million; and thus gross investment, *minus* sales of fixed assets to the Government at 1938 prices, would amount roughly to 40 per cent of depreciation, and gross investment by itself to something like 50 per cent of depreciation (or more).

The conclusion emerges from our analysis that gross investment in fixed capital was probably at a higher level than 50 per cent of depreciation (part of it, however, was used to make good war damage) and that stocks and working capital in the 'civilian sector' were not reduced more than porportionately to output. The latter explains why the considerable reduction of inventories did not affect the functioning of production and distribution in that sector.

It should be stressed that the disinvestment both in fixed and in working capital discussed above applies only to the *private* sector of the economy.[1] It is quite possible that the Government has *accumulated* stocks of goods in war-time. As to Government investment in fixed capital not only have many State-owned factories been built, but also the Government has financed a large amount of investment in privately-owned establishments and this investment is *not* accounted for either in the White Paper figures of disinvestment or in our guesses. It is, of course, difficult to assess to what extent this investment will remain useful for the economy after the termination of hostilities.

Personal Savings

The aggregate personal income may be divided into three components: (a) direct tax payments, inclusive of those due for repayment after the war but exclusive of death duties and stamps on the transfer

---

[1] Disinvestment in fixed capital, however, includes that in the *non-war* sector of public authorities (mainly local authorities).

H

of property; (*b*) personal expenditure on consumption; (*c*) gross personal savings. The latter in turn may be subdivided into: (1) death duties, etc.; (2) excess of direct tax liabilities over tax payments; (3) costs involved in the acquisition and transfer of property and life assurance by persons; (4) net personal savings. Gross savings provide a measure of savings out of current spendable income, if we make the plausible assumption that people budget their expenditure on the basis of their incomes net of taxes *paid*. The personal savings ratio on this assumption will be that of gross personal savings to personal income after payment of direct taxes (inclusive of those due to repayment after the war but exclusive of death duties, etc.). This ratio was as follows in the period 1938–43:

The Saving Ratio

	1938	1939	1940	1941	1942	1943
Per cent	7·7	9·4	16·5	20·4	22·5	25·0

If we deduct these percentages from 100 we obtain the percentage part of spendable income consumed. The White Paper gives further the indices (1938 = 100) of real personal consumption, that is, of the personal consumption in terms of constant prices. If we divide them by the percentages of spendable income consumed and relate the series obtained at the 1938 level, we obtain what may be called an index of real personal spendable income:

Real Consumption and Real Income

		1938	1939	1940	1941	1942	1943
Real personal consumption (1938 = 100)		100	100	88	81	80	78
Consumption out of spendable income	%	92·3	90·6	83·5	79·6	77·5	75·0
Real personal spendable income (1938 = 100) ..		100	102·5	97	94·5	95·5	96·5

The percentage of spendable income saved increased very considerably in spite of a slight fall in the real spendable income. This increase is thus entirely due to war-time conditions, because normally a fall in real income reduces the saving ratio. In 1940 it was mainly the voluntary effort which increased the saving ratio, while rationing and general uncertainty (which discouraged buying of household goods, etc.) played only a secondary rôle as stimulants of saving. The increase in the saving ratio in the subsequent years, however, was probably due mainly to limitation of consumption by rationing and shortages.

We shall now compare the rise in personal savings with that in so-called small savings (Savings Bank Deposits, National Savings

Certificates, and 3 per cent Defence Bonds). We take personal savings net of death duties, etc., and costs of acquisition and transfer of property, but gross of the excess of tax liabilities over tax payments. To the 'small savings' should be added the rise in coin and note holdings in the hands of 'small men' which most probably constituted a substantial part of the increase in the note and coin circulation. As there is no way of estimating precisely what part it was, we show in the Table both 'small savings' proper, and small savings plus the increase in the coin and note circulation. The adjusted figure of 'small savings' is somewhere in between. For both these two variants we calculate the difference as compared with 1938 level, and compare the result with the corresponding difference in personal savings, by calculation the ratio of the latter to the former.

'Small Savings' and Personal Savings

			1938	1940	1941	1942	1943
1. Small Savings	..	.. £m.	4	467	601	600	719
1a. Rise over 1938 level		.. £m.	0	463	597	596	715
2. 'Small Savings' plus increase in cash circulation[1]	..	.. £m.	−3	541	744	769	886
2a. Rise over 1938 level		.. £m.	0	544	747	772	889
3. Personal savings net of death duties, etc.	..	.. £m.	183	712	1,006	1,274	1,521
3a. Rise over 1938 level		.. £m.	0	539	823	1,091	1,338
4. Percentage (1a) : (3a)	..			86	73	54	54
5. Percentage (2a) : (3a)	..			101	91	70	67

[1]The increase in cash circulation is calculated as the difference of coin and note circulation outside banks in January of the next year and January of the year considered (Source: Statistical Summary of the Bank of England).

In 1940 and 1941 these ratios in both variants are much higher than in 1942 and 1943. This may be explained by the great rôle played in 1940 and 1941 by transfers from other assets and investment of current savings of large savers. This process, however, could not continue indefinitely, because of the exhaustion of transferable assets of small savers and the reaching of the statutory limit of the respective small savings holdings by the large ones.

THE PROBLEM OF 'SMALL' SAVINGS

by M. Kalecki

FROM BULLETIN, VOL. 5, No. 16 (NOVEMBER 20, 1943)

THE recently published inquiry of Mr. Madge into the 'War-time Pattern of Saving and Spending'[1] provides some interesting data which contribute to the elucidation of the character of 'small savings.' The object of a budget and interview inquiry[2] were two large samples of manual workers' and small salary earners' families in Leeds, in the periods February–May and June–August, 1942, respectively. The results of this survey show that about 4 per cent of gross incomes was devoted to National Savings (p. 34). In an Appendix Mr. Rothbarth introduces a correction to this figure based on the fact that in the budget inquiry and in the interview inquiry in the second half of the survey (June–August) the percentage of saving was much higher than in the interview inquiry in the first half of the survey. He attributes this difference to the greater reliability of the budget inquiry and to the improvement of interviewing in the second half of the survey. The correction he introduces raises the percentage of savings in relation to gross income to about 5 per cent (p. 133). This figure gives a basis for estimating the total rate of National Saving of manual workers and small salary earners by applying the above percentage to the appropriate aggregate income. The results of such a calculation must, however, be treated with great caution for two reasons: (1) Leeds may not be representative for the whole country, and (2) what is probably more important, the above percentage of savings obtained for Leeds may be too low because some people refused to be interviewed, and this may introduce a certain bias into the sample; for, as Mr. Rothbarth puts it, 'thrift and secretiveness may correlate'.

This second objection to the validity of the results of the survey may, however, be accounted for by estimating a plausible upper limit for the bias in question. Out of all budgets and interviews attempted in the second half of the survey, 63 per cent were successful, 9 per cent doubtful or inadequate, and 28 per cent were refusals[3] (p. 28).

[1] National Institute of Economic and Social Research, *Occasional Paper*, IV.

[2] The Budget inquiry was based on regular family budget records. The interview inquiry applied where people refused to keep budgets; it attempted to obtain data on income, spending, and saving in the past week, by interviews.

[3] 15 per cent total refusals, and 3 per cent cases where the husband refused information about the money retained by him.

The cases classified as doubtful and inadequate are those where the total amount of income did not square with spending, tax payment and saving. From various particulars given about this category in the report, it does not seem that these people were particularly heavy savers. We shall therefore assume that the percentage of saving in this category is the same as in successful budgets and interviews. It is in the case of refusals where we may suspect a correlation between secretiveness and thrift. We shall assume that half of the refusals were very heavy savers, and the other half saved at a normal rate. This assumption probably exaggerates the connection between secretiveness and thrift, because there are quite a lot of other reasons for not being interviewed, the simplest of which being that people may not like to be bothered. It follows from the above assumptions that 86 per cent are taken to save at the rate of 5 per cent of their income while the remaining 14 per cent are much heavier savers. We shall assume for them a rate of saving of 20 per cent. The resulting average rate of saving would then be 7 per cent. On this basis the Leeds rate of National Saving in 1942 was between 5 and 7 per cent of income. Of course, this rate of saving may still not be representative for Great Britain as a whole; still, the amount obtained from the application of this percentage to the wage-bill and small salary bill will not be devoid of significance.

According to the White Paper (Cmd. 6623) the wage-bill (exclusive of pay and allowances to H.M. Forces) was in 1942 £2,708 million and the salary bill £1,381 million. Further, it may be estimated that in 1938 salaries below £250 a year constituted less, but not very much less, than 40 per cent of the total salary bill.[1] Thus, if we add to the wage-bill 40 per cent of the salary bill we obtain a reasonable figure for the wage and small salary bill. On this assumption we obtain £3,260 million.[2] Apply to this 5–7 per cent, obtained above as the rate of National Savings in relation to income, we arrive at £160–230 million. We may thus say that if the Leeds percentage of saving is representative for Great Britain the contribution of manual workers and small salary earners to National Savings in 1942 was of the order of £200 million. This compares with the aggregate of about £600 million of small savings in 1942. It is more correct, however, to compare the £200 million working-class savings with the £465 million invested

[1] From 'Changes in Salaries in Great Britain', by Joan Marley and H. Campion, *Studies in the National Income*, edited by A. L. Bowley in conjunction with the data on the aggregate salaries of shop assistants (whom we classify throughout as salary earners) and on the total salary bill.

[2] The percentage error in this figure caused by an even relatively large error in the small salary bill is of no importance.

in National Savings Certificates and Post Office and Trustee Savings Banks, because manual workers and small salary earners are not likely to buy National Defence Bonds, the subscriptions to which amounted to about £135 million. Thus, working-class saving would make 40 to 50 per cent of the increase in Savings Bank Deposits and National Savings Certificates. It may be asked how the rest of the small savings assets were absorbed. A certain part could still, even in 1942, be transfers from other assets. But this part is not likely to have been large in 1942. The rest might be current saving out of incomes of pensioners, wives of service men, of small shopkeepers and farmers— which again is not likely to amount to much—and out of medium and large incomes, in particular that done by wives and juniors.

2. Mr. Madge's report includes also an inquiry into a sample of Post Office Savings Bank accounts in Glasgow and Aberdeen. The changes in deposits were examined in half-yearly intervals from November, 1938, to May, 1941. Its results are therefore unfortunately not comparable with those of the Leeds survey. The Savings Bank inquiry indicates that in the period November, 1939, to May, 1941, about one-third of Post Office savings in Glasgow and about 40 per cent in Aberdeen was due to increases in individual deposits by £150 or more in any half-yearly interval examined (p. 89; actually these rates of one-third and 40 per cent relate to the balance of increases and decreases in deposits by £150 or more in any half-year examined). Clearly this part of deposits corresponds to transfers or current savings of large savers. Out of the remaining increase in deposits 55 per cent in Glasgow and 68 per cent in Aberdeen was due to manual and black-coated workers; the rest were savings of traders (24 and 14 per cent) or juniors (21 and 18 per cent). It follows that the current savings of manual and black-coated workers in Glasgow and Aberdeen were of the order of 40 per cent[1] of the total increase in Post Office Savings bank deposits. Mr. Madge states repeatedly that working-class savings are invested to a much greater extent in Savings Banks than in National Savings Certificates; thus the share of workers in small savings, even excepting National Defence Bonds, must have been appreciably less than 40 per cent in the period November, 1939, to May, 1941. This compares with 40 to 50 per cent obtained above on the basis of the Leeds inquiry for 1942.

[1] By multiplying 2/3 by 55 per cent and 0·6 by 68 per cent we obtain 37 per cent and 41 per cent for Glasgow and Aberdeen respectively. Corrections for two factors should be introduced here: working-class 'savings' may still, and most probably do, include transfers amounting to less than £150 in half a year; some of the junior savers are certainly working class. Both corrections are probably not very large and act in opposite directions.

3. The results arrived at above will be helpful in the analysis of the trend of small savings which is shown in half-yearly intervals from 1940 up to date.

TABLE I

RATE OF SMALL SAVINGS

£ million

		3 per cent Defence Bonds	National Savings Certificates*	Savings Bank Deposits†
1940.	April–September	94	88	71
1940–41.	October–March	96	97	102
1941.	April–September	90	109	111
1941–42.	October–March	92	136	117
1942.	April–September	55	99	115
1942–43.	October–March	56	125	145
1943.	April–September	69	170	146

* Inclusive of the accrued interest.
† Inclusive of the accrued interest not credited to depositor's account.

After small savings reached their lowest level in the middle of 1942, they have shown since that time a spectacular increase. In an earlier article[1] we attributed the fall in 1942 to many medium and large investors having reached the statutory limit in National Defence Bonds and National Savings Certificates, and we took it as an illustration of the considerable share of transfers and large savers in the National Savings. To what, then, is to be attributed the reversal of the tendency since that time? Let us analyze National Defence Bonds, National Savings Certificates, and Post Office and Trustee Savings Banks separately.

With regard to National Defence Bonds we notice that the high level of 1941 has not been regained. The relatively high figure of the period April–September, 1943, is swollen by the Wings for Victory Campaign (March–June, 1943), and the consideration of the period after its end shows that the average for the calendar year 1943 will be appreciably lower. The position of National Savings Certificates is more complicated. It is now obvious that the low level in April–September, 1942, was partly a reaction to the 'effort' made in the Warship Weeks Campaign which swelled the figure for October–March, 1941–42. During saving campaigns some people probably transfer money to National Savings assets from other investments, but in the subsequent period they partly offset it by investing their current savings in the latter. After elimination of this factor the level of savings in National Savings Certificates in April–September, 1942, would probably be close to the (half-yearly) average for the calendar year, 1942, which was £115 million. A corresponding figure for

[1] 'The Fall of Small Savings', p. 113.

April–September, 1943, is—judging from the period preceding and following the Wings for Victory campaign—something of the order of £150 million (instead of £170 million).

This figure, however, is not strictly comparable with that of 1942 for another reason: it includes subscriptions to the new issue of National Savings Certificates the interest on which is not tax-free and which was made for the benefit of investors who have reached the statutory limit in the old National Savings Certificates. In the period January–June, 1943, the subscriptions to this new issue of Savings Certificates made about 10 per cent of the total increase in Savings Certificates.[1] Thus, £115 million in 1942 is comparable to something like 90 per cent of £150 million, that is, to £135 million in 1943. We thus obtain the following picture:

TABLE II

ADJUSTED SAVING IN NATIONAL SAVINGS CERTIFICATES (OLD ISSUE)

Half-yearly rate £ million

Mid–1941	..	109*
Mid–1942	..	115
Mid–1943	..	135

* The figure April–September, 1941, from Table I; it differs little from the average of 1941 which was £107 million.

The net sales of National Savings Certificates thus adjusted show a continuous rise which was, however, much greater from mid-1942 to mid-1943 than in the preceding period. The same tendency can be noticed in the Post Office and Trustee Savings Bank Deposits. (See Table I; adjustments like those made for National Savings Certificates are not necessary here, because Warship Weeks and Wings for Victory Campaigns did not disturb this series to a great extent.) We are thus still left with the question why the increase of small savings between 1942 and 1943 was considerably higher than between 1941 and 1942. With regard to National Savings Certificates the explanation may be the combination of two tendencies: (1) working-class savings increased steadily throughout the period considered, (2) many medium and large investors reached the statutory limit between mid-1941 and mid-1942. The latter factor cannot affect the trend of Savings Bank Deposits, because in these not the total amount of deposits but the yearly increase is limited (to £500). In both types of assets the slowing down from 1941 and 1942 could also be due to the saturation of transfers of small investors who exhausted their transferable assets.

[1] Cf. *Banker*, October, 1943, p. 12.

THE FALL IN 'SMALL' SAVINGS

by M. Kalecki

FROM BULLETIN, VOL. 4, No. 15 (OCTOBER 31, 1942)

1. IN the Summer and Autumn of this year 'small' savings showed, for the first time since the beginning of the war, a definite tendency to decline. The fact was widely commented on in the financial press, and it is interesting to inquire in some detail into the character and causes of this phenomenon.

In the table below the various types of 'small' savings (3 per cent Defence Bonds, National Saving Certificates, and Savings Bank Deposits) are shown separately in half-yearly intervals.

RATE OF SMALL SAVINGS
£ million

		3 per cent Defence Bonds	National Saving Certificates[1]	Savings Bank Deposits[2]
1940.	April–Sept.	94	88	71
1940–41.	Oct.–March	96	97	102
1941.	April–Sept.	90	109	111
1941–42.	Oct.–March	92	136	117
1942.	April–Sept.	55	99	115

[1] Inclusive of the accrued interest.
[2] Inclusive of the accrued interest not credited to depositor's account.

As we see, the various types of savings were very differently affected by the recent fall. It was very strong in the net sales of 3 per cent Defence Bonds and the level of this type of savings is much below the corresponding figure for last year. The fall of investments in National Saving Certificates was also considerable, but still much smaller than in Defence Bonds, and the level reached was not much below that of the corresponding period of last year. Finally, the increase in Savings Bank Deposits remained nearly stable, and was higher than the level in the same period of 1941. To understand this divergency we must first say something about the general character of small savings.

2. It has been repeatedly stated in the Bulletin that so-called small savings are by no means really the current savings of 'small men'. This may easily be confirmed by comparing the total amount of small savings in 1941 with a crude estimate of these savings of workers and small salary earners in that year. It follows from the White Paper

(Cmd. 6633) that the total wage and small salary bill in 1941 was something like £3,000 million. Further, according to the provisional estimate of Mr. Madge, the percentage of income saved by the working-class in the shape of 'small' savings may be estimated at less than 5 per cent. This would mean that these savings of wage and small salary earners in 1941 amounted to less than £150 million. However, total 'small' savings in 1941 were £601 million, so that the savings of wage and small salary earners contributed only about 25 per cent to the total of small savings, if the above estimate is correct.

It should be noted, from what information is available, that 3 per cent Defence Bonds are in general not bought by working-class savers, but the above estimate of their share in 'small' savings is much lower even than the savings in National Certificates and Savings Bank Deposits only, which amounted in 1941 to £427 million.

It is thus clear that a major part of 'small' savings is to be accounted for either by transfers from other investments or by the current savings of large savers. This is not only due to the savings campaign, which makes people think that it is particularly patriotic to invest as much as possible in small savings at the expense of other types of investment, but to the very advantageous terms which small savings offer to an investor. All three types of small savings have terms of withdrawal not very different from bank deposits, on which the rate of interest is negligible, while the rate offered on small savings assets is about the same or much higher (for National Saving Certificates) than on medium- and long-term Government securities. One may wonder whether, because of the limits of this type of investment, it is worth while for a large or medium investor to take this advantage into account. It is, however, easy to see that the total amount which could have been invested by a family in small savings, over the three years of the war, is not at all so small. A person can invest in 3 per cent Defence Bonds up to the limit of £1,000, in National Certificates up to the limit of £375, and in Savings Bank Deposits £500 each year.[1] That means that over three years the total amount which could have been invested was £2,875, and for a family of four it would be £11,500. This amount may be quite considerable, even for a rather wealthy person, especially with regard to the investment of his new savings during the three years of war.

3. Referring back to the table, we see that savings in 3 per cent

---

[1] Actually, if a person has accounts both in the Post Office Savings Bank and in the Trustee Savings Banks he may increase his saving deposits at a rate of £1,000 p.a.

Defence Bonds maintained a steady level up to the Summer of 1942. As Defence Bonds are probably bought mainly by large and medium investors it may be asked why all the transfers were not made, say, in the first year and, after the limit had been reached, why they did not stop. The answer is, that the advantages offered by Defence Bonds might have been insufficient for many people to induce them to sell their other investments. However, when they considered how to invest new savings or the proceeds out of the compulsory sales of foreign securities called up by the Government and the redemption of home securities, it was quite natural for them to invest up to the limit in the securities which offered the greatest comparative advantage. But, of course, with the lapse of time, more and more people reached the limit and finally a decline in this type of investment was bound to occur.

The position with regard to National Saving Certificates was different in so far as a considerable proportion of these is accounted for by really small savers who have no chance to reach the limit for quite a considerable time. Their savings increased owing to the rise in the wage-bill and the difficulty of spending the increased earnings on account of rationing, shortages of goods and so on. This was sufficient to create a permanent rise in National Saving Certificates in spite of the fact that here also the limiting factor for large and medium investors made itself felt.[1] The effect of this latter factor on the recent fall of investment in National Saving Certificates may be partly due to the high pressure of the savings campaign during the London Warship Week in March, 1942, which was responsible for the high figure in the October–March period of 1941–42. This pressure might have induced many transfers to National Saving Certificates and in this way accelerated the process of reaching the limit. However, the fall in National Saving Certificates was less drastic than in Defence Bonds owing to the important part played by small savers.

The position of Savings Bank Deposits is, of course, quite different from that of 3 per cent Defence Bonds and National Saving Certificates, because what is here subject to the limit is not the total amount but the yearly increase in deposits. This explains why the Savings Bank Deposits were not affected by the recent fall in 'small' savings. The increase in this type of savings in the earlier period was

[1] As stated by the Chancellor of the Exchequer 60 per cent of the persons who acquired National Savings Certificates during the war, and who by now have reached the limit, bought the maximum amount at one time.

to a great extent due, as in the case of National Saving Certificates, to a strong rise in the current savings of the working-class.

4. In discussions about the fall in small savings it has often been suggested as a remedy that the limit for National Saving Certificates should be raised in order to enable the 'small' saver to carry out his task.

If, however, the 'small' saver is really small it is highly unlikely that his war-time savings could reach the limit of National Saving Certificates even if we do not take into account the fact that for a family the limit is proportionately higher. For imagine a worker who, starting to save on a large scale only in war-time—and this is the case with most of the workers—has saved up till now £375. That would mean that he must save £125 a year, and because it is highly unlikely that he can save more than 20 per cent of income this would mean that he must have earned over £600 (tax free) a year, which does not seem to be a very plausible figure. And, indeed, as stated recently by the Chancellor of the Exchequer, 95 per cent of the owners of National Saving Certificates have not reached the limit.[1]

The effect of raising of the limit for the National Saving Certificates would be in fact: (1) to secure on paper a high level of savings which would result from the advantageous terms of National Saving Certificates; and (2) to provide for investors an additional profitable opportunity at the expense of the Treasury. Fortunately the Government did not fully assent to this demand. The new issue of Saving Certificates, announced recently, yield less than a half as compared with the old issue. It is a little more advantageous than Savings Bank Deposits after deduction of standard income tax, but a little less profitable than 3 per cent Defence Bonds after the same deduction. The limit for the new issue is £187½. However, even this limited concession is superfluous. If the public is anxious about the fall of 'small' savings, the remedy is not to force them up at the expense of other investments and at an additional cost to the Treasury, but to explain that the figures of 'small' savings are misleading, and may show a fall, although the total amount of personal savings (and in particular that of genuine small savings) is on the rise.

---

[1] 40 per cent out of the remaining 5 per cent bought the maximum amount in one lump. (The figure of 60 per cent mentioned in the preceding footnote applies only to persons who bought their certificates during the war.)

THE DISTRIBUTION OF WORKING-CLASS SAVINGS

by Henry Durant and J. Goldmann

FROM BULLETIN, VOL. 7, No. 1 (JANUARY 13, 1945)

IN discussing the incidence of savings among wage-earning families *The Economist* recently commented that 'the problem can obviously only be settled by means of a much wider survey of the total savings accumulated in individual families'. Such a survey has, in fact, been carried out; an account of its results is given below.

1. *The Sample*

The enquiry was undertaken by The British Institute of Public Opinion in the Spring of 1944. The findings are derived from a national sample of 1,153 working-class families who revealed both their weekly net family income and their total holdings of savings. The method of selection was that of stratified sampling described elsewhere.[1]

In a national survey comprising 3,465 interviews, 2,575 were obtained with either householders or their wives; 1,921 of these were classified as working-class.[2] Families with no adult earner (mainly families of old-age pensioners and of men in the Forces) were excluded; they numbered 292. Of the remaining 1,629 working-class contacts 15 per cent were unable to give information on their family income, or refused. (Some of them answered the question on savings). Another 14 per cent, while supplying information on their family income, did not reply to the question about savings. Thus we arrive at an effective sample of 1,153 working-class families with at least one adult wage-earner.

2. *The Distribution of Savings*

The term 'savings' referred to holdings of savings and was not restricted to National Savings. Contacts were asked to state what

[1] See p. 299.

[2] Altogether 4,143 persons were approached; of these 16 per cent refused to give an interview. This is not much different from the proportion refusing to answer surveys containing only questions on opinion. Moreover, the interviews proceeded for some time until the questions about savings and income were reached. Therefore, these refusals to give an interview at all, may be held to be unrelated to savings and income.

The classification into working-class and others is made by the interviewers on the spot, using a combination of occupational and income characteristics.

kinds of money savings their families had, but only 21 per cent of those saving mentioned savings other than National Savings Certificates, Post Office and Trustee Savings Banks, and Saving Stamps. These were savings through Co-operative Societies, Banks, Clubs. by holding cash, Government Bonds and through Building Societies (deposits or share capital). Interviewers were specially instructed to confine the enquiry to money savings; any saving through insurance societies or through repayments of mortgages was excluded and so were other types of savings in the form of real assets.[1]

Table I gives (*a*) the distribution of families according to the size of their accumulated savings and (*b*) the share of aggregate working-class savings held by each group.

TABLE I

DISTRIBUTION OF WORKING-CLASS SAVINGS

Range of Savings £	Percentage of families within this range	Share in Aggregate Savings Per Cent
None	13 ⎫	0 ⎫
Up to 25	23 ⎬ 52	3 ⎬ 9
„ 50	16 ⎭	6 ⎭
„ 75	9	6
„ 100	15	16
„ 200	12	19
„ 300	5 ⎫	14 ⎫
„ 400	2	7
„ 500	1	5
„ 600	1	5
„ 700	1 ⎬ 12	4 ⎬ 50
„ 080		
„ 900	1	6
„ 1,000		
Over 1,000	1 ⎭	9 ⎭
	100%	100%

From the Table it will be seen that 52 per cent of the families, the poorer half of the sample when the families are arranged in order of the magnitude of their savings, own only 9 per cent of aggregate savings, while 12 per cent of the families, at the other end of the scale, own 50 per cent of aggregate savings. These results broadly confirm the conclusions obtained for the *rate* of national saving by Charles Madge in the Leeds Enquiry (see 'War-time Pattern of Saving and Spending', p. 67). If the families without earners had been included, the degree of inequality in the distribution of savings would have been slightly increased. They were not included or subjected to further analysis because it was believed that the size of their savings was scarcely related to their present conditions. Their inclusion

[1] In a few exceptional cases an endowment policy was included when it was nearing maturity.

TABLE II

FREQUENCY DISTRIBUTION OF FAMILIES BY SAVINGS AND BY INCOME GROUPS

Size of Savings (£)

Family Income (£)	None	-25	-50	-75	-100	-200	-300	-400	-500	-600	-700	-800	-900	-1,000	1,000—	No. of Families	Average Savings
Up to 2	15	5	2		1	1										24	15·6
Up to 3	24	38	10	2	8	5			1	2						90	44·2
Up to 4	57	88	28	21	27	20	4	2	1							248	44·3
Up to 5	26	53	45	30	39	21	6	3			3	2				230	80·0
Up to 6	25	47	41	24	40	32	13	3	2	1	1	1			1	230	82·9
Up to 8	4	22	41	17	36	31	19	6	2	1	1					183	121·7
Up to 10	3	4	5	12	21	12	10	2	2	2			2		2	78	188·1
Up to 12	2	4	6	1	11	8	2	3	2	2	2	1			3	46	221·7
Up to 15		2	1		2	3	3	2	1	2				1	2	15	235·8
Over 15			1	1	2	3		1							1	9	236·1
All families	156	263	180	108	187	136	57	22	11	10	7	4	2	1	9	1,153	91·7

would have tended to veil the relationships which it has been attempted to isolate.

3. *The Effect of Income*

Only a very loose correlation is to be expected between the present income and the stock of past savings. Yet there is a fairly regular relationship between average family income (net of Income Tax and Social Insurance contributions) and average savings held (see Diagram A).[1] Family Savings increase with rising family income but at a faster rate.[2]

Such a relationship, even if it is not very regular as the diagram shows, cannot necessarily be expected *a priori*. We know that income is correlated with the rate of saving.[3] There is, however, no reason to suppose that current income should be closely correlated with the total accumulated stock of money savings.

DIAGRAM A

STOCK OF FAMILY SAVINGS BY FAMILY INCOME

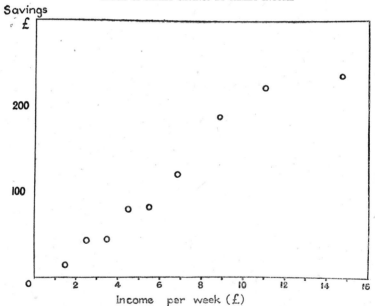

[1] Table II contains a summary of the information on which this and the following diagram are based. The two highest income groups were combined in Diagram A and the last point has the ordinates £14·7 and £235·9.
[2] The correlation coefficient between net family income and family savings is + 0·35. The skewness of the distribution restricts, of course, the usefulness of the correlation coefficient.
[3] See Madge, loc. cit., and Income and Spending and Saving of City Families in Wartime, U.S. Department of Labour, Bulletin, No. 724, p. 11.

There are grounds, however, for expecting that money savings accumulated during the war, when the possibilities of spending have been severely restricted, would be fairly closely correlated with current income. Since we find a correlation present, it seems reasonable to suggest that the total present savings held by the working-class consist, in fact, largely of savings made during war-time.

4. *The Effect of the Number of Children*

Within each income group there is still a considerable scatter of savings about the group average. To isolate, so far as possible, the influence of differences in family structure, the savings of each income group were further classified according to the number of children under sixteen in the family (see Diagram B).[1]

DIAGRAM B

FAMILY SAVINGS BY FAMILY INCOME AND NUMBER OF CHILDREN UNDER 16

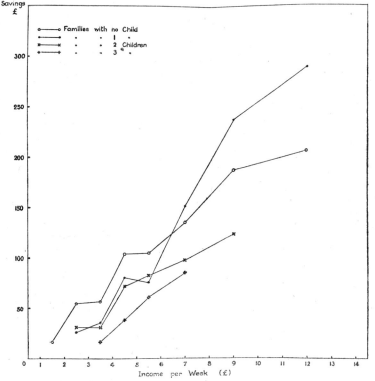

[1] Because of the low cell frequency in the upper end of Table 2, the last three income groups have been aggregated in Diagram B.

I

As might be anticipated, the Diagram indicates that, for the lower ranges of income, savings within any income group tend to decrease as the number of children increases. Unfortunately, the sample is too small to test the validity of this generalization for the higher income ranges. There is, for instance, some indication that with rather high incomes one-child families tend to save more than families without children.[1]

5. Checks on the Sample and the Results

The average size of the family in the effective sample is 3·6, and the average number of children is 1·0, against 3·77 and 1·15, respectively, in the Ministry of Labour Budget Enquiry, 1937-38. The call-up would, of course, tend to reduce the average size of the family. Families where all the earners are in the Forces and the wife not working would tend to have a larger number of children under sixteen. Their exclusion thus reduced the average number of children in the sample.

As the original data were already grouped (in £1, £2, or £3 intervals for family income and in £25 or £100 intervals for family savings) there are some difficulties in estimating average income and average savings from the data. If it is assumed, as has been done in the Tables and Diagrams, that the group averages coincide with the mid-points of the group intervals, average family income is £5. 9s. 0d. and average savings £92. There is, however, some evidence that quite frequently, say, the letter 'C' on the check card handed to the contact was taken to stand for a family income of 'about £4' instead of 'up to £4.'[2] If this practice were general

FAMILY INCOME—Per week

A	up to £2
B	up to £3
C	up to £4

the group averages would accordingly coincide with the upper limits of the intervals, and average family income would be £6. 2s. 0d., and average family savings £112. The correct figures are probably

[1] The effects of income and number of children on savings were singled out not because it was thought that they are the only determinants of savings, but because they are probably the most important ones, and also because they are more easily handled than other factors, such as family history, occupation, age, etc. A breakdown by additional characteristics would also require a far larger sample.

[2] During the interview a check card was handed to the contact, with letters printed against the income and savings scales. The contact was asked to call out the letter printed against his income group and saving group. It has been proved that such a procedure considerably reduces the rate of refusals. The first part of one check card read as follows:

between these limits. In any case, the assumption made about the position of the group average has only a very slight influence on the shape of the distribution of either incomes or savings.

The average net family income of between £5. 9s. 0d. and £6. 2s. 0d. compares with an average net family income of £6. 2s. 0d. in the 1943 Enquiry of the Institute of Statistics; but it should be borne in mind that the latter Enquiry was in the main restricted to families with at least one *male* earner and strictly confined to families with at least one dependent child.

6. Conclusion

It is probable that among those who refused to answer there was a higher proportion of big savers than amongst those who did answer. This would tend to raise the general average of savings, but would only slightly affect the degree of inequality in the distribution of savings.[1] In other words, whilst some facts relating to savers may not have come to light, the results of the enquiry—after allowing for errors in this sampling method—do suggest that the bulk of the working-class population have comparatively insignificant holdings of money savings.[2]

---

[1] The average income of those who refused to state their family savings but gave their family incomes was £5. 15s. 0d., against £5. 9s. 0d. for those who revealed both income and savings (taking mid-points as group averages).

[2] The converse is also true, of course, that there is a fairly small section of the working-class with rather high holdings of savings.

THE BURDEN OF THE NATIONAL DEBT

by M. Kalecki

FROM BULLETIN, VOL. 5, No. 5 (APRIL 3, 1943)

1. THE problem of the burden of the National Debt has three important implications. It is, firstly, more or less generally accepted that it is essential in war-time to keep the budget deficit as low as possible in order that the future interest payments on the debt should be reduced. This consideration plays an important rôle in war-time increases in indirect taxation of necessities and semi-luxuries, which can hardly constitute a proper device to fight inflation because they themselves contribute to the rise in prices.

The other two implications affect not the war finance proper but the discussion of post-war economics, as, for instance, the Beveridge Plan. It is frequently maintained that the burden of the debt has increased very much up till now and this, together with the future rise, will make it impossible to embark upon costly reforms. And even more general is the conviction that it is impossible to have a budget deficit in peace-time whenever it is necessary to maintain full employment, if this leads to a long-run rise in the burden of the debt.

We propose in this paper to show: (1) that in spite of the great increase in the amount of the National Debt in the course of this war up to the present, the future 'burden' of the present debt is not likely to be higher than in 1938–39; (2) that it is possible to devise special taxes for financing the interest on National Debt which will render its increase harmless in the sense that it will have no repercussions on output and employment; that therefore it is not necessary to consider the reduction of the budget deficit as such to be an important problem of war finance; and that a regime under which budget deficits would be used whenever necessary to maintain full employment does not involve insuperable difficulties.

2. In the financial year 1938–39 the interest on National Debt was £223 million.[1] Not all this sum can be considered a 'financial burden' because a part is returned to the Treasury through income tax and surtax paid on this income. (The precise definition of the amount returned by taxation is that it is equal to the loss of yield of

---

[1] Inclusive of interest accruing on National Saving Certificates.

income tax and surtax if the payment of the interest on National Debt were suspended). This amount may be roughly estimated as standard income tax charged on the interest on National Debt, because the balance of the influence of income tax exemptions, allowances, and reduced income tax rate on one side and of surtax on the other is probably relatively small.[1] With the standard rate of 5s. 6d. in the £ in 1938–39 the tax-free interest on National Debt may be thus estimated at £162 million.

In 1942–43 the interest on National Debt was about £330 million. Now, the post-war standard rate of income tax may be conservatively assumed—7s. 6d. in the £. Taking into account that in the £330 million[2] there is about £20 million of tax-free interest on National Saving Certificates, we may estimate, on the above assumption, the future tax-free interest on the present National Debt at £214 million. But this is not the end of the story. The post-war level of prices will be hardly less than 30 per cent higher than pre-war, and the 'tax yielding capacity' may be assumed to increase in roughly the same proportion. Thus, to compare the future 'burden' of the present debt with the pre-war 'burden' it is necessary to deflate £214 million by 1·30, which gives £164 million as compared with £162 million of the pre-war tax-free interest on National Debt.[3]

It may be objected to this calculation that, since a large part of the National Debt is in the form of floating debt, the future 'burden' of it would be higher if the short-term rate of interest increased after the war. To that it may be replied that the present short-term rate is higher than in the last seven pre-war years; and that the short-term rate of interest may be easily controlled by the Government in combination with the Bank of England. There is thus no reason to expect its rise in the future as compared with the present level.

3. We have shown that the future 'burden' of the present National Debt is, on plausible hypotheses, approximately the same as it was before the war. But the war is not yet over, and, as endeavours are made to keep prices stable and thus no further reduction in the 'real' value of the National Debt can be expected, the 'burden of the debt' will certainly rise. This will continue for a few years after the termina-

---

[1] The influence of income tax exemptions, allowances, and reduced income tax rate was in 1938–39 greater than that of surtax for unearned incomes as a whole. (As a result the average rate of income tax and surtax on unearned income was of the order of 4s. in the £, while the standard rate was 5s. 6d. in the £). It must not be forgotten, however, that if interest on the National Debt were suspended it would 'come off the top'.

[2] Inclusive of interest accruing on National Saving Certificates.

[3] Even considerable changes in the rate adopted for the calculation of the tax-free interest on National Debt are of small importance for the results of this comparison, if these changes are proportionate for the two cases compared.

tion of hostilities, in particular in connection with the payment of compensation for destroyed property and of post-war credits. Thus, it is important to consider the general problem of dealing with the 'burden of the debt'.

Imagine, first, that interest on National Debt incurred after a certain date, for instance, from now onwards, will be financed by a special annual capital tax on all private capital (inclusive, of course, of Government securities). A rise in the National Debt will increase the amount of capital tax to be collected, but will, at the same time, increase the interest yielding assets in private possession, which would not have come into existence if the budget had been balanced. The capitalists, as a body, gain by an increase in the National Debt as much in interest as they lose in capital tax.

Moreover, it may be shown that the increase in the National Debt does not involve any disturbances in output and employment if interest on it is financed by a capital tax. The current income after payment of capital tax of some capitalists will be lower and of some higher than if the National Debt had not increased, but their aggregate income will remain unaltered and their aggregate consumption will not be likely to change significantly. Further, the inducement to invest in fixed capital is not affected by a capital tax, because it is paid on any type of wealth. Whether an amount is held in cash or Government securities or invested in building a factory, the same capital tax is paid on it and thus the comparative advantage is unchanged. And if investment is financed by loans it is clearly not affected by a capital tax because it does not mean an increase in wealth of the investing entrepreneur. Thus, neither capitalists' consumption nor investment is affected by the rise in the National Debt if interest on it is financed by an annual capital tax.

4. We shall now briefly consider the order of magnitude and the administration of the annual capital tax. As we propose this for financing the interest on the National Debt incurred after a certain fixed date, say from now onwards (the interest on the 'old debt' being already accounted for in the budget), the relevant interest on the National Debt may be assumed to be about 2 per cent, as this is approximately the present average cost of (short-term and long-term) borrowing and there is no reason to assume that it would be increased in the future.[1] The annual capital tax will thus be substantially lower

---

[1] The Government can continue to have on tap the long-term and medium-term issues and finance the rest by floating debt. It is true that the cost of borrowing will increase if sales of long- and medium-term issues rise in proportion to the budget deficit, but then nothing prevents the Government from reducing the rate of interest on these issues.

than 2 per cent, because the tax to finance the interest on the 'extra debt' will be collected from all types of privately-owned capital, of which the 'extra debt' constitutes only one item. If, for instance, this debt were one-half of all privately-owned assets the annual capital tax would amount to 1 per cent. Moreover, it should be noticed that even if there is a long-run increase in the National Debt as a result of a 'full employment policy', the rate of the annual capital tax need not necessarily increase. Indeed, permanent full employment in conjunction with the increase in population and technical progress will certainly cause expansion in private capital equipment. Whether the *rate* of capital tax will rise or not depends on the relation between the budget deficit necessary to maintain full employment and the rate of expansion of capital equipment.

The above argument still requires some elucidation. It seems reasonable to deduct the capital tax from income before income tax is paid, as is done in the case of capital depreciation. For instance, if an asset yields 4 per cent, and the capital tax is 1 per cent, the income of 3 and not 4 per cent would be subject to income tax. This causes, of course, a certain reduction in the average yield of income tax, but this is offset by the income tax yielded by the interest on National Debt. If the National Debt increases, the national income being constant, and the interest on National Debt is financed by a capital tax, the aggregate yield of income tax is unchanged. It is true that it is being reduced by the increasing amount of capital tax, but it is being *pro tanto* raised by the increasing interest on National Debt.

The annual capital tax would have to be higher if small property were exempted from it. This would be desirable both for social and administrative reasons. If, for instance, property below £1,000 were exempted, the rate of capital tax would have to be increased by something like one-fifth.[1]

The simplest way to administer the capital tax would probably be to collect it by taxing on capital of enterprises and persons, not including shares and debentures in the valuation of wealth. The balance sheets of enterprises in combination with existing valuations of fixed assets by tax authorities would then provide the basis for the valuation of the great part of private capital. The smallness of the capital tax as shown by the above estimates will facilitate the collection of the tax.

5. If, however, the administration of the capital tax is considered likely to involve serious difficulties, it is possible to replace it by a

[1] See Campion, 'Public and Private Property in Great Britain'.

modified income tax, the influence of which upon the national economy as a whole would be more or less equivalent to that of a capital tax. This income tax would be imposed on unearned income only and thus would affect the same people as the capital tax. However, income tax, as opposed to capital tax, weakens the inducement to invest because it reduces the net rate of profit. The following modification may remove this adverse effect. Imagine that income tax is charged on gross unearned income, that is, before deduction of depreciation. On the other hand all investment on fixed capital, whether for the sake of replacement, or expansion, is deducted from the taxable amount. (If it exceeds the taxable income the excess is carried over for deduction in the next years.) It is easy to show that such a tax does not affect the rate of profit expected on new investment. Indeed, suppose that an entrepreneur expects for each £100 invested in fixed capital a gross profit of £10 per annum. One shilling in the £ of our income tax reduces this expected profit to £9½ per annum. But, by investing £100 he gets £5 reduction in his current income tax and thus the cost of investment is reduced to £95. Consequently, the expected gross rate of profit is the same 10 per cent per annum as if the tax were not in existence. Thus, the repercussions of the 'modified income tax' will be more or less the same as those of the capital tax.

6. It follows that if the interest on National Debt incurred after a certain date is financed by a special annual capital tax or by a special 'modified income tax' the rise in the National Debt will not involve a 'burden' and will not have any significant repercussions on output and production. Consequently, to keep down the Budget deficit in war-time in order to reduce the increase in the National Debt ceases to be the primary objective of war finance. And, if to maintain full employment in peace-time requires budget deficits there is no reason to be scared by the rising National Debt.

THE IMPACT OF THE WAR ON INDIA

by J. Steindl

From Bulletin, Vol. 4, No. 5 (April 4, 1942)[1]

1. It is intended in the following to give an outline of the economic changes which the war has produced, and is likely to produce in the near future, in India.

India is a predominantly agricultural country. In 1931, 88·5 per cent. of the principal earners of income in British India were living in rural areas, and 70 per cent. were directly dependent on agriculture. The proportion of agricultural income in the total income of British India was 53 per cent., the proportion of the income of rural areas in the total about 70 per cent. (Rao, *National Income of British India*, 1931–32). The Indian States are certainly of an even more rural character. It is unlikely that the last decade has produced a *fundamental* change in the proportions.

The production of armaments in India is rendered difficult by the limited size of organized large-scale industries, as compared with the size of the population and the wealth of raw materials (e.g., iron ore, manganese, bauxite). The number of workers employed in large-scale industries (those establishments which come under the Factories Act) was 1,750,000 in 1939, only 200,000 more than in 1929. Production of finished steel was of the order of one million tons in 1939–40, and output of coal 25 million tons in the same period. Since the beginning of the war industrial capacity has been expanded to some extent, under the recommendations of the Chatfield Commission, and industrial output has increased.

What is the difficulty in the way of a substantial increase in the production of war material? In contrast to other countries engaged in the war, India has an abundant supply of labour. This takes the form of 'disguised unemployment', i.e. people are employed in occupations of very low productivity, domestic service, handicraft, small-scale trade, and last but not least, they are crowding the land and splitting it up into uneconomically small holdings, a considerable part of the present population being completely surplus, so

---

[1] The tables and figures in this article have been revised and brought up to date, but the contents remain substantially unaltered.

that their withdrawal from agriculture would not involve any reduction in the output. What makes the transfer of this surplus into industry difficult is the lack of equipment and the difficulty of training, but apart from this there is a more fundamental problem. A considerable increase in war production (which would, in fact, amount to a part-industrialization, would require an increase in the production of food. This is directly due to the fact that industrial workers earn a higher income than workers in other occupations; more fundamentally it is due to the fact that the industrial workers, if they are to be of any use in production, require, on purely physiological grounds, a higher standard of living and especially a better diet than the people engaged in low productivity occupations with a sub-marginal standard of living. A substantial transfer of labour from 'disguised unemployment' to industrial employment will therefore increase the demand for consumption goods, amongst other things, also the demand for food. The quantitative importance of this increase in demand for food will, of course, depend on the amount of labour drawn into industrial employment, and on the increase in total industrial income resulting from the expenditure of the newly employed workers. It will be additional to other food requirements brought about by the war: the net additional food required by the increasing army in India, and the necessity of food exports to provide the armies of the middle east. Even if the additional food requirements are small as compared with the total food production, the effect may be noticeable, as the demand will be largely concentrated in big populated places, and the area from which the food supply of these centres is drawn is in practice only a part of the total agricultural area of the country.

TABLE I

				Yield				
	Area under Food Grains	Rice (cleaned)	Wheat	Cotton	Jute	Linseed	Ground Nuts	Sugar
1929/30 ..	100	100	100	100	100	100	100	100
1930/31 ..	101	104	90	96	109	99	117	117
1931/32 ..	102	106	87	67	54	109	96	145
1932/33 ..	101	100	91	86	75	107	127	171
1933/34 ..	103	99	90	93	77	99	141	178
1934/35 ..	100	97	93	93	83	110	80	187
1935/36 ..	100	91	91	98	70	102	96	216
1936/37 ..	102	104	93	105	93	110	121	236

It seems to be a feature of agricultural production in India that it is rather inelastic. An Indian expert on the subject writes: 'Production is no measure of activity in the case of agriculture, especially in India where virtually the same area is cropped every year so that production is practically independent of the price obtained. . . . While acreage remains constant, so does the yield per acre.'[1] That there are no substantial variations in acreage can be seen from the statistics; Table I gives the area under food grains in British India, in percentages of 1929–30, and shows that the variations amount only to a few per cents. The course of actual output is more difficult to judge, because the statistics are unreliable; the estimates of agricultural production in British India are based on sample estimates of yield per acre in different districts. Table I gives the output figures, for what they are worth, of important crops, again in percentages of 1929–30. There is obviously an important difference in the behaviour of so-called 'commercial crops' (cotton, jute), which show a definite dependence on price and the state of trade (which is largely due to a change in acreage of these crops with varying price), and the food grains which show no such influence. While the statistics are inconclusive the assumption of a high inelasticity of food production can be supported by general information about Indian agriculture. Production, especially in the case of such important food crops as rice, is very labour intensive, using extremely little equipment, and the technique remains unchanged year by year. It is plausible to assume that under these conditions the yield, apart from the influence of the weather, is stationary. A rapid expansion of total acreage cannot be expected, because it would require heavy capital outlay. A changeover of area from surplus industrial crops to food crops is advisable, but it is not likely to come about automatically, without assistance to the agriculturalist; the area devoted to oilseeds, cotton and jute is about 18 per cent of the area devoted to food grains, but only a part of the industrial crops are surplus.

2. Owing to the inelasticity of agricultural production, an expansion of purchasing power in India must very largely have the effect of increasing prices. By 'increase in purchasing power' is meant the generation of additional money income, either by construction of industrial equipment, or by accumulation of stocks, or by a government deficit, or finally by an excess of exports over imports. The last of these factors, the *foreign balance*, is by far the most important in the case of India, so that the others can, as a first approximation,

[1] Sen Gupta, in *Economic Problems of Modern India*, by Prof. Mukerjee, p. 329.

be neglected (the budget deficit will be taken into account at a later stage). It is necessary in the following to consider India and Burma together, because the two countries for financial purposes are difficult to separate.

To evaluate this foreign balance (Table II) for the last years account must be taken not only of the surplus of exports over imports, on private account, but also of the purchases of British and other Empire governments which are not included in the statistics of private merchandise trade, and of the payment of Britain for the construction of plant, for the army, etc.   On the other hand, the remittances of the Indian government to London on account of interest, pensions, etc. (so-called 'home charges'), and the remittances of private firms for interest, dividend, etc., must be deducted. The remaining 'foreign balance' finds its counterpart in the accumulation of sterling balances (mostly British treasury bills) in the Reserve Bank of India. In part this sterling balance was used for repatriation of the sterling debt of the Government of India, and the foreign balance for the last years can therefore be obtained by adding up the increase in sterling assets in the Reserve Bank and the sums used for repatriation of the sterling debt (line 1 and line 2 in Table II). Roughly, the same result must be obtained, if H.M. Government's *net* requirements of sterling exchange are deducted from (or its *net* refunds of sterling are added to) the purchases of sterling by the Reserve Bank. The latter item results from the surplus of private merchandise and treasure export, the counter value of which is sold in the form of sterling exchange to the Reserve Bank, after private requirements for transfer of interest, dividend, etc., have been covered.

Having thus obtained the foreign balance it is necessary to make one adjustment in order to estimate the amount of new purchasing power generated. Part of the foreign balance is due to a surplus of treasure exports which merely constitutes the exchange of one form of assets (gold coin, ornaments, etc.) into another (notes, securities, etc.), but not the generation of additional incomes. The surplus of treasure export must therefore be deducted from the foreign balance, to obtain the *net addition to purchasing power* due to the foreign balance. From 1940–41 on statistics of private treasure exports are not available; it is, however, certain that they have declined considerably during this period, owing to the increase in prices of precious metals in India. We can, therefore, regard the foreign balance, uncorrected for treasure exports (Table II, line 6), as sufficient indication for our purposes in these years. It will be seen from Table II that in the two years preceding the war the foreign balance was a negative quantity; the net effect of the foreign balance was deflationary. In 1939–40 the figure was about 50 crores of rupees,[1] and in 1940–41, probably somewhat higher. In the financial year ended March 1942 the foreign balance was about 250 crores of rupees. As to the year 1942–43, it was mentioned in the Budget speech that large sums would be paid by Britain for purchases, and the foreign balance is bound to rise to even higher levels (see Table II).

TABLE II

THE FOREIGN BALANCE

(Financial Years, April–March)

(in crores of rupees)

	1936–37	1937–38	1938–39	1939–40	1940–41	1941–42	1942–43	1943–44
1. Accumulation of sterling	+15	−18	−13	+66	+2	+140	+227	+434
2. Repatriation of sterling securities	—	1	—	22	89	110	160	16
3. Purchases of sterling by the Reserve Bank	71	33	34	97	76	98	122	140
4. H.M. Government's net requirements (—) or refunds (+) of sterling	−55	−50	−48	−10	+15	+152	+265	+310
5. Balance of private treasure export[1]	+15	+15	+23	+41	—	—	—	—
6. Foreign balance including treasure exports (1+2) or (3+4)	+15	−17	−13	+87	+91	+250	+387	+450
7. Foreign balance excluding private treasure exports (6—5)	+0	−32	−36	+46				

Sources—*Reserve Bank of India.* Report on Currency and Finance 1944–45, p. 38, and earlier reports; and Statistical summary.

[1] Not available from 1940–41 onwards.

Beside the foreign balance the budget deficit is also contributing to the creation of additional purchasing power. In pre-war times the budget was practically balanced, heavy 'retrenchment finance' being practised during the depression. Owing to war expenditure an increasing deficit has now appeared. If this deficit is added to the net foreign balance the following figures are obtained:

Crores of rupees	1939–40	1940–41	1941–42	1942–43
Foreign balance	45	60	250	387
Budget deficit (+) (surplus —)	−8	+8	+13	+145
	40	70	260	530

Only the order of magnitude of these figures is significant. They show that the net additional purchasing power 'injected' into the

[1] 1 crore is 10 million; 1 rupee =1/6 (10 million crores of rupees = £7·5 million).

system has increased considerably in 1941–42, and will rise to an even higher level in the course of 1942–43. There is no doubt that it will constitute a considerable financial problem for India.

3. Both the foreign balance and the budget deficit must be financed by new saving, which must either find its way into the banking system and form there the counterpart of the increased holding of sterling assets and of government securities. The following table gives the increase in circulation and bank deposits during the war:

Crores of rupees	1939–40	1940–41	1941–42	1942–43
Increase in circulation of notes and rupee coin	+62	+57	+165	+318
Increase in deposits in Scheduled Banks	+21	+26	+51	+172
	+83	+83	+216	+490

It appears that in 1939–40 and in 1940–41 the increase in all forms of money is about as great as the total foreign balance including of treasure exports, and in 1941–42 it amounts to a large proportion of the latter. The new saving has thus taken primarily the form of holding liquid assets. This is probably largely due to the increased requirements of money for the purposes of transactions, owing to the increasing price level and the expanding sphere of monetary transactions.

The rupee securities created as counterparts for the repatriated sterling debt in March 1941 have, in the first instance, been taken over by the Reserve Bank, and by the government. Subsequently a large part seems to have been absorbed by the banks. The counterparts for the new repatriation in March 1942 have largely been taken over by the Reserve Bank.

4. The sum of foreign balance and budget deficit—it may be called 'Investment' in the sense of Mr. Keynes' General Theory—must create an equal amount of saving to finance it. Under the conditions of inelastic supply prevailing in India this saving will largely be created by an increase in prices, which raises the profit margins and the excess of the peasants' cash receipts over their expenditure until the necessary saving is forthcoming. As far as the scanty evidence with regard to prices goes, it supports the view that the Rs. 260 crores of 'investment' in 1941–42 have already produced a noticeable increase in prices.

The cost of living index for Bombay has risen by 25 per cent from

August 1939 to August 1941, the cost of living indices for Ahme-
dabad and Sholapur by 26 per cent. and 18 per cent respectively
in the same period. The difference in the development in different
towns is due to different composition of the index; for large industrial towns the Bombay index is more representative than the Sholapur index. It must be kept in mind that retail price statistics are
rather unreliable in India, but as the Bombay cost of living index
is used widely as a basis for wage negotiations (dearness allowances),
it is not likely to overstate the increase in prices. Part of the price
increase, especially at the beginning of the war, is due to increased
import prices and reduction of imports. The quick rise in summer
1941 seems, however, largely influenced by increased war purchases
and production.

It may be expected that the further increase in 'investment' in
1942–43 will have a noticeable influence on the cost of living.
The amount of money spent is large in proportion to the Indian
economy, and it will be largely concentrated in certain centres.[1] The
corresponding saving will have to come partly out of increased
profit margins of industrial entrepreneurs and merchants, partly out
of increased cash receipts of peasants which will thereby be enabled
to repay debt or to hoard. It is impossible to say to what extent
merchants and industrialists on the one hand and peasants on the other
hand will contribute to this saving.

The increased cost of living will almost certainly affect the condition of the workers adversely. Owing to lack of any wage statistics
it is impossible to say how far it has been offset by wage increases.
Payment of a bonus for increased cost of living is widely used,[2] but
the adjustment of this bonus can always be effected with a certain
lag only. As always in the case of inflation, the increase in money
wages will not catch up with the price increase, because the necessary saving can be squeezed out only by permanently higher profit
margins.

On the other hand, the rise in prices to be expected will affect
the burden of debt which weighs particularly heavily on the
peasantry. The indebtedness of Indian agriculture was estimated
by the Banking Enquiry Committees in 1929 at about Rs. 900 crores
for 1928–29, and it was put at about Rs. 1,200 crores for 1933.[3]

---

[1] The national income of British India and Burma was estimated at Rs. 1,600 to 1,800
crores in 1931–32, of which about Rs. 500 crores was income of urban population. Since
then the income must have increased considerably on account of price increases and increase
in production.

[2] See *International Labour Review*, December 1941.

[3] Mr. P. J. Thomas in *Economic Problems of Modern India*, p. 176.

A considerable rise in prices would depreciate the real value of this debt.

5. It appears from the preceding analysis that a substantial increase in the war production of India is not only dependent on the help which the United States can give in the form of machines, tools, experts, etc., but that it also constitutes a considerable financial problem for India. The main reason for this is the inelasticity of supply; in part this can be overcome by using more of the available labour: for example, to provide additional housing for workers in war industry. To a large extent, however, this elasticity is rooted very deeply in the existing structure of the Indian economy, and it is therefore likely that the increase in expenditure will produce an appreciable price rise.

III. CONSUMER'S RATIONING AND PRICE CONTROL

GENERAL RATIONING

by M. Kalecki

FROM BULLETIN, VOL. 3, NO. 1 (JANUARY 11, 1941)

THE PROBLEM

THERE are indications that in the second half of the year the financial situation was 'inflationary': stocks of consumption goods were run down and/or a rise in prices of these goods out of proportion with costs took place. After a certain time this development must lead to scarcity of goods and still greater price increases, and the only way in which this may be prevented is by the curtailment of total expenditure on consumption.

Broadly speaking there are two ways, other than the *laisser faire* method of inflation, of adjusting consumers' spending to available supplies: taxation and rationing.

The common disadvantage of all *taxation* schemes is that their effect is not much different from that of price increases. This is quite clear in the case of flat income taxation, which affects the real consumption of the various income groups in much the same way as a rise in prices. The difference between these two ways which is in the back of the mind of people who advance such proposals is probably based on a rather arbitrary assumption that workers will not ask for higher wages when taxed while they usually do it when the cost of living rises, and thus the 'vicious spiral' will be prevented. Even granted that the assumption is right, the only people for whom the difference is essential are those with fixed incomes. For workers it does not, of course, matter whether their wages will be cut by 10 per cent. by taxation or whether prices will rise by 100 per cent. and wages by 80 per cent.

Is taxation of the higher incomes an adequate solution of the problem of fair curtailment of consumption? Such taxation will undoubtedly tend to reduce to some extent the expenditure of the well-to-do, but to what extent is most uncertain, for the latter are likely to reduce the amount currently saved and in many cases even to dissave. Moreover, they may curtail their expenditure in an unhelpful way by cutting, say, education and entertainment while the actual problem is the scarcity of food, clothing, etc.

Mr. Keynes' scheme does not differ essentially from income taxation. For the working class the consolation offered by prospective post-war enjoyment of compulsory savings is of a rather shadowy character. As to the well-to-do, on whom in the last version of Mr. Keynes' scheme falls the chief burden of compulsory saving, it is even less efficient than income tax in cutting their consumption: seeing compulsory savings accumulating on blocked account they are more likely to save less on a voluntary basis or to dissave than they would if taxed to the same extent.

The most direct way of controlling expenditure is *specific rationing* over a wide range of shop goods, on the lines of the existing rationing schemes for, say, butter or meat. But here also the disadvantages are serious. To be comprehensive such a scheme must embrace an enormous number of commodities which involves considerable inconvenience for consumers and shopkeepers, as also difficulties in control. Moreover, it is difficult to prevent the transfer of coupons from poorer people, who do not fully consume their rations, via shopkeepers or otherwise, for the benefit of those who can afford to consume more, and among the latter this 'surplus' is distributed in a haphazard and unfair way. Finally, at the moment when the rationing is introduced shopkeepers are in possession of certain stocks of commodities which they are able to sell without coupons unless their inventories are permanently watched; and a general running down of stocks is obviously undesirable.

THE GENERAL RATIONING SCHEME

Is there another way of restricting consumers' spending which is free from the disadvantage of specific rationing of individual groups of commodities?

It seems to us that a scheme limiting consumers' total expenditure in shops attains the end by a less cumbrous way and with less inconvenience to consumer and shopkeeper. The scheme is based on a simple principle. A total maximum expenditure in retail shops is fixed at, say, 25s. a week for an adult and 15s. for a child under 14.

Expenditure on services is not included in our scheme, because some of them are not scarce (e.g. education, entertainments) while others may, if necessary, be controlled much more simply by direct methods: dwelling space by billeting; travelling by reducing the number of trains and abolishing first class; gas and electricity by direct rationing; domestic services by fixing the maximum number of servants, etc., etc.

Apart from services, certain categories of goods could be bought coupon free: (1) medicines; (2) newspapers and books; (3) repairs. For people who have lost their chattels as a result of bombing, newly-married couples, etc., a special allowance should be made. The coupons required for the purchase of meals in restaurants must be only a certain definite proportion of their price, since it includes the cost of service.

THE PROBLEM OF COUPON DISTRIBUTION

If all people are issued coupons for the same amount those of low income grades will not be able to use them fully and might sell the residue to the well-to-do (or buy goods on their account). This problem may be handled in two ways. As in the case of specific rationing of commodities, we may make the transfer of coupons a punishable offence. Nevertheless, transfer may take place to some extent. The reduction in expenditure, which can be fully relied upon, is then limited to the difference between the present actual expenditure and that which would ensue from the full use of their coupons by all people. The possible transfer of coupons from the poor to the better-off people is undesirable for the same reasons which were mentioned in the discussion of specific rationing of commodities: the 'surplus' coupons will be redistributed among the well-to-do and the rich in a haphazard and unjust way.

One may, however, take another course and reduce the possibility of the transfer of coupons in the following way: the Government distributes the spending coupons at the flat rate, but at the same time declares that it is prepared to buy back unused coupons at the values to which they relate. As a result, any one who is unable to use a certain amount of his coupons because his income is too small, will be able to sell *half* of the unused coupons to the Government and, with the proceeds, make use of the other half for purchases.[1] This arrangement has the following advantages:

(1) The transfer of coupons from the poorer to the richer popula-

[1] He will be able, of course, to adopt another policy: he may, e.g., sell more than half of the unused coupons and increase his expenditure on services.

tion is prevented. For a poor man, being able to sell his coupons to the Government on the above terms, is likely to prefer to do this, rather than sell them illegally, even if the price offered were higher. On the other hand, the rich will be discouraged from buying coupons illegally because they will have to pay for the coupons more than their face value, and thus pay for the purchase of any particular good more than *twice* its price.

(2) Under the system allowances are granted automatically to the lower income groups.

(3) All this is done without any administrative machinery, such as census of incomes, etc.

It is true that this scheme implies some increase in Government expenditure, but after allowing for this increase, the curtailment of total expenditure in shops is still greater than it would be if all people used all their coupons. This is because only *half* the amount of coupons which the poor, at present, could not spend because of insufficient income, would, under the above arrangement, be used for purchases, while the other half would be given up to the Government.

ADMINISTRATION OF THE SCHEME

A certain difficulty in the running of the scheme may arise from the possible destruction of coupons by bombing. This may be prevented by issuing not actual coupons but books of Post Office Savings Banks model, in which the maximum expenditure for a certain period is credited to the owner, and on which he may draw the actual coupons from the Post Office, the procedure being exactly the same as with Post Office Savings Banks.

The most difficult problem is to ensure that goods are not sold without coupons. For this purpose a Retailers' Controlling Office might be established to which the retailers return all coupons received and obtain there 'retailers' coupons' which they must, in turn, surrender to wholesalers when buying from them. These return the 'retailers' coupons', which must cover their full turnover as ascertained for payments of Purchase Tax, to the Authorities. The Retailers' Controlling Office will be in this way in possession of data on purchases of each retailer and will be able to compare them with the amount of 'consumers' coupons' surrendered. The amount of consumers' coupons should exceed that of retailers' coupons by an amount corresponding to retailers' margin *plus* the fall in retailers' stocks or *minus* their rise. The retailers will be requested to supply, in addition, the value of their stocks at certain intervals, and so the Retailers' Controlling Office will be able to see whether a retailer's margin—as calculated from his purchases, coupons returned and changes in his stocks—is at a level customary for his line of business. In all doubtful cases an investigation of the actual margin must be carried out on the spot and heavy fines imposed if the case of selling without coupons is proved. Also the declared value of stocks must be checked by samples and fines imposed if a misleading declaration is discovered.

FINAL REMARKS

This scheme presents, I think, certain definite advantages. First and foremost it constitutes a real safeguard against inflation, and it can easily be adapted to the most stringent supply situation. Secondly, it is comprehensive and more convenient than the specific rationing of a corresponding range of goods; instead of struggling with an avalanche of coupons, for boots, clothing, electric torches, pots and pans, etc., etc., the consumer and the shopkeeper have to master only one set of coupons. Finally, although for particular reasons—e.g., nutrition—some goods must be rationed specifically, among the remainder the consumer has, in our scheme, the widest possible freedom of choice. Against this must be set the disadvantage of complex administration, although it must be stressed that the administrative problem of our scheme will be simpler than that involved by the specific rationing of all goods.

Although income tax and specific rationing of commodities have been criticized above as methods for curtailment of general expenditure, they not only do not interfere with this scheme but actually supplement it. The savings accumulating as a result of the functioning of the scheme should be at least partly collected not by borrowing but by taxation, and for this reason the income tax rate should be raised. In some cases this will bring a certain pressure on expenditure and so reduce the possibilities of evasion from our scheme.

The rationing of some essential commodities is necessary also within our scheme, because the latter only reduces but does not abolish fully the inequality of expenditure. For this reason it may also be advantageous to 'differentiate' our scheme by introducing food and non-food coupons.

RATIONING AND PRICE CONTROL

by M. Kalecki

FROM BULLETIN, VOL. 6, No. 2 (FEBRUARY 5, 1944)

IT has been stated time and again that price control without rationing is not effective in combating inflation.[1] The inflationary tendency arises when the demand for consumption goods exceeds their supply at current prices, and therefore prices tend to increase. If they are fixed at the existing level the discrepancy between demand and supply must show itself in queues and shortages and the distribution becomes haphazard. The reply to the opposite question, whether rationing makes price control unnecessary, is much less obvious. We shall start from the simple case of rationing of one commodity and then pass to the more complex one of the point rationing scheme.

1. Imagine that rationing of a certain commodity has been introduced. The first requirement that it shall be effective in preventing the increase in price of this commodity is that the rations should be fixed at such a level as to match the available current supplies. If the ration is 'too high' the price will tend to increase. In some cases, however, prices may rise after rationing even if the ration *has* been properly matched with the available supply.

Imagine that rationing is introduced at the stage where there is a *tendency* for inflationary price increases, that is, for the rise of prices out of proportion with prime costs, but that this has not happened in the past. In other words, the ratio of price to prime costs is still 'normal' but there is a tendency for this ratio to increase under the pressure of demand. The introduction of rationing brings into equilibrium the quantities demanded and supplied. Prices may nevertheless increase for a different reason. It seems fairly likely, at least for some commodities, that rationing reduces the sensitiveness of customers to price differences as between various sources of supply. Thus, the market becomes more imperfect; competition becomes less keen; and the price may increase although the disequilibrium between demand and supply has been removed by rationing. To prevent this, price control is required.

2. We see that there are some reasons for accompanying rationing

---

[1] cf. M. Kalecki, 'What is Inflation?' (See p. 80.)

by price control if we want to keep the price at the level which prevails at the time when rationing is introduced. We are going to show now that price control is even more important if we want to reduce the price. Such will be the case, for example, when rationing is introduced after a certain measure of inflation has taken place, that is, after the price of a given commodity has risen appreciably in proportion to its prime costs under the pressure of demand. Can we expect that rationing by itself will do the trick? The reply is rather negative.

First, rationing is usually combined with a quota system, that is, the allocation of supplies to firms in certain fixed proportions. As a result, after rationing which matches the current supplies has been introduced the firms cannot tend to increase their sales by competing with one another. But even if we assume that this factor is not effective because rations have been fixed somewhat below the level matching the available supply, there is another reason why it is very uncertain whether prices would fall. As already mentioned, rationing may cause the market to become much more imperfect and this will prevent competition from getting the price down.

The most effective way, then, to reduce the prices to the 'normal level,' that is, to the level which shows a 'normal' ratio to prime cost, is price control. It should be added, however, that if prices are reduced considerably below the level they have previously reached, it may necessitate some reduction in the ration. For the reduction in price may increase demand somewhat by inducing those people who at the old price did not use fully their coupons to increase their purchases.

To sum up: in order to reduce the inflated price it is necessary to accompany rationing by price control. The ration in general must be somewhat lower than that which would match current supplies at the price which was in existence at the moment of introduction of rationing.

3. All the conclusions arrived at above are applicable to a point scheme. The ration in terms of points must match the current supplies in terms of points. Price control is desirable if it is intended to keep the prices at the level prevailing at the moment when rationing is introduced. It is necessary if it is intended to reduce the prices below this level. There are, however, additional problems to be considered. We are now dealing not with one good but with an aggregate of goods. That demand and supply are equilibrated by rationing for all goods in terms of points does not mean that such an equilibrium

exists for each of the goods in question taken separately. Demand and supply for single goods may be adjusted either by the automatic movement of uncontrolled prices or by changes in points values, that is, in points necessary to purchase a unit of a given good.

We shall argue that the latter is the preferable way. The system of prices should be controlled while demand and supply for single commodities should be brought into equilibrium by varying the relative point values. This may be supplemented by changes in the relations of controlled prices.

It may be shown that if such adjustments are left to the 'free play' of prices it is by no means certain that the price index of the commodity group considered would not increase. Take, for instance, the case when we have two commodities A and B in the point scheme. Let us assume that the total number of points in the ration is divided equally between these two commodities, and so is their value in terms of money. Imagine now that the demand shifts from A to B, while the supply of either commodity is fixed. Imagine further that A has closer substitutes among the commodites outside the group than B. Then the relative price rise in B will be higher than the relative price fall in A and the price index of the group will rise. Of course, when demand shifts from B to A there will be a decrease in the price index of the group.

There is, however, a factor which makes for a tendency for the price index of the group rather to rise than to fall when demand shifts from one commodity to another. So far we have assumed that price changes have to be such that the volume of sales of either commodity would remain unchanged. In fact, that will be true only of the commodity in greater demand if its supply cannot be increased. But, the price of a less demanded commodity may not fall at all or at least not enough to prevent a decline in the volume of its sales; the fall in demand may cause a reduction in supply or an increase in stocks.

It follows that the best way to stabilize the price index of the group is to keep the price of commodities concerned under control and change the relative point values until equilibrium of supply and demand is achieved for all commodities. It may be useful to supplement this measure by changes in the relations of the controlled prices, in particular when a large part of the consumers do not use their coupons fully and thus are not subject to the influence of changes in relative point values. We may thus conclude that in the case of a point scheme, price control is desirable for additional reasons and that it should be combined with variable point values.

4. An interesting illustration of the above may be found in the developments which took place in the first years of rationing of clothing and footwear when it was unaccompanied by price control. After the introduction of rationing in June, 1941, the retail price index of the Ministry of Labour continued to rise until March, 1942, the total rise in that period having been about 10 per cent. It is true that in the same period there was some rise in the prices of raw materials and wages in this sector, but from all that we know the order of these changes was not such as to justify the increase in the prices of finished products by 10 per cent. We also know that in the same period a shortage of cheaper goods was noticeable and probably it is mainly their prices that caused the increase in the price index.

The rise in prices after the introduction of rationing might have been due to the rations being too high in relation to the available supply. But the shortage of cheaper goods points to another factor which might be even more important in this context. The shortage of cheaper goods was most probably due to a *relative* shift in demand. The rationing of clothes and footwear cut severely the consumption of the higher income groups while that of the poor was little or not at all affected.[1] The structure of production, however, did not adapt itself to this change for some time. (The quota of firms specializing in production of cheap and expensive clothing were probably reduced in the same proportion initially). As a result there was a tendency for cheaper goods to increase in price while the prices of more expensive goods did not fall.[2] Thus there was a tendency for the price index of clothing to increase even independently of the fact that the rations might have been fixed a little too high in relation to the available current supply.

After a certain time, in order to accelerate the change in the structure of production, price controlled utility goods were introduced. As a result after March, 1942, the price of clothing ceased to rise and, in September, started to fall. The analysis of the extent to which this fall was due to the pressure of price control or to the reduction in costs of production of utility goods and their exemption from purchase tax is beyond the scope of this paper.

5. It follows from the above argument that it is always useful and in most cases necessary to supplement rationing by price control.

---

[1] This influence was probably more important than the tendency of individuals to buy better quality goods for their coupons.

[2] The increased market imperfection resulting from rationing, in particular in goods bought by richer people whose consumption has been cut by rationing much below the level they could afford out of their incomes, may have contributed to this.

This conclusion is of some practical importance for the post-war transition period. As long as some commodities are in scarce supply both rationing and price control must be maintained. And even after rationing is made unnecessary by ample supplies, price control may be usefully applied for pressing down prices which are 'high' owing to a considerable degree of market imperfection or the existence of industrial monopolies.

INFLATION, WAGES AND RATIONING

by M. Kalecki

REPRINTED FROM 'THE BANKER' (October, 1941)
BY KIND PERMISSION OF THE EDITOR

THE inflation controversy that has been in progress ever since war began was recently carried a stage farther by the White Paper on Price Stabilization and Industrial Policy, which in effect advocated stabilization of wages as the remedy. My object in this article will be to examine this proposal and to advocate comprehensive rationing as a preferable alternative. The problem of inflation arises in war-time because the volume of employment is maintained or even increased, whereas the output of consumption goods falls considerably, partly because man-power must be diverted from civil to armament production, partly because of difficulties in importing food and raw materials. Thus, unless the consumption of those other than wage-earners is reduced (to the full extent of the decline in consumption goods output, or even more) the amount of goods purchased by workers for their hourly wage must fall. Consequently, prices rise in relation to wages so as to equilibrate the demand for and supply of consumption goods. In an endeavour to restore the previous level of real wages, the workers demand higher money wages, which leads to the 'vicious spiral'—not, it will be noted, as the cause, but only as a symptom of inflation, in the sense of a deficiency of goods relatively to the volume of purchasing power.

What happens in this situation if money wage rates are stabilized? Prices must increase in the first instance up to the point at which real wage rates are reduced sufficiently to equate the demand for consumption goods to their supply. But because wages are kept stable no *subsequent* rise of prices ensues. Real wages are reduced, but this no longer sets in operation the 'vicious spiral'. It is important to notice that *real* wages will not be stabilized at the lower level they first reach. Any further fall in the supply of consumption goods will automatically cause a further decline in real wages. If, for instance, the deficiency in the output of consumption goods is at first made good to a certain extent by depletion of stocks, the rise in prices and fall in real wages may be moderate. But after stocks are exhausted, prices must rise to a level which equalizes demand and current output. Or if because of increased difficulties of importing food there is a further fall in supplies, real wages decline again correspondingly.

Thus both *laisser-faire* inflation and stabilization of money wages will have this in common: that the lower income grades are hit, and it is the reduction in their consumption which keeps in balance the demand for and supply of consumption goods. This is not only an evil in itself, but it tends also to reduce the productivity of labour both in the war sector and in consumption goods industries. There is consequently a danger that the war effort is impaired and the output of consumption goods falls further still, causing an additional rise in prices and fall in real wages.

It is sometimes assumed that inflation may be stopped directly by an all-round control of prices. No decrees about prices can, however, increase the supply of goods. The outcome of price-fixing measures is either that prices continue to rise illegally or that the discrepancy between demand and supply is reflected in a shortage of goods and queues. Inflation still exists, but its shape is altered. In this form it victimizes chiefly the people who have no time—or servants—to make the best of the state of haphazard distribution: in other words, those who work hard and have low incomes. That such a state of affairs is detrimental to the war effort need hardly be pointed out.

All this leads us to rationing as the true remedy against inflation. Comprehensive rationing of goods in short supply avoids rising prices, depletion of stocks and also haphazard distribution. For demand is now adjusted to supply by the direct curtailment of expenditure. And in contrast with the position under *laisser-faire* inflation, wage stabilization, or price control without rationing, the largest cut in consumption is exacted from those with the highest standard of living. Of course, rationing of all goods by description would be quite impracticable. However, the purpose may be achieved *grosso modo* by rationing retail spending in the aggregate. This was the essence of my plan, the final version of which was presented at the beginning of this year.[1] Since that time, the piecemeal rationing of food has been considerably extended and rationing of clothing introduced. To superimpose rationing of total retail expenditure upon the amount of piecemeal rationing now in

---

[1] See page 137.

existence would create a system of great complexity, because for a wide range of goods two types of coupons would have to be surrendered. I have therefore suggested that the rationing of expenditure should now be used for closing the gaps in the existing rationing system.

The most important of these gaps is unrationed food—which still represents two-thirds of the total expenditure on food, drink, and tobacco. Rationing of joint retail expenditure on these items would have two important advantages over a further extension of specific rationing in this field: first, further additions to the list of rationed foodstuffs would render the rationing system very complicated and cumbrous; secondly, and more important still, whereas the commodities so far rationed are universally consumed, this is not the case for many of the commodities at present unrationed. It is, therefore, important to secure freedom of choice in consumption of these remaining goods.

The control of rationing by value is in general more difficult than rationing by weight or points, because of differences in wholesale and retail prices. However, in the case of food, drink and tobacco, this difficulty may be easily overcome, since in this field most retail prices have a uniform level all over the country. It is, therefore, possible to enforce the following rule: when the shopkeeper buys these goods from the wholesaler or manufacturer he must surrender coupons for the amount representing their *retail* value. In this way, rationing by value would operate much like rationing by points, and could be organized by the Ministry of Food and the Board of Trade on the same lines as the rationing schemes now in existence.

The value of the 'expenditure ration' to cover food not rationed specifically, drink and tobacco, must be fixed at such a level that: (i) running down of stocks ceases; (ii) prices in general cease to rise, and in the case of such commodities where the price advance up to now has been very sharp, should actually fall; (iii) acute shortages, queues and so on, should become uncommon. Restaurant meals must be included in food rationing, but the total value of coupons surrendered should be equal not to the price of the meal—which includes the cost of cooking, and all the other services involved—but to the retail value of the ingredients. In addition, I suggest: (i) supplementing the point rationing of clothes and footwear by prohibiting the manufacture (or import) of goods over a certain price limit, which would render rationing by points rather more similar to rationing by value; (ii) the immediate introduction of a stringent combined point rationing of coal, gas, and electricity.

Finally, I propose the following solution to the problem of people with low incomes being unable to purchase the full ration. The Government should declare that it will buy unused coupons of every description at the values to which they relate (in the case of point coupons for clothes and footwear their 'average' value would be paid). As a result, any one unable to use a certain part of his coupons because his income is too small would be able to sell *half* of the unused coupons to the Government, and so obtain the wherewithal for using the other half. In this way, allowances are granted automatically to the lower income groups, while at the same time the transfer of their coupons to richer people by sale on a black market is prevented.[1] This scheme implies, it is true, a certain increase in Government expenditure, but every coupon bought by the Government makes sure that the consumption of rationed goods will be to that extent below the level corresponding to full use of coupons issued.

The above measures would, I believe, create a fairly comprehensive and equitable system of distributing goods in short supply, though it would probably be desirable to include in the rationing system some additional categories of non-food goods and services. On the other hand the scheme outlined would probably give rise to objections of various kinds. It might first be asked why it is necessary to curtail expenditure on consumption by the troublesome means of comprehensive rationing. Could not income tax or Mr. Keynes' plan do the job? The answer to this is that an increase in income tax or the imposition of 'blocked saving' may result *chiefly* in a reduction in 'free saving' or even in dissaving. Still more important, perhaps, is that even if expenditure *is* curtailed, this may happen in an unhelpful way: for example, people may spend less, say, on entertainment and education, whereas it is food which is actually scarce. To achieve the same result as the direct rationing of food expenditure by taxation or any other indirect methods is for these reasons impossible.

Another question is: What will be the repercussion of possible wage increases on the system of comprehensive rationing? It must first be emphasized that what drives wages up in the 'vicious spiral' is the rise in the cost of living. Once this problem has been tackled by comprehensive rationing, the rise in wages will have the

---

[1] Such a black market already exists in clothing coupons.

character of adjustments and thus will be on a moderate 'peace-time' scale. Further, wage increases could then affect the demand for goods in scarce supply only in so far as they made possible a fuller use of their rations by the lower income groups. This might conceivably entail some reduction in the general ration. But if the system of granting allowances by buying up of unused coupons is adopted, such changes could be only small. In other words, the problem of a rise in wages is to a great extent divorced from that of the demand for goods in scarce supply.

There still remains to be considered, however, the influence of a rise in wages on prices *via* costs. But this is only a special case of a more general problem; a rise in the price of foreign raw materials would create exactly the same difficulties. It is here that the policy of price control and subsidies may play its proper part. While these measures cannot solve the problem of inflation arising out of the scarce supply of goods, they may be used effectively to prevent price increases coming not from the demand but from the cost, side. Lastly, it may be objected that comprehensive rationing considerably reduces the incentive to work harder or more efficiently, because it makes it impossible to spend earnings over a certain limit. It must be noticed first that there still remains the accumulation of savings as an incentive, and that a certain range of goods, and particularly services, would remain unrationed. In addition, however, the incentive may be strengthened by differential rationing. It has now been officially recognized that heavy workers need higher food rations. A more refined differentiation could be introduced in addition based upon working time, etc. Nor would there be anything to prevent the introduction of non-food coupon premia for extra work or more efficient work. It is finally important to stress that comprehensive rationing of food would remove those *obstacles* to work which at present result from shortages and queues.

THE PROBLEM OF PRICE AND WAGE CONTROL

by J. Steindl

From Bulletin, Vol. 4, No. 14 (October 10, 1942)

A S the fear of inflation in the Unites States grows more acute, the discussion of the remedies reaches a new stage; after the imposition of a (partial) price ceiling in May, 1942, the immediate issue is that of farm prices and of wages. The Canadian experiment of stabilization of all prices and wages, begun in December, 1941, is looked upon as an example. Great Britain is in a much more advanced stage of a war economy and has had more experience than either of these countries; in spite of this the policy of a wage stop, which was proposed and dismissed over a year ago, is again attracting attention.[1]

1. The Canadian Experiment

Since December 1, 1941, no retailer, wholesaler, or manufacturer in Canada is allowed to sell any commodity at a price higher than the maximum price at which he sold it in the basic period (September 15th to October 11, 1941); a revision of this ceiling is only possible with the permission of the War-time Prices and Trading Board, and all traders were licensed for the purpose of control. Simultaneously, no employer may pay wage rates higher than those in force on November 15, 1941 (or any higher rate in force before that date—but this is in practice unimportant); he may depart from this only with the permission of the War Labour Board. This Board may grant an increase on one of two grounds: if wages are low as compared with the same or a substantially similar occupation in a comparable locality; or it may grant a cost of living bonus. This bonus is based on the official cost of living index, but it does not provide for a stable real wage in

---

[1] Sir John Wardlaw-Milne, speaking in the House of Commons on September 9, 1942, about the necessity of controlling wages as well as prices, said: 'The Government are creating a vested interest in carrying on the war, and that is an extremely dangerous situation.' (*Financial News*, September 10th.)

The Chancellor of the Exchequer stated on September 29th that the Government 'continues to rely on those concerned with wage negotiation in industry and on tribunals to handle claims for wage alterations with the full sense of responsibility which they share for safeguarding national and not merely sectional interests. If that sense of responsibility were to break down, the price stabilization policy would become impossible and the Government would have to reconsider the position.' (*Manchester Guardian*, September 30, 1942.)

terms of this index. First, the adjustment is considered only at quarterly intervals; secondly, the bonus provided for a 1 per cent increase in the cost of living amounts in many cases to less than 1 per cent of earnings.[1] The wage stop was supplemented afterwards by a stop on salaries (including managerial salaries). The necessary corollary of the wage policy is a strict essential works order, and the recent introduction of 'rationing' of labour to non-essential industry. Though the wage stop within the terms of the order is extremely strict, it would not prevent an inflatory spiral if the attempt to stabilize the cost of living were to break down.

The most important aim is therefore the preservation of the present ceiling on *retail prices* (including services and rents). Where the necessity for an adjustment has arisen, the retail price has been chosen in most cases as the fixed point, and wholesale and manufacturing prices have been 'rolled back'. Such adjustments have become necessary for various reasons, for example, seasonal price variations, rise in import prices, and the fact that some retail prices were not yet adjusted to the increased wholesale prices at the time of the imposition of ceilings. No doubt there are other factors which will make adjustments necessary also in the future (for example, cost increase due to less efficient labour). Three ways were open for dealing with the problem: squeezing of profit margins, reduction of cost, and subsidies. The 'squeeze' has in many cases been distributed in some way between retailers, wholesalers, and manufacturers; reduction of cost by simplification, elimination of 'frills', and standardization is playing a very important part, and is a desirable effect of the pressure exerted by the ceiling.[2] This pressure will also help to bring about concentration, both in production and in distribution.

Subsidies have been granted in a number of cases to offset cost increases. The sum has so far been rather small, but it seems to be growing. For the financial year 1942–43 the total cost of subsidies is estimated at $50 million. In the administration of these subsidies an interesting practice has been developed, for example, in the grocery trade.[3] The subsidy, calculated so as to offset the cost increase, is in the case of each individual firm reduced by the amount by which the firm's net profits exceeded its standard profit under E.P.T. before

[1] The bonus is 25 cents weekly (for 1 per cent increase in cost of living) in the case of adult male workers; it is therefore less than 1 per cent for all those whose earnings are above $25 a week; but for female workers whose earnings are below $25 and for youths under 21 years the bonus is 1 per cent of earnings.

[2] The policy described above is similar to the price and wage stop policy pursued in Germany from 1936 onwards.

[3] See *Canadian Labour Gazette*, April, 1942, p. 431.

L

the cost increase occurred; that is, in so far as the cost increase absorbed only excess profits, it is not compensated by a subsidy. If this arrangement becomes general, there would be a tendency for reduction or elimination of excess profits with rising cost and the subsidies would tend to establish standard profits (or the profits in the basic period of the price control, if they are lower than standard profits), provided that the firm continues to work with the same efficiency as before.

On the surface it appears that the ceiling policy has so far been successful. The official cost of living index kept remarkably stable at 115·8 in June, 1942, against 115·4 in November, 1941 (on the basis of September, 1939 = 100). This success must not be overestimated. To quote an American commentator: 'Relative stability in the *index of living cost*, however, does not necessarily indicate that the *cost of living* has not gone up. There have been persistent reports that low profit lines have been discarded for those on which higher profits could be made. While these reports cannot be verified there would seem to be little reason to doubt such a development.'[1] The cost of living index will less and less reflect the real deterioration in the standard of living with a given money income as scarcities appear and the consumer is forced to substitute more expensive or less satisfactory commodities for the customary ones, or finds it impossible to substitute anything at all.

This leads to the main problem of the Canadian price policy, that of the inevitably appearing scarcities which have already led to a hesitant adoption of rationing in some cases (sugar, tea, coffee, gasoline). While retail sales were strongly increasing up to the first months of 1942, the supply of civilian goods has been reduced, and will certainly be cut down further. In some lines (mainly durable goods) the restriction of supplies has been felt already by the consumer; the sales of radio and electrical stores show a significant decline as compared with last year, an indication of existing scarcity in view of the generally increased demand. If these scarcities spread, the price policy will come up against its real test.

2. *Price Policy in the United States.*

The principle of the general price ceiling in U.S., effective since May, 1942, is the same as in Canada: no seller may enhance the price of a commodity above the maximum price which he asked in the basic period (March, 1942), except with the permission of the Office

---

[1] Jules Backman, 'Six Months of Canadian Experience under a General Price Ceiling,' *Duns Review*, August, 1942, p. 10.

f Price Administration. Control by the consumer is facilitated in he case of about two hundred essential goods ('cost of living com- nodities') by the obligation to exhibit prices visibly together with he goods. The control extends to all stages, manufacturing and listribution. Exempted are most farm products, wages, and those ;oods the prices of which are specifically controlled (all essential raw naterials).

The Conference Board, New York, made a survey of two months' xperience under the ceiling policy.[1] Its conclusions are that there ias been 'a fairly general decline in profit margins', due to increase n cost; in part, however, the increase in cost is due to reduction in)utput. Subsidies would be required, but many executives are)pposed to the principle of subsidies and prefer stabilization of all :ost items. For companies which are highly taxed most of the cost ncrease is borne by the Treasury.

The policy of standardization, cost reduction, and concentration ias hardly been started as yet, but it will become very important in /iew of the considerable reduction of civilian supplies. It can be :oreseen that as this policy develops there will be more and more ipecific price control, with scheduled maximum prices for standard- zed commodities, and the general ceiling will appear as a temporary :ramework at a later stage. This may also make it possible to depart :rom the rigidity of the ceiling policy which leaves no room for :elative price changes.

Farm prices on the average had reached 100 per cent parity by mid- May,[2] but many individual farm products were much below parity (for example, rye, wheat). Under the February legislation, no farm price could be made subject to ceiling until it had reached 110 per :ent parity. Those farm prices which were above 110 per cent parity were to be kept at the existing price. This led to a conflict between the President, who wanted to set up a ceiling for farm prices at 100 per :ent parity, and the 'farm-block' of Congress members who wanted, in effect, a higher parity (they proposed to change the calculation of parity by including *all* farm labour, also unpaid family labour, in the goods bought by farmers, and 100 per cent parity according to this new calculation amounts, it is said, to about 112·5 per cent parity in terms of the old formula). The legislation which was passed at the beginning of October establishes the principle of 100 per cent parity

[1] Quoted from *Commercial and Financial Chronicle*, August 6, 1942.
[2] Parity is the relation between the price of a farm product and the average price of all goods which farmers buy, expressed as a percentage of the same relation as it existed in the average of the years 1910 to 1914.

but allows for an increase in farm prices in accordance with an increase in cost of production.

There are two ways of meeting the demands of the farmers: either the whole price ceiling is raised, or else the farm prices are kept at existing levels and the farmers granted *subsidies* which give them substantially the same advantage as the higher prices would. In this way the requirement of an incentive for farmers could be met, and at the same time the subsidies could be so devised as to provide an incentive in just those lines where production is needed; whereas the rigid principle of parity is purely irrational from this point of view. It may be objected that such a policy would increase purchasing power; but as it will be necessary anyhow to control demand directly by means of rationing and licensing, this argument is not decisive.

Up to now *wage rates* have been subject to control in so far as wage disputes were referred to the National War Labour Board (formed in January, 1942). The Board formulated the principles of wage control on the occasion of the 'Little Steel Case'; the real wages of January, 1941, are regarded as peace-time standard; the cost of living since that time increased by 15 per cent, and any group of workers who did not receive a corresponding increase in wages between January, 1941, and now, are entitled to it. Apart from this, adjustments are allowed on the grounds of inequalities and abnormally low standards of living.

3. *The Question of Wage Control*

At present the U.S. administration seems to have given way to the critics of its former policy, who argued that the continuation of bargaining and the consequent wage increases would break the price ceiling and create inflation.

There are two ways in which wage increases could endanger the price ceiling: the one is by the action of the increasing wage bill on the demand for consumption goods, the other by the increase in cost of production. We shall deal with these two factors in turn. A wage increase will indeed increase the demand for consumption goods, and, if civilian supply is limited, an 'inflationary gap' will appear; but it is by no means the only factor which can create such a gap; the most important under the present conditions in the United States is probably the restriction of civilian supply. Apart from this, the wage bill will rise, even with fixed wage rates, for various reasons.[1]

If the wage stop in itself is no guarantee against inflation the

[1] Cf. Kalecki, 'Inflation, Wages, and Rationing,' p. 147.

position of labour under such a policy must be fairly considered. They have reason to fear that they will be delivered up to open or hidden inflation with their hands bound by the wage stop. Against the first danger, that of open inflation, they may be partly secured, if the wages are in some way bound up with the cost of living, as in Canada. But there is hardly any means of securing them against the more 'subtle' forms of inflation: deterioration in quality of goods, enforced substitution of more expensive and less useful goods, for those which are included in the cost of living index, and scarcities which make it often impossible to get essential goods for any but the lucky or leisured buyers. It is therefore easily understandable that labour is hostile to a wage stop. Moreover, as the policy is inadequate for preventing inflation, it only serves to delay and to sabotage the adoption of really effective means. It has been shown by the British experience that the adequate way of preventing inflation is the elimination of excess demand by comprehensive rationing. The United States will have to follow substantially similar lines, or they will find it difficult to avoid inflation in one form or another. It remains to consider whether the wage stop is useful as a supplementary measure, provided that not only prices but also qualities and rations are guaranteed; or, alternatively, whether there are specific reasons against a wage stop even under these conditions. This leads to the second effect of a wage increase on prices, its effect *via cost*.

In so far as wage increases take place in industries which are working for government account, they will only be reflected in the prices which the Government has to pay for armaments. In so far as they take place in the civilian sector, in which prices are subject to the ceiling, the wage increase will 'squeeze' the profit margins. The resulting problem is in principle not new, because a squeeze on profit margins exists, as the Canadian experience shows, even in spite of a wage stop. It may be dealt with in the following way: after having considered the possibilities of taking up the squeeze by economies through standardization, etc., the Government may decide to give a subsidy on the product in question which compensates (partly or wholly) the increase in cost. This subsidy should be calculated so that it gives a company working with reasonable efficiency and full use of its available labour supply the possibility to earn just their standard profits under E.P.T., but not more. In this way, cost increases would be allowed to absorb excess profits and would only be compensated by subsidies in so far as they would make it impossible for a firm to earn standard profits with reasonable efficiency. The advantage of this arrangement is that it would provide for a greate incentive. Firms earning just standard profits would at least have much greater incentive for not slackening their efforts than firm earning excess profits.[1]

Wage increases are therefore by no means incompatible with policy of price stabilization. Under a rigid price ceiling most of th wage increase will be paid, directly or indirectly, by the Treasury If the demand for consumption goods is controlled by rationing, th increased wages will largely be saved (except in so far as wage in creases will enable some groups of workers to use their full ration and therefore lead to a somewhat greater national debt.

As there is no reason why wage stabilization should be a necessar part of a policy to prevent inflation, the arguments which spea against it may be given due weight. If wages are fixed, the incentiv of wage differentials to bring about shifts of labour to essenti: occupations cannot be made use of fully (this is of great importanc under present conditions in the United States). Reliance must the be put *exclusively* on the shifting of labour and tying of workers t jobs by methods of compulsion; and the situation resulting ma sometimes be exceedingly harmful to production (tying of labou to industries where the workers get lower wages than they coul easily get elsewhere, compulsory shifting of labour to lower pai occupations). Giving up the method of bargaining involves regimer tation of labour to a degree which cannot be decided upon lightly i view of its repercussions on production.

Finally, there is one consideration which is obviously of gre: importance for the United States, but no less applicable also t Great Britain: the policy of wage stabilization is an inadequate polic for fighting inflation, but this is not generally realized. There i therefore, a danger that it may be used to delay the adoption c effective means. Discussions in both Houses of Parliament show tha it affords distinct relief to turn away from the sterner tasks of fu rationing, and to 'try it this way'. A policy of wage stabilizatio apart from the harm it would cause directly in the field of labou policy, could only serve to distract attention from the problems c rationing and equitable distribution which to a large extent hav still to be faced.

[1] This is an application of the principle developed by M. Kalecki ('The Problem of Pro Margins', p. 382). The practice, developed in Canada in some cases and described earlier i the text, of deducting from the amount of subsidy due to a firm the excess profits which tl firm earned before the cost increase, has a degree of resemblance to this principle. It wou tend to bring the firm down to standard profits, on the basis of its *present efficiency*; a deterio tion in efficiency would then lead to the loss of part of the standard profit.

RATIONING AND INDEX NUMBERS

by J. L. Nicholson

The following article is based on one which appeared in
The Review of Economic Studies, Vol. X, No. 1, Winter
1942–3. It is included here by kind permission of the
Editors of that Journal.

WHEN rationing is introduced, the consumption of certain
commodities is restricted and the consumer, in deciding how
to spend his money, is unable to exercise the same freedom of
choice as he did before. At the prevailing prices, it cannot be
assumed, therefore, that he would purchase the same goods, and in
the same quantities, as he would in the absence of rationing. When
estimates are made of changes in real income, some allowance
should, strictly speaking, be included for the effects of such limitations on the consumer's freedom of choice.

A method is developed, in the first part of this article, by which
the loss in real income caused by rationing may be approximately
estimated. The second part gives a diagrammatical representation
of the problem, as well as an analysis of different types of demand
curve. An attempt is made, in the third part, to apply the method;
but, since the data which are available are very fragmentary, the only
purpose of making an estimate is to give some idea of the probable
order of magnitude involved.

I. DERIVATION OF THE METHOD[1]

Let X and Y represent rationed and unrationed goods respectively.
Let x_1 and y_1 be the quantities consumed at the first date, prior
to the introduction of rationing, and x_2 and y_2 the quantities consumed at the second date, after rationing has been introduced.

Let P_x and P_y be the prices at the first date, and px and py the
prices at the second date, of X and Y respectively.

It is assumed that the quantities consumed before the introduction of rationing can be represented by a point of equilibrium on a
particular indifference curve connecting X and Y. Suppose that this
indifference curve is represented by a function of x, denoted by
$f(x)$, so that $y_1 = f(x_1)$. The introduction of rationing causes the

[1] The non-mathematical reader may omit this section.

consumption of X to be reduced from x_1 to x_2. In order that real income should remain constant, the consumption of unrationed goods would then have to increase from $f(x_1)$ to $f(x_2)$, and the difference between $f(x_2)$ and y_2 provides an indication of the change in real income between the two dates.[1] Thus, if we can determine $f(x_2)$, we can obtain a measure, though not necessarily the only possible measure,[2] of the loss in real income caused by rationing.

Further notation must now be introduced.

Write $R = -f'(x)$ for the marginal rate of substitution of X for Y,

and let $R_1 = -f'(x_1) = \dfrac{P_x}{P_y}$

Let $E = x_1 P_x + y_1 P_y$ and let $\kappa_x = \dfrac{x_1 P_x}{E}$ the proportion spent on X

at the first date.

Let $r = \dfrac{x_1 - x_2}{x_1}$, the proportionate reduction in the consumption of X.

Write $\sigma = \dfrac{d \log\left\{\dfrac{f(x)}{x}\right\}}{d \log R}$ for the elasticity of substitution between

X and Y, and σ_1 for the elasticity of substitution at the point (x_1, y_1).

Let $\rho = \dfrac{d \log\left\{\dfrac{f'(x)}{x}\right\}}{d \log f''(x)}$, a second order elasticity of substitution, and

let ρ_1 be the value at the point (x_1, y_1).

Then $\sigma = -\dfrac{R}{x} \cdot \dfrac{dx}{dR}\left\{\dfrac{xR}{f(x)} + 1\right\}$,

so that $f''(x) = -\dfrac{dR}{dx} = \dfrac{R}{\sigma}\left\{\dfrac{R}{f(x)} + \dfrac{1}{x}\right\}$.

[1] It is assumed, throughout this discussion, that there is no difference between income and total expenditure.

[2] The indifference curve passing through the point (x_2, y_2) would, theoretically, provide an alternative measure, but we have even less knowledge about the shape of this curve than we have of the indifference curve which passes through the initial point of equilibrium (x_1, y_1).

It can also be shown that

$$\rho = \frac{1}{f'''(x)}\left[\frac{\{f''(x)\}^2}{f'(x)} - \frac{f''(x)}{x}\right],$$

so that $f'''(x) = -\dfrac{R}{\rho\,\sigma}\left[\dfrac{R}{f(x)} + \dfrac{1}{x}\right]\left[\dfrac{1}{\sigma}\left(\dfrac{R}{f(x)} + \dfrac{1}{x}\right) + \dfrac{1}{x}\right].$

By Taylor's Theorem, we have

$$f(x_2) = f(x_1) + (x_2 - x_1)f'(x_1) + \frac{(x_2 - x_1)^2}{2}f''(x_1)$$

$$+ \frac{(x_2 - x_1)^3}{6}f'''(x_1) + \ldots$$

$$= f(x_1) + (x_1 - x_2)R_1 + \frac{(x_1 - x_2)^2 R_1}{2\,\sigma_1}\left\{\frac{R_1}{f(x_1)} + \frac{1}{x_1}\right\}$$

$$+ \frac{(x_1 - x_2)^3 R_1}{6\,\rho_1\,\sigma_1}\left[\frac{R_1}{f(x_1)} + \frac{1}{x_1}\right]\left[\frac{1}{\sigma_1}\left\{\frac{R_1}{f(x_1)} + \frac{1}{x_1}\right\} + \frac{1}{x_1}\right] + \ldots$$

$$= f(x_1) + rx_1\frac{P_x}{P_y} + \frac{r^2 x_1}{2\,\sigma_1}\cdot\frac{P_x}{P_y}\cdot\frac{1}{1-\kappa_x}$$

$$+ \frac{r^3 x_1}{6\rho_1\sigma_1}\cdot\frac{P_x}{P_y}\cdot\frac{1}{1-\kappa_x}\left\{\frac{1}{\sigma_1(1-\kappa_x)} + 1\right\} + \ldots$$

Now write $LE = x_1 p_x + y_1 p_y$, where L is Laspeyre's formula for the change in the cost of living between the two dates, and let

$$IE = (L + \lambda)E = x_2 p_x + f(x_2)\,p_y\ .$$

I is then an index of the cost of living based on the indifference curve $f(x)$, and λ indicates the reduction in real income caused by rationing, expressed as a proportion of total expenditure at the first date.

Thus $\lambda E = p_x(x_2 - x_1) + p_y\left\{f(x_2) - f(x_1)\right\}.$

Substituting the expression for $f(x_2)$ given by Taylor's expansion as far as the second differential, and rearranging the terms, we obtain, as a first approximation:

$$\lambda = r\kappa_x\left\{\frac{P_y}{P_y} - \frac{P_x}{P_x}\right\} + \frac{P_y}{P_y}\cdot\frac{r^2\,\kappa_x}{2\,\sigma_1(1-\kappa_x)} \quad \ldots (1)$$

Using Taylor's expansion as far as the third differential, we obtain, as a second approximation:

$$\lambda = r\kappa \left\{\left(\frac{p_y}{p_y} - \frac{p_x}{p}\right) + \frac{p_y}{p_y} \cdot \frac{r^2}{2\sigma_1(1-\kappa_x)} \left[1 + \frac{r}{3\rho_1}\left(\frac{1}{\sigma_1(1-\kappa)} + 1\right)\right]\right\} \dots(2)$$

Thus, provided we have separate price indices for the various commodities, and provided we know the proportion which is initially spent on the goods which are subsequently rationed, the measurement of changes in real income depends on the possibility of obtaining estimates for parameters such as σ and ρ, which characterize the form of the indifference curve connecting the two groups of rationed and unrationed goods. It should be added that the formulae given here are strictly applicable only if the proportionate reduction in consumption is the same for all rationed goods; if this is not the case, some allowance should properly be made for variations in the shape of the individual indifference curves, relating to particular rationed goods.

2. INDIFFERENCE CURVES AND DEMAND CURVES

Diagrams 1 and 2 illustrate the relationship between demand curves and indifference curves. In Diagram 1, the amounts of different commodities, X and Y, are measured along the two axes. I_1N_1 and I_3N_3 are indifference curves of the normal type. I_2P_2 and I_3P_1 are price lines, indicating the possible combinations of X and Y which can be purchased with a given expenditure, at a given set of prices. I_2L_2 and I_3L_3, in the terminology of Hick's *Value and Capital*, are price-consumption curves, which join the points of tangency to indifference curves of various price lines, all passing through the same point on the Y-axis. X and Y are taken to represent rationed and unrationed goods respectively, and the consumer is supposed to have been in equilibrium, before the introduction of rationing, at the point P_1, where x_1 and y_1 are the amounts consumed of the two groups of commodities.

It is assumed that the introduction of rationing causes a reduction in the consumption of X from x_1 to x_2. If prices and money income remain the same as before, the individual will then be able to increase his consumption of unrationed goods from y_1 to y_3, as indicated on Diagram 1. But, in order to obtain the same satisfaction as before, the consumption of unrationed goods would have to be increased to $\bar{y}_2$, so that he could reach the point P_2, on the same indifference

[1] Differences between money income and total expenditure being ignored.

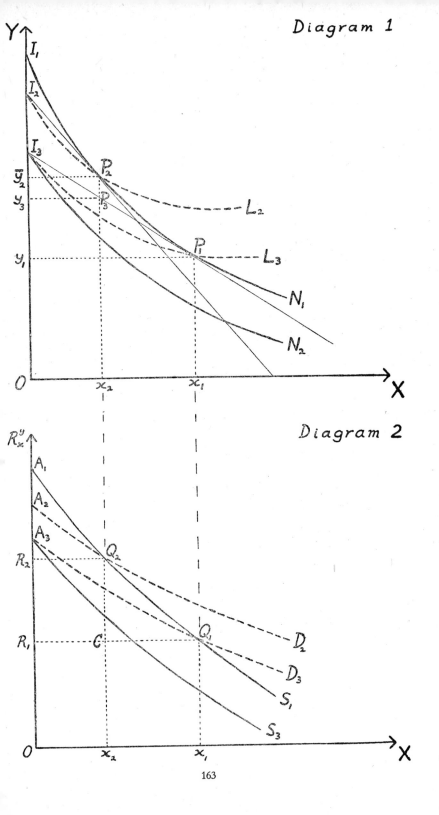

Diagram 1

Diagram 2

163

curve as P_1. Thus, if there were no changes in price, the loss in real income would be given by $\bar{y}_2 - y_3$.

The loss in real income can also be illustrated on Diagram 2, which shows different types of demand curve. In this diagram rationed commodities, represented by X, are measured, as before, along the horizontal axis. Along the vertical axis are measured different values of R_x^y, the marginal rate of substitution of X for Y, which is defined by the slope of the indifference curve at a particular point. The curves A_2D_2 and A_3D_3 correspond, respectively, with the price-consumption curves I_2L_2 and I_3L_3 in Diagram 1; for any point on I_3L_3, the curve A_3D_3 relates the marginal rate of substitution[1] of the indifference curve at this point to the amount consumed of X. Let R_1 denote the marginal rate of substitution at P_1. The corresponding point on A_3D_3 is Q_1, drawn vertically below P_1, with co-ordinates R_1 and x_1. Similarly R_2 denotes the marginal rate of substitution at P_2 and the corresponding point on A_2D_2 is Q_2, having co-ordinates R_2 and x_2. Any number of similar curves may be drawn, corresponding to the various price-consumption lines of the indifference curve map.

If the prices of X and Y are denoted by $p(x)$ and $p(y)$ respectively, for any point of equilibrium we have $R_x^y = \dfrac{p(x)}{p(y)}$. Suppose that $p(y)$ is constant and the level of money income is given. The curves A_2D_2, A_3D_3 and other similar curves will then represent ordinary demand curves for X, each of which is constructed on the assumption that money income and the prices of all other goods are constant, while the different curves relate to different levels of money income.

Defining real income as equivalent for all points on the same indifference curve, we can now construct a different type of demand curve, based on a constant real income. The curves A_1S_1 and A_3S_3 in Diagram 2 are intended to correspond, respectively, with the indifference curves I_1N_1 and I_3N_3. If the curve I_1N_1 is defined by the function $f(x)$, the curve A_1S_1 will be defined by $-f'(x)$. Thus, the co-ordinates of any point on A_1S_1 are the marginal rate of substitution and the amount of X, indicated by the corresponding point on I_1N_1; A_3S_3 is derived, in a similar way, from the indifference curve I_3N_3. Curves of this type, which can be constructed from any of the indifference curves, may be termed *indifference* demand curves.

---

[1] This phrase will henceforward be used as short for 'the marginal rate of substitution of X for Y.'

Comparing the curves A_3D_3 and A_3S_3, the former shows changes in the demand for X as real income increases along the price-consumption line I_3L_3; the latter shows changes in the demand for X on the assumption that changes in price are continuously offset by changes in money income, so that the level of real income, defined by the indifference curve I_3N_3, remains constant.[1] The ordinary demand curve shows both the 'income' and the 'substitution' effects of changes in price; the *indifference* demand curve shows only the 'substitution' effect. From these two curves it would also be possible to construct a third, showing the 'income' effect alone.

In the notation of the previous section, we have

$$\bar{y}_2 - y_1 = f(x_2) - f(x_1) = \int_{x_1}^{x_2} f'(x)dx = \int_{x_2}^{x_1} R_x^y \, dx,$$

that is the area under the curve A_1S_1 between x_1 and x_2. Also $y_3 - y_1 = f'(x_1)(x_2 - x_1) = R_1(x_1 - x_2)$, that is the rectangular area $CQ_1 x_1 x_2$.

It follows that, if all prices remain constant, the loss in real income, defined by $\bar{y}_2 - y_3$, can also be represented as the area Q_2Q_1C. The formula (1) above, which gives a first approximation to the loss in real income caused by rationing, implies that, over the relevant range (between x_1 and x_2), the indifference curve I_1N_1 can be represented by a parabola, so that the indifference demand curve A_1S_1 is a straight line, and Q_2Q_1C is a triangle.

It is worth noting that a simple connection exists between the elasticity of the indifference demand curve and the elasticity of substitution. Writing $\xi = -\dfrac{R}{x} \cdot \dfrac{dx}{dR}$ for the elasticity of the indifference demand curve, and otherwise preserving the same notation as before (see page 160), we have:

$$\sigma = \xi \left\{ \frac{xR}{f(x)} + 1 \right\} = \frac{\xi}{1 - \kappa_x}, \quad \text{or } \xi = \sigma \left(1 - \kappa_x\right).$$

Now writing e for the price-elasticity of demand and η for the income-elasticity of demand for X, the relation between e, η and σ is given by:[2]

$$e = \kappa_x \eta + \left(1 - \kappa_x\right) \sigma \, .$$

[1] The curve A_3S_3 must lie below the curve A_3D_3, except when X is an 'inferior' good. For 'intermediate' goods (neither 'inferior' nor 'superior') the two curves would coincide.
[2] Cf. Hicks and Allen, *A Reconsideration of the Theory of Value*, Economica, 1934, p. 201.

The elasticity of the indifference demand curve, as we should expect, is independent of the first term in this expression.

3. APPLICATION OF THE METHOD

Applying formula (1), shown above (page 161), we can obtain a rough idea of the effects of rationing on the cost of living of the working-class, during the first few years of the war. The computation necessarily involves a certain amount of guesswork and is given mainly for purposes of illustration.

We shall consider only rationed foods, since the rationing of clothing has probably had little effect on most working-class households. According to the Ministry of Labour's family budget inquiry in 1937–38, relating to industrial working-class households, expenditure on rationed foods amounted to about a quarter of total expenditure.[1] For the period between 1938 and 1941, it has been estimated that, allowing for goods which are not included in the official index, the cost of living of wage earners increased by 33 per cent.[2] Prices of rationed foods, as given by the Ministry of Labour, increased by 26 per cent in the same period, so that prices of un-rationed goods increased by 35 per cent. The average reduction in the consumption of rationed foods, including foods which are no longer obtainable, appears to have been between a half and one-third. The elasticity of substitution between rationed foods and all other goods has been roughly estimated[3] from American data at between 0·6 and 0·8. Substituting these figures in formula (1), we can estimate the additional increase in the cost of living, on account of rationing, at between 4 and 11 per cent. Thus, the final index, for the period from 1938 to 1941, is raised from 133 to between 137 and 144. This estimate does not allow for the rationing of goods other than food. Even so, it is evident that rationing has had an appreciable effect on real income, as here defined.

It is interesting, finally, to see what the relative prices would have to be in order that the point P_2 (shown on Diagram 1) should represent a position of equilibrium under a system of free market prices. The required condition is that the prices of rationed goods, relatively to those of unrationed goods, should increase in the ratio $R_2 : R_1$. Using the figures given above, and the relations previously obtained between σ, κ_x and R, this ratio is found to lie between 1·56 and

---

[1] *Ministry of Labour Gazette*, December, 1940.   [2] See p. 214.
[3] C. E. V. Leser, 'Family Budget Data and Price Elasticities of Demand', *The Review of Economic Studies*, November 1941, p. 57.

2·11. Since the average prices of unrationed goods increased between 1938 and 1941 by 35 per cent, the prices of rationed foods would have had to increase, over the same period, by between 111 and 185 per cent, or roughly to between two and three times their former level. It may also be deduced that, in order to be as well off as before, the consumer would have to increase his consumption (in real terms) of unrationed goods by between 14 and 26 per cent.

POINTS, PRICES AND CONSUMERS' CHOICE

by G. D. N. Worswick

FROM BULLETIN, VOL. 6, No. 3 (FEBRUARY 26, 1944)

WHEN a woman went shopping in peace-time she came home with a basket-full of goods whose marginal rates of substitution one for another were equal to the ratios of their prices. Should she feel the slight dizziness which is the symptom of 'disequilibrium', it was not difficult to effect a cure by a slight alteration in her subsequent purchases. The introduction of 'point' rationing, where 'point' values are not proportional to prices, has brought a new problem into the domestic economy. For now the average housewife has not only to make the best of her money, but also of her points. That there exists a position of maximum satisfaction, or, more correctly, a preferred position in the point-money economy, is witnessed by the sober behaviour of shoppers. But, although the instinct of the rational housewife has brought her to this position, and a serious epidemic of 'disequilibrium' need not be feared, it is of some interest to try to discover her secret.

1. Consider first two commodities X and Y, whose prices per unit are respectively a and b shillings, and for which r and s points respectively must be surrendered. Suppose in addition that the consumer spends on these two commodities m shillings and p points in the given period.

The consumer can buy either $\frac{m}{a}$ of X and no Y, or $\frac{m}{b}$ of Y and no X.

The equation of the *price line* is therefore $ax + by = m$.

The equation of the equivalent *point line* is $rx + sy = p$.

The *price* line and *point* line will intersect in a point P whose co-ordinates are:

$$x = \frac{ms - pb}{as - rb} \qquad y = \frac{pa - mr}{as - rb}$$

Suppose that the slope of the price line is steeper than that of the point line, i.e. X is *relatively* more expensive in terms of money than in points.[1] Then as $-rb$ will be positive. The conditions that both x and y, the co-ordinates of P, should be positive are:

$$\text{for } x: \quad \frac{m}{p} > \frac{b}{s}$$

$$\text{for } y: \quad \frac{m}{p} < \frac{a}{r}$$

Now $\dfrac{m}{p}$ is the ratio of the *total* money outlay to the *total* 'point' outlay, while $\dfrac{b}{s}$ and $\dfrac{a}{r}$ are the ratios of the prices to the 'point' values of the two commodities Y and X. Thus, for both co-ordinates of P to be positive the ratio of total money outlay to total points must lie between the ratios of price to point values of the two commodities. The condition is:

$$\frac{a}{r} > \frac{m}{p} > \frac{b}{s}$$

If this condition is not satisfied then one, and only one, of the co-ordinates of P will be negative.[2] This would mean that there is, in fact, no way in which the consumer could spend *all* his money and *all* his points. He could spend all of one and still have a surplus of the other.

In Figs. 1 and 2 we illustrate the case where $\dfrac{a}{r} > \dfrac{m}{p} > \dfrac{b}{s}$. MM' RR' are respectively the *price line* and equivalent *point line*, intersecting in P. The curved line represents the indifference curve passing through P.

(i) Suppose the indifference curve through P lies in the angle MPR, i.e. the marginal rate of substitution at P lies between the ratio of prices and the ratio of point values. In this case, given that the consumer is willing to spend his full money outlay m, and/or all his points p, P will be his preferred position. For although there are higher indifference curves which he could 'afford' either in

---

[1] We can always draw our diagrams in such a way that this will be the case. This condition is equivalent to the condition that the ratio of the price of a unit of X to its point value should exceed the corresponding ratio for Y.

[2] Since, if $\dfrac{m}{p} > \dfrac{a}{r}$ it must also be $> \dfrac{b}{s}$; and similarly if $\dfrac{m}{p} < \dfrac{b}{s}$. We exclude throughout the case where the point and price ratios are the same.

M

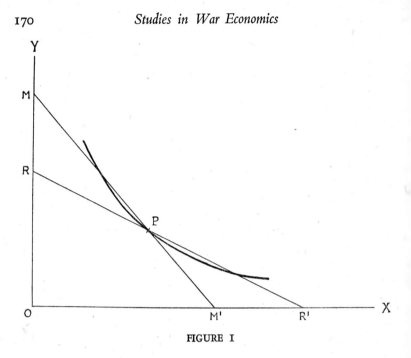

FIGURE I

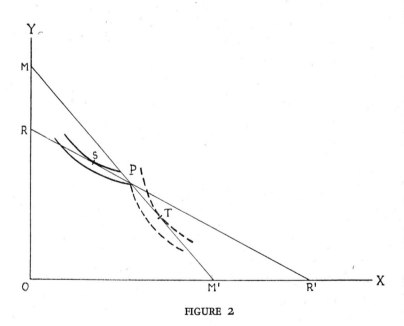

FIGURE 2

terms of money or of points, there is none on which he can afford both simultaneously. (Fig. 1).

(ii) Suppose now that the marginal rate of substitution at P is greater than both the ratio of prices and of point values of the commodities. The slope of the indifference curve through P will now be steeper than that of both MM' and RR' (Fig. 2, dotted lines).

In this case P, although it denotes the only position where the consumer can spend all his money and all his points, will not be the optimum position. The latter will be the point T where an indifference curve touches the price line MM'. In this case the consumer will spend all his money and still have points to spare. The opposite would be the case if the marginal rate of substitution at P were *less* than the ratio of both prices and points (Fig. 2). The optimum position would now be S, where an indifference curve touches the point line, and this time the consumer, after spending all his points, would still not spend all the cash he was willing to do.

2. The conclusions arrived at above can be used to illustrate for two commodities the practical case where the total number of 'points' is fixed, but the money outlay is variable. In Figure 3 RR' is the point line; that is to say, if all points are spent on X quantity OR' is obtainable, and if all are spent on Y quantity OR is obtained. M_1M_1' is the first position of the price line. Clearly in this case all the points cannot be spent and so the consumer will lay out his money without regard to points and choose position T_1. Now, as the consumer's money outlay rises the price line will move upwards (remaining, of course, parallel to M_1M_1'). The point of tangency T will trace out the 'income-consumption' curve. Let this curve intersect the point line RR' at T_2. The price line through T_2, M_2M_2', will, of course, touch the indifference curve through T_2. With a money outlay which will buy either OM_2' of X or OM_2 of Y, the consumer will, in fact, choose the combination represented by T_2, and will also *just* spend all his points.

If there were no rationing a further increase in money outlay would simply lead to an extension of the 'income-consumption' curve (T_2T_3). But the 'points' impose their own limit to the way in which the consumer can lay out his money. The income-consumption curve, in fact, takes a sharp turn at T_2 and runs along the point line RR'. It will continue as far as the point Q, where an indifference curve touches the point line. However much money the consumer has, he cannot go beyond the point Q. That the 'income-consumption' curve does, in fact, run along RR' from T_2 to

Q is easily shown. At T_2 the marginal rate of substitution is equal to the ratio of *prices*, at Q it is equal to that of *points*. Between T_2 and Q the marginal rate of substitution lies between the price-ratio and the point-ratio. Hence, in accordance with case (*i*) in the previous section, the preferred position lies on the point line.[1]

It follows from the above argument that for some consumers point rationing (where the point values are not proportional to prices) causes a loss of satisfaction. The extreme case is where the consumer is at Q, when his money alone would indicate the point T_3; for Q, involving the same outlay of money, is on a lower indifference curve than T_3. There is a loss for all consumers whose consumption lies on the T_2Q part of the 'income-consumption' curve, increasing from T_2 to Q. It would appear that the loss is greater, the greater the difference between the ratio of points and the ratio of prices. There is, of course, no loss for those who have not enough money to take up all their points (T_1).

3. It is customary in indifference curve analysis to take, not two commodities, but a single commodity X and a composite commodity Y, representing all other goods; it is then possible to study the effect of a change in price of the single commodity. Can we take this step for both money *and* points? The problem only exists for consumers whose money outlay puts them on the T_2Q part of the 'income-consumption' curve. Persons with a higher money outlay take notice only of points: persons with a lower take notice only of prices. So long as we are restricted to a given income the comparison can be made. We calculate the average money outlay per point for all goods except X. This average, of course, will vary, for a given consumer, with his income, but we may use it to study changes in the point value or price of one good, for it will enable us to draw on the *same* diagram the point line and the price line, with the same scale.

Which does the consumer prefer, a reduction of, say, 1 per cent in the point value of the good or a 1 per cent price reduction? Let us suppose that in terms of Figure 3 the consumer is on the T_2Q part of the income-consumption curve (we shall see below that this is the significant case). In Figure 4 the consumer's outlay of points and money is represented by the point P, the intersection of the point line RR' and the price line MM'. RR_1' is the new point line corresponding to a reduction of 1 per cent in the point value of X;

---

[1] It should perhaps be stressed that at no point along T_2Q is an indifference curve tangential either to the price line or the point line.

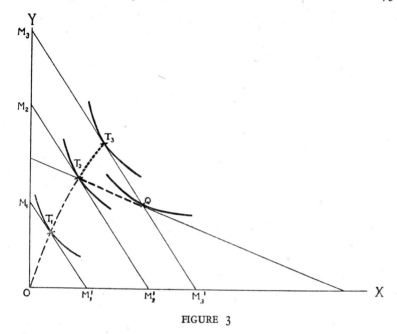

FIGURE 3

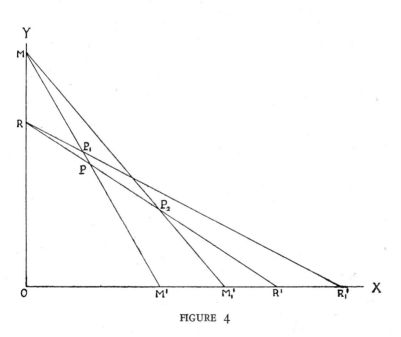

FIGURE 4

MM_1' is the new price line which shows the corresponding 1 per cent price reduction of X (as defined above). In the first case the new equilibrium position is P_1, in the second P_2. The preference of the consumer depends upon whether P_2 is on a higher or lower indifference curve than P_1. A glance at Figure 3 shows[1] that at T_2 any reduction in the point value of X would leave the consumer unmoved. He would still remain at T_2 since here the indifference curve touches his *price* line. On the other hand, if the price were reduced at all, his equilibrium point would be to the right of T_2 on the point line, and so upon a higher indifference curve. At the other end of the scale at Q the consumer, while being unable to take advantage of a reduction in price, would be better off if the point value was reduced. Somewhere in between T_2 and Q is a position where the consumer is indifferent to point or price changes of equal proportions. We note that for low money outlays (on the OT_1T_2 section of the 'income-consumption' curve) the consumer, being unable to take up all his points, is unaffected by changes in point ratios. Similarly the relatively well-to-do who would spend more money if it were not for the rationing, will operate only with points in their purchasing, and are therefore unaffected by relative price changes. Consumers therefore fall into three categories:

1. Low incomes—these prefer downward adjustment in prices.
2. Medium incomes—of these some prefer a price reduction, others a point reduction of equal proportion.[2]
3. High incomes—these prefer downward adjustment in point values.

The categories, low, medium and high, are related to the particular rationing scheme. In some cases most people may be in category 1, in others in category 3. This conclusion is, of course, in accordance with everyday experience. For example, the Ministry of Food may wish to dispose of surplus stocks of food included in the 'points' scheme. If many people are not taking up their full quota of points, the depointing of the particular item may prove an insufficient measure and may have to be accompanied by a reduction in price.

---

[1] In Fig. 3 we originally had two single commodities. We now take Y to represent the composite commodity.

[2] The comparison of equi-proportional price and point changes is, of course, arbitrary. Other criteria of comparison could be taken. But whatever the criterion, the same conclusion would be reached, that of the 'medium income' group, some consumers would be more sensitive to prices, others to points.

DIFFERENTIAL RATIONING

by M. Kalecki

FROM BULLETIN, VOL. 4, No. 11 (AUGUST 8, 1942)

THE necessity for differential rationing may arise for two reasons:(*a*) some workers, because of the character of their work, may require more than the average of a particular product; (*b*) flat rationing may be unjust to poor people, either because the product in question represents a higher proportion of their consumption than of that of the more well-to-do; or, because the higher income groups may more easily compensate for the reduction in the consumption of this product by more expensive substitutes; or, finally because the rich may be in possession of some stocks of this product.

1. A good example is offered by rationing of bread and flour (including spaghetti and biscuits) which may become necessary in this country as a result of the shortage of shipping space. Not only do manual workers require more bread, which is an energy food, but also flat rationing would mean a much greater hardship for poor people than for the well-to-do. The rations of manual workers should therefore be *considerably* higher than those of the rest of the population, not only on account of their greater physical effort but also because, in general, they belong to the poorer strata of the population. Even so, the workers' families with many children will be at a great disadvantage both because they are usually the poorest and because the higher bread ration would be given to *earners*. This, however, can be partly remedied by giving relatively high rations to children in general, and would also be mitigated by the fact that large families would usually find it easier to substitute potatoes for bread. These considerations do not aim, of course, at minimizing the importance of the 'technical' problem of compensation for greater physical effort, and this requires that rations should be differentiated also among manual workers: heavy workers, for instance miners, should get higher rations than other manual workers.

2. What would be the repercussions of the reduction in bread consumption upon consumption of other food? The consumption of potatoes will increase; this does not present any particular difficulty

because the supply of potatoes is ample and may be easily increased.[1] However, there would also most probably be a certain pressure in the demand for other goods. This may necessitate some additional rationing, in particular of products which are more or less substitutes for bread, as for instance cake. Cake can be included in the points scheme or the scheme for sweets. This measure is, in any case, over-due quite apart from the problem of bread rationing. To relieve the position of the poorer population, it would be advisable to reduce the prices of products included in the points scheme. This would enable people who do not at present use their ration to buy more. If the supply of 'points foods' is kept constant this would, of course, necessitate the reduction of the ration.

As indicated in another article,[2] the problem of bread rationing would be made very much easier if a small part of the shipping space saved thereby could be used for larger imports of cheese or dehydrated meat. It is generally known that bread consumption in war-time is much higher than in peace-time because people compensate in this way for the deficiency in protein foods. The increase in the supply of the latter would reverse this development and thus it would allow of lower bread rations without imposing great hardship, and would also relieve the pressure on the market for other goods. It is, however, by no means certain whether such a scheme is possible. Larger imports of cheese are dependent on rationing of cheese in the United States.[3] As to the dehydrated meat it is difficult, on the one hand, to estimate the possibilities, and on the other hand it will perhaps be necessary to use this import to compensate for reduced imports of fresh meat as a result of losses in refrigerator ships. But even if we abstract from the possibility of increasing imports of cheese and meat, there still remains a way of easing the bread position to a certain extent by differential rationing of meat.

3. Actually, the differential rationing of meat already exists, but it is of a peculiar character. At present all people who have meals in restaurants and canteens enjoy a differential ration of meat, because no coupons are surrendered when eating out. This privileged position of people taking meals in restaurants can hardly be justified. As to the canteens, they *are* a substitute for differential rationing in favour of manual workers, but even here the rationing is of a haphazard nature, not all workers being able to use the facilities of canteens.

[1] The substantial admixture of potato flour in bread which is sometimes proposed to save wheat is really equivalent to a flat rationing of wheat bread, and should therefore be rejected on the same grounds.

[2] Cf. 'Shipping—The Bottleneck', by F. Burchardt. (See p. 186.)   [3] Ibid.

The situation should be ordered by making it obligatory to surrender meat coupons in restaurants and canteens,[1] and use the surplus of meat saved in this way for increasing uniformly the rations of the manual worker.

This would mean, of course, shifting a certain amount of meat from the better-off population to the workers. In the event of bread being rationed this would permit a certain reduction in the workers' bread ration. But differential rationing of meat is useful from the point of view of shipping space even if bread is unrationed. If workers were to receive higher meat rations now this would probably cause a reduction in their present consumption of bread, which has increased, as mentioned above, in war-time as a result of the deficiency in protein foods. On the other hand, people eating in restaurants are unlikely to compensate the cut in their consumption of meat by substantially increasing their consumption of bread. They will rather direct their demand to other goods which may—just as the differential rationing of bread—necessitate some expansion in the scope of rationing.

4. It has frequently been proposed that clothes rationing should be on a differential basis because rich people are in possession of considerable stocks. The most satisfactory solution of this is, I think, that proposed by Mr. Burchardt in the article quoted. He argues there that 'Sir William Beveridge's idea of permitting the use of clothing coupons for fuel purchases (in the case of older people) may well be capable of wider application and may be operated the other way round too. The poor could use excess fuel coupons for buying clothes, the rich clothing coupons for buying fuel. Such a combined rationing by points would permit avoidance of differential rationing of each group taken separately, and it should be possible to devise a scheme which saves imports of clothing materials and does not throw coal consumption out of gear'.

I should like now to elaborate this proposal in some detail, namely the problem of fixing the point relation between clothing and coal. Suppose that the number of clothes coupons, after a moderate reduction as compared with the present level, is a, and the unknown number of coupons to be added for coal is x. The total number of interchangeable coupons will be $a + x$. Let us denote further the amount

---

[1] A rough solution of the administrative problem involved is to fix a certain flat coupon value per meat meal. The caterer will then have to make his meat meals in such a way as to cover his meat purchases, for which he will have to surrender coupons according to general rules. He may, of course, try to give meals short of their actual coupon value, but this will probably be to a great extent prevented by competition.

of fuel per coupon by y. A poor man will not be able to cut his consumption of clothing and footwear, therefore his fuel consumption will be xy. If we denote by b the level at which we want to fix it we have the equation:

$$xy = b$$

Now, a very rich man may abstain from buying clothes at all and spend all his coupons on fuel. His fuel consumption will therefore be $(a + x) y$. Let us now assume it is decided that he should not exceed the fuel consumption of the poor by more than m per cent. We then obtain the second equation:

$$\left(a + x\right) y = b \left(1 + \frac{m}{100}\right)$$

It may easily be obtained from these two equations that $x = a \cdot \dfrac{100}{m}$ and $y = \dfrac{b}{a} \cdot \dfrac{m}{100}$. If, for instance, m is 75 per cent, then $x = 1 \cdot 33a$ and $y = \dfrac{b}{1 \cdot 33a}$.

The scheme would also have the advantage of settling the difficulty arising out of the fact that families with many children require more clothes, but usually less fuel, because they will be able to spend more of their coupons on clothes and less on fuel.

The value b of the fuel consumption per head of a poor household must be determined so as to balance the total demand for and supply of fuel for household use. The difference in climatic conditions of various regions may also be accounted for by varying the number of clothes-fuel coupons distributed in these regions.

DIFFERENTIAL RATIONING IN PRACTICE

by J. Goldmann

FROM BULLETIN, VOL. 4, NO. 14 (OCTOBER 10, 1945)

IN view of the prospective worsening of the food position and the 'inevitable and very considerable changes in the matter of food', forecast by Lord Woolton, the problem of differential rationing has become increasingly important. While the theoretical aspects of the problem have already been discussed,[1] it may be interesting to review the experience gained in differential rationing during the last war, as well as the various schemes which are in force at present, in this country and elsewhere.

1. In the last war the issue of supplementary food rations to heavy workers was not considered in this country until it became probable that bread would have to be rationed, and it was carried into effect, against strong opposition, in anticipation of such an emergency. As long as bread was freely available, it was held, with little justification, that additional calorie requirements of certain sections of the population could be covered by a larger consumption of breadstuffs; when, however, a shortage in cereal supplies seemed imminent and the strictest economy of shipping space became imperative, simple rationing at a flat rate had to be abandoned.[2]

The principal food rationed differentially was bacon,[3] of which supplementary rations were not issued for more than a few months. In fact, additional supplies of bacon were made available to certain consumers, not so much for their own sake, but in order to get the population classified and to have those already marked who were qualified for special consideration so that bread rationing could, if necessary, be introduced at short notice.

On the basis of a detailed classification of occupations according to food requirements, the Ministry of Food estimated that 6 million heavy workers would claim and receive supplementary rations, and about 1·6 million adolescent boys. In fact, only 3 million supplementary books were issued to heavy workers, and 350,000 to boys.

---

[1] See p. 175.
[2] Sources for the last war are Sir William Beveridge, British Food Control, and the *National Food Journal*, 1918. Specific references have been omitted.
[3] And meat other than butcher's meat.

The inverse relation that existed between the price of bacon and its palatability upset official expectations. A short time after the inception of the scheme large supplies of bacon from America enabled the Ministry to free it altogether from the ration at a stage when it became certain that the supply of wheat was safeguarded until the harvest, and thus well into the next year.

Differential rationing, when it came into operation, had a mixed reception. On the grounds that it introduced discrimination between one class of workers and another, it was strongly opposed by the Parliamentary Committee of the Trade Union Congress, although many individual Unions declared in its favour, especially those of miners, railwaymen and transport workers. A straw poll among the more important food committees arranged by the Ministry resulted in a majority of 320 to 98 in favour of the new scheme.

2. In this war the Trade Union Congress seems to have taken a similar line. The general policy of the Government 'to allow the maximum possible rations for all consumers generally, rather than give a supplementary ration to any particular class at the expense of the rest of the community',[1] was confirmed in the House of Commons after a special Trade Union Congress Committee had been consulted. But, in spite of its obvious advantages, the present canteen system can hardly be said to supply fully the additional food requirements of all classes of heavy workers, in view of the technical difficulties involved in catering for agricultural workers, railwaymen, and similar categories. Moreover, the inadequate capacity of many of the existing canteens cannot be improved as quickly as would be necessary, if a sufficient standard of nutrition for the workers is to be secured now, in conditions which include prospective further cuts in total consumption. A more satisfactory solution could be obtained if the present policy were combined with the issue of supplementary rations to all heavy workers, while the surrender of coupons were made compulsory in every catering establishment, canteen, or restaurant.

There seems to be a tendency to overrate the difficulties connected with any scheme that differentiates between various classes of workers. Actually, such differentiation already exists at the present, in clothing and in cheese rations, and few complaints have been made. Outside Great Britain, two countries with a similar political structure, that is, Sweden and Switzerland, have adopted the differential rationing of food to a large extent (meat and fat in both countries; bread in

[1] Major Lloyd George, *Hansard*, October 2, 1941.

Sweden; sugar, cheese, and pulses in Switzerland). Under these schemes heavy workers draw, for example, twice as much meat, and of fats roughly half as much again as the ordinary consumer. In Russia, too, there is differentiation between ordinary consumers (household duties), office workers, and manual workers.[1]

Another attempt at differential food rationing has been made in this country in the preferential treatment of industrial canteens. Even so, assuming that Major Lloyd George's hope to double the meat allocation for canteens catering for very heavy workers, with similar increases in the allocation of some other foods,[2] has materialized, it still seems doubtful whether the meat consumption of these workers exceeds the ration granted to corresponding classes of consumers in Germany or the Protectorate. In fats, particularly important for those engaged in heavy work, the 'heaviest worker' in Britain is at a disadvantage compared with his opposite number in Germany, in spite of his additional supplies through the canteen.[3]

Insufficient as the extra canteen supplies may be, almost 50 per cent of the workers of this country are not able to obtain meals in canteens at all, and many of them who have no opportunity to eat in other catering establishments are actually worse placed than the normal consumer who is in no need of additional supplies. These workers, and their number is very large, are still dependent for their special food requirements on bread and potatoes, apart from the special cheese allowance for some categories. But, 'to suggest that the heavy worker can remain really efficient, happy, and healthy on the same diet as the sedentary worker plus a little extra bread, is like suggesting that a Rolls Royce car can run on the same petrol as a seven h.p. car with the addition of a little coal'.[4]

The provision of new canteens and expansion of existing ones, however necessary and desirable, cannot offer a speedy and comprehensive solution of the feeding problem of the heavy worker, which will be aggravated by the need for further cuts in consumption. Experience gained in this country, and elsewhere, would suggest that differential rationing according to needs, combined with compulsory surrender of coupons for meals taken out, is fair to everybody and in accordance with scientific requirements.

[1] *Daily Herald*, September 23, 1942.   [2] *Hansard*, October 2, 1941.
[3] British ration: 8 oz. plus 3 oz. through canteen, and fat content of bacon and cheese; German ration: 20 oz. (for very heavy workers).
[4] Professor A. V. Hill, *Hansard*, October 2, 1941.

FUEL RATIONING

FROM BULLETIN, VOL. 4, NO. 7 (MAY 16, 1942)

TWO problems are involved in the question of fuel rationing: (1) whether fuel rationing is necessary, either at the present time or in view of a possible deterioration in the situation in the future; (2) whether the particular scheme proposed by Sir William Beveridge cannot be simplified. In the recent discussion these two issues have been confused. The violence of the opposition to the rationing scheme is, indeed, rather surprising. Starting from the complexities of Sir William's scheme, much of the opposition appears to assume that such complexities are inherent in *any* rationing scheme, and goes on to argue that therefore rationing is impracticable altogether, and that the only way out of the difficulty is to appeal for voluntary saving in domestic use of fuel and to increase the output of coal. In this note we shall discuss the two issues separately.

1. If the subject is examined dispassionately it is clear that a reduction of domestic fuel consumption is necessary and, as Sir William convincingly demonstrates, the only way of distributing the reduced supplies is by rationing. It is true that certain increases in production can be obtained by particular measures. The release of miners from the Forces which is now strongly advocated in many quarters (including, curiously enough, some people who were strongly opposed to such a release before fuel rationing was threatened) can remedy the situation only to a minor degree. Output might be increased by concentrating production in the best seams and in the best pits. The miners themselves could be assured of a better standard of nutrition, thereby increasing their productivity. These steps might have been taken in the past: they were not, however, and even if they were to be taken at once it would be some time before output increased.

Against this potential increase, moreover, we are confronted with three offsetting items. The first is the necessity to pension old miners, which, from a humanitarian point of view, far outweighs the minor discomforts which will be caused by fuel rationing. The second is the continuously increasing demand for coal by the armament industries, to which should be added any development of substitute production, for example, oil, rubber, which the acute shipping position may necessitate. Thirdly, whatever increase in output may be achieved, the need to build up large and dispersed stocks is of great importance. Thus, although it is possible to increase the production of coal, the problem of curtailing domestic consumption loses none of its urgency.

2. Curtailment of consumption is thus necessary and rationing is the fairest way of distributing the reduced supplies. Let us consider, first, the scheme as given in the White Paper. Its main disadvantage is that it tries to be too perfect, to give to every one an allowance corresponding precisely to his needs. As a result the scheme is administratively complicated. (It should be emphasized, however, that the 15,000 workers required by Sir William Beveridge for a short period to initiate the scheme are less 'wasteful' than the number of miners who would be required to produce, year in, year out, the extra coal needed to maintain domestic consumption.) A pointer to a simpler scheme is given by food and clothing rationing.

Suppose, first of all, that every one receives the same personal ration, and that there is no basic household allowance at all. *A priori* children need the same ration as adults; they may consume less light, but need as much fuel for heating and a little more for washing. The obvious objection to this scheme is that the consumption of fuel does not increase proportionately with the number of persons in a family, because a great part of this consumption is, so to speak, overhead consumption (this is true not only of heating and lighting but also of cooking). A certain element of elasticity must therefore be introduced into the scheme so as to reduce the number of coupons available to large families. These usually include a good many children. One could achieve *approximately* the required aim by reducing the allowance for children under fifteen to, say, 50 per cent. This is not, be it noted, because children need less fuel, but is simply a device to make the family ration increase less than proportionately to the number of children in the family.[1] Babies and children under five or six (not attending school) need more than children attending school and should therefore be treated as adults. Sir William's idea of permitting invalids and old people to exchange clothes coupons for fuel coupons should definitely be incorporated in the scheme. Climatic conditions also can be accounted for, as in Sir William's plan. The precise demarcation of the 'special' categories needs, of course, careful and detailed consideration and the above examples are mentioned only to show that a considerable element of elasticity can be intro-

---

[1] For this reason if a family consists of only one adult and one child, the latter should be treated as an adult.

duced with a scheme based on the personal ration. Even with these modifications, such a scheme is not perfect. There will be some cases of great hardship; there will be others where the family ration is too high. The former can be remedied by instituting offices for appeals for special allowances; the latter, inherent in any rationing scheme (for example, some people *need* no clothes coupons at all because they already own large stocks), can only be met by the voluntary 'saving' campaign. The return of unused coupons, and the encouragement of saving within the ration, might, indeed, be assisted if the Government offered to buy back unused coupons for a small sum.

There remains the problem of coupon control. We envisage the following situation. The coupons should be on a points basis for all rationed fuels. For gas and electricity it is enough to collect coupons when the meter is read. For coal, the registration with one merchant which is now almost universal, should be completed, and coupons should be tendered when bills are paid. There is still the problem of preventing the sale of unused coupons to other people. This can, in theory, be obviated by comparing for each consumer the ration with the number of coupons actually used during the rationing period, for in each case the number of coupons used on gas, coal, or electricity is known (oil is a special case and might require registration). In practice it would be impossible to do this for all consumers, but a sample test, coupled with heavy penalties for any infringement thus revealed, should be sufficient.

So far no mention has been made of offices and institutions such as hospitals, schools, etc. For these some simple assessment such as floor space should be used, and, in order to prevent the over-statement of needs, a sample test should be made of the correctness of the estimate by the institution, coupled with a penalty for falsification. An alternative for institutions, etc., would be to cut consumption by some percentage of the previous year, the cut being varied according to the type of institution.

This last alternative suggests a possible modification of the general scheme of domestic rationing, if fair rationing on a *personal* basis is rejected. In our above proposal we allowed for appeals for extra fuel to be made to a Fuel Officer and it is possible that the number of such appeals, especially from the larger houses with few inhabitants, would overload the administrative machinery. The objection to rationing on a 'personal' basis on these grounds may lead to a rejection of the whole principle, but it is possible to modify the above scheme to get over this difficulty. The consumer could be given he choice of taking the uniform personal ration as described above, or of accepting a certain substantial percentage cut in his consumption of gas, electricity, and coal below the level of the last year. For most mall houses the basic personal ration would be more favourable, while some of the larger domestic consumers would prefer the latter alternative. In this way the scheme would become less complicated to administer but, it must be admitted, at the expense of fairness.

N

SHIPPING—THE BOTTLENECK

by F. A. Burchardt

FROM BULLETIN, VOL. 4, NO. 10 (July 18, 1942)

SHIPPING commitments of the Allied Nations have increased with Japan's entry into the war and with organized supplies to Russia. Shipbuilding, particularly in the U.S.A., is on the increase but behind schedule, and will not reach the target peak in the near future. Shipping losses for the first half of 1942 are grievous (according to American sources, greater than in any other period of this war); in American waters and in the Pacific and Indian Oceans greater than on the Atlantic route. Losses in recent months seem to have exceeded additions to the merchant fleet. Even discounting statements such as that of the American journal, *Iron Age*, that finished war goods are piling up at the docks of both coasts and at inland war plants for lack of shipping, it is clear that the rapid expansion of American war output makes it imperative to speed up its transport to battle areas. The battle for seaborne supplies is, and will remain in the coming months, a decisive factor in Allied economic strategy, and will greatly influence military strategy, as recent British-American discussions indicated. To make the most economical use of shipping is therefore of the greatest importance at this stage of the war.

Three main lines of policy are generally envisaged to relieve the strain on shipping resources: (1) better protection of merchant ships plying in the seven seas by escorts and extended patrols; (2) a speeding up of new construction and repairs; (3) the saving of shipping space by adjusting the economic policy of Allied countries to this bottleneck. The first two seem to have been among the main topics of the discussion between Churchill and Roosevelt, and will not concern us here. Some aspects of the third one, the contribution of economic policy towards relieving the shipping bottleneck, will be discussed in the following paper. But we shall disregard the important questions of organization, in particular the interlocking of the responsibilities of the Inter-allied Shipping Board with the conflicting policies of the Service and Civil Departments in the two main countries. The newly-established 'Combined Production and Resources Board' and

the 'Combined Food Board' may lighten to some extent the formidable task of inter-allied shipping authorities, provided (which seems
doubtful) they have sufficient executive power over all other departmental decisions, and bear the shipping bottleneck constantly in mind.
Better organization in itself will, however, not deliver the goods if
the principles of policy are undefined and not strongly impressed on
the supply departments.

If shipping is the limiting factor, and if it is desired to secure the
maximum flow of arms to the battlefield not in 1944, but in 1942, and
1943, with a declining or slowly growing merchant fleet, a saving in
shipping may be attempted on three main lines: (1) Imports of
unessential goods may be drastically curtailed, whereby past notions
of the degree of essentiality must be revised in the light of
the present emergency. (2) Dense and concentrated goods may
be substituted for bulky goods as far as possible; this applies particularly to raw materials and civilian goods, food in particular. (3) The
distribution of arms production between the Allied Nations may be
adjusted so as to minimize shipping.

Little can be said about the last case. The recent decision to specialize
on fighter production in Britain while the U.S.A. concentrate on
bombers which can, in some cases, be flown to the battle areas, requiring only shipments of spare parts, is a good example of a division of
labour which saves shipping space. The concentration of shipbuilding
in the United States, though presumably dictated by other motives,
could be cited as another instance. Agreements on types and speedy
standardization of parts would obviously operate in the same direction. Weapons requiring large quantities of bulky raw materials of
which a considerable part is wasted in the production process (for
example, ores), and a small value added, should be manufactured
near the location of raw materials provided that the final product is
not extremely bulky. As far as production facilities overseas permit,
Britain should import alumina not bauxite, or at least highly concentrated ores or semi-manufactures instead of ores with a low metal
content. This has not been neglected in the past, but greater savings
are possible, particularly as before America's entry into the war
Britain could not fully adopt such a policy for security reasons. Even
now the possibilities are limited, though by no means negligible. But
the matter is a highly technical one and requires adjustment of
production facilities both here and overseas which may not be practicable to a great extent in the very short run.

The policy of substitution of concentrated goods for bulky goods, which has some scope in the armament sector, can be applied, however, over the whole field of raw materials and foodstuffs. Bulk reduction by concentration is one obvious line; the second—the replacement of bulky goods by different goods of higher density. A few examples from the food front may illustrate the two methods. Meat has been imported hitherto either frozen or tinned. Refrigerator ships are in short supply, and tin has become a scarce material. Tin could be saved by replacing the tin-wasting small containers by large containers (tin consumed increases with the square, when the volume is cubed), or by replacing tin altogether, if health reasons permit, by other packing material. Dehydration promises to save even more shipping space: by reducing the moisture content of the meat its weight and bulkiness are reduced and at the same time the problem of packing materials is solved. To provide the principal meat suppliers with dehydrating equipment may turn out to be a major contribution to 'shipbuilding' or 'shipping' in the medium run. The powdering of eggs and milk has been adopted in the past, and might be supplemented, if possible, by concentrating oranges and other vitamin concentrates, by dehydration of vegetables and so forth. To import pills, powders, and dry goods and to add the water here is obviously to save shipping (and inland transport and storage) without lowering the objective standard of nutrition.

The same applies to the substitution of high quality foods for bulky foods. Bread consumption increased considerably when meat and cheese supplies were reduced. But cereals are very bulky imports. If it were possible to reverse the trend, shipping would be relieved. Again, the policy was inaugurated long ago but now needs speeding up and special measures here as well as in America. Cheese supplies from U.S.A. seem to have been determined on the basis of extended output without substantial reduction in American consumption before December, 1941. There seems to be a case now for rationing cheese and, if necessary, meat in U.S.A. to free greater quantities for Britain and Russia. American deficiencies may partly be made good by return freights of dairy products from New Zealand and Australia. To put it harshly, the Americans should live more on wheat and the British more on cheese and meat. Shifts in production to implement such a policy, and shifts in consumption habits enforced by rationing, imply sacrifices on the part of the Americans; but it may be argued that both the shipping situation and the war situation require them.

But Britain cannot come off scot-free, and sacrifices must be asked of the population to relieve the shipping situation. Britain is the best fed, best clothed nation in Europe, and enjoys a standard of living in other fields (fuel, household goods, smoking, etc.) which exceeds that of most other belligerent countries except U.S.A. and Canada. Considerable reductions are indispensable in order to save shipping space, and can be secured without undue hardship both in the food and in the non-food sectors. A few hints will be sufficient to illustrate this point.

If the Americans are asked to eat less cheese and more bread, the British may be asked to eat less bread and cake and more home-grown potatoes. Such a demand will clearly necessitate the intro-duction—or rather the systematic application—of differential ration-ing, giving more of certain categories of food, for instance bread or meat, to some groups of workers than to other people. The import-ance and implications of differential rationing are discussed more fully in a later paper. But some instances may be given to show the possibilities. It would appear practicable to reduce the clothes ration to save shipping space.[1] A uniform reduction of clothing points would cause hardships for the lower income groups and for the youngsters, while the stocks possessed by the more well-to-do might allow almost a 100 per cent cut without causing undue hardship for a certain period. On the other hand, the middle and upper classes would feel a uniform fuel ration more than the lower classes. Sir William Beveridge's idea of permitting the use of clothing coupons for fuel purchases (in the case of older people) may well be capable of wider application and may be operated the other way round too. The poor could use excess fuel coupons for buying clothes; the rich, clothing coupons for buying fuel. Such a combined rationing by points would permit avoidance of differential rationing of each group taken separately, and it should be possible to devise a scheme which saves imports of clothing materials and does not throw coal con-sumption out of gear. Alternatively licences for individual purchases (on the continental model) may be introduced for clothes and house-hold goods which in effect would also amount to differential rationing.

But the net saving obtained by differentiating according to needs must in many cases be supplemented by some general cuts. It is not generally known that sugar equivalent to the personal sugar ration of the whole population is grown in this country; but about a million tons of sugar[2] is imported for other purposes. As cake and sweets

---

[1] It is estimated that cloth rationing saved 250,000 tons of shipping space annually (*Manchester Guardian*, May 18, 1942).

[2] Sugar has a high calorie value per ton of shipping. Rather than add it to cake made from imported wheat or flour, it may be used to increase the personal ration.

figure largely in the consumption of sugar, cake rationing seems to be overdue. Various other instances could be given, and it seems regrettable that a separate 'Combined Food Board' has been established while shipping questions are the main domain of the Combined Resources Board. Lord Woolton, more than anybody else, could assist the shipping authorities by strict husbanding of his stocks and resources.[1]

In the non-food sector potential economies are almost equally large. We have already referred to textile materials and ores. But timber is looming even larger on the import side and calls for strictest economy, and the allocation of timber by the Control and a survey of its uses may reveal sources of economy. A tightening up of waste collection of paper and rags but equally of all other materials might also add appreciably to home supplies; and finally, a substantial reduction of advertising would certainly not affect the standard of living in this country nor impair the war effort and would still save thousands of tons of shipping. The recent restrictions in petrol consumption—adopted rather late in view of the tanker situation—and the insistence on fuel economies in industry should set the pace for economies in all other important materials, especially those which require shipping. Home produced substitutes (plastics, straw, etc.) should help to mitigate the cuts which have to be made.

To work out more detailed plans requires more data on imports, shipping capacities and strategic plans than are available; but the main principles are clear. Beginnings have been made in all directions to adjust the allied countries to the shipping bottleneck. To carry them out rigorously and speedily is the immediate task ahead.

The main conclusions would seem to be: (1) the greatest and most immediate saving in shipping space can be obtained by concerted action of the Ministry of Food and the Board of Trade mainly by the following methods: (*a*) a drastic cut of unessential imports which neither help the war effort nor maintain the standard of living (for example, paper for advertising); (*b*) a reduction in civilian supplies accompanied by wider differential rationing; (*c*) a substitution of concentrates (food, ore, etc.) for bulky goods, combined with suitable price adjustments, to enable everybody to buy his ration, and a drive for increased home supplies (potatoes for cereals, paper, etc.). (2) The next biggest but not immediately realizable source of saving would seem to be the production departments. Shifts in production

[1] That at this time of plentiful supplies of fresh vegetables, milk and other unrationed goods the total food points have not been greatly reduced, might well cause concern to the shipping authorities.

facilities and specialization take time in the industrial and raw material sector and even more in the agricultural sector. But the setting up of new plants should be carefully scrutinized in view of the shipping situation and desirable transfers of plant and specializations should be initiated in order to reap the benefit in shipping relief in six or twelve months' time. Adjustments in the armament sector (specialization on types of weapons and standardization of parts), though important, will require more time, particularly as the readjustment must not be allowed to slow down current arms output appreciably. In the long run, however, it should give good results.

Expectations of reduced losses, whether justified or not by the events of the next nine months, and the steady expansion of new construction, can in the most favourable circumstances not dispense with the task of the Combined Resources and Food Board to save shipping space by proceeding speedily and by action, rather than by persuasion, along all three lines outlined above.

RATIONING AND SURPLUS GOODS

by J. Steindl

FROM BULLETIN, VOL. 3, No. 15 (NOVEMBER 1, 1941)

THE purpose of this note is to set out the advantages which the method of rationing of expenditure has in countries with substantial surpluses of some consumable goods. Australia may be taken as an example, but the argument can be applied equally well to New Zealand, also to South Africa.[1]

The underlying problem was touched upon when the late Australian Government indicated its desire to solve the problem of surplus goods (in part) by inducing Australians to consume more of the surplus food in substitution for imported food or highly processed food which uses up scarce factory labour.[2] The surplus goods are mainly meat, sugar, butter, fruits. To the scarce consumer's goods belong first all those which are imported (textiles, and a great variety of smaller items); and, second, goods which are needed for the war effort (for example, the product of wool manufacture, probably also cheese which is needed for export to the United Kingdom) or which need labour which could be diverted to war production.[3] The dual aim of restricting the consumption of the scarce goods and keeping up, or increasing the consumption of surplus goods, can be solved by rationing the total expenditure on scarce goods, on the lines of Mr. Kalecki's scheme,[4] while leaving people free to spend on surplus goods as much as they like. The effect of this scheme would be to direct the additional income, resulting from the increasing war outlay, into channels where expenditure is innocuous and does not produce shortages.

On what grounds should we expect an increase in consumption of surplus foods? Most of them belong to the kind of foods which wage-earners consume in increasing quantities as their income increases. There is no investigation of consumption at various income

[1] It should be noted that the above article refers to the situation existing before the war in the Pacific began.

[2] *Monthly Summary of Bank of Australasia,* July, 1941, p. 5.

[3] We take it for granted all the time that the farmers who produce the surplus goods cannot be diverted to war production, and that it would be unwise to leave the farms and their equipment to deteriorate; otherwise the problem of surplus would not arise.

[4] For the details of this scheme, see p. 137.

levels for Australia, but there are such investigations for several other countries (including the United States) and they show that, within the ordinary range of wage-earners' incomes, consumption of meat, milk, and dairy products, and fruit, probably also of sugar, increases with increasing income.[1] It is true that with higher incomes there will probably be a limit to this increase, but even in Australia this limit is not likely to be reached by a large number of incomes. Any increase in the lower incomes resulting from the war expenditure will then lead to an increase in the consumption of surplus goods. But if expenditure on other goods is rationed then the rise in consumption will be greater than it otherwise would be. Not being able to spend a part of the increase in income on scarce goods, people will probably buy surplus goods in great quantities in order to get some immediate satisfaction out of their income. The total increase in consumption of surplus food resulting from the rationing scheme would depend on the following factors: the increase in lower and middle-sized incomes resulting from the war expenditure, the extent to which expenditure on scarce goods is restricted, the rise in surplus goods consumption with a given rise in income levels, and finally the extent to which people will, as it were, forcibly substitute surplus goods for other goods which they are not able to buy in greater quantities.

If the problem of simultaneous scarcity and surplus is left to be solved by the price mechanism, there will be inflation in the sector of scarce goods, while the prices of surplus goods will rise little (in practice this state of affairs would probably lead to the granting of subsidies to farmers, to enable them to keep up their real income). The price discrepancy between surplus goods and scarce goods would lead to substitution of the former for the latter, and this would mitigate the inflation, and at the same time increase the consumption of surplus goods. But the 'substitution effect' of the price discrepancy would be limited, and a large part of any increase in money income would be spent on scarce goods, with the only effect that their prices would rise again.

In the case of rationing, however, inflation in the scarce goods' sector will be prevented by fixing the expenditure ration for scarce goods so as to equal their supply. Any spendable surplus above this expenditure ration could only be used for surplus goods (and perhaps services) or for saving. Scarce goods above the expenditure ration

---

[1] Workers' Nutrition and Social Policy, International Labour Office, *Studies and Reports*, Series B, No. 23 Geneva, 1936, p. 65.

having, as it were, an infinitely high price, the substitution will be carried out to a far greater extent than the price mechanism could achieve, and the effect on surplus goods consumption will therefore be greater.

It appears that in countries with consumable surplus goods the method of financing the war by taxation (or compulsory saving) imposed partly on middle and lower incomes, involves even more obvious disadvantages than elsewhere. If the taxation prevents a rise in lower incomes, it prevents at the same time a rise in consumption of surplus goods; if it actually cuts down lower incomes in order to reduce consumption of scarce goods, then the consumption of surplus goods likewise falls, and the pressure on their markets increases. Orthodox war finance is unable to cope with this problem.[1]

What would happen if the rationing scheme were introduced and lower incomes were increased until all the surplus would be absorbed? There is little danger of this with respect, for example, to Australian meat, but wherever it would happen a kind of secondary scarcity would arise. The answer to the problem is to apply the same technique again: ration expenditure on those surplus goods which become scarce, by fixing a separate expenditure ration for these goods. There would then be one expenditure ration for goods of primary scarcity, and another expenditure ration for goods of secondary scarcity.

In practice any such scheme would have to be coupled with strict price control of surplus goods in all stages.

---

[1] For an example of successful new methods to cope with surplus goods, independent of rationing, see S. Moos, 'The Two Stamp Plan', p. 195.

THE TWO-STAMP PLAN
A NEW METHOD OF DISTRIBUTION

by S. Moos

From Bulletin, Vol. 3, No. 11 (August, 1941)

EIGHT years have passed since, in the framework of the sweeping New Deal legislation, a law was passed in the U.S.A. which enabled the Agricultural Adjustment Administration (A.A.A.) to pay, out of processing taxes, compensation to farmers who submitted to the regulation of production by the Federal Government. By restricted production the New Deal intended to adjust supply to effective demand and thus avoid the accumulation of commodity surpluses. The Act was, however, abolished in January, 1936, by a 6:3 vote of the Supreme Court which declared the processing taxes to be unconstitutional. The U.S.A. Government was indicted of having infringed the rights of the individual States which, sovereign in their territories, were alone responsible for the agricultural policy to be pursued.[1] Thus, this great attempt at organized agricultural production was defeated because it involved the bigger and still undecided issue of States' authority against the Federal Government.

The regulation of production having failed, another scheme for the disposal of surpluses was tried out with a certain measure of success. When commodity markets weakened under the pressure of supplies for which no sufficient demand was forthcoming, agricultural surplus products were bought by the Government and sent to relief agencies for distribution to relief clients. This scheme was opposed, especially in derelict areas, by tradesmen whose turnover decreased in proportion to the relief deliveries by the State.

In 1939, a new scheme was put into operation, this time based on the principle of adjusting demand to supply. The gap between potential and effective demand was to be bridged by selling surplus products to people who otherwise would not be able to buy these goods. The scheme, known as the Food Stamp Plan, or Two-Stamp Plan, was, in May, 1939, begun experimentally in one town, Rochester, and has since become one of the most successful economic experiments carried out by the New Deal Administration, expanding

[1] See E. A. Radice, *Fundamental Issues in the United States*, Oxford, 1936.

so rapidly that it is expected to reach soon 4–5 million customers. Extending to 14 areas only, in November, 1939, it had, in the Spring of 1941, spread to 250 areas, including Greater New York where it was inaugurated on March 1, 1941.

The Two-Stamp Plan allows special categories of people on relief or in need of assistance to purchase, at local relief district stations, books containing from 8 to 56 orange-coloured stamps worth 25 cents each. These orange stamps entitle the holder to buy any food from any grocer, butcher, or dairyman taking part in the scheme. For every $1·0 worth of orange stamps the buyer receives *free*, in addition, 50 cents worth of blue stamps. The weekly minimum of orange stamps to be bought by one person has been fixed at approximately $1·0, an amount which is taken to represent the average weekly expenditure of poorer families on food. According to research of the Department of Agriculture about 20 million people spend 5 cents a meal only. $1·50 per family have been allowed as the upper limit for the purchase of orange stamps. The free blue stamps can be used only for the purchase of commodities on the Government surplus list. Mainly relief recipients with cooking facilities are qualified for the purchase of stamps and receive the authorization by mail. Those retailers who have applied to the Surplus Marketing Administration (S.M.A.) for participation in the scheme— over 200,000 retail food stores in poverty-stricken districts are, at present, taking part—accept both the orange and blue stamps instead of cash and receive from the Government, directly or through the wholesaler, their full value redeemed.[1]

The Government raises the sums required for this purpose partly by using 30 per cent of all customs receipts as provided by tariff laws, obtaining in this way about $100,000,000 a year, and, if necessary, by additional grants. From May, 1939, until May, 1941, some $80,000,000 of surplus foods were bought with blue stamps. In September, 1940, more than 2,000,000 relief recipients used $4·6 million worth of blue stamps, while in January, 1941, 3,000,000 recipients spent $7·0 million on surplus products, equalling a yearly expenditure of $28 per person and a total expenditure of $84 million.

---

[1] The surplus is to be measured not by physical units but by economic standards based on prices. Thus, surplus means that quantity of an agricultural product which, if sold on the market, would lower prices under a level remunerative to producers. The surplus, therefore, increases or decreases correspondingly with the fall or rise of the remunerative or 'parity' price. A price is considered remunerative if the purchasing power obtained by the agricultural producer by selling a certain quantity of his crops enables him to buy the same amount of goods as in the base period August, 1909—to July, 1914. Changes in interest-, tax-, and freight-rates are also to be taken into account.

TABLE I

SALE OF SURPLUS PRODUCTS AND INCREASE IN FAMILY EXPENDITURE RESULTING FROM THE SCHEME

Product	Percentage inc. in family exp.due to the scheme	Quantities in million lb.		Total Production		Assumed sale of surplus as per cent of production
		Sold in Jan. '41 to 3 mil. recipients	Sold yearly assuming 7·5 million recip.	Quantity	Year	
Fruit	14·0					
Potatoes .. ⎱		27·8	850	28,884	1934	3·0
Dry Beans ⎰	12·0	3·5	100	1,122	1934	8·9
Other Vegetables ⎰		6·6	200			
Eggs	13 0	3·6[1]	110[2]	2,161	1934	5·1
Butter	14·0	2·7	80	1,786	1938	4·5
Flour ⎱ ..		24·0	700	20,600	1937	3·4
Other Cereals ⎰ ..	16·0	8·6	250			
Lard	6·0	4·7	140	1,700	1938	8·2
Pork	25·0	10·5	300	7,600	1938	4·0

[1] Sold in February, 1941: 7·2 mill. lb. apples, 1·2 mill. lb. dried prunes, 1 mill. lb. raisins, 6·1 mill. grape fruits, 2·1 mill, doz. oranges.
[2] Mill. dozen.

Not more than 25 per cent of total funds are to be spent on any one surplus commodity. In the period December, 1939 to January, 1940, 34 per cent of the funds available were spent on butter and eggs, 23 per cent on pork; flour and pork lard came next. Of fruit mainly oranges and grapefruit were designated as surplus food. From time to time commodities are added to or taken off the surplus list which, in December, 1939, included sixteen commodities. Since the Summer of 1940 such changes may be carried out on a regional basis so that a regional surplus can be absorbed in a similar way as a large-scale national one.

We may conclude from Table I, which shows a marked increase of family expenditure on agricultural products, that the Two-Stamp system has succeeded where other plans have failed, in stimulating the consumption of additional quantities of surplus goods. If the Plan is extended to another 4·5 millions in receipt of relief, so that $100 million out of customs and $100 million out of State grants would be spent, considerable quantities of surplus products will be absorbed. If, on the other hand, the American re-armament programme absorbs many of those now receiving relief, the scheme may decline in importance. Its scope, however, could be considerably increased by the inclusion of low income groups. Their exclusion actually tends to remove the incentive for accepting or even remaining in low-paid work which deprives workers of the benefits of the Food Stamp Plan. But an attempt, undertaken in Oklahoma, to include families with an income below $19–50 a week in the scheme, was strongly opposed as 'socialism', 'fascism', 'relief for non-reliefers', etc. The Chamber of Commerce feared increasing State interference in normal trade channels, while those benefiting from the extension of the Plan resented being counted in the same social category as 'reliefers'. Even of reliefers entitled to receive blue stamps, one-quarter on the average do not use this opportunity.

The Two-Stamp Plan is not forced upon communities but introduced on application only. A guarantee must be given by the local authorities not to cut the cash payments due to reliefers who receive blue stamps and to bear the administrative costs of the Plan, amounting to about $500 for 10,000 persons. The minimum and maximum limits ($1·0 and $1·50) for the purchase of orange stamps are adjusted to local conditions in such a way that in very poor communities blue stamps are distributed without orange stamps having been bought. These cases are, however, exceptional since the general obligation to acquire orange stamps is designed, as mentioned above, to prevent purchasing power released by the free issue of blue stamps being shifted from food to other items.

Merits of the Plan

It is true that producers who would receive almost the total Government subsidy if they restricted production, and some 75 per cent of the subsidy if surpluses were directly distributed by the State to those in need, obtain under the Two-Stamp Plan only 45 per cent.[1] But under the latter system a rather stable price level is maintained while direct distribution tends to undermine prices of agricultural products, purchasing power being diverted by those benefiting from food grants to other fields of consumption. Although this tendency is considerably lessened in the Two-Stamp Plan by the compulsory continuation of normal expenditure as a condition for the grant of surplus products, this loophole has to receive the constant attention of the S.M.A. On the other hand, the scheme, by removing the pressure of surplus supply on the market, favours price increases. Such a trend became especially marked in connection with possible Government purchases under the Lease-Lend to Britain programme,

[1] The other 55 per cent being used for administrative costs and for payment of the margin between producers' costs and retail prices.

so that in March, 1941, the S.M.A. decided in future to withhold information on its daily purchases of butter, lard, eggs, cheese, and other surplus food products. Increased costs of distribution may be considered another disadvantage of the scheme.

No doubt these tendencies, as far as they do not cancel each other, may jeopardise the scheme which, at the same time, is not safe from being misused by those benefiting from it. Many of those living near or below the subsistence level attempt, in spite of prohibitions, to exchange their blue stamps against cash instead of against commodities, thus defying the purpose for which they received the blue stamps. In March, 1941, a plot was discovered to counterfeit food stamps, orange and blue, and sell them at a discount of 70 per cent of their value to retailers who could pass them on as genuine stamps. The plot was discovered in time by the Treasury Secret Service, the printing and engraving equipment was confiscated and the men responsible were arrested. But the possibility of fraud represents a constant danger to the Food Stamp Plan. It has been met by counter-measures which, so far, have proved efficient. Areas which administer the plan in an improper manner, for example, introduce arbitrary conditions in selecting prospective stamp holders, can be deprived of the distribution of surplus commodities. Anybody taking part in the scheme, including retailers and wholesalers, who infringes the regulations can be refused further participation in the scheme. A more severe form of punishment may be inflicted by treating the misuse of the scheme, such as the raising of false claims, as a criminal offence.[1]

Against these drawbacks must be set the advantages of the plan, which successfully improved the nourishment of low-income families and the turnover of the retail trade, thus absorbing commodity surpluses without the opposition and even with the consent and support of the trades concerned.

The voluntary basis and the adaptability to local conditions have largely contributed to the success of a scheme original in its conception as well as in its execution. The surplus products are neither destroyed nor distributed to people in need without regard to their actual desires, nor does this distribution upset the normal market. By subsidizing the consumer instead of the producer the Government satisfies consumer, distributor, and producer at the same time. Surplus products are absorbed by purchasing power being transferred from

[1] See S. Herman, *The Food Stamp Plan, The Journal of Business of the University of Chicago*, October, 1940–January, 1941.

the consumers of imported goods to the consumer of home production.

Surplus products are distributed through normal trade channels without leading to a slump in prices and profits. The Two-Stamp Plan, originating in the theory of price differentiation and discriminative marketing, thus represents a decisive step forward in the development of the economics of distribution, though final judgment must be postponed until more data are available and until general economic conditions have become more normal than in a world at war.

Application to Great Britain

The principles applied in the scheme could, with possibly similar success, be applied to problems of a war-economy, such as rationing and food subsidies. These measures, in spite of the unequal distribution of purchasing power, are at present carried out according to the principle of price equalization, that is, of prices equal in all markets, and are based on a theoretical equality of rations. But, in practice, those possessing sufficient purchasing power can buy high-priced un-rationed goods while, on the other hand, rations are not being fully consumed by those with restricted means. Food subsidies are paid in such a way that those with high purchasing power profit to the same degree as the poorer classes. In order to improve these conditions special categories of buyers, say wives and children of members of the armed forces, evacuees, or low-paid workers in war industries, could receive special 'dividend cards' instead of ordinary ration cards, the stamps representing a bonus on their purchases, so that goods obtained by these stamps could be bought at reduced prices. The Ministry of Food would, in future, announce not only the quantity of the weekly ration of a commodity, but also the money value represented by the dividend stamps. While purchases on normal ration cards would be marked in the ration book, as practised now, the quantity-value stamps of dividend cards would be cut and collected by retailers, as at the beginning of the rationing scheme, and redeemed by the Food Office, directly or via the wholesaler or bank. The additional costs involved would be of a comparatively small magnitude since subsidies now paid to producers and wholesalers would be used for financing the scheme. In Table II we give estimates of the cost of such a scheme according to the value of the 'dividend' and the number of persons benefiting. To these figures an allowance for administrative costs has to be added. Part of the dividend stamps could be used for important unrationed foods such as cocoa, vegetables, or if available, fruit.

TABLE II

ESTIMATE OF ANNUAL EXPENDITURE ON 'DIVIDEND' STAMPS

Number of persons benefiting			Annual cost with a weekly dividend of 2/-	3/-	4/-
			£ million		
3,000,000	..	..	15·6	23·4	31·2
5,000,000	..	..	26·0	39·0	52·0
10,000,000	..	..	52 0	78·0	104·0

By applying the principle of discriminative marketing in this way a more equal distribution of the food available and improved nourishment of large sections of the population could be achieved.

O

IV. WAGES AND NATIONAL INCOME

EMPLOYMENT AND NATIONAL INCOME DURING THE WAR

by J. L. Nicholson

FROM BULLETIN, VOL. 7, NO. 14 (OCTOBER 13, 1945)

IN the following pages, a general account is given of changes in employment, incomes, consumption and prices, which have been brought about in this country during the war. An estimate is also made of the distribution of the financial 'war burden' between wage earners and others.

1. EMPLOYMENT

First, we consider the changes that have taken place, between 1938 and 1944, in the number of insured persons employed in industry. The estimated number of persons insured against unemployment under the General, Special or Agricultural Schemes, in the first week of July, are shown in Table I. It should be noted that all the figures in this Table refer to persons in the United Kingdom, aged 14 and over. The first line shows the numbers actually insured at the time of the annual exchange of cards. Owing to changes in the scope of insurance, certain adjustments were necessary in order to obtain a continuous series of comparable figures. From September 1940, unemployment insurance was extended to include non-manual workers earning between £250 and £420 a year, estimated to number 364,500 in July 1941. Also, women over 60 ceased to be insurable against unemployment from July 1940. After adjusting the figures for these two changes,[1] the index number shown in the second line is obtained. From April 1942 women employed part-time[2] were exempted from unemployment insurance; the numbers so employed in previous years must have been comparatively small, so that this index effectively repre-

---

[1] Index numbers before and after each change were joined by the chain method; in this way, it was implicitly assumed, for instance, that the proportion of non-manual workers earning between £250 and £420 p.a. was constant from July, 1941 onwards, the actual numbers after this date not being available.

[2] i.e. for not more than 30 hours a week.

sents the numbers insured against unemployment in July of each year, excluding part-time workers and after eliminating changes in the scope of insurance.

For the purpose of comparing estimates of national income with changes in employment, it would be useful to know the average number of insured persons in employment throughout each year, but these numbers are not available. Estimates were therefore made of the average number of insured persons in each year by interpolating from the July figures;[1] the results, expressed as index numbers, are shown in line 3 of Table I. The average numbers of insured persons who were wholly unemployed (including casuals) or temporarily stopped, which are ascertained once a month, were then subtracted from the average numbers insured, in order to obtain estimates of the average numbers of insured persons in employment. Adjustments were made for the classes of domestic servants which were brought into insurance in April 1938, and for a minor change in the method of counting unemployed men at Government training centres,[2] as well as for the two changes in the scope of insurance, mentioned above.[3] Further, since the numbers of insured persons unemployed, after August 1940, are available for Great Britain but not for the United Kingdom, it was assumed that the number of unemployed persons in Northern Ireland, relatively to the number in Great Britain, remained constant after this date. Since the number in question was then small in relation to the total number employed (about 0·6 per cent), and must have subsequently declined, no substantial error could thus have been introduced. The estimated average numbers of insured persons employed, not including part-time women, are shown in the form of index numbers in line 4 of Table I. The estimated average number of insured persons in employment in 1938, corresponding to the scope of unemployment insurance in July of that year, was 13,873,500.

The number of part-time workers was 380,000 in July 1942, 756,000 in July 1943, and 900,000 in July 1944.[4] When these are

---

[1] If n_1, n_2, n_3, are the numbers insured at the beginning of July, in three successive years, using linear interpolation between these dates, the average number in the second year is given by $\frac{1}{8}$ $(6n_2+n_1+n_3)$.

[2] See *Ministry of Labour Gazette*, 1940, p. 223.

[3] It was assumed that there was no unemployment among non-manual workers earning between £250 and £420 a year. Continuity in the insurance figures is also disturbed by the fact that, in a period of rising incomes, persons who were insured at one date may not, if their incomes increase beyond the upper limit, be insurable at a later date. This would have made the index numbers, if anything, slightly too low.

[4] These figures were kindly supplied by the Ministry of Labour. It is not clear why the proportion of part-time women workers appears to have been much less in the industries covered by the Ministry of Labour earnings inquiries.

TABLE I

Insured Persons, aged 14 and over, in the United Kingdom
General, Special and Agricultural Schemes

	1938	1939	1940	1941	1942	1943	1944
1. Number insured in July[1] (000's)	15,742.85	15,898.3	15,121.75	15,240.2	15,406.5	15,002.5	14,514.3
2. Index of No. insured in July[2]	100	101.0	96.3	94.7	95.8	93.0	90.2
3. Index of av. No. insured in year[2]	100	100.3	96.7	95.1	95.4	93.2	90.6
4. Index of average No. insured employed[2]	100	102.5	102.4	104.9	106.7	104.7	102.0
5. Do. including part-time workers[3]	100	102.5	102.4	104.9	108	107½	105
6. Index from insurance conts.[2]	100	102	100½	105	106	101½	
7. Index of working time	100	101½	105	107	109	107½	104½
8. Index of volume of employment (5 × 7)	100	104	107½	112	117½	115½	109½

[1] Actual numbers, unadjusted for changes in the scope of insurance.
[2] Adjusted for changes in the scope of insurance, but not for part-time workers.
[3] Including two part-time workers as equivalent to one full-time worker.

TABLE II

Numbers of Males aged 14-64 and Females aged 14-59 Employed in Great Britain
(mid-year figures, in thousands)

	1938	1939	1941	1942	1943	1944
Males 14-64 employed in industry		13,086	11,520	10,992	10,438	10,136
Females 14-59		4,837	5,848	6,502	6,706	6,569
TOTAL (above groups)	17,400	17,923	17,368	17,494	17,144	16,705
Do. expressed as index numbers	100	103.0	99.8	100.5	98.5	96.0
Men in Armed Forces[2]	400	477	3,271	3,785	4,284	4,497
Women in Auxiliary Services		—	103	307	461	466
Full-time Civil Defence (M. & F.)	—	80	383	384	323	282
TOTAL in Forces, Auxiliary Services and full-time Civil Defence	400	557	3,757	4,476	5,068	5,245
TOTAL employed in Industry, Forces, Civil Defence, etc.	17,800	18,480	21,125	21,970	22,212	21,950
Do. expressed as index numbers	100	104	119	123	125	123

[1] Excluding Domestic Servants; including women employed part-time, two counted as one.
[2] Excluding prisoners and missing.

ncluded, counting two part-time workers as equivalent to one ull-time worker, the final index number, shown in line 5, is obtained.

It is interesting to compare the index of the number of insured persons employed with the index number which was derived from employees' contributions to unemployment insurance,[1] which hitherto provided the only means of estimating war-time changes in the volume of employment. The latter, which is shown in line 6, is not adjusted for part-time women and may be compared, therefore, with the index in line 4.

These two series would not be expected to give exactly the same results, for several reasons:

(i) As mentioned above, the index in line 4 does not refer exactly to the average number of insured persons employed (the average number insured were estimated by interpolation and the average numbers unemployed were based on figures relating to a particular day in each month).

(ii) The index derived from insurance contributions does not allow for changes in the proportions belonging to different sex and age groups, which pay varying contributions; it appears, however, from the data relating to insured persons (employed and unemployed) that such changes would have caused only a very slight reduction in this index (by not more than 0·5 per cent in 1943).

(iii) Agriculture was not included in the index based on contributions, and as the number of women employed in agriculture has risen considerably during the war, this index would be slightly too low (by not more than 1 per cent in 1943).

(iv) Persons temporarily stopped for only part of a week, who are not included in line 4, would continue to pay contributions.

These reasons could probably explain the differences between the two series, which agree very closely for 3 of the 5 years, and differ by not more than 3 per cent in the other two years. The results appear to justify the method which was previously used.

The index relating to insured persons employed (line 5 of Table I) will be used in subsequent analysis as indicating changes in the number of wage earners employed. Insured persons include small salary earners, but do not include most domestic servants, or men over 65 and women over 60. It is estimated[2] that the number of

---

[1] The method of construction was described in BULLETIN, Vol. 3, No. 13, p. 294. The effects of changes in the rates of contribution and in the scope of insurance were eliminated.
[2] Sir Godfrey Ince, *Mobilization of Man-power in Great Britain for the Second Great War*, Manchester Statistical Society, 1945.

persons over these ages in industrial employment in Great Britain increased, during the war, by over 400,000. The number employed as indoor domestic servants was probably reduced by a roughly similar amount, so that these two factors approximately cancel each other, while any change which may have occurred in the relative number of salary earners with less than £420 a year could have had only a slight effect on the index.

There is, however, a further qualification which should be mentioned. During the war, the number of persons who are permanently employed in Government service, or on the railways, and who are not insurable against unemployment has declined, while the number of temporary employees, who are insured, has increased. To the extent that the former have been substituted by the latter, the index number overstates the increase in the numbers employed. A comparison of the changes in the total number of persons employed in Government service with the changes in the number of insured persons so employed shows a comparatively small discrepancy, so that, at least as far as Government employees are concerned, this point does not, in fact, appear to be very important, and is therefore neglected.

An estimate was also required of the increase in average hours worked. This was based on data obtained from the Ministry of Labour inquiries into earnings and hours of labour in mining (except coal), manufacturing and building industries, supplemented by information relating to the average number of shifts worked by coal miners.[1] The resulting index is shown in line 7 of Table I and, when multiplied by the index of the average numbers employed (line 5), provides an estimate of changes in the volume of employment (line 8).

An idea of the total mobilization of man-power, in industry and the Forces, is provided by figures which have been made available for Great Britain[2] (but, oddly enough, not for the United Kingdom), and which are shown in Table II. Comparison with Table I shows that the number of insured persons employed has increased relatively to the total number of persons employed in industry; the number of persons employed but not insured must have declined considerably. This is partly explained by the substitution of permanent for temporary employees in government and railways (see above). The

---

[1] *Statistical Digest*, 1944, published by the Ministry of Fuel and Power (Cmd. 6639).
[2] See *Statistics relating to the War Effort of the United Kingdom* (Cmd. 6564) and Table 12 of the White Paper on National Income (Cmd. 6623). The number in the Forces in 1938 was indirectly estimated from their total pay and allowances.

total number of persons employed in industry, the Forces, auxiliary services and full-time civil defence,[1] at the peak, in 1943, was 25 per cent greater than in 1938.

2. Consumption and Prices of Main Items

Next we consider changes between 1938 and 1944 in consumption and prices of the main groups of items for which estimates are given in the White Paper on National Income (Cmd. 6623). For the main categories of expenditure, Table III shows changes in consumption (in real terms) and in market prices (including the effects of indirect taxes and subsidies). The data relate (as far as possible) to expenditure out of personal incomes. The figures for individual categories relate to purchases in the United Kingdom, including those of tourists and Dominion and Allied Troops and excluding expenditure abroad of British tourists and members of the armed forces. The final totals, however, are adjusted so as to relate to purchases out of British incomes.

Income in kind received by the forces[2] is included in the total, but not in the separate groups. Thus, the decline in food consumption, shown in Table III, is partly the result of the gradual increase in the number of persons in the forces and auxiliary services.

The figures relating to beer consumption, given in the White Paper, are expressed in terms of bulk barrels. In order to eliminate the effects of dilution, it is necessary to reckon the consumption of beer in terms of standard barrels[3] and this is also more consistent with the procedure adopted for other goods, where, 'as far as possible, and in nearly all cases of merchandise sales, the value of expenditure at 1938 prices takes account of the changed quality of the goods sold' (Cmd. 6623, p. 27). Standard barrels have accordingly been used in calculating the index numbers shown in Table III; this affects the prices and consumption of beer as well as of all goods combined.[4] Since in many cases it must have been impossible to make full allowance for changes in quality, it may be assumed that more correct index numbers would show greater increases

---

[1] Excluding domestic servants.

[2] This is stated to include food and clothing only. Housing and travel met at Government expense are apparently excluded from both income and expenditure. It is assumed that the price index for all other goods and services can be applied to income received in kind.

[3] Expenditure on beer in terms of standard barrels at 1938 prices, according to information kindly supplied by the Central Statistical Office, was £ million: 180, 186, 179, 189, 180, 184, 194 in the years 1938 to 1944 respectively.

[4] The price index of beer is raised, through this adjustment, by about 35 points and the price index of all items combined by about $1\frac{1}{2}$ points.

in price, and correspondingly larger reductions in consumption, than are indicated by the present estimates.[1]

The two sets of figures relating to rent, which show very little change compared with 1938, are probably not altogether reliable. The Ministry of Labour index, which shows an increase of only $2\frac{1}{2}$ per cent since 1938, refers mainly to working-class dwellings and does not include furnished houses, so that it very probably understates the increase in the general level of rents over the whole country. It is possible, also, that rent from lodgers, evacuees or from sub-letting may not always have been recorded in income tax returns, and this would partially explain the apparent stability in the total income from rent.

Index numbers of consumption and prices of all goods and services combined are affected by the weights which are applied to the constituent items. Of the two index numbers of total consumption, shown in Table III, one is the result of combining different items according to their market prices (including the effects of indirect taxes and subsidies) and the other is the result of using factor prices (excluding indirect taxes and subsidies) as weights It can be seen that the former index is slightly higher than the latter, one showing a fall in consumption of about 18 per cent, and the other of about 20 per cent, between 1938 and 1944. This is because items which are subject to indirect taxation are given greater weight when valued at market prices than when valued at factor cost, and on the whole the consumption of these items has increased, relatively to that of most other goods. From the consumer's point of view, the index of consumption based on market prices is more appropriate; when considering the factors engaged in production, the index based on factor prices is more appropriate.

The results are also influenced by changes in the distribution of expenditure, the effects of which on the indices of market prices of all consumption goods are indicated by the three series, shown in lines 4, 5 and 6 of Table VI, below. If 1938 weights are applied, in all years, to the main groups of expenditure distinguished in the White Paper,[2] the series shown in line 4 is obtained; if the price index for a given year is calculated on the basis of weights relating

---

[1] It is interesting to note that earlier estimates of the consumption of 'other alcohol' (spirits and wines), which were indirectly derived from the yield of customs and excise duties, agree closely, except for 1941, with the official estimates now available. The index numbers obtained by this method were 101, 94, 81, 76 (1938 = 100) for the years 1939 to 1942 respectively. The method was described in BULLETIN, Vol. 5, No. 10, pp. 162–5.

[2] If separate data were available for all the items within each group, different results might have been obtained.

TABLE III

INDEX NUMBERS OF PERSONAL CONSUMPTION AND MARKET PRICES

	1939	1940	1941	1942	1943	1944
	Index Numbers of Consumption (1938 = 100)					
Food	100·9	85·5	78·1	82·5	77·9	82·8
Beer (Standard barrels)	103·3	99·4	105·0	100·0	102·2	107·8
Other Alcohol	103·4	93·2	94·3	76·1	75·0	68·2
Cigarettes	104·2	103·4	114·6	120·8	120·8	121·5
Other Tobacco	100·0	93·8	100·0	100·0	90·6	87·5
All Tobacco	103·4	101·7	111·9	117·0	115·3	115·3
Rent	102·9	103·5	102·4	101·2	101·0	100·8
Fuel and light	101·0	102·6	103·1	101·0	95·3	95·3
Furniture	94·7	69·1	46·1	31·6	23·7	19·7
Hardware	91·5	72·0	54·9	40·2	35·4	35·4
Footwear	104·1	93·2	79·5	76·7	72·6	72·6
Men's and boys' wear ..	100·0	81·1	55·1	54·3	44·9	54·3
Women's and infants' wear.. ..	98·0	81·7	59·8	60·2	55·7	62·2
All clothing	99·6	83·4	61·7	61·2	55·4	61·7
Travel	92·3	57·7	59·2	63·4	65·5	65·8
Services	99·3	86·8	79·4	74·6	71·1	71·1
Other goods	100·7	93·2	80·4	70·0	70·7	73·2
TOTAL CONSUMPTION*						
Index based on market prices ..	100·4	88·9	82·4	81·3	79·4	81·9
Index based on factor prices ..	100·1	87·9	80·5	79·7	77·0	79·8
	Index Numbers of Market Prices (1938 = 100)					
Food	102·5	120·1	133·7	132·6	134·3	134·5
Beer (standard barrels)	104·8	141·3	168·5	207·8	232·6	235·6
Other Alcohol	103·3	122·0	139·8	180·6	209·1	216·7
Cigarettes	112·0	144·3	160·0	197·1	236·8	244·0
Other Tobacco	112·5	156·7	171·9	225·0	272·4	282·1
All Tobacco	112·1	146·4	161·9	201·5	241·9	249·3
Rent	101·0	102·4	102·4	102·6	102·4	102·6
Fuel and light	101·0	111·7	118·2	122·2	126·8	133·3
Furniture	101·4	132·4	182·9	237·5	230·6	226·7
Hardware	102·7	123·7	153·3	181·8	193·1	193·1
Footwear	102·6	132·4	156·9	173·2	164·2	169·8
Men's and boys' wear ..	103·2	133·0	165·7	178·3	177·2	181·2
Women's and infants' wear.. ..	103·3	133·8	166·7	180·4	175·9	182·4
All clothing	103·1	133·3	164·4	178·4	173·7	179·6
Travel	100·4	110·4	119·0	118·9	119·4	119·3
Services	100·4	114·6	128·0	137·8	147·1	152·4
Other goods	101·4	113·8	136·4	153·1	157·1	158·5
TOTAL*						
Index of market prices	102·3	119·8	135·3	145·4	151·1	153·4
Index of factor prices	101·7	118·6	131·3	137·6	143·0	145·4

* Including income in kind of Forces and adjustment to correspond with expenditure out of British incomes. Beer reckoned in standard barrels.

to the same year, the series shown in line 5 is obtained; if the weights are based on the average quantities consumed in 1938, and in the given year, the series shown in line 6 is obtained.[1] Since relative

[1] Writing p_0 and q_0 for prices and quantities in 1938, and p_1 and q_1 for prices and quantities in the given year, the formulae are respectively:

$$\frac{\Sigma\, p_1\, q_0}{\Sigma\, p_0\, q_0} \quad \text{(line 5);} \qquad \frac{\Sigma\, p_1\, q_1}{\Sigma\, p_0\, q_1} \quad \text{(line 4);} \qquad \frac{\Sigma\, p_1\, (q_0 + q_1)}{\Sigma\, p_0\, (q_0 + q_1)} \quad \text{(line 6).}$$

Reasons for preferring the last formula are given by Professor Bowley, *Economic Journal*, 1928, p. 216.

changes in consumption have been negatively correlated with relative changes in price (groups which, in general, have shown the greatest reductions in consumption having also shown the greatest increases in price, and vice versa), the use of 1938 weights results in higher price indices than the use of weights in later years.

The index of total consumption based on market prices, shown in Table III, is indirectly obtained from the market price index based on average weights. The index of factor prices and the corresponding index of consumption, shown in the same table, are apparently based on Fisher's 'Ideal' formula, which is the geometric mean of the indices resulting from the use of weights in the base year and in the current year.[1]

3. CONSUMPTION OF FOOD[2]

Some additional information is available regarding the consumption of different kinds of food. Table IV shows the percentage distribution of the total expenditure of all households on food in 1938 and 1943, together with the corresponding percentages in working-class family budgets[3] in 1937–38 and in middle-class households[4] in 1938–39. The items included in the different groups are not always defined in detail, but the majority of items are easily classified, and the dividing lines can be assumed to be practically the same, therefore, in all three cases. Expenditure on alcoholic drinks and meals away from home are excluded. Since there were few changes in prices between October 1937 and January 1939, the first and last dates of the working- and middle-class inquiries respectively, the first three sets of figures shown in the Table should be on a comparable basis.

In a few cases, such as the sugar group and dairy products, where the proportions in total household expenditure appear to be substantially higher and lower, respectively, than in working- or middle-class households, the differences are difficult to explain; otherwise, the distribution of expenditure on the various groups is surprisingly similar in the three cases.

As might have been expected, the proportion spent on bread and cereals is higher in working-class than in middle-class and other

---

[1] The two index numbers shown here are based on figures given in the White Paper (Table 14), but include an adjustment for beer (see above).

[2] This section is reprinted from *Bulletin*, Vol. 6, No. 13, with the substitution of more recent figures in Table V.

[3] Those of industrial workers. See the *Ministry of Labour Gazette*, December 1940.

[4] *Journal of the Royal Statistical Society*, vol. cv, Part III, 1942.

TABLE IV

DISTRIBUTION OF HOUSEHOLD EXPENDITURE ON FOOD

	Industrial Working–Class Households 1937–38	Middle–Class Households 1938–39	All Household Expenditure United Kingdom 1938	1943
	Percentages of Total Household Expenditure on Food			
Bread, Cereals, etc.	16·3	13·3	14·6	19·7
Meat, Bacon, etc.	24·6	22·5	24·4	23·9
Fish	4·2	4·4	3·8	3·1
Oils and Fats	10·3	8·6	8·7	5·0
Sugar, Preserves, etc.	5·0	6·2	9·6	9·2
Dairy Products	18·6	20·9	16·8	17·8
Fruit	5·5	9·5	7·0	3·1
Vegetables	7·5	7·0	7·4	11·0
Beverages	5·6	4·5	4·8	4·0
Other Foods	2·4	3·1	2·9	3·2
Total Household Expenditure on food	100·0	100·0	100·0	100·0

households generally, and the proportion spent on fruit is smaller. Changes in the proportions spent on different items during the war, as shown by the last two columns in the Table, are the result of changes in relative prices as well as in quantities consumed. But the very slight decline in the proportion spent on the meat group is unexpected.

More interesting than the index of total food consumption out of personal expenditure, which is shown in Table III, are the figures of average quantities consumed per head of the civilian population, which have been published in considerable detail.[1] These figures have been combined into nine groups,[2] for which index numbers are given in Table V, based on average quantities consumed in the years 1934–38. An index of average consumption per head for all these foods combined has also been estimated, the different groups being weighted according to their relative importance in total household expenditure in 1938, as shown in column 3 of Table IV. It is implicitly assumed that the inclusion of foods consumed outside the household would not affect the relative importance of the different groups.

The consumption of cereals, dairy products and vegetables is

[1] *Food Consumption Levels in the United States, Canada and the United Kingdom,* U.S. Dept. of Agriculture, 1946. The figures, which are described as 'per capita supplies of food moving into civilian consumption' have been interpreted as referring to actual consumption.

[2] Eggs were combined with other dairy products, and potatoes with other vegetables, according to their relative expenditure in industrial working–class budgets in 1937–38. In other cases, weights were added together. Meat and fish are included according to edible weights, dairy products according to the amount of milk solids, eggs according to shell-egg equivalent, oils and fats according to fat content, etc.

TABLE V

INDEX NUMBERS OF AVERAGE CONSUMPTION PER HEAD OF CIVILIAN POPULATION, UNITED KINGDOM

	1940	1941	1942	1943	1944	1945
			(average 1934–1938=100)			
Bread, Cereals, etc.	107	122	116	118	119	119
Meat, Bacon, etc.	90	77	78	73	80	72
Fish	64	58	62½	68	76	89½
Oils and Fats	91	88	88	84	85	81
Sugar and Syrups	71	65	66	65	69	68
Dairy Products	98	96	114	118	118	121
Fruit	89	46	69½	60½	71	66
Vegetables	94	105	119	123	134	132
Beverages (tea, coffee, cocoa)	106	99	95	79	87	93
All Food (1938 weighting) ..	92	87	92	91	95	94

considerably higher than before the war, of fish and fruit much smaller. The estimated reduction in the average consumption per head of all food[1] is considerable; on the other hand, there is evidence that nutritional standards have been maintained remarkably well, and in some cases have even been improved, during the war.[2] The supplies of nutrients, however, as a result of war-time changes in diet, have not, in general, fallen as much as this.

The gradual divergence, during the period studied, between the index of total food consumption, shown in Table III, and that of average food consumption per head, shown in Table V, reflects the gradual reduction in the size of the civilian population. But, apart from the difference in base period, which is probably unimportant, the method of calculation in the two cases was not the same. In the second case, the different commodities within each group were brought on to a common basis of comparison, in terms of weights, by the use of conversion factors which were based on edible contents. In Table III, on the other hand, the reduction in the index of food consumption is partly a reflection of the substitution of less expensive for more expensive kinds of food (e.g. margarine in place of butter, dried eggs in place of shell eggs), while the total amounts, irrespective of quality, would not have declined to the same extent.

4. THE COST OF LIVING OF THE WORKING-CLASS

The cost of living index published by the Ministry of Labour, according to the official description, shows 'the average percentage increase in the cost of maintaining unchanged the standard of living

---

[1] The only items excluded form a very small fraction of the total.

[2] Cf. Sir John Boyd Orr, *Food & the People* (Target for To-morrow Series), pp. 21–3.

prevailing in working-class families prior to August 1914.' During recent years, this index has lost its representative character; in particular, goods of which the prices are subsidized are over-weighted and goods which are subject to indirect taxation are very inadequately represented (tobacco having a weight of only 0·8 per cent and drink being completely excluded). During the war, attempts have been made, admittedly with incomplete data, to calculate a revised index of changes in the working-class cost of living, and the results are shown in line 2 of Table VI.

A further estimate can now be made, using the price indices shown in Table III. The weights applied to these indices were taken from the Ministry of Labour inquiry of 1937–38 into the family budgets of industrial workers,[1] but in the cases of drink, tobacco and coal the family budget data[2] were not acceptable, and figures derived from an independent source were substituted. The weights used (in percentages) were as follows:

Food	.. 39·0	Fuel & Light	6·6	Rent	.. 12·4	Household	
Drink	.. 3·5	Clothing ..	9·3	Services	.. 11·8	goods	0·7
Tobacco ..	5·1	Travel ..	2·6	Furniture ..	2·6	Other goods	6·4

TOTAL   .. 100·0

The results of applying these weights to the price indices shown in Table III (the price index for beer was used for all drink) are given in line 3 of Table VI. Lines 4 and 6 in this Table show the effects on the general market price index of different systems of weighting, which were discussed above, while lines 1 to 3 show different estimates of the cost of living of the working-class.

The earlier estimate of the cost of living of wage earners agrees very closely with the revised estimate, while the Ministry of Labour index is seen to be much lower than either. The differences between the revised estimate for wage earners (line 3) and the most comparable general market price index (line 4) are also relatively small. This is partly, of course, because the price indices for the main groups were the same in both cases, but the results show that, although the distribution of working-class expenditure is known

[1] *Ministry of Labour Gazette*, December, 1940.
[2] The following is the distribution of expenditure, excluding contributions to national insurance, shown in the Ministry of Labour family budgets (industrial workers):

Food	.. 40·7	Fuel & Light	7·7	Rent	.. 12·9	Household	
Drink	.. 0·9	Clothing ..	9·8	Services	.. 12·3	goods	0·8
Tobacco ..	3·0	Travel ..	2·7	Furniture ..	2·7	Other goods	6·5

TOTAL   .. 100·0

TABLE VI

INDEX NUMBERS OF THE COST OF LIVING (1938 = 100)

	1939	1940	1941	1942	1943	1944
1. Ministry of Labour Index	101	118	128	128	128	129
2. Wage earners' index (earlier estimate) ..	—	120	133	140–145	145–150	—
3. Wage earners' index (present estimate, 1938 weights)	102·5	119·7	134·9	143·2	147·9	150·1
General Market Price Indices:						
4. 1938 weights	102·3	119·8	136·1	146·7	151·9	154·2
5. Weights in later years ..	102·3	119·7	134·4	143·8	150·1	152·3
6. Average weights ..	102·3	119·8	135·3	145·4	151·1	153·4

to be very different from that of the whole community, the difference does not appear to have much effect on the final index.

The evidence suggests that the White Paper index does not differ significantly from the best available estimate of changes in the cost of living of wage earners. And, since this is a general index, if it applies to one section of the community as a whole, it must also apply to the remainder as a whole. It will be assumed, therefore, that for the purpose of estimating changes in real income the index of general market prices, shown in line 6 of Table VI, can be applied to the incomes both of wage earners and of non-wage earners.[1]

None of these price indices makes any allowance for the effects of rationing and shortages in reducing the consumer's freedom of choice.[2] It is not possible to obtain accurate estimates of the effects of rationing, but the reader should bear in mind that, if this factor were taken into account, the indices of real income would be lower, and the estimates of the war burden higher, than are shown below.

5. SUBSIDIES AND THE COST OF LIVING

Further light on the problem of the cost of living index is provided by information which has been published, showing the effects of subsidies on the prices of foodstuffs.[3] Table VII shows the market prices of the main foods which are subsidized and estimates of what the prices would become if subsidies were removed. Detailed information has been provided for two dates, February, 1944 and June, 1945.

[1] Strictly speaking, the incomes of non-wage earners should be deflated by an index which includes the prices of investment goods. But since savings are not a very large proportion of income, and since the increases in the prices of investment goods during the war have not been very different from those of retail prices, this point can be neglected.

[2] For a discussion of this problem, see page 159.

[3] See the statements in Parliament given by the Financial Secretary to the Treasury, February 2, 1944, and by the Minister of Food, June 1, 1945.

TABLE VII

FOOD PRICES WITH AND WITHOUT SUBSIDIES

	February, 1944 Market Price	February, 1944 Price without Subsidy	June, 1945 Market Price	June, 1945 Price without Subsidy
	s. d.	s. d.	s. d.	s. d.
Bread, per 4 lb.	9	1 2	9	1 1
Flour, per 6 lb.	1 2¾	1 9¼	1 3	1 9¼
Meat, home-killed, per lb.	1 1¾	1 5	1 0¾	1 4½
Meat, imported, per lb.	8¼	9¼	†	†
Potatoes, per 7 lb.	6¾	10¼	7	10¾
Eggs (large), per doz.	2 0	3 9½	2 0	3 6¼
Eggs (small), per doz.	1 9	3 6½	1 9	3 3¼
Sugar (domestic) per lb.	4	5½	4	6
Milk, per quart	9	9½	9	10
Cheese, per lb.	1 1	1 3¼	1 1	1 4
Bacon, per lb.	1 10½	1 11	1 10½	1 11
Tea, per lb.	2 10	3 0*	2 10	3 0

* Inferred from the amount of the subsidy.

† Ratio of unsubsidized to subsidized price assumed the same as in February, 1944.

It is interesting to estimate what the Ministry of Labour Index of Food Prices would be, firstly, if there were no subsidies, and, secondly, if subsidies were spread evenly over all foodstuffs. The results are shown below, for three dates for which the data are available.[1] The unsubsidized index is calculated from the data in Table VII, using the same weights as the Ministry of Labour. The corrected index at market prices, assuming even distribution of subsidies, can then be calculated from the unsubsidized index, and the amount spent on subsidies in relation to the total expenditure on food. Thus, for February 1944, the amount spent on food subsidies was 15·3 per cent of the total expenditure on food and 151·5 ÷ 1·153 = 131·4. The error, found by comparing the official index with the corrected index, shows the extent to which the application of subsidies is biased in favour of items which are included, or overweighted, in the index. The error is seen to be considerable, amounting to between 8 and 10 per cent.

	Expenditure on Food Subsidies Amount	*Expenditure on Food Subsidies* Per cent of Total Food Expenditure	*Ministry of Labour Food Index (1938 = 100)* Actual	Unsubsidized	Corrected	Error per cent
October, 1942	£127 mm.	9·6	115·3	138·8	126·6	9·8
February, 1944	£206 mm.	15·3	119·6	151·5	131·4	9·9
June, 1945	£225 mm.	16·8	121·0	152·5	130·6	7·9

[1] The calculation for October, 1942, is based on the statement made by Mr. E. Bevin in the House of Commons, October 15, 1942, that 'if the cost of items included in the cost of living index, in respect of which subsidies are being paid by the Ministry of Food, were to increase by amounts equivalent to those subsidies, the cost of living index would be increased by about 20 points, or 10 per cent over its present level.'

It must be remembered that the correction applied here does not allow for various foods (such as cakes, fruit and vegetables) which are not represented in the index and which have increased considerably in price.

No doubt the distribution of subsidies is designed to favour the lower income groups, and in this sense is progressive. On the other hand, the incidence of indirect taxes, which are known to fall most heavily on low incomes, is regressive and the yield of indirect taxes has increased much more than the amount spent on subsidies. It should not be assumed, therefore, that the increase in the cost of living in recent years has been less for low income groups than for others.

In the case of food, surveys in Oxford which have been conducted since 1941, show the following changes[1] in the minimum cost of a 'human needs' diet (taking the average figure for April and November each year, with 1938 as 100).

Index of Cost of 'Human Needs' Diet

1938	1941	1942	1943	1944
100	129	131	136	140

It is seen that the increase in cost up to 1943 and 1944 is not less than that of the index of general food prices, shown in Table III.

6. THE DISTRIBUTION OF THE WAR BURDEN

We proceed, on the basis of the official estimates of the national income of the United Kingdom, given in the White Paper (Cmd. 6623), to estimate the changes between 1938 and 1944 in the net incomes of wage earners and of non-wage earners, and then to estimate the financial 'war burden' which has fallen on each of these classes. The results differ from those obtained previously because some of the earlier estimates have since been superseded, and on certain points, noted below, the procedure has been changed. A prefatory warning is given that all estimates of national income, and resulting calculations, are bound to be approximate and sometimes even tentative in character. We are not, however, usually interested in the exact figures, but in making general comparisons, or revealing the trend over a number of years; and, for these purposes, the data are probably accurate enough.[2]

---

[1] Cf. page 275.

[2] The present analysis is based, almost entirely, on the official estimates prepared in the Central Statistical Office. No doubt it might be possible to improve on these estimates and, for particular purposes, it might be appropriate to use a definition of national income which is different from that adopted in the White Paper. In order to estimate changes in

Estimates are required of the net money income which remains after deducting direct taxes on current income. The net income of wage earners is obtained by deducting income tax payments and contributions to insurance, which are a form of direct taxation, from total wages. For insurance contributions, it is convenient to use the figures given in the White Paper (Table 27) which include voluntary as well as compulsory contributions. Although voluntary contributions should, strictly speaking, be excluded, the effect on the final results would be negligible. We deduct income tax payments on wages, not the tax liabilities, the difference having effectively disappeared on the introduction of 'pay-as-you-earn'. Table VIII shows the estimates of total wages (line 1), direct tax payments (lines 2 and 3) and money wages, net of direct taxes (line 4). Net money wages are also expressed in the form of index numbers (line 5) and after deflating by the index of general market prices (Table VI, line 6), an index is obtained showing changes in the real net income of wage earners (line 6).

As the present analysis is concerned with incomes derived from industry, the pay and allowance of members of the Forces and auxiliary services are excluded, and non-wage incomes (line 7) cover profits (including undistributed profits), interest, rent and salaries (including earnings of shop assistants). To obtain direct tax liabilities on non-wage incomes, it is necessary to deduct, from the total of direct tax liabilities on current income (line 8), the direct tax payments of wage earners (line 9, equal to the sum of lines 2 and 3) and income tax on the pay of Forces and auxiliary services, which can only be very roughly estimated (line 10). Death duties and stamps on the transfer of property, which cannot properly be considered a charge on current income, are excluded. Total non-wage incomes net of direct taxes (line 11; equal to line 7, less line 8, plus lines 9 and 10) are then expressed as index numbers (line 12), which are deflated by the index of general market prices in order to obtain an index of the real net income of non-wage earners (line 13).

It has been customary to regard interest on the national debt as a transfer payment and not as part of the net national income. In earlier studies this point of view was accepted and income tax payable in respect of this interest was accordingly deducted from the direct tax liabilities on non-wage incomes. It appears to be more

investment, for instance, an adjustment would be necessary for the valuation of stocks. But for problems connected with the distribution of the national income, this adjustment does not seem to be necessary. Cf. pages 99–100.

P

logical, however, and more consistent with the treatment of other types of interest to regard interest on the national debt as negative Government income, and as part of the income of holders of the national debt.[1] In this way, the arbitrary distinction, implicit in the former method, between so-called productive and unproductive loans is avoided. The present analysis, therefore, does not include the adjustment which was previously made.

It remains to estimate the financial war burden on wage earners and others. The conventional method of assessing the cost of the war in terms of the total amounts paid in direct and indirect taxation suffers, on both theoretical and practical grounds, from a number of objections. On the one hand, there are serious pitfalls in estimating the division of indirect taxes between different income groups; and, on the other hand, the sum of direct and indirect taxes does not (necessarily) represent the whole of the war burden. The method which will be used here, and which avoids these difficulties by making use of a broader concept, was suggested by Mr. Kalecki.

In normal conditions, if there are no great changes in the relative importance of different industries, we should expect the real income, both of wage earners and of non-wage earners, to vary approximately in proportion to changes in the volume of wage-labour in employment, adjusted for changes in productivity. For the share of wages in the national income has remained fairly stable over a long period, and it may be assumed that, before the war, industry was working under more or less constant returns.[2] In this way, we can estimate an index of *potential* real income, showing the increase in real income which might reasonably have been expected under peacetime conditions. If we then compare this with the actual changes in real income of the two classes, the difference, expressed as a percentage of the index of *potential* real income, may be regarded as measuring the financial sacrifice imposed by the war.[3]

An estimate has already been given of changes in the volume of employment (Table I, line 8), the index referring to insured labour, which is taken as synonymous with wage-labour (see pp. 205–6). The results of the censuses of production in 1924 and 1935 provide some idea of the normal rate of increase in productivity under peacetime conditions. Among the industries included in the censuses,

[1] Cf. T. Barna, *Redistribution of Incomes through Public Finance*, pp. 32–4. The total net national income is unaffected by the change in treatment.
[2] Even if this assumption were incorrect, the proportionate distribution of the total net output could scarcely be affected.
[3] A fuller explanation of the method is given below, page 221.

TABLE VIII

Estimates of Wages and Non-Wage Incomes (£ million) and the Distribution of the War Burden

	1938	1939	1940	1941	1942	1943	1944
1. Total wages, gross	1,735	1,835	2,115	2,419	2,708	2,916	2,930
2. Income tax payments on wages	2	3	5	28	112	185	235
3. Insurance contributions	51	53	56	61	65	64	64
4. Total wages, *net*	1,682	1,779	2,054	2,330	2,531	2,667	2,631
5. Index of total wages, *net*	100	105·8	122·1	138·5	150·5	158·6	156·4
6. Index of real wages, *net*	100	103·4	101·9	102·4	103·5	105·0	102·0
7. Total non-wage incomes, *gross*	2,806	3,011	3,412	3,836	4,041	4,164	4,233
8. Total Direct tax liabilities (excluding Death Duties, etc.)	478	627	986	1,464	1,765	1,955	2,093
9. Direct Taxes on wages	53	56	61	89	177	249	299
10. Income tax on Forces (approx.)	—	—	—	10	30	60	90
11. Total non-wage incomes, *net*	2,381	2,440	2,487	2,471	2,483	2,518	2,529
12. Index of non-wage incomes, *net*	100	102·5	104·5	103·8	104·3	105·8	106·2
13. Index of real non-wage incomes, *net*	100	100·2	87·2	76·7	71·7	70·0	69·2
14. Index of *potential* real income	100	105½	111	117	125	124	120
15. War Burden on wage earners (per cent)		2	8	13	17	16	15
16. War Burden on non-wage earners (per cent)		5	21	35	43	44	42

average net output per manual operative increased by about 35 per cent during these 11 years.[1] Average weekly hours of work increased, in the same period, by $4\frac{1}{2}$ per cent, so that productivity (net output per man-hour) increased by about 29 per cent, or at an average rate of 2·3 per cent per annum. The industries covered by the censuses provided less than half of the national income and in other industries and services changes in productivity would probably have been much less. For industry as a whole, it seems reasonable to assume a normal rate of increase in productivity of $1\frac{1}{2}$ per cent per annum.

When the index of the volume of employment is adjusted to allow for a steady increase in productivity, at this assumed rate, an index of *potential* real income is obtained (Table VIII, line 14). By comparing this index with the indices of real net income (lines 6 and 13), estimates are obtained of the financial war burden, expressed as percentages of *potential* real income (lines 15 and 16). Since these estimates are very approximate and the concept of a financial war burden is, to some extent, conjectural, the results need to be interpreted with caution. There is evidence, however, that the burden on wage earners, relative to the burden on non-wage earners, remained fairly constant, in the ratio of about 2:5, throughout the war. If the effects of rationing had been included[2] both sets of estimates would be raised and the burden on wage earners, relative to non-wage earners, would also be increased. The financial burden of the war apparently reached its highest level in 1942 or 1943.

[1] A. L. Bowley, *Studies in the National Income*, p. 146.　　[2] See page 159.

MEASURING THE COST OF THE WAR

by M. Kalecki

FROM BULLETIN, VOL. 4, No. 1 (JANUARY 10, 1942)

THE question 'Who pays for the war?' is frequently answered by the compilation of direct taxes paid by various classes of the population. And in this way the rather biased result is arrived at that the poor do not pay for the war at all because they are not subject to income tax. Any serious attempt, however, to answer this question concerning the financial war burden on various classes should obviously take account of indirect taxation also. This calculation is, however, very difficult, because of the lack of reliable statistical data on consumption by the poor and the rich of drink and tobacco, which are the most important items of indirect taxation. Indeed, the sources of information of the shares of various income groups in the consumption of particular commodities are family budgets, in which the items of drink and tobacco are known to be understated. But apart from this technical difficulty there is a general objection against measuring the war burden by tax payments, even if indirect taxation is accounted for.

The payment for war is not limited to the payment of taxes. A good example of this is the repercussions of sinkings of cargoes by the enemy. The loss is covered by insurance, the cost of which is added to the price of imports. The resulting higher price paid for consumption goods surely means paying for the war. Another important example is a rise in prices disproportionately with costs, owing to the scarcity of goods. Assume that the extra profits arising in this way are taxed away. Although technically paid by producers or merchants, these taxes, in fact, are a charge on the consumer.

These and similar difficulties may be avoided if we introduce a broader concept of paying for the war. Imagine that it is possible to estimate approximately how the real income of a certain class of the population would change if employment had risen as it actually has during the war and there were no war-time abnormalities. We can then calculate that the *potential* real income of this class—i.e. the real income they would get at the present level of economic activity in normal conditions—is higher by a per cent than in the year preceding the war. Further, we calculate by how much their *actual* real income is reduced. If we denote this latter percentage by β, the potential real income is $100 + \alpha$ (taking the year preceding the war equal to 100) and the actual real income is $100 - \beta$. The discrepancy between these two items may then be taken as the amount paid for the war by the class of the population considered.[1]

---

[1] The application of this method is illustrated on pp. 216–20.

EARNINGS AND HOURS OF LABOUR,
1938–1945
by J. L. Nicholson

FROM BULLETIN, VOL. 8, NO. 5 (MAY 1946)

THE present article contains a summary of the changes in earnings and hours of labour between 1938 and 1945, and a discussion of the different factors responsible for these changes. Earnings inquiries have been conducted by the Ministry of Labour at six-monthly intervals since July 1941, and in October 1938 and July 1940. These inquiries cover the main industries engaged in mining (except coal mining), manufacturing, building and public utilities, which will be referred to as the Principal Industries. They do not include agriculture, coal mining, railways, the shipping service, port transport, the distributive trades, catering, or domestic and other services. Information is available, however, about the earnings of coal miners and railway workers since before the war, as well as of dock labourers since 1942. Data on working hours were collected in October 1938, July 1943, and in subsequent inquiries, but not at the intermediate dates.

The average weekly wages of men, boys (under 21), women, girls (under 18) and of all workers together, in the industries covered by the Ministry of Labour inquiries, are shown below, for the three dates: October 1938, July 1944, when the peak level was reached, and July 1945. These averages were obtained by weighting the different industries according to the numbers currently employed at the respective dates. It should be remembered that the figures relate to actual *earnings* in a given week, including any extra payments for overtime, Sunday or night work, as well as earnings on piece work, and must be distinguished from *wage rates*, which are based on a full ordinary week's work and do not include any of these additional payments.

TABLE I
Average Weekly Earnings in the Principal Industries

	Men		Boys		Women		Girls		All	
	s.	d.	s.	d.	s.	d.	s.	d.	s.	d.
October 1938 ..	69	0	26	1	32	6	18	6	53	3
July 1944 ..	124	4	47	4	64	3	34	11	96	8
July 1945 ..	121	4	45	6	63	2	35	1	96	1

Part-time women workers (those employed for not more than 30 hours a week), whose average weekly earnings in July 1945 were 31s. 4d., are included, throughout this survey, on the basis of two part-time workers representing one full-time worker.

Index numbers of average earnings, for all the dates at which inquiries have been held since October 1938, are shown in Table II. The first set of figures was obtained by applying weights proportionate to the numbers in the different industries, and in the four sex and age groups, in 1938. The figures in the second part of the table are based on the numbers currently employed at the respective dates, the index number for a particular date representing the ratio of the average earnings prevailing at that date to the average earnings in October 1938.

For the sake of comparison, the Ministry of Labour index of wage rates in the same group of industries is also shown. If this index were extended to include the main industries not covered by the inquiries, namely agriculture, coal mining, railways and merchant shipping, it is stated that the figure for July 1945 would be raised to 151.

Average earnings in January in the building and contracting industries are affected by the fact that working hours are shorter in winter than in summer. In order that the January figures should be more closely comparable with those at other dates, the index numbers were adjusted by assuming that average earnings of builders at each of the January inquiries were mid-way between the averages recorded at the July inquiries of the same and the preceding year; the unadjusted and adjusted figures have both been shown.

From the second set of figures, it is evident that, except for girls, average earnings reached their peak in July 1944. Over the period from 1938 to 1945, the average earnings of women and girls are seen to have risen more than those of men and boys. This is partly because, during the war, women have frequently taken over work which was formerly done by men, so that the proportionate numbers of women employed in different occupations within a given industry have probably changed considerably. The same may also be true of boys, whose average earnings, in the first few years of the war, increased faster than those of men, although the average age of boys in employment must have fallen, those in the older age groups being liable to conscription.

Comparison of the two sets of figures shown in Table II shows the effects on average earnings of transferences from relatively low

TABLE II

Index Numbers of Average Weekly Earnings in the Principal Industries

Based on numbers employed in 1938

	Men	Boys	Women	Girls	All	Index of Wage rates
October 1938	100	100	100	100	100	100
July 1940	126	132½	118	118	125	110½
July 1941	140	155½	129	132½	139½	118
January 1942 (unadjusted)	140½	156½	134½	140	140½	122
January 1942 (bldrs. adj.)	144	161½	—	—	144	—
July 1942	153	169	151	159	154	124
January 1943 (unadjusted)	154	165	158½	166	155½	126½
January 1943 (bldrs. adj.)	156	168	160	—	157½	—
July 1943	164	173	167	176	165	130
January 1944 (unadjusted)	165	172	170½	178½	166½	132
January 1944 (bldrs. adj.)	166½	173½	171	—	167½	—
July 1944	169	175	174	183	170½	135½
January 1945 (unadjusted)	164	165	173	178	165½	138½
January 1945 (bldrs. adj.)	165	166	174	—	166½	—
July 1945	169½	172	180	187½	171½	143

Based on numbers currently employed

	Men	Boys	Women	Girls	All
October 1938	100	100	100	100	100
July 1940	129·0	134·5	119·7	120·7	129·9
July 1941	144·1	160·7	135·1	135·1	142·4
January 1942 (unadjusted)	147·8	162·9	146·2	145·0	146·0
January 1942 (bldrs. adj.)	151·0	167·6	—	—	150·2
July 1942	161·5	177·0	166·7	163·5	159·9
January 1943 (unadjusted)	164·9	172·8	180·0	173·4	165·1
January 1943 (bldrs. adj.)	167·0	176·0	181·8	—	167·6
July 1943	175·7	180·8	191·3	182·9	175·7
January 1944 (unadjusted)	179·2	179·6	196·2	185·1	179·5
January 1944 (bldrs. adj.)	180·6	181·0	196·7	—	181·2
July 1944	180·2	181·5	197·7	188·7	181·5
January 1945 (unadjusted)	172·8	169·0	194·3	182·0	176·0
January 1945 (bldrs. adj.)	174·0	170·4	195·1	—	177·4
July 1945	175·8	174·4	194·4	189·6	180·4

paid to relatively high paid industries, as well as, in the case of the averages for all workers, the effect of changes in the relative proportions of men, boys, women and girls.[1] In the industries covered by the inquiries, the percentage numbers in these four sex and age groups, in October 1938, and in January and July 1945, were approximately as follows:

	Percentage Numbers Employed			
	Men	Boys	Women	Girls
October 1938	61½	12	19¾	6¾
January 1945	60	8½	27	4½
July 1945	61	8½	26¼	4¼

The proportion of women employed in these industries has in-

[1] Writing N_0 and N_1 for the relative numbers ($\Sigma N_0 = \Sigma N_0 = 1$) and W_0 and W_1 for wages at the two dates, the formulae are respectively:

$$\frac{\Sigma N_0 W_1}{\Sigma N_0 W_0} \quad \text{and} \quad \frac{\Sigma N_1 W_1}{\Sigma N_0 W_0}$$

The ratio of the latter to the former is $1 + \Sigma(N_1 - N_0) W_1$ which depends on the correlation between changes in numbers and the level of earnings at the later date.

creased and the proportions of boys and girls have declined; the proportion of men, on the other hand, has remained surprisingly stable.

With the help of these figures, we can separate the effects, on the average earnings of all workers, of relative changes in sex and age groups from those of transferences between different industries. The results are given in Table III.

The fact that the proportion of women increased during the war, while the proportion of men declined, caused a reduction in the average earnings of all workers combined, which was only partly counterbalanced by the fall in the proportions of boys and girls. At the last two dates, however, the net effect of changes in the proportions in these four groups, partly because the proportion of men began to increase and that of women to decline, has been to raise the general level of earnings.[1]

The effects of changes between industries on the average earnings of men and women apparently reached a maximum in January 1944, since when the movement has been reversed in the direction of industries where wages are relatively low. The effects of such transferences have been greatest in the case of women, mainly, no doubt, because new entrants have been attracted to the more highly paid industries, and least in the cases of boys and girls.

TABLE III

Effects of Different Factors on Average Earnings in the Principal Industries

	Changes between Industries.					All Workers Changes in Sex-age Groups	Misc.	
	Men	Boys	Women	Girls	All		Hours	Factors
	Percentage Increase or Decrease (—) *in Earnings*							
July 1940	2½	1½	1½	2½	2¼	+1·5	13·4	
July 1941	3	3½	4½	2	3	—0·9	18·1	
Jan. 1942	5	4	8½	3½	5½	—1·6	18·6	
July 1942	5½	4½	10½	3	6	—1·9	24·0	
Jan. 1943	7	5	13½	4½	7½	—1·3	24·7	
July 1943	7	4½	14½	4	7¾*	—1·3	7·0	18·8
Jan. 1944	8½	4½	15	3½	9†	—1·0	5·9	20·1
July 1944	6½	3½	13½	3	7¼‡	—0·5	4·5	20·6
Jan. 1945	5½	2½	12½	2	6‡	+0·4	1·7	18·4
July 1945	3½	1	8	1	4‡	+1·2	1·9	17·6

* Of which 0·5 per cent was due to differences in hours.
† Of which 0·9 per cent was due to differences in hours.
‡ Entirely due to differences in earnings.

Average hours of work in the principal industries in October 1938, and the percentage changes since that date, are shown in Table IV.

[1] The contrary statement, which appears in *The Ministry of Labour Gazette* for February 1946, is not borne out by the results of our calculations.

The figures relate to the average number of hours actually worked and exclude, for instance, recognized intervals for meals. This information is not available for any date between October 1938 and July 1943, but it is known that in some cases working hours were reduced before the latter date. The effect of the seasonal factor in the building and contracting industries has again been eliminated, so far as possible, by recalculating the percentages on the assumption that average hours in building, at each of the January inquiries, were mid-way between the averages at the two adjoining dates. The percentage changes in the average hours of all workers are shown, weighted according to the relative numbers in different industries, and in different age and sex groups, in 1938, and also according to the relative numbers currently employed. From July 1944 onwards, the difference between the results obtained from the two methods of weighting was negligible.

TABLE IV

Average Weekly Hours of Work in the Principal Industries

	Men	Youths	Women	Girls	All	All 1938 Wts.
			Current Weights			
October 1938	47·7	46·2	43·5	44·6	46·5	—
		Percentage Increase or Decrease (—) *since October 1938*				
July 1943	10·9	3·9	5·5	1·1	7·5	7·0
Jan. 1944 (unadjusted) ..	9·0	1·9	3·9	0	5·8	4·8
Jan. 1944 (bldrs. adj.) ..	10·1	2·6	4·6	—	6·8	5·9
July 1944	7·3	1·1	2·5	—0·9	4·5	—
Jan. 1945 (unadjusted) ..	3·6	—2·2	—0·9	—3·6	1·1	—
Jan. 1945 (bldrs. adj.) ..	4·4	—1·7	—0·7	—	1·7	—
July 1945	4·2	—1·3	—0·5	—2·5	1·9	—

Of the various factors which have been responsible for the increase in the average weekly earnings of all workers in the principal industries, it has thus been possible to obtain separate estimates for the following, the percentage changes between October 1938 and January 1944 being shown for the sake of illustration:

	Changes between October 1938 and January 1944
Effect on Average Weekly Earnings of:	
(i) Wage rates	+32%
(ii) Changes in numbers employed in different industries:	
(*a*) owing to differences in hours	+0·9%
(*b*) owing to differences in earnings	+8%
(iii) Changes in hours of work in given industries	+5·9%
(iv) Changes in relative numbers of men, women, boys and girls ..	—1·0%
(v) All remaining factors, including extra payments for overtime and night work, changes between different occupations within each industry and changes in age structure within the four sex and age groups (estimated as a residual)	+20·1%

Index of average earnings of all workers (October 1938 = 100):

$$132 \times 1{\cdot}009 \times 1{\cdot}08 \times 1{\cdot}059 \times {\cdot}99 \times 1{\cdot}201 = 181{\cdot}2 \text{ (approx.).}$$

The estimated effects of each of these factors, for all dates for which the relevant information is available, are shown in Table III. The relative importance of the different factors on the average earnings of all workers is also shown, in pictorial form, in Diagram A. The logarithmic scale has here been used, so that equal vertical distances represent equal percentage changes. The width of any band corresponds to the relative strength of the particular factor and the vertical summation of all the bands (allowing for the effect of changes in sex and age groups being negative over a large part of the period) represents the increase in average earnings. Before July 1943, it is not possible to separate the effect of increases in hours from that of miscellaneous factors.

It can be seen that, while wage rates have shown a steady increase, at an average rate of about $5\frac{1}{2}$ per cent per annum, the influence of transferences between different industries began to fall during 1944, hours have been reduced almost to their pre-war level, and the effects of residual factors has also begun to decline. As industries

DIAGRAM A.—ANALYSIS OF INCREASE IN EARNINGS

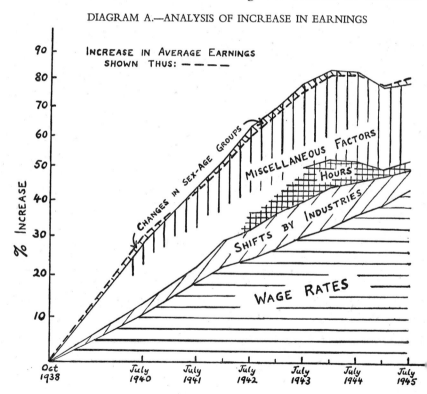

return to more normal conditions, and overtime working, for example, becomes less common, some of these tendencies can be expected to continue beyond July 1945. The effects of changes in the relative importance of different industries would, however, remain if a wage policy were adopted which was designed to attract labour into the expanding industries. The increase in wage rates will probably continue, but the declining importance of other factors can be seen from the fact that in January 1944, when earnings had reached a peak level, changes in all factors other than wage rates were responsible for raising the average level of earnings by as much as 37 per cent, while in July 1945 they were responsible for raising the average level by about 26 per cent.

Table V contains information about weekly and hourly earnings of men (21 and over) and women (18 and over) in the sixteen groups of industries covered by the Ministry of Labour inquiries. Up to July 1943, the greatest increases in men's earnings were in engineering, miscellaneous manufacturing industries and government industrial establishments; the smallest increases were in paper and printing, which had relatively high earnings in 1938, and in transport, building and public utilities. Since then, weekly earnings of men in Government establishments have fallen, owing to a reduction in hours, while textile workers and brick makers, whose earnings were relatively low in 1938, have experienced some improvement.

When the different groups of industries are arranged in order, according to the level of men's hourly earnings, their relative positions show comparatively little change. The relative positions of men engaged in the treatment of non-metalliferous mine and quarry products, in the brick, pottery and glass industries, and in miscellaneous manufacturing, have improved, while the relative positions of builders and transport workers have declined, but the positions of the remaining eleven groups have shown little or no change.

The order of the different groups of industries, when arranged according to the level of women's hourly earnings, shows greater changes. Women engaged on non-metalliferous products, in engineering and in miscellaneous manufacturing industries have improved their relative positions, while the relative positions of those engaged in the leather, clothing and paper industries, and in public utility services, have declined.

In nearly all groups of industries, the percentage of women's to men's hourly earnings is seen to have risen. For all the industries

TABLE V. Average Weekly and Hourly Earnings in the Principal Industries

Average Weekly Earnings

	Men						Women					
	Oct. 1938	July 1945	Index Nos. (Oct. 1938 = 100)				Oct. 1938	July 1945	Index Nos. (Oct. 1938 = 100)			
	s. d.	s. d.	July 1941	July 1943	July 1945		s. d.	s. d.	1941	1943	1945	
Mining, quarrying of iron, stone, etc.	60 6	103 6	139	163	173		29 8	62 11	151	199	212	
Treatment of non-met. products	66 5	116 5	142	165	175		27 10	51 9	139	177	186	
Brick, pottery, glass	63 2	111 1	140	165	176		32 8	62 10	138	195	192	
Chemical, paint, oil, etc.	69 3	122 10	142	168	177		33 4	69 1	144	210	207	
Motor engineering, shipbuilding	75 0	133 0	150	184	177		31 9	58 2	132	167	183	
Textiles	57 3	104 7	142	169	183		34 11	54 6	115	146	156	
Leather, fur, etc.	64 1	107 6	134	156	168		32 9	55 7	126	153	170	
Clothing	64 3	110 8	130	154	172		32 11	56 7	122	154	172	
Food, drink, tobacco	65 3	110 4	134	156	169		33 8	62 4	127	169	185	
Woodworking	66 3	110 7	131	154	167		34 1	54 7	116	150	160	
Paper, printing, etc.	84 3	122 11	115	134	146		—	—	—	—	—	
Building, contracting, etc.	66 0	111 4	147	164	169		31 9	60 5	135	187	200	
Miscellaneous manufacturing	69 0	126 6	144	178	183		34 11	63 7	170	205	234	
Transport, storage, etc.	70 0	114 10	132	149	164		27 8	51 5	135	173	186	
Public Utility Services	63 1	98 6	123	140	156							
Government industrial	75 0	127 1	147	176	169		44 9	80 11	121	181	181	
All the above	69 0	121 4	144	176	176		32 6	63 2	135	191	194	

Average Hourly Earnings

	Men							Women					
	Oct. 1938 d. (order)	July 1943 d. (order)	July 1945 d. (order)	Index Numbers (Oct. 1938 = 100)				Oct. 1938 d. (order)	July 1943 d. (order)	July 1945 d. (order)	Per cent of Men's Hourly earnings		
				1943	1946						1938	1943	1945
Mining, quarrying of iron, stone	15.6 (13=)	23.9 (13)	25.9 (13=)	153	165			7.8 (13=)	15.8 (5=)	17.1 (7=)	45.8	62.7	62.6
Treatment of non-met. products	16.0 (11)	25.2 (6)	27.3 (8)	158	171			7.8 (13=)	13.3 (15)	14.3 (15)	50.0	54.1	53.2
Brick, pottery, glass	15.6 (13=)	24.6 (8=)	26.9 (9)	158	173			8.9 (9)	17.1 (4)	17.1 (7=)	51.7	64.3	59.8
Chemical, paint, oil, etc.	17.2 (4=)	26.6 (5)	28.6 (6)	155	166			9.1 (6=)	17.9 (3)	19.1 (3)	48.7	58.3	59.0
Motor engineering, shipbuilding	18.7 (2)	30.7 (1)	32.4 (1)	164	173			8.6 (10=)	13.6 (12=)	15.6 (11)	59.7	60.2	62.4
Textiles	14.4 (16)	22.6 (15)	25.0 (15)	157	174			9.1 (6=)	13.6 (12=)	15.3 (13)	56.2	56.2	58.0
Leather, fur, etc.	16.2 (10)	24.2 (11)	26.4 (12)	149	163			9.6 (3)	13.7 (10=)	15.8 (10)	55.8	54.6	55.1
Clothing	17.2 (4=)	25.1 (7)	28.7 (5)	146	167			8.6 (10=)	13.4 (14)	15.5 (12)	54.1	57.0	59.8
Food, drink, tobacco	15.9 (12)	23.5 (14)	25.9 (13=)	148	163			9.1 (6=)	15.4 (8)	17.7 (5)	53.5	62.6	64.1
Woodworking	17.0 (8)	24.6 (8=)	27.6 (7)	145	163			9.2 (4=)	13.7 (10=)	15.1 (14)	41.8	49.1	49.5
Paper, printing, etc.	22.0 (1)	27.9 (3=)	30.5 (3)	127	139			—	—	17.3 (6)	—	65.0	65.0
Building, contracting, etc.	17.1 (7)	24.3 (10)	26.6 (11)	142	155			8.6 (10=)	15.8 (5=)	17.8 (4)	50.6	55.6	58.2
Miscellaneous manufacturing	17.0 (8=)	27.9 (3=)	30.6 (2)	164	179			9.2 (4=)	18.5 (2)	21.4 (2)	53.5	76.8	80.1
Transport, storage, etc.	17.2 (4=)	24.1 (12)	26.7 (10)	140	155			10.1 (2)	13.8 (9)	15.9 (9)	65.6	65.4	66.5
Public Utility Services	15.4 (15)	21.1 (16)	23.9 (16)	137	167			12.0 (1)	21.3 (1)	22.9 (1)	65.9	74.0	75.3

combined, this percentage has risen from about 52 in October 1938 to about 60 in July 1945. This is partly explained by the fact that women have been taking over work which was formerly done by men (cf. above, p. 148), but the same tendency has also been observed over longer periods. The average earnings of all females in 1906, for example, was 43 per cent of the average of all males and by 1924 the proportion had risen to 48 per cent.[1]

Apart from the industries which are included in the Ministry of Labour inquiries, the only data on earnings which are available relate to coal miners and railway and dock workers. The data on coal miners' wages, which are summarized in Table VI, cover all classes of workers, including juveniles, and the averages for 1938 to 1944 refer to the whole of each year, not to sample weeks, as in the Ministry of Labour inquiries.

TABLE VI

Average Wages in Coal Mining in Great Britain[1]

	Av. Earnings per Man-shift	Index of Av. earnings per Man-shift	Average Weekly earnings	Index of Average weekly Earnings
	s. d.		*s. d.*	
1938	11 8·02	100	57 11	100
1939	11 11·99	102·8	61 9	106·6
1940	13 6·05	115·7	71 2	122·9
1941	15 5·11	132·2	82 9	142·8
1942	18 0·18	154·4	96 2	166·0
1943	19 8·54	168·9	103 3	178·3
1944	22 4·75	191·9	113 0	195·0
1945[2] (1st half) ..	23 9	203·6	118 5	204·5
(3rd qtr.) ..	24 6	210·0	110 10	191·4

[1] All the figures include the value of allowances in kind.
[2] Provisional.

During the war, average weekly earnings of coal miners have risen more than those of most other workers, so that, whereas in 1938 the average weekly earnings of miners were less than those of any of the groups, with the exception of textiles, shown in Table V, by 1945 they were not far below the average level of men's earnings in these other industries.

The average earnings of railways workers, at all the recent dates for which information is available, are shown in Table VII, the figures in each case relating to one week in March. In calculating the averages, all workers receiving adult rates of pay were classified as men or women, and those paid at junior rates were classified as

[1] These averages relate to a normal working week. Cf. A. L. Bowley, *Wages and Income in the U.K. since 1860*, p. 16.

boys or girls. This, and the effects of recruitment to the Forces, must have caused a lowering of the average age of boys classified as such, and would thus provide a partial explanation for the increase in boys' earnings being less than the increase in men's earnings.

TABLE VII

Average Weekly Earnings in the Railway Service

			Men s. d.	Boys s. d.	Women s. d.	Girls s. d.	Men Index	Boys Numbers (Mar. 1939 = 100)
March 1939	..	..	..	68 9	28 10	—	—	100	100
March 1942	..	..	..	96 2	35 10	63 1	40 2	140	124
March 1943	..	..	..	105 4	38 6	74 2	47 5	153	133½
March 1944	..	..	..	114 0	40 4	79 8	50 2	166	140
March 1945	..	..	..	116 10	42 3	82 8	48 8	170	147

The average weekly earnings of women railway workers were 66 per cent of men's average earnings in March 1939 and 71 per cent in March 1945, a much higher proportion than in most other industries. The corresponding figures for all the industries included in the Ministry of Labour inquiries were 47 per cent in October 1938, and 52 per cent in July 1945.

The average weekly earnings of all classes of dock labourers, during three months of each year from 1942 to 1945 were as follows:

						s. d.
July–September	1942	..	..	..		127 6
,,	,,	1943	..	..	..	153 10
,,	,,	1944	..	..	..	161 8
,,	,,	1945	..	..	..	136 7

The averages recorded for the last three years compare favourably with the average earnings of engineers (cf. Table V). No comparable figures are available for any pre-war date, but the position of dockers, relative to workers in other industries, has certainly improved.

It is noticeable, in fact, that the greatest increases in wages have been in industries, such as coal mining and agriculture, where the level of wages in 1938 was relatively low; and these industries played, of course, a particularly important part in the war effort.

To complete this survey, a rough estimate may be made of the average increase in earnings for the industries included in the Ministry of Labour inquiries, combined with agriculture, coal mining and railways. For agriculture, figures of earnings are not available, but Professor Bowley's index of wage *rates* shows an increase of 103 per cent between 1938 and July 1945. The average wage *rate* of dock labourers in 1938 was 72s. 10½d.,[1] and, assuming

[1] As shown by Professor Bowley's Index of Wage Rates.

that at that time there were no extra payments, the increase in average earnings of dockers from 1938 to the third quarter of 1945 would be 87½ per cent. For coal mining, railways (men and boys) and the other industries, we use the figures quoted above.

The average earnings of all workers in these industries, when weighted by the relative numbers employed in 1938, are estimated to have risen by about 75 per cent between 1938 and July 1945, and by about 83 per cent over the same period when weighted by the relative numbers currently employed at the respective dates. These estimates do not include distribution, domestic service and certain other industries, in which the increase in earnings has probably been less. But assuming that the estimated increase in earnings is representative of all wage earners, and using the data contained in the latest White Paper on the National Income (Cmd. 6784) concerning the change in the level of retail prices, and proportion of wages taken by income tax and national insurance contributions, we obtain the following estimates of changes in money and real wages, before and after direct taxation.

	Percentage change 1938 to 1945
Average money wages, before taxation	+83%
Average real wages, before taxation	+19%
Average money wages, after direct taxation	+69%
Average real wages, after direct taxation	+10%

There has apparently been some increase, therefore, in average real wages, after allowing for direct taxation, during the war; these estimates do not, of course, take account of the effects of rationing in reducing the consumer's freedom of choice.[1]

[1] cf. Rationing and Index Numbers, page 159.

THE DISTRIBUTION OF INCOMES

by J. L. Nicholson

From Bulletin, Vol. 6, No. 2 (February 5, 1944)

1. The Distribution of Private Income in 1940–41 and 1941–42

THE data which are available on the distribution of incomes in this country are, in several respects, incomplete. The White Paper on War Finance (Cmd. 6438) gives estimates, relating to the financial years 1940–41 and 1941–42, of the total private income, before and after direct taxation, in broad income ranges. The number of incomes is given for the ranges above £250 per annum, but not for the large group of incomes under £250. Also, the incomes of husband and wife are reckoned as one, so that the figures do not refer exactly to the number of income recipients; nor do we have the distribution of incomes per family. If all individual incomes were reckoned separately, and those of wives counted apart from their husbands, the number of incomes in the lowest group would be substantially increased, while the aggregate income in this group would be only slightly increased.[1] On the other hand, the incomes of juveniles are included on a par with those of adults and it might be held that their incomes are not strictly comparable.

It is further stated that 'The whole of transfer payments other than National Debt interest has been included in the incomes below £250.'[2] If transfer incomes are to be included, this is a reasonable assumption to make, so long as it is remembered that, in effect, transfer payments are then included twice in the total of incomes before taxation.

Working on the basis of the figures given in the White Paper, an estimate requires to be made of the total number of incomes, and hence of the number of incomes under £250 p.a. The total number of persons, aged 14 to 64, who were gainfully employed in September 1943 was given by Mr. E. Bevin as 22·75 million, including 700,000 part-time women; he also stated that 1 million men and women over 65 were in full-time paid employment in

---

[1] Through the transfer of some incomes at present included, together with husbands' incomes, in the higher ranges.

[2] Cmd. 6438, p. 11.

the war effort.[1] This gives a total, excluding those over 65 who were employed, but not in the war effort, of 23·75 million. The number of married women in full-time gainful employment in April 1943 was given as 2½ million.[2] The incomes of husband and wife being reckoned as one, we must exclude married women, assuming their husbands are all gainfully occupied, from the total number of employed persons. Women employed part-time (some of whom may be married) are also best excluded; their incomes are included, but the amount is sufficiently small to be ignored. The total number of incomes in 1943 may be estimated, therefore, at approximately 20·5 million[3] and we shall assume the same number for the financial year 1941–42. For the previous year, when the number would have been slightly less, we shall assume 20 million. These are quite rough estimates, which, however, do not affect most of the subsequent analysis. They are probably too low, rather than too high, since a number of persons with transfer incomes are excluded, in addition to the categories already mentioned.

The distribution of private incomes in 1940–41 and 1941–42, that is, of incomes *received* in these years, is shown in Table I. The terms gross and net income refer to incomes before and after direct taxation, at the rates current in each year.

The effects of income tax and surtax are shown in the quite different distributions of gross and net income; the changes between the two years being partly the result of reductions in allowances and increases in the rates of income tax in July 1940 and April 1941, and partly the result of a general increase in the level of incomes.

Unfortunately, it is not possible to compare these figures with those published for 1938–39 and 1941–42.[4] The earlier statement referred to income tax assessments for each year, which are based partly (under Schedules D and E) on incomes received in the previous year, and excluded a large part of incomes in the lowest ranges, as well as transfer payments. It is known, also, that some of the estimates have been considerably revised.

It appears, from these figures, that the average gross income in the lowest grade, of incomes under £250 p.a., was £214 in 1940–41

---

[1] Statement in the House of Commons, September 23, 1943.
[2] Statement by Mr. E. Bevin, April 30, 1943.
[3] This figure excludes retired persons, some of whom are included in the numbers shown in the White Paper.
[4] Statement by Captain Crookshank in the House of Commons, July 23, 1942.

TABLE I

The Distribution of Private Income

Range of Gross Income £ p.a.	Number of Incomes ooo's	per cent	Aggregate Gross Income £ mn.	per cent	Aggregate Net Income £ mn.	per cent
			1940–41			
Under 250	15,580	77·9	3,328	57·5	3,302	63·7
250—500	3,295	16·5	1,069	18·5	984	19·0
500—1,000	770	3·9	516	8·9	411	7·9
1,000—2,000	250	1·2	345	6·0	245	4·7
2,000—10,000	97	0·5	360	6·2	197	3·8
over 10,000	8	0·04	170	2·9	48	0·9
Total	20,000	100	5,788	100	5,187	100
			1941–42			
Under 250	14,610	71·3	3,398	52·3	3,307	59·8
250—500	4,450	21·7	1,490	22·9	1,276	23·1
500—1,000	1,050	5·1	685	10·5	495	9·0
1,000—2,000	285	1·4	400	6·2	245	4·4
2,000—10,000	97	0·5	360	5·5	170	3·1
over 10,000	8	0·04	170	2·6	35	0·6
Total	20,500	100	6,503	100	5,528	100

and £233 in 1941–42. It is unlikely that the averages in this grade were, in fact, as high as this, so that the total number of incomes, from which the number in this grade is derived, has probably been under-estimated, as mentioned above. Both for this reason and because the numbers do not include married women, the degree of inequality in the distribution of incomes, according to the number of persons, would be greater than the table indicates. It is important, also, to remember that no information is available regarding the distribution of quite a large portion of private income, such as undistributed profits; and that, if this income were allocated to the persons to whom it belongs, the inequality in the distribution of incomes would be rather greater than the available figures suggest.

From the data in Table I, we can obtain approximate estimates of the additional yield in taxation which would result from limiting the maximum level of income. For a typical family, say a married couple with two children, a gross earned income of £2,000 corresponds to a net income of about £1,200. For larger families, or families having some investment income, a gross income of £2,000 would correspond with a somewhat smaller net income, but at these levels of income the variations in allowances are comparatively unimportant. In 1941–42, the number of incomes above £2,000 gross was 105,000 and the corresponding aggregate net income was

£205 million. Thus, if gross incomes were limited to £2,000, which means that net incomes would be limited to roughly £1,200, the additional yield in taxation would be of the order of £80 million per annum. The conclusion has a hearing on taxation policy (cf. page 90).

2. PARETO'S AND GIBRAT'S FORMULAE

The present data, though not as complete as might be desired, can be used to throw some light on the problem of representing the distribution of gross incomes by a mathematical curve. In its simplest form, Pareto's well-known law can be written:

$$\log y = \log A - a \log x,$$

where y is the number of incomes above £x. This formula has been applied to the figures given above, with results which are shown in Table II, under the heading: Pareto I.

In a more general form, Pareto's law can be written:

$$\log y = \log A - a \log (x - x_0),$$

where x_0 is some arbitrary point, to be determined from the data. This formula has also been applied, with results which are shown in Table II, under the heading: Pareto II. It is clear that the second and more general form, in which x_0 is given the value of 40, yields better results than the first.

These formulae cannot be applied to incomes under £250, since it is not known what is the lowest income. But, according to the Pareto law, in either of these two forms, the numbers increase as income diminishes and it is most unlikely, therefore, that the law would apply to the lowest range of incomes. In the present case, it was also found that the law did not apply very well, in either form, to incomes over £10,000 p.a.

When the aggregate incomes in each range are estimated from the equations to the second form of Pareto's law, the agreement is found to be fairly close for the four highest groups, but not for incomes below £500, in 1940–41. In 1941–42 it is fairly close only for incomes between £500 and £10,000 p.a. Incomes estimated from the first form of the law, as may be seen from the Table, do not agree so well.

An alternative method of representing the distribution of incomes, which is derived from the Normal Curve of Error, has been suggested by Gibrat.[1] If the Normal Curve is denoted by

$$N(z) = \frac{N}{\sqrt{2\pi}} e^{-\frac{1}{2}z^2}$$

and the derived curve by $N(x)$, the transformation is made by substituting

$$z = a \log (x - x_0) + b$$

and equating areas on the two bases, dz and dx, so that

$$N(z)\, dz = N(x)\, dx.$$

The introduction of logarithms causes the normal curve to be transformed into a skew curve, which Gibrat calls the law of proportional effect. 'La loi de l'effet proportionnel se traduira donc par le fait que les logarithmes de la variable seront répartis suivant la loi de Laplace.'[2]

When this curve is applied to the present data, against the number of incomes, the values of z and of $\log (x - x_0)$ are found to lie approximately on a straight line when $x_0 = 170$. As shown in Table II, the numbers given by the formulae agree fairly closely with the original data, except for the top range, of incomes over £10,000 p.a.

When the corresponding incomes are estimated, it is found that the law does not apply to the group of incomes under £250, and it is known, indeed, that the minimum income is not as high as £170. The Gibrat formula accounts quite well, however, for the distribution between £250 and £10,000 p.a.

The equations, from which the figures given in Table II were derived, are given below, with the notations mentioned previously. These equations were estimated by the method of least squares, but in each case the top point, corresponding to incomes above £10,000, since it was found to lie off the line formed by the remainder, was excluded from the computation. Here, logarithms all refer to the base 10.

1940-41

Pareto I $\log y = 10{\cdot}9033 - 1{\cdot}7850 \log x$
Pareto II $\log y = 10{\cdot}5013 - 1{\cdot}6641 \log (x - 40)$
Gibrat $z = 1{\cdot}3141 \log (x - 170) - 1{\cdot}7316$

[1] R. Gibrat, *Les Inégalités Economiques*, Paris, 1931.   [2] Op. cit., p. 64.

1941-42

$$\text{Pareto I} \quad \log y = 11.3887 - 1.9314 \log x$$
$$\text{Pareto II} \quad \log y = 10.9517 - 1.7999 \log (x - 40)$$
$$\text{Gibrat} \quad z = 1.4800 \log (x - 170) - 2.2532$$

The degree of equality or inequality in the distribution of incomes is indicated, in Pareto's formulae, by the value of a, the coefficient of $\log x$ or of $\log (x - x_0)$; and in Gibrat's formula by the value of a, the coefficient of $\log (x - x_0)$. The increase in the value of each of these parameters between 1940–41 and 1941–42 is evidence of a slight, but significant,[1] reduction in inequality. Since the value of a in the first form of Pareto's law was found[2] to be approximately 1·68 in 1938–39, there appears to have been a continuous tendency, during the war, for inequality in the distribution of *gross* incomes to become slightly reduced. Changes in the inequality of distribution of *net* incomes, reflecting increases in direct taxation, have, of course, been more marked.

TABLE II

The Distribution of Private Income—Comparison of Data and Formulae

Range of Gross Income £ p.a.	No. of Incomes (000's)	Nos. (000's) given by formulae:			Aggregate Gross Income £ mn.	Aggregate Gross Income (£mn.) given by formulae:		
		Pareto I	Pareto II	Gibrat		Pareto I	Pareto II	Gibrat
1940-41								
Under 250	15,580			15,584	3,328			2,973
250—500	3,295	2,980	3,159	3,271	1,069	1,000	925	1,088
500—1,000	770	865	829	792	516	581	524	544
1,000—2,000	250	250	241	247	345	338	314	344
2,000—10,000	97	97	98	102	360	334	341	358
Over 10,000	8	6	7	4	170	132	176	79
Total	20,000			20,000	5,788			5,386
1941-42								
Under 250	14,610			14,625	3,398			2,854
250—500	4,450	4,221	4,474	4,435	1,490	1,411	1,303	1,457
500—1,000	1,050	1,106	1,058	1,043	685	740	664	699
1,000—2,000	285	290	278	294	400	387	361	394
2,000—10,000	97	98	100	100	360	333	340	330
Over 10,000	8	5	6	3	170	95	128	41
Total	20,500			20,500	6,503			5,775

[1] The sampling errors of the differences, in the cases of both Pareto II and Gibrat, are associated with probabilities of less than 1 in 20.

[2] BULLETIN, Vol. 4, No. 12, p. 225.

3. On the Significance of the Formulae

The equations of Pareto and Gibrat are different in appearance and may be thought to have different implications. Pareto himself had contrasted his formula with the Normal Law of Error and argued that chance factors could not explain the form of the distribution. 'La répartition des revenus n'est pas l'effet du hasard,' he wrote.[1] This conclusion was challenged by Gibrat, who showed that a curve which was derivable, by means of a logarithmic transformation, from the Normal Law, gave an adequate description of the distribution of incomes in many cases. It may be interesting, therefore, to compare the forms of the two curves.

In the Gibrat formula, shown above, the number of incomes at a particular level is given by:

$$N(x) = N(z)\frac{dz}{dx} = \frac{N}{\sqrt{2\pi}} \cdot \frac{a}{x - x_0} exp\left[-\tfrac{1}{2}\left\{a \log (x - x_0) + b\right\}^2 \right]$$

Therefore

$$\log N(x) = \log\left(\frac{Na}{\sqrt{2\pi}}\right) - \tfrac{1}{2}\left\{a \log (x - x_0) + b\right\}^2 - \log (x - x_0)$$

and this is of the form:

$$\log N(x) = b_1 + b_2 \log (x - x_0) - b_3 \left\{\log (x - x_0)\right\}^2$$

where natural logarithms are now referred to.

According to the Pareto law, in the second form mentioned above, the number of incomes at x is given by:

$$-\frac{dy}{dx} = \frac{a}{x - x_0}. \quad y = n, \text{ say,}$$

so that:

$$\log n = \log a + \log A - (a + 1) \log (x - x_0),$$

which is of the form:

$$\log n = c_1 - c_2 \log (x - x_0).$$

Gibrat's formula can therefore be represented by a quadratic function, Pareto's by a linear function, of $\log (x - x_0)$. The values of x_0 which give the best fit in each case will not, however, generally be the same; in fact, we can expect the value obtained from Pareto's equation to be less than that obtained from Gibrat's formula. It

[1] *Cours d'Economie Politique*, p. 315.

should be noted, also, that b_2, b_3 and c_2 are essentially positive, so that the coefficients of the independent variables have the signs indicated. It is only, therefore, over the range where the number of incomes declines, as income increases, that the curves could both describe any given distribution of incomes. The Gibrat curve, expressing log $N(x)$ as a function of log $(x - x_0)$, within a certain range, gives approximately a straight line; and the curvature of the line can, of course, be reduced by altering the value of x_0.

Thus, the form taken by the distribution of incomes, at any rate over a wide range, can be derived from the Normal Curve; and the relation given above provides at least a partial explanation of why the distribution often conforms, also, to the simpler equation given by Pareto. It is worth noting that Edgeworth[1] had suggested, as a possible explanation of the Pareto Law, that if means and faculties were originally distributed according to the law of chance, an abnormally protuberant curve might eventually result from an application of the principle: Unto him that hath shall be given.

When, however, Pareto's law is used to deduce generalizations, such as that the distribution of incomes is, in some sense, inevitable, it is apparently done in defiance of the warning which Pareto himself gave: 'Ce n'est là qu'une loi empirique.'[2]

While the formulae, which have here been discussed, can be used to account for the distribution of incomes over most of the range above £250, they do not, evidently, explain the distribution of incomes below this level. But, in order to determine the form of the distribution of the smaller incomes, in this country, it would be necessary to have information in greater detail than is at present available.

[1] Journal of the Royal Statistical Society, 1924, vol. lxxxvii, p. 573.
[2] *Cours d'Economie Politique*, Preface, p. iv.

V. CONSUMPTION AND PRICES

INCOME AND HOUSEHOLD EXPENDITURE OF WORKING-CLASS FAMILIES WITH CHILDREN

By T. Schulz

FROM BULLETIN, VOL. 8, NOS. 2 AND 3 (FEB., MARCH, 1946)

THE importance of a comprehensively planned food policy in war time was demonstrated during the first world war when, through the absence of such a policy, incidences of malnutrition became evident. When hostilities broke out in 1939, public opinion was thus prepared for and in favour of food rationing. It was introduced by the end of the year, and was soon extended so as to cover all the main foodstuffs that were in short supply. These foods, however, only represented part of the nation's diet—in terms of calories and second-class proteins by far the smaller part. It therefore became important to understand how the rations allowed to the individual dovetailed into his consumption of unrationed foods and whether he could obtain a satisfactory diet.

The need for such a survey was one reason that induced the Institute of Statistics to start a series of inquiries into working-class household expenditure in May 1940.[1] A further reason was the desire to obtain a picture of the changes in the cost of living as reflected in the outlay on the main groups of household expenditure and to study the trend of expenditure in general.

We realized from the outset that the sample on which such a continuous survey could be based would have to be small. For the keeping of a detailed household account, even over a short period, is an exacting task for the busy housewife that is not accustomed to it. Moreover, the collecting and checking of such accounts requires skilled supervisors, and war-time conditions enhanced the difficulties of finding suitable people for the task, which was undertaken voluntarily through all the years. With these limitations in view

---

[1] The inquiry was initiated by Professor A. L. Bowley, who at that time was Acting Director of the Institute.

we decided to aim, as far as possible, at a homogeneous sample, by trying to obtain our household accounts from one clearly defined type of family.

So far, seven inquiries have been undertaken, but we hope to collect two more samples and conclude this survey in 1947. The seventh inquiry, with which this paper deals, was carried out in June–July, 1945. Except for the first year when the sampling was repeated after an interval of six months, the inquiries were made once a year. Their purpose is to ascertain in detail working-class household expenditure during a fortnight within a fixed sampling period. A survey over four weeks would, of course, have been preferable; but very few housewives were willing to keep a daily account of every single item of expenditure for so long. Even for the shorter period the number of contributions has remained small. We do, however, believe—and the picture obtained from every additional inquiry has confirmed us in this conviction—that our samples are representative of a particular type of urban working-class family, viz., that within the lower or medium income range with, as a rule, one or more dependent children.

A number of the families that supplied the household accounts in 1944 were directly affected by the attacks of the flying bombs. In some instances, houses were damaged, and the families had to live in temporary quarters; in other cases, people had given shelter to evacuees, and several families kept house together. In summer, 1945, many of those who had a home to go back to had returned to it. Others had relinquished unsatisfactory temporary quarters—perhaps rather expensive ones—for more suitable accommodation. It was, therefore, of considerable interest to compare household accounts for these two years in order to see whether and to what extent these more stable conditions were reflected in the families' mode of living, as expressed in the pattern of their household expenditure.

PART I: INCOME AND EXPENDITURE ON NON-FOOD ITEMS

1. *The Structure of the Sample*

(*a*) General

In 1944, in spite of the prevailing difficulties, we obtained a maximum in our six years' series of samples, of 226 household accounts, supplied by families from 17 different towns. In 1945, only 155 families from 14 towns contributed to our sample. The Investigators in Bristol, Reading, and Edinburgh, who had assisted us in previous years, were unable to do so in 1945, and it proved impossible to find any one suitable and willing to take their places. War-tiredness, the readjustment of family life consequent to the ceasing of the European hostilities, and the impending elections, affected the readiness and, often, the ability of the housewives to keep a detailed account during the stipulated period.

Nevertheless, the total number of families that completed a budget for us in both 1944 and 1945, was about as high as the number of parallel budgets obtained for 1943 and 1944: 84 families whose structure had remained *unchanged* from one sampling period to the following one, had supplied accounts for the years of 1943 and 1944, and 85 families did so for 1944 and 1945. From families whose structure had *changed*, either because of the birth of a child, the calling up or demobilization of a member of the family, or for some other reason, we obtained 33 accounts in 1943 and 1944, and 26 in 1944 and 1945. But there were in 1944, 109 *new* families that had not previously contributed to our sample, and only 44 of such families in 1945. We again accepted for our sample *new* families only if they were not supported by Public Assistance or charity organizations, had at least one dependent child at home, and did not keep boarders on a profit basis.[1] The inclusion in a family of a relation, friend, or evacuee, who only repaid the actual expenses incurred on his or her behalf, was not deemed to vitiate the homogeneity of our sample.

(*b*) Geographical distribution

That the reduction in the total number of accounts kept has little interfered with the general structure of our sample in 1945, as compared with that of 1944, becomes evident from the data in the two bottom rows of Table I, which compare some of the characteristic average figures for the two years. The Table sets out the distribution by towns of the families that supplied an account in 1945. They are subdivided into *unchanged*, *changed*, and *new* families.

It will be seen that half of the *new* families came from Liverpool, which, in 1945, was represented by 27 accounts, as compared with 31 in 1944.

In 1944, the majority of the Liverpool budgets were obtained through schools from the parents of girls aged between 13 and 14

---

[1] There is, however, amongst the *changed* families one that was in receipt of Public Assistance in 1945, and a few of the *unchanged* families no longer had children under 14 years of age, although this was the case in the first year when they contributed to our inquiry, with one exception.

TABLE I

Geographical Distribution of Families

	Un-chgd.	*Chgd.*	*New*	*Total*	*No. of Persons per family*	*'Man' value per Person*	*Expenditure on* Food per 'Man' per week	*Expenditure on* Rent[1] per family	*Expenditure on* Fuel and light per week
(1) Birmingham	6	3	—	9	4·7	0·73	15/0¼	9/11¼	6/3
(2) Dundee ..	1	—	—	1	2·0	0·73	17/10¼	4/7	6/3
(3) Glasgow ..	7	1	4	12	4·1	0·73	14/11¼	12/0¾	7/4
(4) Leeds ..	10	2	1	13	4·2	0·81	14/11½	14/–	5/9¼
(5) Lincoln ..	1	4	—	5	6·8	0·76	12/0½	11/5¾	8/0¼
(6) Liverpool ..	2	3	22	27	5·3	0·79	13/3	13/6	10/7
(7) London ..	5	2	1	8	4·6	0·75	15/5½	15/3	8/8¼
(8) Manchester ..	11	4	2	17	4·9	0·74	14/6¼	11/6	6/6¼
(9) Newcastle ..	6	1	—	7	3·6	0·78	14/0½	10/4	4/4½
(10) Oxford ..	6	—	3	9	4·7	0·74	13/5½	11/6¾	7/8
(11) St. Helens ..	7	1	4	12	4·6	0·75	12/8	11/8¼	7/5½
(12) Sheffield ..	7	1	—	8	5·0	0·80	12/6½	14/2¾	6/10½
(13) Southampton	13	2	6	21	4·0	0·80	16/6	17/5½	9/1
(14) Swindon ..	3	2	1	6	3·5	0·80	14/10¼	16/4½	8/6½
Total 1945 ..	85	26	44	155	4·6	0·77	14/2½	13/–	7/10¼
Total 1944 ..	84	33	109	226	4·7	0·77	13/10¼	13/2¾[2]	8/2

[1] Excluding the following 17 families living rent free or buying their houses: Leeds 2; Liverpool 2; Manchester 1; Newcastle 1; St. Helens 1; Swindon 2; Southampton 8.
[2] Average for 204 families.

years, and, unfortunately, contact had been lost with most of these families. Yet in spite of the fact that 22 out of the 27 budgets in 1945 came from *new* families, the average figures of family structure and expenditure on food and rent were fairly similar for this town in both years; in 1945, the number of persons per family was 5·3, the 'man' value per person[1] 0·79, food expenditure per 'man' 13 shillings 3 pence, and rent per family 13 shillings 6 pence, as against the following values in 1944: number of persons 5·2, 'man' value 0·80, food expenditure per 'man' 13 shillings 1¾ pence, and rent 14 shillings 2½ pence. Only the figures for fuel and light were markedly different for the two years, viz., 10 shillings 7 pence in 1945, and 9 shillings 7¾ pence in 1944, per family per week, thus exhibiting an apparent rise by nearly 10 per cent, while average expenditure on this item of the whole sample in 1945 was approximately 4 per cent below that of our sample in 1944. However, outlay on fuel and light during the summer months is largely determined by the purchases of coal that is stored for later consumption—

[1] The average 'man' values are based on the following scale: adult male, 1·00; adult female, 0·85; children, from 0·33 to 0·70, with an average of 0·55. The values for children are set out in more detail in part II of this paper. This scale of 'man' values is employed always, except where explicit reference is made to a different scale.

at present often more dependent on conditions of supply than of demand—and there is no reason to assume that differences in the outlay on fuel and light point to any fundamental difference in the socio-economic type of the Liverpool budgets for the two years, which, indeed, is most unlikely to exist.

The average figures for the families from one town may, of course, conceal very considerable differences in the food expenditure of the individual families; yet in conjunction with the data in Table II, they will convey some idea of the economic type of the families with which our sample is concerned.

TABLE II

Expenditure on Food Compared with Other Household Expenditure

1945 Outlay on Food per 'Man' per Week	*1944* Number of Families	*1944* Persons per Family	1945 *Number of Families*	1945 *Persons per Family*	1945 *'Man' Value per Person*	1945 *Average Outlay on Food per 'Man' per Week*	1945 *Total Househ. Outlay*[1] *ex Housg. p. 'Man' p. Week*	1945 *Outlay On Rent per Family*[2] *p. Week*
under 9*s.*	*4*	*7·8*	—	—	—	—	—	—
9*s.*—10*s.*	*6*	*5·7*	4	5·8	0·73	9/5½	20/6½	11/10½
10*s.*—11*s.*	*12*	*6·4*	9	5·3	0·82	10/6½	19/0¼	14/6¼
11*s.*—12*s.*	*27*	*5·7*	19	5·7	0·77	11/7¼	20/1¾	11/10½
12*s.*—13*s.*	*36*	*5·2*	20	5·5	0·75	12/5¾	22/7¼	11/9½
13*s.*—14*s.*	*29*	*4·4*	18	5·0	0·78	13/6	23/5½	13/8½
14*s.*—15*s.*	*25*	*4·8*	22	4·5	0·79	14/6¾	27/11¼	12/9¾
15*s.*—16*s.*	*23*	*4·3*	20	4·1	0·76	15/6½	32/7¼	15/6¾
16*s.*—17*s.*	*24*	*4·1*	7	3·7	0·78	16/6¼	27/7	15/1¾
17*s.*—18*s.*	*11*	*3·5*	12	3·8	0·77	17/3¾	32/3¾	11/6¾
18*s.*—19*s.*	*13*	*3·5*	8	3·4	0·78	18/6¾	40/1½	11/8
19*s.*—20*s.*	*8*	*3·6*	6	3·2	0·75	19/6¼	39/5¼	12/5¾
20*s.*—22*s.*	*3*	*4·0*	6	3·3	0·67	20/11¾	40/11¾	12/8¾
22*s.* and over	*5*	*2·6*	4	3·5	0·80	24/2½	43/4½	12/10¼
Total	*226*	*4·7*	155	4·6	0·77	14/2½	30/2¼	13/–[3]

[1] Including outlay on food.

[2] Excluding 17 families living rent free or buying their houses, in the following food expenditure groups: 11*s.*—12*s.*, 2 families; 12*s.*—13*s.*, 1 family; 13*s.*—14*s.*, 3 families; 14*s.*—15*s.*, 3 families; 15*s.*—16*s.*, 3 families; 16*s.*—17*s.*, 1 family; 18*s.*—19*s.*, 2 families; 19*s.*—20*s.*, 1 family; 22*s.* and over, 1 family.

[3] Average per family per week of 138 families.

(*c*) The economic outline

In the absence of full information regarding income, expenditure on food is, perhaps, the best single pointer to the standard of living of a person or a family, and in Table II our sample is surveyed from that angle. The numbers of families and their average structure are shown ranged according to their expenditure on food per 'man', and with expenditure on food is compared total household expenditure per 'man', including expenditure on food but excluding cost of housing, i.e., of rent, rates, and mortgage charges. This latter item has been deducted since, for the individual family, cost of housing is not a variable in the short run, as are all the other major items of household expenditure. The last column in Table II gives the average outlay per family per week on rent only (including rates). In both 1944 and 1945, little less than two-thirds of the families spent on food per 'man' per week from 11 shillings to 16 shillings.

The expenditure on food per 'man' per week of all the 155 families in 1945 was 14 shillings 2½ pence, while that of the 226 families in 1944 was 13 shillings 10¼ pence. This slight apparent increase results mainly from the dropping out of our sample of some of the poorest families; there were in 1944, four families with a weekly food expenditure per 'man' of less than 9 shillings, but none in 1945; and only one of the families that kept an account in both years spent less than 9 shillings in 1944. No rise occurred in the expenditure on food per 'man' of the *unchanged* families, and that of the *changed* families declined by 3 per cent, as will be seen from the indices in Table IV.

DIAGRAM A

Cumulative Frequency Curves of Families and Persons in Relation to their Expenditure on Food

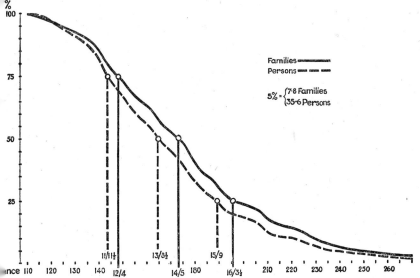

Expenditure on Food per 'Man' per Week

In Diagram A the proportion of families below or above a given food expenditure per 'man' is compared with the proportion of persons below or above that point. The lower and the upper quartiles of the total number of persons and the total number of families, lie more closely together than the two medians, thus indicating that the families between the first quartile and the median of the number of persons, are of an average size larger than those below the first quartile, a fact that is not obvious from the figures in Table II. In 1944, the quartiles and medians found for 226 families—1064 person—were, for persons: lower quartile, 11 shillings 9 pence; median, 13 shillings 4½ pence; upper quartile, 15 shillings 7 pence; for families: lower quartile, 12 shillings 2¾ pence; median, 13 shillings 10¼ pence; upper quartile, 16 shillings 3 pence.

TABLE III

Average Structure of Families

	Age Group	Unchanged Families (85)		Changed Families (26)		New Families (44)	All Families (155)
		1944	1945	1944	1945	1945	1945
Males..	18 and over	0·91	0·95	1·19	1·19	1·16	1·05
Females	18 and over	1·11	1·11	1·42	1·31	1·20	1·17
Males..	15—17	0·15	0·16	0·31	0·27	0·11	0·17
Females	15—17	0·12	0·14	0·27	0·27	0·23	0·19
Children	6—14	1·15	1·20	1·54	1·62	1·41	1·33
Children	under 6	0·67	0·55	0·89	1·04	0·77	0·69
Persons p. family		4·11	4·11	5·62	5·70	4·88	4·60
'Man' value per Person		*0·76*	*0·78*	*0·77*	*0·75*	*0·77*	*0·77*

Table III analyses the composition of the 85 *unchanged*, 26 *changed*, and 44 *new* families, that kept an account in 1945. There was little change in the average structure of the 111 families that were represented in the sample of 1944 as well as in that of 1945. Some members advanced, of course, to a higher age group, with the result that the 'man' value per person of the *unchanged* families is somewhat higher for 1945 than for 1944. The 'man' value per person of the *changed* families shows a slight decline owing to the larger number of young children per family in 1945. Apart from other changes in their composition, nine children were born to these 26 families, between June, 1944 and June, 1945.

2. *Household Expenditure and the Cost of Living Index*

The household expenditure per 'man' of the *unchanged*, *changed*, and *new* families, is broadly surveyed in Table IV. In Table V, the

TABLE IV

Household Expenditure of Three Groups of Families

				Per 'Man' Unchanged Families 1945	Per Week Changed Families 1945	Per Week New Families 1945	Index of Expenditure (1944 = 100) Unchanged Families	Changed Families
Food	..	..	..	14/4	13/11	14/2½	100	97
Housing	..			4/–	2/10	3/6	99	92
Clothing	..			2/2¾	2/4¾	2/6½	87	119
Fuel and Light	..			2/2¾	1/8	2/7	86	93
Miscellaneous	..			8/0¼	5/6¼	8/10½	98	101
Total	..	..	..	30/9¾	26/4	31/8½	97	99

relative household expenditure of all the 155 families in 1945 is compared with that of the 226 families that kept accounts in 1944, and, further, with the 'weights' applied by the Ministry of Labour for its cost of living index, adjusted for the differences in the rise of prices in the several groups, since July 1st, 1914. The last two rows in Table V give the actual outlay as ascertained by us, per family

TABLE V

Weekly Family Expenditure

	1944 226 Families incl. Miscellaneous per cent	excl. Miscellaneous per cent	1945 155 Families incl. Miscellaneous per cent	excl. Miscellaneous per cent	1944 Ministry of Labour Cost of Living Index Weighting[1] incl. Miscellaneous per cent	excl. Miscellaneous per cent	1945 incl. Miscellaneous per cent	excl. Miscellaneous per cent
(1) Food	48	62·7	47	63·4	50·4	53·5	50·5	53·5
(2) Housing ..	12	16·1	12	16·2	13·1[2]	13·9[2]	12·9[2]	13·7[2]
(3) Clothing ..	8	11·0	8	10·5	20·6	21·9	20·3	21·5
(4) Fuel and Light	8	10·2	7	9·9	10·1	10·7	10·7	11·3
(1)—(4)	76	100·0	74	100·0	94·2	100·0	94·4	100·0
(5) Miscellaneous	24		26		5·8		5·6	
Total Outlay ..	100		100		100·0		100·0	
Weekly Outlay ..	s. d.		s. d.					
per Family ..	105 0½[3]		106 6¾					
per 'Man' ..	28 10¾		30 2¼					

[1] Corrected for the rise in prices from July 1, 1914, to June–July, 1944 and 1945.
[2] Rent only (incl. rates).
[3] In 1944, the family consisted of 4·7 persons with an average 'man' value of 0·77.

and per 'man', for 1944 and 1945. It will be noticed that all the figures for the two years have remained remarkably steady, and, also, that the relative data obtained by us differ considerably from the Ministry of Labour 'weights'. Although only 111 families of our sample supplied budgets in 1944 and 1945, the differences between the actual expenditure figures of both years is small.

R

The outlay per family was 1 shilling $6\frac{1}{4}$ pence higher in 1945, and the outlay per 'man' 1 shilling $3\frac{1}{2}$ pence, the relatively closer approach in the outlay per family reflecting the fact that the average family in 1945 contained about 0·1 'man' less than in 1944.[1]

In this first part of our paper we shall consider only the groups of non-food items in Tables IV and V, reserving the analysis of the outlay on food for a subsequent section.[2]

3. *Expenditure on Non-Food Items*

(*a*) Cost of housing and rent.

A decline in the outlay on housing per 'man', of 8 per cent, is shown in Table IV, for the *changed* families. This appeared at first somewhat surprising, for rents are controlled and there was no proportionate rise in the average 'man' value per family. Had this been the case it might have accounted for the lower average outlay per 'man', since cost of housing is an overhead charge for the family and its total unaffected by variations in the number of persons. But there occurred, in fact, for six of the families substantial reductions in their outlay on housing—from 2 shillings to 15 shillings a week—in most instances because of the family's relinquishing of temporary and rather expensive accommodation.

The much higher cost of housing per 'man' of the *unchanged* families as compared with that of the *changed* and the *new* ones, appears in a different aspect if we consider the cost of housing per family instead of per 'man'. Then the lowest outlay is still found to obtain for the *changed* families—none of which lived rent free— with 12 shillings per week. The central position, however, is now taken by the *unchanged* families, with an average of 12 shillings 9 pence; this group includes two families that paid nothing for their housing accommodation. Another two families that also paid no charges at all were found in the group of *new* families, which, including these two families, had an average outlay on housing of 13 shillings 2 pence.

The average cost of housing per family per week for all the 155 families in 1945 amounted to 12 shillings $9\frac{1}{4}$ pence, as compared with an average weekly rent (including rates) of 13 shillings paid by 138 families. Of the remaining 17 families, four paid nothing and thirteen paid mortgage charges and/or rates, in six instances

[1] The average weekly cost of maintenance for 0·1 'man' in 1945 being just over 3 shillings, the total difference for a family of the same size as in 1944 would amount to 4 shillings 8 pence.
[2] Part II.

substantially more, and in six substantially less, than the average cost of rent. One family spent exactly 13 shillings per week on rates and mortgage charges. In 1944, an average rent of 13 shillings 2½ pence was found to obtain for 204 families. In that sample, exceptionally high rents paid by a few families were counterbalanced by the low rents of some of the poorest families that did not keep an account in 1945.

The outlay on rent per family is given for the different towns represented in our sample, in Table I. These figures cannot, of course, be taken as characteristic of the relative levels of rent charges in these towns. They merely indicate in conjunction with the figures of food expenditure and expenditure on fuel and light, some strategic points in the cost of living pattern of the families of our sample. There is no perceptible interrelation between these three sets of figures in Table I, although some relation between rent and expenditure on food seems to emerge in Table II, where the families are arranged in ascending order of food expenditure per 'man'. Rent there tends towards a peak for the central groups of food expenditure, while for the higher groups it again falls off.

(b) Clothing

The average outlay on clothing per 'man' per week for the three groups of families was 2 shillings 2¾ pence for the *unchanged*, 2 shillings 4¾ pence for the *changed*, and 2 shillings 6½ pence for the *new* families (Table IV). These figures, however, represent only part of the actual expenditure on clothing. They comprise little more than what the housewife disburses in payment into clothing clubs, or for shoe repairs and small items of apparel purchased largely for herself or for the children. The main outlay on clothing is usually met by the earners directly, either out of their pocket money or out of savings, and does not appear in the housewife's account of household expenditure.

(c) Fuel and Light

Similar to the outlay on housing, the outlay on fuel and light is considered better as a charge incurred per family than per person or per 'man', since variations in the size of the family make generally little or no difference to the household consumption of light or heating of the families of our sample, while the concomitant alterations in the consumption of fuel for cooking and washing are, as a rule, too slight to cause any substantial changes in the total outlay on fuel and light, taken together. In 1945, this outlay had declined fairly sharply for the *changed* as well as the *unchanged*

TABLE VI

Weekly Family Expenditure on Fuel and Light

Group of Families	Total Fuel and Light Outlay	Index (1944 = 100)	Coal Outlay	Gas Outlay	Electricity Outlay	Other[1] Outlay
Unchanged (85)						
1944	8/1¼	100·0	4/2	2/0½	1/6½	4¼
1945	7/1¼	87·8	3/5	1/10	1/6	4¼
Changed (26)						
1944	7/8½	100·0	3/10½	2/2¼	1/4½	3¼
1945	7/1¼	92·2	3/4	2/1¾	1/2¼	5¼
All Families (155)	7/10¼	—	3/7¾	2/2	1/7¾	4¾

[1] Including firewood, matches, etc.

families, but from the figures in Table VI it appears that this was mostly the result of a decline in the outlay of coal. Hence the lower index figure may rather picture temporary changes in supply than in potential consumption, for part of the coal that is bought during the summer months is stored for the cold season. During the twelve months lying between our two inquiries, the Ministry of Labour index of the cost of fuel and light had gone up by 9 per cent, from 253 to 275, a rise brought about by an increase in the price of coal of approximately 12 per cent, and of gas by 6 per cent. The volume of coal purchased in 1945 per family of our sample was therefore 73 per cent of that of 1944 for the *unchanged* families, and 77 per cent for the *changed* families, during the sampling period.

(e) Miscellaneous items

The biggest difference for the several groups of families in Table IV appears in the outlay on 'miscellaneous' items, which includes a very wide range of expenditure, e.g., purchases of household goods, seeds and garden implements, cleaning materials, laundry charges, contributions to voluntary insurances and clubs for unspecified purposes, payments to doctor, dentist, and chemist, cost of education, amusements, newspapers, drink, and tobacco. Many of these expenses tend to appear only in part in the household accounts, being largely defrayed by the earners themselves and, to that extent, unknown to the housewife. One would, however, be inclined to assume that—*ceteris paribus*—the larger the average number of persons per family with pocket money of their own the smaller the outlay of housekeeping money on 'miscellaneous' items. There is, indeed, an indication of this with respect to the *unchanged* and *changed* families. The former contained, on the average, 1·36 persons over 14 years old, excluding the housewives, whether earners or non-earners, and the latter 2·04 of such persons. If the expenditure on 'miscel laneous' items of the two groups of families is weighted by these numbers the resulting indices are very nearly the same for the two groups. For the *new* families, however, this index figure is 35 per cent above that of the *changed* and 38 per cent above that of the *unchanged* families.

The average weekly outlay per family *out of housekeeping money* on some of the largest single items of the 'miscellaneous' group will be found in Table VII. For the data of this Table, the families have first been subdivided into two main groups, viz., those stating their total income and those stating their household expenditure only.

TABLE VII

Expenditure on Miscellaneous Items out of Housekeeping Money

	99 Families Stating Income			*56 Families Stating Household Outlay Only*		
	Families Buying as per cent of 99 Families	*Weekly Outlay per Family: Actually Buying*	*Weekly Outlay per Family: Average of Group of 99 Families*	*Families Buying as per cent of 56 Families*	*Weekly Outlay per Family: Actually Buying*	*Weekly Outlay per Family: Average of Group of 56 Families*
Drink	47	2/–	–/11½	50	3/0¾	1/6½
Tobacco	65	9/5¾	6/2¾	55	9/9	5/4¾
Newspapers	96	1/6¾	1/6	98	1/5½	1/5¼
Amusements . .	77	4/9	3/7¾	64	4/5¾	2/10½
Insurance and Clubs[1] . .	99	4/5½	4/5	96	4/7¼	4/5¼
Total Average Outlay			16/9			15/8¼

[1] Excluding compulsory insurances and 'clubs' for specific purchases, *viz.*, clothing coal, furniture, etc.

Secondly, for each individual item the number of families that declared any expenditure on it, has been counted and expressed as a percentage of the total number of families in the respective group. We thus were able to calculate two sets of figures of average expenditure, the one referring only to the number of families that actually spent some money on the item, and the other based on the total number of families in the whole group. The pattern of household expenditure of the families that revealed their total income will be discussed below; here we are only interested in a comparison of the absolute and relative figures given in Table VII for the two groups of families. The percentage of families that showed in their household account some expenditure on tobacco, amusements, and insurances and clubs, was somewhat higher for the group stating total income than for that stating household expenditure only. Since a similar relative picture emerged in previous years, it seems to indicate that when the housewife knows what everybody in the family earns she is more likely to be entrusted with providing certain personal items for the earners, either for their own or for the family's benefit, e.g., cigarettes and tobacco, or a family visit to the cinema. It is worth noting that with the exception of expenditure on drink—which in any case represents only a small fraction of the actual outlay on this item—the average figures for the two groups, relating to the number of families actually stating an outlay on these items of expenditure, approach closely to one another.

4. *Household Expenditure and Income*

In analysing accounts of household expenditure that are divorced from the background of family income, there always remains a strong element of doubt as to how the data obtained should be interpreted. Thus it is impossible to say whether a rent high in relation to food expenditure does actually affect the level of food expenditure; or, to take another example, whether a low expenditure on clothing implies lack of purchasing power due to poverty or only lack of purchasing power out of housekeeping money. It is therefore fortunate that we received statements of their total net income[1] from 99 out of the 155 families, so that we can try to place our analysis of household expenditure in a wider perspective. Of the 99 families, 50 *unchanged* and 9 *changed* families had supplied statements of their income also in 1944, while 13 *unchanged* and 6 *changed* families only made them in 1945. These latter 19 families had consequently to be included in the group of 'new' families for the purpose of all the Tables referring to total income, in which, therefore, 'new' families has a meaning different from that employed generally in this paper, viz., families that kept a household account for us for the first time in the year referred to.

The figures of absolute outlay in Table VIII square reasonably well with those in Table IV, even as regards the extremely small group of *changed* families in Table VIII. Owing mainly to the higher outlay on 'miscellaneous' items of the families that stated their income, the figures of relative outlay give a smaller 'weight' to the other items, as compared with those in Table V, for all the families taken together. Nevertheless, the approximation to one another of these several sets of figures is sufficiently close to allow us to assume that a similar margin between income and household expenditure, of something between a fifth and a quarter of the total

[1] 'Net' income in this context excludes taxes, compulsory insurances, and contributions to trade unions.

TABLE VIII

Expenditure of Income of 99 Families

	50 Unchanged Families				*9 Changed Families*				*40 New Families*[1]	
	1944		*1945*		*1944*		*1945*		*1945*	
	Per 'Man' per Week				*Per 'Man' per Week*				*Per 'Man' per Week*	
Food		14/2¾		14/8		14/3¾		14/3½		14/9¾
Housing		4/1¾		4/2¾		4/–		3/3¼		3/8
Clothing		2/10		2/6¼		1/11¼		3/8		2/7¼
Fuel and Light ..		2/5½		2/3		1/10¼		1/9¼		2/5¾
Miscellaneous ..		8/11¾		8/8½		8/6½		8/0½		8/0½
Total Household ..		32/7¾		32/4½		30/7¾		31/0½		31/7¼
Savings[2]		–/8½		–/8½		–/1¾		–/6¼		–/3¼
Unspecified		7/0½		8/5¾		8/11		7/7		9/9¾
Total Income ..		40/4¾		41/6¾		39/8½		39/1¾		41/8¼
	Relative Expenditure of Income									
Food	43·6	35·2	45·3	35·3	46·7	36·0	46·1	36·5	46·8	35·5
Housing	12·7	10·3	13·1	10·2	13·0	10·1	10·5	8·3	11·6	8·8
Clothing	8·7	7·0	7·8	6·1	6·4	4·9	11·8	9·4	8·2	6·2
Fuel and Light ..	7·5	6·1	6·9	5·4	6·0	4·6	5·7	4·6	7·9	6·0
Miscellaneous ..	27·5	22·2	26·9	20·9	27·9	21·5	25·9	20·5	25·5	19·3
Total Household ..	100·0	80·8	100·0	77·9	100·0	77·1	100·0	79·3	100·0	75·8
Savings[2]		1·8		1·7		0·4		1·3		0·7
Unspecified		17·4		20·4		22·5		19·4		23·5
Total Income ..		100·0		100·0		100·0		100·0		100·0
	Per Family per Week									
Total Income ..		125/9		132/3¼		149/1		152/5¼		140/1½
Housing		12/11		13/5½		15/–		12/8½		12/4¼
Fuel and Light ..		7/7¾		7/1¾		6/11		6/11¼		8/4¼

[1] Including Unchanged and Changed Families that did not state their total income in 1944.

[2] Contributions to street and school savings clubs out of housekeeping money.

income, also exists on the average for the remaining 56 families. Indeed, it may even be somewhat wider for these families, since, as appears from the figures in Table X, they had 15 per cent more adult male earners per family than the families that stated their total income. It is not possible for us to attempt any definite conclusion in this respect, since the 9 *changed* families had the highest number of adult male earners and yet the smallest margin between income and household expenditure. But this group is too small to be taken by itself as typical, and a comparison of the structure and the outlay of the 50 *unchanged* and the 40 'new' families does, in fact, reveal the wider margin for the group with the larger number of adult earners, viz., the 'new' families.

The increase in weekly income per family of the 50 *unchanged*

TABLE IX

Structure of 99 Families in Table VIII

	50 Unchanged Families		9 Changed Families		40 New Families[1]
	1944	1945	1944	1945	1945
	per Family		*per Family*		*per Family*
Earners, 18 and over					
Male	0·92	0·94	1·11	1·22	1·00
Female[2] ..	0·33	0·30	0·44	0·22	0·37
Earners, 16—18:					
Male	0·04	0·10	0·22	0·11	0·03
Female ..	0·06	0·08	—	—	0·12
Earners, under 16	0·10	0·08	0·22	0·33	0·03
Non-Earners[3] ..	0·77	0·80	1·01	1·01	0·75
Depend. Children[4]	1·86	1·78	1·67	2·11	2·10
Total No. in Family	4·08	4·08	4·67	5·00	4·40
'Man' value p. Person	*0·76*	*0·78*	*0·80*	*0·78*	*0·76*

[1] Including Unchanged and Changed Families that did not state their total income in 1944.
[2] Including housewives in receipt of army allowances.
[3] Housewives and invalids.
[4] Including children at school over 14 years old.

TABLE X

Distribution of Earners and Non-Earners in Families Stating Income and Families Stating Household Outlay Only

Members in Family		Families stating Income	Families stating Household Outlay Only	All Families
		(99)	(56)	(155)
Earners:				
18 and over {	Male	0·99	1·14	1·04
{	Female	0·32	0·26	0·30
16—18 {	Male	0·07	0·05	0·06
{	Female	0·09	0·04	0·07
Under 16	Male and Female	0·08	0·13	0·10
Non-Earners[1]:		0·80	0·96	0·87
Dependent Children[2]:		1·94	2·55	2·16
Persons per Family		4·29	5·13	4·60

[1] Housewives and Invalids.
[2] Including children at school over 14 years old.

families, by about 6 shillings 6 pence, shown in Table VIII, does not indicate for these families a general trend towards increased individual earnings, but is due mainly, on the one hand, to the decline in the number of dependent children and the concomitant increase in that of earners, and, on the other, to the advance of some of the young earners in these families to a higher wage group, from 1944 to 1945.

The figures of family structure in Tables IX and X have been compiled for the purpose of distinguishing between the earning and the non-earning members of these families. The picture which they convey is therefore somewhat different from that obtained from Table III, where the only distinction made is between age and sex groups. In Tables IX and X, the figures for dependent children include boys and girls at school over 14 years old, of which there were 0·14 per family. This does not, however, imply that about every seventh family of our sample had a child at a secondary school; some of these dependent children had apparently only just attained their fourteenth birthday and were due soon to leave school. A housewife is counted as a full earner in Tables IX and X only if her income was at least 50 shillings per week,[1] and as a half earner if it was at least 25 shillings. Earnings below this amount were disregarded.

The difference between the actual and the potential standard of living of a family is indicated, although only in a very broad way, by the relation between food expenditure and income. The proportion of the family income spent on food ranged, for the 99 families that stated their total income, from 20 per cent to 60 per cent, the former representing an outlay on food of 16 shillings 2 pence per 'man' per week, by a family of three persons, and the latter a corresponding outlay of 14 shillings 6 pence by a family of eight persons. In general, expenditure on food seemed independent of the absolute amount of income. Among the 99 families a central group of 39 families stood out with an expenditure on food from 12 to 16 shillings, which absorbed between 30 and 50 per cent of the family income. For all the 99 families, the average proportion of income allotted to the purchase of food amounted to 35·5 per cent, but the scatter around the central group was loose.

Yet although no correlation was found to exist between our data of food expenditure and their relative magnitude with respect to income, a strikingly 'normal' distribution can be obtained if we break down the figures in a different way, ignoring the absolute outlay on food and, instead, considering its relative magnitude and relating it to the size of the family. This has been done in Table XI. The tendency of the relatively larger families to spend a larger proportion of their income on food is, of course, nothing un-expected, not only because large families tend to be relatively poorer than small ones of a similar type but also because, if the larger family

[1] A housewife is also counted as an 'earner' if, in the absence of her husband, she drew an army allowance.

TABLE XI

Outlay on Food Compared with Income

Families Size	Total No.	under 20 per cent	per cent 20—30	per cent 30—40	per cent 40—50	per cent 50—60	per cent 60 and over
		Food expenditure representing of income					
Under 5 Persons	66	1	18	27	18	2	—
5—7 Persons	27	—	4	11	11	1	—
Over 7 Persons	6	—	—	1	2	2	1
All Families	99	1	22	39	31	5	1

contains more earners than the small one, such expenditure as cost of housing, and fuel and light, is likely to take up a smaller proportion of the total family income than it does for the family of fewer persons. Of the six families of over 7 persons in Table XI, four had an outlay on food per 'man' of between 12 and 14 shillings, one—spending slightly over 50 per cent of the total income on food—of about 11 shillings 9 pence, while the family with the highest expenditure—14 shillings 7 pence—employed about 62 per cent of their total income for the purchase of food.

PART II: OUTLAY ON FOOD AND NUTRITION

1. *Total Outlay on Food in 1944 and 1945*

(*a*) Outlay per person and its relation to outlay per 'man'

It has already been shown in Part I that the average food expenditure per 'man'[1] of the families that supplied comparable budgets for 1944 and 1945, was nearly the same for both years. Indeed, as regards the families whose structure had remained *unchanged*, the figures for both years were practically identical, while a decline of three per cent occurred in the outlay on food of those families whose structure had *changed*, since 1945. 'Man,' however, is an artificial unit, and in dealing with specific data relating to two successive periods the picture is simplified if, instead, we can refer to the natural unit, 'person'. This seems permissible so long as the proportion of families whose structure underwent some fundamental change during the time considered, remains relatively small; for it makes, of course, a considerable difference to the cost of a diet of a given nutritional standard whether the person for whom it is bought is an infant or a grown-up man. Thus, the outlay on food per 'man' of the *unchanged* families was 3 per cent above that of the *changed* families, in 1945; yet their outlay per person was 7 per cent

[1] For the scale of 'man' values applied, see Table XX, *Institute of Statistics Scale*.

higher, in consequence of the higher 'man' value per person of the *unchanged* families, viz., 0·78 as compared with 0·75.

DIAGRAM B

Changes in Expenditure on Food per Person per Week of 111 Families[1]

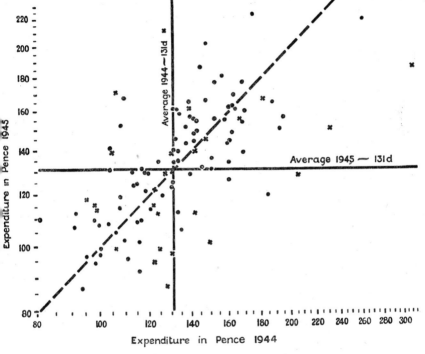

[1] Outlay in Pence: 1944 horizontal, 1945 vertical. Logarithmic scales. Dots signify *unchanged*, crosses *changed* families.

In Diagram B, we have employed different signs for the two types of families; *unchanged* families are indicated by dots, and *changed* ones by crosses. For all these 111 families—85 *unchanged* and 26 *changed*—the average weekly outlay on food per person was the same in both years, amounting to 10 shillings 11 pence.

(*b*) Changes in outlay on food and structure of family

Those families whose outlay of food remained constant, whatever its absolute figure, will be found in Diagram B along the diagonal. It will be noticed that the marks appear in a fairly dense scatter around that line, thus indicating that for the majority of the families the differences in the outlay on food, for the two periods under survey, were moderate. The Diagram also shows clearly that most of the extreme variations in the expenditure on food occurred with respect to the *changed* families, whose increase or decrease in numbers was frequently unaccompanied by proportionate changes in income. This fact stands out less in the data in Table XII, in particular as

TABLE XII

Changes in Food Expenditure since 1944

Food Expenditure 1945 per Person per Week		under 85	85–94	95–104	105–114	115–124	125 and over	Total
		Index of Food Expenditure per Person: 1944 = 100						
		Number of Families						
under 9s.	Unchanged	2	4	4	1	–	–	11
	Changed	5	1	1	–	–	–	7
9s.—10s.	Unchanged	2	1	4	3	3	1	14
	Changed	1	1	1	1	1	–	5
10s.—11s.	Unchanged	1	4	2	6	–	1	14
	Changed	1	–	2	–	–	–	3
11s.—12s.	Unchanged	2	3	4	2	–	1	12
	Changed	–	–	1	1	–	1	3
12s.—13s.	Unchanged	1	2	5	4	–	1	13
	Changed	1	1	1	–	–	–	3
13s.—14s.	Unchanged	1	2	3	2	4	–	12
	Changed	–	1	–	–	1	–	2
14s. and over	Unchanged	1	–	1	1	2	4	9
	Changed	1	–	–	–	–	2	3
Total	Unchanged	10	16	23	19	9	8	85
	Changed	9	4	6	2	2	3	26

regards increases in food expenditure, since, in order to save space, all the families showing an increase of 25 per cent and more, are summarized in one column. There were, in our sample of 111 families, two *changed* families whose weekly outlay on food per person, in 1945, was 166 and 160 per cent respectively, of that in 1944. The next two in this sequence were *unchanged* families, with and outlay on food in 1945, of 153 and 140 per cent of their outlay in 1944. Conversely, at the lower end, there were five *changed* families that in 1945 spent less than 70 per cent of their outlay on food in 1944, and only one *unchanged* family.[1]

The two bottom rows in Table XII give the numbers of families in relation to their food expenditure per person in 1945, as compared

[1] The percentage change from 1944 to 1945 is measured by the vertical distance from the diagonal in Diagram B. The percentage scale is contained in the left hand scale of the Diagram, beginning at 100.

with 1944. The distribution indicates a 'normal' pattern for the *unchanged* families. For the reasons discussed no 'normality' could be expected as regards the numbers of *changed* families

(c) Changes in outlay on food resulting from changes in supply

Expenditure on food is, of course, the more flexible, in relation to non-food expenditure, the larger the margin available for luxuries and semi-luxuries. A family whose income is too low to allow for the purchase of anything but the bare necessities, will tend to exhibit for two periods with approximately identical price level, a much more rigid pattern of expenditure than one that can exercise a certain amount of choice. The variations in the total expenditure of the latter type of family are likely to be the more erratic the less normal the conditions of supply, and semi-luxury foods—cake, the more expensive kinds of fish and vegetables, etc.—may be substituted for unobtainable non-food luxuries, or, even, necessities, or *vice versa*. We have an indication of this in the somewhat looser scatter of dots—signifying *unchanged* families, few of which seemed to have experienced substantial changes in income—in the quadrant enclosing the families with an expenditure above the average in both years, while in that referring to expenditures below the averages it was mainly changes in the structure of a family that caused substantial alterations in the outlay on food per person. If, in these cases, the addition to the family was a new-born infant, a decline in the standard of nutrition, as expressed in the outlay per person, may be more apparent than real.

2. The Pattern of Food Expenditure and Consumption

(a) Changes in relative expenditure on food groups

In Table XIII, the relative outlay on the main categories of foods is set out for the *unchanged, changed*, and *new* families. In the lower part are given the weekly expenditure on food per person and per 'man', and this is compared with the corresponding total household expenditure. The group 'bread and cereals' includes flour, cake, biscuits, ready-to-eat breakfast cereals, rolled oats, rice, semolina, macaroni, and similar products. That of 'meat and meat products' comprises butchers' meat, bacon, cooked, tinned, and potted meat, offals, sausages, and meat pies. 'Fish' refers to all kinds of fish—wet, cured, potted, fried, and tinned. 'Dairy produce' is taken to mean not only milk, cheese, butter, and eggs—dried and in shell—but also margarine; the 'fat' group therefore only represents the outlay on lard, cooking fat, dripping, and suet. Amongst 'other vegetables

TABLE XIII

Relative Expenditure on Food Groups

	Unchanged Families (85)		Changed Families (26)		New Families 44
	1944	1945	1944	1945	1945
Bread and Cereals	15·1	15·4	15·1	16·9	16·8
Fats[1]	1·1	0·6	1·1	0·5	0·7
Meat and Meat Products	21·6	19·1	22·6	20·6	19·4
Fish	4·1	5·2	5·7	5·4	3·9
Dairy Produce	21·6	20·6	21·6	21·1	20·6
Groceries	8·9	7·7	8·2	7·6	7·6
Potatoes	4·8	5·6	4·2	5·1	6·1
Other Vegetables and Fruit	9·6	13·2	8·0	10·9	10·7
Other Foods[2]	13·2	12·6	13·5	11·9	14·2
Total	100·0	100·0	100·0	100·0	100·0

Weekly Expenditure on Food and Total Expenditure

Food Expenditure:					
per Person	10/11	11/1¼	10/11½	10/4¾	10/11
per 'Man'	14/3½	14/4	14/3¾	13/11	14/2½
Total Expenditure:					
per Person	24/2½	23/11½	20/5¼	19/8	24/4½
per 'Man'	31/8½	30/9¾	26/8	26/4	31/8½

[1] Cooking fats only; butter and margarine are included under Dairy Produce.
[2] Including canteen meals, meals at school, etc.

and fruit' are included also dried legumes, tinned vegetables, and dried fruit. Sugar, tea, cocoa, jam, syrup, and honey, constitute the 'groceries' group. 'All other foods' include all meals bought away from home, besides condiments, all kinds of fancy foods, and sweets.

It will be noticed that there occurred some slight but distinct shifts in the relative outlay on some of the food groups, in the budgets of the comparable families—the *unchanged* and the *changed* ones. The most marked of these shifts is the upward movement in the outlay on other 'vegetables and fruit'. It reflects the consumption of larger quantities of relatively expensive spring vegetables and salads, and does not indicate the purchase of larger quantities of vegetables in general. Very little fresh fruit was obtainable during the period of our inquiry. Outlay on potatoes was increased because old potatoes were scarce and new potatoes were released in larger quantities in 1945 than during the slightly earlier period in 1944. The decline in the outlay on 'fats' is concomitant to the reduction in the ration of cooking fat, which ration amounted, per person per week, to one ounce, in 1945, and to two ounces, in 1944. Smaller purchases of cooked meat, rationed or points, account for the smaller share in total food expenditure of the 'meat 'group, in 1945.

(b) Consumption of the main rationed foods and of milk

Table XIV deals with the main foods—excepting the staple carbo-hydrate foods and vegetables—bought per ordinary ration book, i.e., per ration book of a person over 5 years old.[1] The list includes, besides the main rationed foods, also unrationed fats and milk, of which latter the supply is somewhat elastic in response to demand during the months of June and July.[2] Of cheese the consumption is shown after deducting all special rations allowed to heavy workers, the inclusion of which would, of course, distort the averages. Weekly milk consumption is given, first, for all milk per person, and, secondly, for Government milk and school milk only, in relation to the number of children entitled to it. Since the school milk is actually consumed at school, the averages per child for this item are more significant than those for Government milk, which is received by the families at home and may or may not go entirely to the infants entitled to it.[3]

Smaller quantities were obtained in 1945 than in 1944, of bacon, fats, jam, and some of the 'points' foods. All these changes are connected more or less directly with changes in the rations allowed per person over 5 years old. In June and July 1945, only three ounces of bacon per week could be bought instead of four in 1944, and only one ounce of cooking fat instead of two. The combined sugar and jam ration in 1945 was 12 ounces per week, sugar and jam being interchangeable weight per weight. In 1944, the ration was the same if taken up in the form of sugar, but twice the weight

[1] In both, summer 1944 and 1945, a child up to the age of five could obtain no tea and was only allowed half of the adult meat ration. On the other hand, it was entitled to a pint of Government milk a day, at 2 pence a pint, and to a special allowance of eggs.

[2] At least for those who are fortunate enough to be supplied by a retailer whose production of milk is high during this period.

[3] In analysing the data of milk consumption further, the disquieting fact emerges that while the majority of the families of our sample had a consumption in accordance with their nutritional needs and, in some instances, even well above normal requirements, a minority of families with young children was consuming decidedly too little milk. Of the 73 families of our sample with children in receipt of Government milk, 8 families, including 8 infants and 13 children of school age, had an average domestic consumption per head of fresh milk of under 3 pints per week, including the milk supplied under the Government scheme. If we omit this special milk and the infants for whom it was supplied, we find that 13 of the 73 families bought for the other members—including 17 children of school age—less than 2 pints per head per week. Two of these 13 families had no other fresh milk besides that obtained under the Government scheme. Of the remaining 82 families with no infants, two, with 5 children of school age, had a domestic milk consumption of less than 2 pints per head per week, while 18, with 38 children at school, consumed over 2 but under 3 pints per head per week. In several families, however, a low domestic consumption of milk was accom-panied by a high consumption of milk at school, the children buying at school two-thirds of a pint per day on five days a week. The figures of milk consumption of the families of our sample for 1945 are discussed in detail in the *Appendix* to Part II of this survey, in BULLETIN, Vol. 8, No. 3.

in jam. The number of 'points' available per person per week had declined from 6 to 5, which may account for the decline in the purchases of certain points foods, enumerated in Table XIV.[1]

(c) Changes in the number of 'points' and the effect on demand

The figures for cereals in Table XIV exclude rolled oats and oatmeal, and refer mainly to ready-to-eat breakfast cereals. It is interesting to find that while less of these foods were bought in 1945 more oat products were eaten, possibly because they require fewer 'points': for a lb. of oats two 'points' have to be surrendered, while twelve ounces of breakfast cereals need four. Also, rolled oats are much cheaper than the breakfast cereals, of which twelve ounces cost approximately a shilling, while a lb. of rolled oats costs $3\frac{1}{2}$ pence; but the prices for these two types of food were the same in 1944 and in 1945, and are thus unlikely to have affected the relative demand in 1945. The consumption of rolled oats is given in Table XV, together with that of other foods that bring variety into the diet, and some of which—fish other than tinned fish and cocoa—supplement the rationed foods. The quantities are shown per family per week: first, in relation to those families only that purchased the particular food and, secondly, for all the families of the groups of *unchanged, changed,* and *new* families. The number of purchasing families is expressed, for each year, as a percentage of all the families in the respective group, similar to our procedure of calculating the percentage figures in Table VII, Part I.

Unrationed fish was more plentiful in 1945 than in 1944, and more of it was bought by the *unchanged* families. Biscuits, too, were not so scarce as they had been in 1944, and, although rationed, sweet biscuits require only 4 points per lb., and the demand for them was, in general, still greater than the supply. Tinned milk—especially condensed skimmed and sweetened milk, at four 'points' a tin—could be obtained only in a few places, and was much in demand. Household milk was unrationed during the period covered by our investigation, but it was sold only in those shops that had surplus stocks left. Consumption of dried eggs had slightly declined, but of dried eggs and eggs in shell taken together, about as many were eaten in 1945 and in 1944, as is shown by the figures in Table XIV. Excluding the special allowance of dried eggs for young

[1] The other main rations per week, for a person over 5 years old, were, in June–July 1945; meat, 1 shilling 2 pence worth; tea, 2 ounces; butter (or margarine), 2 ounces; margarine, 4 ounces; cheese, 2 ounces. Supplies of eggs varied, but one-third of a packet of dried eggs—equivalent to three eggs—was available. Extra allowances of eggs were given to young children and expectant mothers, but no adjustment has been made with respect to this in calculating our figures for Table XIV.

TABLE XIV

Weekly Consumption of Foods per Adult Ration Book

	Unchanged Families (85)		Changed Families (26)		New Families (44)
	1944	1945	1944	1945	1945
Meat[1]	17d.	16¼d.	17¾d.	18d.	16¾d.
Bacon ..	3·9 oz.	2·9 oz.	3·7 oz.	2·5 oz.	2·8 oz.
Total Ration, Fats[2] ..	8·0 oz.	7·1 oz.	8·1 oz.	6·9 oz.	7·0 oz.
Butter only	*2·0 oz.*	*2·0 oz.*	*2·1 oz.*	*2·0 oz.*	*2·0 oz.*
Unrationed Fats[3] ..	0·4 oz.	0·3 oz.	0·2 oz.	0·1 oz.	0·4 oz.
Tea ..	2·1 oz.	1·9 oz.	1·9 oz.	1·8 oz.	1·8 oz.
Sugar ...	8·6 oz.	9·9 oz.	8·2 oz.	9·2 oz.	9·4 oz.
Jam[4] ..	5·5 oz.	3·7 oz.	4·8 oz.	3·4 oz.	4·2 oz.
Cheese..	2·0 oz.[5]	2·0 oz.[5]	2·0 oz.[6]	1·9 oz.[6]	1·8 oz.[7]
Eggs, shell[8] ..	1·4 eggs	1·8 eggs	1·2 eggs	1·3 eggs	1·6 eggs
Eggs, dried[9] ..	1·6 eggs	1·3 eggs	1·3 eggs	1·2 eggs	1·1 eggs
Foods Rationed on Points:					
Cooked Meat[10] ..	1·5 oz.	0·9 oz.	1·7 oz.	1·0 oz.	1·1 oz.
Tinned Meat [11] ..	¼d.	½d.	½d.	¼d.	½d.
Tinned Fish ..	¾d.	1d.	1d.	1d.	¾d.
Tinned Peas and Beans	½d.	¾d.	½d.	½d.	¾d.
Cereals[12] ..	2·7 oz.	1·8 oz.	2·6 oz.	1·5 oz.	1·7 oz.
Dried Legumes[13] ..	1·3 oz.	0·5 oz.	1·3 oz.	0·5 oz.	0·3 oz.
Dried Fruit ..	2·4 oz.	2·4 oz.	1·2 oz.	0·9 oz.	1·3 oz.
Syrup and Treacle ..	1·2 oz.	1·0 oz.	0·8 oz.	1·1 oz.	0·6 oz.
Milk Consumption per Person					
Milk, total[14] ..	5·1 pt.	4·8 pt.	4·9 pt.	4·6 pt.	4·8 pt.
Of this:					
Ordinary ..	*3·1 pt.*	*3·0 pt.*	*3·1 pt.*	*2·7 pt.*	*3·0 pt.*
Government ..	*1·1 pt.*	*0·9 pt.*	*1·1 pt.*	*1·3 pt.*	*1·0 pt.*
School ..	*0·7 pt.*	*0·7 pt.*	*0·5 pt.*	*0·5 pt.*	*0·6 pt.*
Tinned[15] and Household	*0·2 pt.*	*0·2 pt.*	*0·2 pt.*	*0·1 pt.*	*0·2 pt.*
Consumption of School and Government Milk per Child per Week					
Children under 6 ..	7·0 pt.	7·0 pt.	7·0 pt.	7·0 pt.	7·0 pt.
Child 6—14 ..	2·5 pt.	2·4 pt.	1·8 pt.	1·8 pt.	2·0 pt.

[1] Including offals, but excluding cooked and tinned meat products, and sausages.
[2] Butter, margarine, lard, and cooking fat.   [3] Suet and dripping.
[4] Including honey and marmalade.   [5] Excluding 6 special rations.
[6] Excluding 3 special rations.   [7] Excluding 4 special rations.
[8] The figures refer to consumption per person. No correction has been made for special allowances for children and expectant mothers. The following numbers of eggs from own hens are included: *Unchanged* families, 1944—0·3; 1945—0·6; *changed* families, 1944—0·03; 1945—0·08; *new* families, 1945—0·5.
[9] One packet of dried eggs equivalent to 12 eggs in shell.
[10] Including small quantities of unrationed cooked meat.
[11] This group overlaps the preceding one. It also includes tinned mixtures of meat and vegetables.
[12] Excluding rolled oats, but including small quantities of unrationed macaroni and semolina. Mainly ready-to-eat breakfast cereals.
[13] Beans, peas, lentils.
[14] The figures in this section show the total quantities of milk obtained per week divided by the total number of persons in the group.
[15] Rationed on points. The combined figures for tinned and Household milk are given in terms of fresh milk.

S

children, the potential consumption of dried eggs per family per week would have been, in 1944, for the *unchanged* families 12·3 and for the *changed* families 16·9 eggs, and, in 1945, for the *unchanged* families 12·3, for the *changed* families 17·1, and for the *new* ones 14·6 eggs. For the latter year, therefore, the actual consumption of dried eggs by the 155 families of our sample amounted to less than 40 per cent of the potential consumption.[1] Purchases of cooked meat, which is dear in 'points', costing a 'point' per ounce, were considerably lower, owing not only to a reduction in the numbers of families buying it, but also to smaller purchases per family.

Dried legumes, which are also rationed on 'points', were apparently partly replaced by fresh peas, which were bought by most of the families.

(*d*) The main unrationed foods

The weekly outlay on vegetables, per 'man' and per person, is given in Table XVI. This Table also summarizes the consumption of the main carbohydrate foods and of the two main unrationed sources of first class protein, viz., fish and sausages. Consumption of both these latter items was higher in 1945 than in 1944, and there was probably still a substantial margin of potential demand that remained unsatisfied because of the limited supply of these foods. Consumption of bread had remained about constant, but fewer potatoes, were bought. This was to be expected, since the potatoes eaten in June–July 1945, were mostly new ones, which have a small amount of wastage, while in 1944 the families bought mainly old potatoes, of which in early summer a large portion has to be discarded in trimmings and peelings. Less flour was purchased in 1945 than in 1944, possibly because the smaller fat ration curtailed home baking and made people resort more to bought substitutes for home-made tea fare.

(*e*) Meals away from home

The numbers of luncheons and dinners bought away from home per person over 14 years old and per child, are given in Table XVII. It will be seen that the *unchanged* families—the most significant group for this item—show a decline in the number of meals for adult and an increase in that of children's meals. It is, of course, not possible to generalize from the data obtained for 85 families; if however, they indicate typical trends it seems to imply that while the habit of school meals is spreading adult people tend to get some-

[1] Since then, the supply was first halved, i.e., reduced to one packet per person every eight weeks, and since February 4, 1946, it has been discontinued.

TABLE XV

Distribution Pattern of Purchases of Certain Foods

	No. of Purchasing Families per cent of Group						*Purchasing Families: Consumption per Family per Week*					*All Families: Consumption per Family per Week*				
	Unchanged (85 Fam.)		*Changed (26 Fam.)*		*New (44 Fam.)*	*Unit*	*Unchanged*		*Changed*		*New*	*Unchanged (85 Fam.)*		*Changed (26 Fam.)*		*New (44 Fam.)*
	1944	1945	1944	1945	1945		1944	1945	1944	1945	1945	1944	1945	1944	1945	1945
Fish (*excl. tinned*) ..	77	80	85	89	84	oz.	25·4	32·1	41·8	35·3	25·6	19·4	25·7	35·4	31·2	21·5
Fish, tinned	44	46	58	50	36	*d*	7½	9½	10¼	11½	10	3¼	4¼	6	5¾	3½
Meat, cooked ..	71	54	81	65	55	oz.	8·7	6·6	11·5	8·7	10·0	6·1	3·6	9·3	5·7	5·5
Meat, tinned	14	12	39	8	18	*d*	7¼	14½	8¾	10	15¼	1	1¾	3¼	¾	2¾
Eggs, dried[1]	66	55	54	54	50	egg[3]	9·9	9·3	13·7	12·9	10·4	6·5	5·2	7·4	6·9	5·2
Milk, tinned	32	19	19	15	27	tin	0·7	1·3	0·7	1·1	1·1	0·2	0·2	0·1	0·2	0·3
Milk, Household[2] ..	13	12	19	15	5	pint[3]	3·1	2·0	3·6	2·5	3·0	0·4	0·2	0·7	0·4	0·1
Dried Legumes ..	40	14	39	19	11	oz.	13·3	14·7	19·2	15·2	14·4	5·3	2·1	7·4	2·9	1·6
Rolled Oats	12	24	27	19	23	oz.	20·8	22·7	17·1	26·4	27·2	2·5	5·3	4·6	5·1	6·2
Biscuits	64	81	81	85	66	oz.	9·2	10·6	13·6	15·1	14·4	5·8	8·6	11·0	12·8	9·5
Cocoa	27	26	58	19	21	oz.	3·7	4·5	4·4	6·4	5·6	1·0	1·2	2·5	1·2	1·1
Dried Fruit	72	67	58	39	57	oz.	13·8	14·8	11·9	13·2	11·4	9·9	9·9	6·9	5·1	6·5
Syrup	34	25	27	39	16	oz.	14·9	16·4	16·0	18·6	18·3	5·1	4·1	4·3	6·5	2·9

[1] One packet equals 12 eggs in shell. [2] One tin equals 4 pints of skimmed fresh milk. [3] Equivalent.

what tired of canteen food and prefer having their main meal a
home, when conditions allow them to do so.

(*f*) Outlay on rationed and unrationed foods

An outline of the weekly expenditure per 'man' on rationed anc
unrationed foods will be found in Table XVIII. The correspondenc
of the outlay on the several food categories by the different groups o
families is striking. The reduction in the purchase of bacon, cookin
fat, and jam, shown in Table XIV in their quantitative aspects, ar
reflected in the decrease in outlay, from 1944 to 1945, on grou
(1) in Table XVIII. The smaller number of 'points' available in 194
lead to a smaller outlay on group (2). Less on the average was als
spent on milk, in summer 1945 than in summer 1944; but for thi
item the decline was small. In spite of the difference in the averag
price of potatoes bought during the periods of our survey in 194
and 1945—1½ pence a lb. in 1944, and 2¼ pence in 1945[1]—the change
in outlay on group (4) were slight. Outlay on potatoes alone ros
by approximately 18 per cent, but it represents only about 40 pe
cent of the total outlay on group (4), and there was a fall in th
outlay on flour, owing to the purchase of smaller quantities, whil
that on bread had remained practically constant. In Table XVIII
again, the increase in expenditure on vegetables stands out.

TABLE XVI

Weekly Consumption of the Main Carbohydrate Foods and of Fish, Sausages, and Fresh Fruit an
Vegetables

	85 Unchanged Families				26 Changed Families				44 New Families	
	per Person		per 'Man'		per Person		per 'Man'		per Person	per 'Man'
	1944	1945	1944	1945	1944	1945	1944	1945	1945	1945
	oz.	oz.	oz.	oz.	oz.	oz.	oz.	oz.	oz.	oz.
Bread	63·6	63·9	83·3	82·1	66·5	66·0	86·8	88·3	68·5	89·1
Flour	9·5	6·9	12·5	8·9	7·9	5·2	10·3	6·9	5·1	6·6
Cake, Buns, Biscuits	8·9	10·2	11·6	13·1	8·5	10·3	11·1	13·8	10·1	13·1
Potatoes, old ..	55·4	11·8	72·5	15·2	52·5	10·1	68·6	13·5	23·9	31·1
Potatoes, new ..	11·6	36·9	15·2	47·4	7·8	37·2	10·2	49·8	35·5	46·0
Rolled Oats	0·6	1·3	0·8	1·7	0·8	0·9	1·1	1·2	1·3	1·6
Fish	4·7	6·3	6·2	8·0	6·3	5·5	8·2	7·4	4·4	5·7
Sausages	3·5	3·7	4·6	4·8	3·4	4·1	4·5	5·5	3·1	4·0
	d.	d.	d.	d.	d.	d.	d.	d.	d.	d.
Outlay on Fresh Vegetables and Fruit (*excl. potatoes*)	10	15¼	13	19¾	8¾	12¼	11½	16¼	12½	16¼

[1] These are the weighted averages for old and new potatoes taken together. Old potatoe
cost about a penny a lb. in both years, but new potatoes were 3¾ pence a lb. in 1944, and 2
pence in 1945.

TABLE XVII

Luncheons and Dinners away from Home

Group of Families	*No. of Meals per Week* per Adult	per Child bought	per Child free	*Average Price per Meal Bought* Adult d.	Child d.
Unchanged					
1944 ..	0·99	1·20	0·16	12¼	5
1945 ..	0·77	1·45	0·17	12¾	5¼
Changed					
1944 ..	0·83	1·71	0·08	15	4¾
1945 ..	0·87	1·34	—	14¼	5
New					
1945 ..	1·17	0·96	0·21	14¼	4¾

TABLE XVIII

Expenditure on Rationed and Unrationed Foods Per 'Man' per Week

	Unchanged Families 1944	*Unchanged Families* 1945	*Changed Families* 1944	*Changed Families* 1945	*New Families* 1945
) Specifically Rationed Foods[1]	4/10½	4/4½	4/10	4/5¼	4/4
) 'Points' Rationed Foods ..	1/1¼	1/–	1/2	–/10¾	–/11½
) All Milk[2]	1/11¼	1/9¾	1/11	1/9½	1/10¼
) Bread, Flour, Potatoes ..	1/11	1/11½	1/9¾	1/10¾	2/1
) Fresh Vegetables and Fruit ..	1/1	1/7¾	–/11½	1/4¼	1/4¼
) Other Foods[3]	3/4½	3/6½	3/7½	3/6½	3/7½
Total(1)—(6)	14/3½	14/4	14/3¾	13/11	14/2½

[1] Including all meat offals.
[2] Including dried Household milk and tinned milk, the former actually belonging, in 44, to group (1) and the latter, in both years, to group (2)..
[3] Including wet fish, kippers, and fried fish, sausages, cake and buns, cocoa, unrationed ts, meals bought away from home.

. *Changes in Nutritional Intake*

(*a*) The standards applied

That the decline in purchases of the foods in groups (1), (2), and)—a decline brought about either by direct changes in rationing r, as regards milk, by a reduced supply of the 'free' market—had me effect on the average nutritional intake, is borne out by the gures in Table XIX. This Table shows the intake of calories and rotein per 'man' per day, calculated, first, by means of the scales sed by us since the beginning of this survey, in 1940, and, secondly, y those supplied to us in 1943 by the Ministry of Health. Both ese sets of scales comprise 'man' values and nutritional values of ods. The scale of war-time food values evolved by the Ministry f Health has now been superseded by a set of Tables published by e Medical Research Council,[1] but, except for very detailed calcu-

[1] War Memorandum No. 14 (H.M. Stationery Office).

TABLE XIX

Nutritional Intake per 'Man' per Day

			Institute Scale (Gross Values)			Ministry of Health Scale (Net Values)		
			Calories	Protein (grammes)		Calories	Protein (grammes)	
Average Requirements:			3,300	100		3,000	70	
Intake:				Total	Animal		Total	Animal
Unchanged Families {	1944	..	3,700	117	55	3,400	95	43
	1945	..	3,400	110	53	3,200	89	41
Changed Families {	1944	..	3,600	118	57	3,300	91	42
	1945	..	3,300	110	53	3,100	85	39
New Families	1945	..	3,400	110	52	3,100	87	40

lations, the older scale is sufficiently precise, and in order to preserv
the continuity of our series we abide by the Ministry of Healt
scale. The 'man' values referring to that scale will be found i
Table XX, together with the 'man' values of the Institute of Statistic
scale. These latter values have been employed by us throughou
this paper for evaluating the relative cost of maintenance withi
the family of a person of a given age and sex group; the Ministry o
Health scale has been used only, beside our own scale, for calculatin
the average nutritional intake, for which it provides a gauge mor

TABLE XX

Scales of 'Man' Values

Institute of Statistics Scale				Ministry of Health Scale		
					Calories	Protein
Adults and Juveniles:				*Age Groups*:		
Male, 14+	..	..	1·00	21+, male	1·00	1·00
Female, 14+	..	..	0·85	21+, female	0·83	0·86
				17—21	1·00	1·29
Children:				15—14	1·00	1·43
10—14	..	..	0·70	12—15	0·97	1·36
6—9	..	..	0·60	7—12	0·70	0·93
3—5	..	..	0·50	3—7	0·50	0·71
under 3	..	..	0·33	1—3	0·37	0·60
				6—12 months	0·27	0·33
				0—6 months	0·20	0·26

precise than our scale. It should be noticed that the figures of nutri
tional intake in Table XIX refer to *gross* requirements and *gros*
intake with respect to the Institute of Statistics scale, while th
figures relating to the Ministry of Health scale give *net* values.

(*b*) Significance of the changes

The decline in calorific intake and in the intake of second-cla
protein revealed by the figures in Table XIX is of minor importanc
In part it is only apparent, reflecting the smaller quantities of—
mainly new—potatoes purchased in 1945, of which, howeve

probably much less was wasted than of the potatoes bought during our survey in 1944, which were mostly old ones. In any case, so long as bread and flour are unrationed and cheap, no real shortage in calories can occur, while a shortage of second-class protein is, at least, very unlikely. But there were small yet significant reductions in the intake of animal protein, although its average supply was still ample for a satisfactory nutrition.

It certainly was by no means impossible to feed a family in a satisfactory way on a small outlay, in summer 1945. Indeed, differences in the expenditure on food per 'man', unless they are either very substantial or else result from expenditure on good canteen meals, may make very little difference to the intake of first-class protein, so long as the main sources of first-class protein are rationed and fresh herrings about as plentiful as the more expensive kinds of unrationed fish.[1] Still, the reduction, from 1944 to 1945, of the bacon ration and the reduction in the number of 'points' with which first-class protein foods might be bought, is likely to have widened the margin of potential malnutrition, for families and for individuals within the families. For apart from the direct curtailment of these foods, the duller the menu the greater the likelihood that it will be rejected in part by members of the family, so that a dietary which gives satisfactory figures of nutritional intake on the average may yet result in practice in unsatisfactory nutrition. Moreover, the smaller the total amount of such first-class protein foods as meat, cheese, and also, eggs in shell, available to a family, the greater the danger that the lion's share of these 'tasty' foods will go to the adult male earners, while—partly from necessity and partly from choice—the housewife and the junior members will subsist largely on starchy and sugary foods. From 1943 to 1944, our surveys had suggested an upward trend in the intake of animal protein, although the absolute figures obtained by us for the whole sample in 1944 were slightly below those given in Table XIX, owing to slight differences in the structure of the samples for the two years.

---

[1] The amount of animal protein available in a family per 'man' is, under conditions of rationing and generally restricted supply, affected mainly by three factors: the housewife's skill of catering, the family's taste, and the structure of the family. In order to see the importance of this last point it must be remembered that a new-born child is entitled to the same food rations as an adult man, with the exception of half of the meat ration, which reduction, however, is much more than counterbalanced by the special allowance of milk and eggs to infants. A family with several young children is therefore able to obtain a considerably larger amount of animal protein per 'man' than a family that has no young children.

CONCLUSION

In summarizing this survey the following main results of our analysis emerge:

In our sample for 1944, some indication was shown of a rise in individual earnings since 1943, but no increase was evident in comparing the figures at our disposal for both 1944 and 1945. Total household expenditure, too, showed very little change, and average expenditure on food had also remained practically constant. Further, average outlay on 'miscellaneous' items purchased out of housekeeping money was nearly identical for both years, for the two groups that allowed of a direct comparison of the household accounts for 1944 and 1945. The most marked variations occurred in the average outlay on clothing and on fuel and light; but the absolute figures involved were fairly small, and we are in no position to offer a satisfactory explanation as to what caused these changes. As regards the outlay on clothing disbursed by the housewife, it may have been merely accidental fluctuations, while the figures for fuel and light point to a reduction in the purchases of coal, which may have been due to the supply position prevailing during our period of sampling. A number of families profited by the more normal conditions in summer 1945, as compared with summer 1944, by finding cheaper housing accommodation. These differences in the cost of housing, for the group of *changed* families, are the only reflex thrown by the changes in the general situation from summer 1944 to summer 1945, on the general structure of the household accounts for the two years.

The standard of nutrition in 1944 was about maintained, though a slight downward trend in the average intake of animal protein was indicated, mainly, it seemed, as a result of slight reductions in the food rations in summer 1945, as compared with summer 1944.

PROPER NUTRITION AT LOW COST

by T. Schulz

FROM BULLETIN, VOL. 7, No. 17 (DEC. 15, 1945)

Introduction[1]

WHEN, after the outbreak of the War, supplies of food were restricted and their distribution controlled by means of rationing, it became evident that changes in the total cost of food of a family were no longer revealed by the Ministry of Labour Cost of Living Index, which, indeed, had already been out of date before the war. The range of foods included in that Index is small, and essential items, such as fruit and vegetables other than potatoes, are altogether omitted. Moreover, it was now no longer consumers' choice that regulated the relative demand for the several foods but the policy of the Government and the general flow of supply under a system of rapidly expanding price control. The rations allowed of individual foods were adjusted from time to time, and it became necessary sometimes to substitute one food for another. Thus, the total cost of food was affected according to whether the rations of relatively cheaper or of dearer foods had been increased or diminished, although no change might have occurred in the actual prices. Luxury foods largely disappeared out of the sight of the ordinary shopper, but the same phenomenon could be observed with respect to the cheapest foods that before the war formed part of the staple diet of poor families. Prices, in general, settled down close to the controlled maximum prices. All these influences together produced a tendency for the cost of food to decline—as compared with its pre-war cost—in the case of families with a pre-war expenditure on food well above the general average, and to rise in that of families whose expenditure had been well below it.

This latter point was of considerable practical importance; for a just distribution of food under conditions of scarcity is attainable only if everybody has the means of buying what he is permitted to buy. The problem, therefore, arose: what is the minimum cost of a satisfactory diet, and how does this cost respond to inevitable changes in supply?

[1] This Introduction was not included in the original article.

In the Spring of 1941 we made an attempt to supply an answer to this question. Our task was simplified by the fact that rationing as well as price control were instituted on a national basis: rations were the same everywhere and prices very nearly the same. We thus compiled a 'human needs' diet that could be purchased by a housewife in Oxford, on the assumption that, at about the same cost, a diet of similar nutritional value would be obtainable in all parts of the country, although its composition might reflect local supply conditions and feeding habits. Our starting point was the 'human needs' diet for a family consisting of husband, wife, and three children, set out by Mr. S. Rowntree in the revised edition of his book, *The Human Needs of Labour*. This edition was published in 1936, and researches into nutritional requirements had since made some progress. It therefore seemed necessary to us to allow for a larger consumption of milk in a 'human needs' diet, and, further, to suggest the use of fresh full cream milk instead of skimmed tinned milk, which latter had, in any case, become very scarce by that time. Other alterations in the pre-war diet were necessary so as to take account of the introduction of rationing and of the general scarcity of many foodstuffs. The minimum cost per week of a diet for a family of five persons was then found to be 33 shillings, in March–April, 1941. This was 27 per cent above the cost of a diet of similar nutritional value in August, 1939.[1] During the same period, the Ministry of Labour Index of food had risen by 23 per cent.

The movements in the cost of a 'human needs' diet since April, 1941, as calculated by us every six months, and the corresponding changes in the Ministry of Labour Index of food are given in Table A. It will be seen that apart from seasonal fluctuations, owing to the fluctuations in the prices of vegetables other than potatoes, the cost of the 'human needs' diet indicated a steadily upward trend until April, 1944. Since then it has settled down at nearly 10 per cent above its cost in April, 1941, or 39 per cent above its pre-war figure. During the same period the Ministry of Labour Index has shown, first, a decided downward swing, and then, since November, 1943, a tendency to get stabilized at its value in April, 1941, that is, at 23 per cent above its pre-war value.

[1] This estimate is based on the cost of the minimum diet for a male adult as suggested by the B.M.A. in 1933, adjusted for changes in the cost of food from 1933 to August, 1939, according to the Ministry of Labour Index. In 1933, the diet per adult male would have cost 5s. 11d. per week, and in August, 1939, approximately 6s. 11d., or, for a family of 3·75 'men' —the standard family assumed by Mr. S. Rowntree—just under 26s.

TABLE A

COST OF A 'HUMAN NEEDS' DIET AND MINISTRY OF LABOUR COST OF FOOD INDEX

(1) *Weekly Cost of a 'Human Needs' Diet for 5 Persons*

	1941 s. d.	1942 s. d.	1943 s. d.	1944 s. d.	1945 s. d.
April	33 0	34 0	34 11¾	37 1¼	36 1½
November	32 10¾	33 2¾	35 6¾	36 4¼	36 1½

(2) *Index of Cost of 'Human Needs' Diet (April, 1941 = 100)*

	1941	1942	1943	1944	1945
April	100	103	106	112	109
November	100	101	108	110	109

(3) *Ministry of Labour Cost of Food Index (April, 1941 = 100)*

	1941	1942	1943	1944	1945
April 1st	100	94	97	99	99
November 1st	97	96	99	99	100

The following article, which is reprinted from the Bulletin, Vol. 7, No. 17, deals with our survey in November, 1945.

Our tenth half-yearly survey of the cost of a 'human needs' diet in Oxford was undertaken in November, 1945. We have again calculated the weekly cost of an inexpensive diet of reasonable variety for a family consisting of husband, wife, one child between 5 and 7, and two children between 7 and 12 years old. Thus, all three children would be entitled to milk at school, at a halfpenny for a third of a pint, but the family would not receive any cheap milk at home under the Government scheme.

From April, 1945, to November, 1945, the Ministry of Labour Index of the cost of food had risen by 0·6 per cent, owing to the rise in the price of potatoes. Nevertheless, the cost of our 'human needs' diet (diet A) has remained constant at 36s. 1½d. per week for the family of five persons, for the increase in the price of potatoes was more than counterbalanced by the seasonal fall in the prices of other vegetables, which are not included in the Ministry of Labour Index. Indeed, were it not for changes in the outlay on other foods, there would be a reduction of 6½ pence, exactly as much as the rise in the cost of potatoes. It will, however, be seen from Table I that this surplus is absorbed.

In calculating the outlay on diet A we have assumed a few items to be purchased in quantities larger than those shown in our diet schedule and carried over two or more weeks; this applies to jam, syrup, haricot beans, and household milk. We do not, however, suggest that potatoes and flour should be bought in bulk, although that would reduce their average prices, since a family with a small weekly income may not be able to do this and, moreover, may lack the necessary storage facilities.

Between April and November, the rations of bacon and cheese were altered, that of bacon being reduced from 4 to 3 oz.[1] and that of cheese being increased from 2 to 3 oz.[2] per person per week. Household milk, which in April, 1945, was no longer issued under the rationing scheme but could be bought freely in Oxford, since substantial stocks were left in the hands of the retailers, was again rationed in November, at a tin—equal to 4 pints of skimmed liquid milk—per ration book every eight weeks. Thus, a family of five persons was able to obtain per week the equivalent of $2\frac{1}{2}$ pints of skimmed milk in November, while in April we had allowed 4 pints of it in the weekly diet. Tinned herrings and pilchards were no longer plentiful and could be found only in some shops. We therefore omitted this item from our basic diet A and suggested instead the addition of 2 lb. of fresh herrings, 8 oz. of pork sausage meat—the cheaper beef sausage meat being almost unobtainable—and 4 oz. of haricot beans. Apples are in season in November, and we included in diet A 8 oz. of cooking apples and an additional 4 oz. of dried fruit, thus raising the total amount of dried fruit to 12 oz., instead of improving the winter diet by 1 lb. of cooking apples, as we suggested in November, 1944. Cooking apples seem to be consumed mostly stewed with a little sugar, and only occasionally to be made up into dumplings or steamed pudding, or even apple tart. Yet it is essential that a sufficiency of calorific food should be offered to the children in an appetizing form, and puddings made with dried fruit are a good way of doing this.

The price of bacon rashers underwent no change from April to November, but cheap rashers at 1s. 6d. a lb were only occasionally to be had, and we therefore raised the price per lb. in diet A to 1s. 9d. in November. The familiar brands of cocoa sold everywhere at $9\frac{1}{2}d.$ for $\frac{1}{2}$ lb., and in many shops no other cocoa was to be had, although in the centre of the town and in two outlying districts cocoa, which made an excellent beverage, was on sale at 1s. 2d. and 1s. 4d. a lb. In general the impression was gained that as a result of the relative shortage of goods housewives give preference to the higher priced foods, many being firmly convinced that a higher price always implies higher nutritional value. This attitude becomes especially obvious as regards the purchase of meat. To this point we shall return further below.

In some places cabbage was only sold at the maximum price of 3d. a lb. In these instances the proportion of wastage was small, and since

---

[1] From May 27th.   [2] From November 11th.

TABLE I

WEEKLY 'HUMAN NEEDS' DIET FOR A FAMILY OF 5 PERSONS

Diet A		Quantity	Price p Unit[1]		Changes since April, 1945 Quantity	'Outlay'	
			s.	d.		s.	d.
(a) Rationed Foods:	1. Meat	7 lb.		10[2]	..	..	
	2. Bacon	15 oz.	1	9[3]	− 5 oz. −		2¾
	3. Margarine	1 lb. 14 oz.		9	..	..	
	4. Lard	10 oz.		9	..	..	
	5. Sugar	3 lb. 8 oz.		4	..	..	
	6a. Jam	4 oz.	1	0	..	..	
	6b. Syrup	1 lb.		8[4]	..	..	
	7. Tea	8 oz.	2	8	..	..	
	8. Cheese	15 oz.	1	1	+ 5 oz. +		4
	9a. Eggs, shell	1 egg		2	..	..	
	9b. Eggs, dried	1¼ pkt.[5]	1	3	..	..	
	10. Herrings, tinned	..		10	−2 tins[10]	−1	8
	11a. Lentils and Peas, split	1 lb.		5	..	..	
	11b. Haricot Beans	1 lb. 4 oz.		6	+ 4 oz. +		1½
	12. Rolled Oats	2 lb. 8 oz.		3½	..	..	
	13. Dried Fruit[6]	12 oz.		9	+ 4 oz. +		2¼
	14. Household Milk	⅝ tin[7]		9	− ⅜ tin −		3¼
	Outlay on Group (a)		18	4¼		− 1	6¼
(b) Liquid Milk:	15a. Ordinary	14 pt.		4½	..	..	
	15b. School	5 pt.		1½	..	..	
	Outlay on Group (b)		5	10½	..	..	
(c) Unrationed Main Carbohydrate Foods:							
	16. Bread	18 lb.		2¼	..	..	
	17. Flour	3 lb.		3	.. +		0½
	18. Potatoes	21 lb.		1[8]	.. +		6
	Outlay on Group (c)		6	1½		+	6½
(d) Vegetables (*exclusive Potatoes*):							
	19a. Swedes	3 lb. 8 oz.		1¼	.. } −		2½
	19b. Carrots	3 lb. 8 oz.		1½	.. }		
	19c. Cabbage	7 lb.		2½	.. −		10½
	Outlay on Group (d)		2	3¼		− 1	1
(e) Other Foods:	20a. Macaroni	8 oz.		7½	..	..	
	20b. Semolina	1 lb. 8 oz.		4	..	..	
	21. Cocoa	4 oz.	1	7[9]	.. +		1¼
	22. Condiments	..		4	..	..	
	23. Cooking Apples	8 oz.		6	+ 8 oz. +		3
	24. Herrings, fresh	2 lb.		7	+ 2 lb. +	1	2
	25. Pork Sausage Meat	8 oz.	1	1	+ 8 oz. +		6½
	Outlay on Group (e)		3	6		+ 2	0¾
	Total Outlay on Diet A		36	1½			

[1] Eggs, in shell, price per egg; dried eggs, price per packet; tinned fish, price per tin; household milk, price per tin; other milk, price per pint; condiments, total outlay; all other

the nutritional values given in Table IV assume it to be 30 per cent of the total we felt justified in including in diet A 7 lb. at the cheaper price at $2\frac{1}{2}d$. a lb., which could be replaced by 5·8 lb. at $3d$. a lb. with only 16 per cent wastage.

Diet A assumes that all the family's rations are bought, excepting only $4\frac{1}{2}$ oz. of tea. Margarine is substituted for butter, and $2\frac{3}{4}$ of the 'points' remain unused. The total expenditure of 'points' in diet A will be found in Table II. The number of 'points' available per week

TABLE II

FOODS RATIONED ON 'POINTS' IN 'HUMAN NEEDS' DIET A

	Quantity	Points
Syrup	1 lb.	8
Lentils and Peas	1 lb.	2
Haricot Beans	1 lb. 4 oz.	$1\frac{1}{4}$
Rolled Oats	2 lb. 8 oz.	5
Dried Fruit	12 oz.	6
Total Points used		$22\frac{1}{4}$
Total Points available		25
Points left over		$2\frac{3}{4}$

had fallen from 6 to 5 per person, since May 27. In April, 24 'points' would have been needed for diet A, which included 2 tins of herrings, at 2 'points' a tin. In November, the herrings are omitted, but $2\frac{1}{4}$ 'points' would be required for the additional purchases of 4 oz. of dried fruit and 4 oz. of haricot beans. Few housewives, however, would like to forgo the use of some of the 'points'; besides, most housewives, irrespective of their housekeeping money per head, are strongly disinclined to buy meat at as low a price as $10d$. a lb. on the average, and additional 'points' foods may help to compensate for the smaller quantity of meat thus obtained per ration.[1]

We have therefore suggested in Table III two modifications of diet A, calling these diet B and diet C. Both these diets utilize all the 'points' available to the family. From diet A is deducted 1 lb. 3 oz. of meat, so that the average price of meat is raised from $10d$. to a shilling a lb. The total outlay on it remains the same. We have further reduced diet A by 4 oz. of haricot beans, assuming that they would have been used with cheap stewing meat. In both diet B and

foods, price per lb.   [2] Average price.   [3] In April, 1945, rashers of American bacon could be bought at 1s. 6d. per lb.   [4] Bought in 2 lb. container.   [5] One packet equivalent to 12 shell eggs.   [6] Seedless raisins, sultanas, stoned dates.   [7] One tin equivalent to 4 pints of liquid skimmed milk.   [8] 8d. for 7 lb.   [9] Bought in $\frac{1}{2}$ lb. tin. In April, 1945, the price of the cheapest cocoa that was generally available was 1s. 2d. a lb.   [10] One tin containing 15 oz.
[1] 1s. 2d. worth per week.

TABLE III

WEEKLY LOW COST DIETS FOR A FAMILY OF FIVE PERSONS

	Diets B and C Quantity	Outlay	'Points' Value
		s. d.	
Diet A		36 1½	22¼
Excluding:			
Meat	1 lb. 3 oz.	. .[1]	. .
Haricot Beans	4 oz.	1½	¼
(—)		1½	¼
(1) *Including* (*Diet B*):			
Pilchards, plain	1 tin	9	3
Bread	9 oz.	1¼	. .
(+)		10¼	3
Total Outlay on Diet B		36 10¼	25
(2) *Including* (*Diet C*):			
Kippers	1 lb.	10	. .
Biscuits, sweet	12 oz.	9	3
(+)		1 7	3
Total Outlay on Diet C		37 7	25

[1] No change in outlay: average cost of meat raised from 10*d.* to 1*s.* a lb.

diet C, the loss of meat is made good by fish, in the former by a tin of pilchards and in the latter by a lb. of kippers. Additional calories are obtained in diet B from 9 oz. of bread and in diet C from 12 oz. of sweet biscuits. These latter may be considered a reasonable luxury for a family with young children. If, instead, bread were eaten, diet C would cost about 1½*d.* more than diet B; but in that case the family would only spend 22 instead of 25 'points' per week. Biscuits were still scarce in Oxford, and people queued for them. Quite good ones could be bought at 10*d.* a lb. in all parts of the town, although not in all shops selling biscuits. Nevertheless, a housewife wanting biscuits rarely inquires after the price but rather considers the length of the queue and the time at her disposal. We have therefore assumed that she will have to pay on the average a shilling for a lb.

In general it was again possible for a particularly careful shopper to save a few pence on any of the three diets. Some housewives could obtain bacon at a lower price, and some could buy 2 lb. of good plum jam at 1*s.* 10½*d.* But for these foods the housewife is tied to the retailer with whom she has registered. Foods that are rationed on 'points' may, however, be bought from any grocery shop. Of these foods, rolled oats could be found at 3*d*. a lb., haricot beans at 5*d*. a lb., and sultanas and stoned dates at 7½*d*. a lb.

Since our last survey in April a *Memorandum* on 'Nutritive Values of War-time Foods' has been published as a White Paper.[1] For the present article we have made use of this publication, in lieu of the provisional data of war-time food values that we obtained from the Ministry of Health. The figures underlying our main calculations of nutritional intake in this article are set out in Table IV. It shows the net values per unit as purchased, that is, the gross values of nutriment contained in any food item *minus* the average proportion of wastage, as given in the last column of Table IV. Protein is measured in grammes; calcium, iron, and vitamin C in milligrammes; vitamin B_1 in microgrammes;[2] vitamin A in International Units. In order to obtain the approximate total of vitamin A potency of a diet, the *Memorandum* suggests that the figures calculated for carotene (marked (*c*) in Table IV) should be divided by 3 before adding them to the values of pre-formed vitamin A, 'but it is stressed that this procedure is provisional and subject to revision'.[3] A deduction of 15 per cent of the total content of vitamin B_1 of a diet is considered necessary so as to allow for losses of this vitamin through cooking. 'For vitamin C, the percentage loss during . . . domestic cooking may be taken as 75 for green vegetables and 50 for other vegetables, but with modern 'conservative' cooking it will be less'.[4] None of these corrections for vitamin potency are included in Table IV; the adjustments there only allow for the presence of inedible matter in the particular food. We have, however, made all the suggested deductions for vitamins in calculating the data for Tables VII, VIII, and IX.

The nutritional values given for meat in Table IV call for a brief explanation. They are somewhat vague approximations, made on the assumption that the housewife buys meat of a rather poor quality—not necessarily the result of buying 'cheap' meat.[5] Indeed, if she purchased all her meat ration in the form of imported breast of mutton, at 4*d*. a lb., she would obtain two and a half times as much in quantity, while the increase in nutrients derived from meat would be as follows: calories 3·9 times; protein 2·1 times; calcium 3·8 times; iron 1·8 times; vitamin A 2·5 times; vitamin B_1 4·9 times. On the

---

[1] Medical Research Council War Memorandum, No. 14 (H.M. Stationery Office).
[2] A millionth part of a gramme.   [3] Op. cit., p. 4.   [4] Ibid., p. 5.
[5] The average values per oz. in the *Memorandum* for all cuts of meat are: beef, 66 calories, protein 4 gm, calcium 3 mgm, iron 1 mgm, vitamin A 12 I.U., vitamin B_1 12 microgm; mutton and lamb, 73 calories, protein 3·4 gm, calcium 3 mgm, iron 0·5 mgm, vitamin A 12 I.U., vitamin B_1 39 microgm.

TABLE IV

NUTRITIVE VALUES OF FOODS

Net Values per Unit as Purchased

	Unit	Calories	Protein gm.	Calcium mgm.	Iron mgm.	Vitamin A I.U.[4]	Vitamin B₁ micro. gm.	Vitamin C mgm.	Deductions made for Non-Edible Portion
Meat[1][2]	oz.	60	3·4	2·0	0·7	12	20	—	—[6]
Bacon, streaky	oz.	129	2·2	3·0	0·3	—	110	—	9%
Margarine	oz.	218	—	1·0	0·1	568	—	—	—
Lard	oz.	253	—	—	—	—	—	—	—
Sugar	oz.	108	—	—	—	—	—	—	—
Jam	oz.	71	0·1	3·0	—	6 (c)	1	0·6	—
Syrup	oz.	81	0·1	7·0	0·4	—	—	—	—
Cheese	oz.	117	7·1	230·0	0·2	369	9	—	—
Eggs, shell	egg	78	6·2	30·0	1·3	500	74	—	12%
Eggs, dried	egg	68	5·4	25·8	1·3	355	48	—	—
Herrings, tinned	oz.	55	6·0	28·0	0·4	9	—	—	—
Lentils and Peas[1]	oz.	83	6·7	12·3	1·7	43 (c)	128	—	—
Haricot Beans	oz.	71	6·1	51·0	1·9	—	128	—	—
Rolled Oats	oz.	111	3·4	16·0	1·2	—	128	—	—
Dried Fruit[1][3]	oz.	63	0·4	16·0	0·4	17 (c)	—	—	—
Household Milk	pint	194	20·4	696·0	0·6	18	222	4·0	—
Liquid Milk	pint	340	18·0	680·0	0·6	600[5]	260	6·0	—
Bread	oz.	70	2·4	17·0	0·3	—	42	—	—
Flour	oz.	98	3 4	23·0	0·5	—	69	—	—
Potatoes	oz.	16	0·4	2·0	0·1	—	26	4·0	25%
Swedes	oz.	4	0·2	10·0	0·1	—	7	7·0	35%
Carrots	oz.	5	0·2	11·0	0·1	4544 (c)	14	2·0	20%
Cabbage	oz.	5	0·3	13·0	0·2	179 (c)	15	14·0	30%
Macaroni	oz.	96	3·0	7·0	0·4	—	21	—	—
Semolina	oz.	96	3·0	5·0	0·3	—	26	—	—
Cocoa	oz.	125	5·8	14·0	4·1	43 (c)	34	—	—
Cooking Apples	oz.	8	0·1	1·0	0·1	9 (c)	10	1·0	20%
Herrings, fresh	oz.	23	2·7	17·0	0·3	26	2	—	40%
Pork Sausage Meat	oz.	73	3·0	9·0	0·3	—	48	—	—

[1] Average values.
[2] The figures are given for cuts of low nutritional value, of beef and mutton.
[3] Seedless raisins, sultanas, stoned dates.
[4] A (c) after the figures in this column denotes carotene.
[5] From 400 to 800 I.U., depending on the feeding stuffs of the herd.
[6] According to cut.

other hand, for cheap stewing beef only, at 10*d*. a lb., the relative figures of nutritional values, as compared with the average figures used for diet A, would be: calories 0·6 times; protein 0·9 times; vitamin A 0·7 times; vitamin B₁ 0·7 times; for calcium and iron they would be unity. If it were possible for the family to obtain a double meat ration, and they spent the whole amount—11*s*. 8*d*.—on best frying steak, they would increase the nutritional values derived from meat in diet A by much less than by spending *only half of it* and laying this money out on breast of mutton; for the improvement would amount to this: calories, calcium, and iron, 1·5 times; protein, vitamin A and vitamin B₁,

T

TABLE V

CALORIES AND PROTEIN IN 'HUMAN NEEDS' DIET A

Calories: Per Cent of Total			*Proteins: Per Cent of Total*		
	April 1945	*November 1945*		*April 1945*	*November 1945*
			Animal Protein:		
Bread and Flour	31 3	31·3	All Milk[3]	15·7	14·8
Margarine and Lard	11·4	11·4	Meat	14·1	14·4
Meat	8·5	8·5	Herrings, tinned	6·7	—
Fresh Milk	8·1	8·1	All Eggs	3·2	3·3
Sugar	7·6	7·6	Cheese	2·6	4·0
Potatoes	6·8	6·8	Bacon	1·6	1·2
Rolled Oats	5·6	5·6	Herrings, fresh	—	3·3
Macaroni and Semolina	3·9	3·9	Sausage Meat	—	0·9
Bacon	3·3	2·4			
All Legumes[1]	3·1	3·5			
Jam and Syrup	2·0	2 0	*Vegetable Protein:*		
Herrings, tinned	2·0	—	Bread and Flour	31·7	32·3
Cheese	1·5	2·2	All Legumes[1]	7·6	8.7
All Eggs[2]	1·4	1·4	Rolled Oats	5·0	5·1
Vegetables (*excl. Potat.*)	1·3	1·3	Potatoes	5·0	5·1
Household Milk	1·0	0·6	Macaroni and Semolina	3·6	3·6
Herrings, fresh	—	1·0	Vegetables (*excl. Potatoes*)	2·1	2·1
Sausage Meat	—	0·7	Cocoa	0·9	0·9
All other foods	1·2	1·7			
			All other foods	0·2	0·3
Total	100·0	100·0	Total	100·0	100·0

[1] Lentils, peas, haricot beans.   [2] One in shell and 15 dried eggs.
[3] Including dried Household milk

1·2 times. On the whole, beef is the least economical meat from the nutritional view-point, and mutton the most economical, if we compare cuts of similar culinary value.

The data for bread and flour in Table IV refer to calcium-fortified 'national' flour of 80 per cent extraction, as used in the ordinary loaf in 1945. For calcium-fortified flour of 85 per cent extraction—the 'national' flour of 1943—the figures are approximately the same for calories, protein, and calcium. For iron they would be about two-fifths and for vitamin B_1 nearly one-quarter above those given by us for bread and flour.

The relative net intake of nutriment from diet A is set out in Tables V, VI, and VII, Table V surveying the calorific intake and the intake of protein, Table VI that of the minerals calcium and iron, and Table VII that of the vitamins A, B_1, and C. These three Tables are arranged in such a way that nutriment derived from foods that are culinary as well as nutritional substitutes appears in one total: thus, dried

TABLE VI

CALCIUM AND IRON IN 'HUMAN NEEDS' DIET A

Calcium: Per Cent of Total			*Iron: Per Cent of Total*		
	April	*November*		*April*	*November*
	1945	*1945*		*1945*	*1945*
All Milk[1]	50·6	47·0	Bread and Flour	24·3	23·8
Bread and Flour	19·4	19·3	Meat	17·2	16·9
Cheese	7·4	11·1	All Legumes[3]	12·7	14·1
Cabbage	4·7	4·6	Rolled Oats	10·5	10·3
Swedes and Carrots	3·8	3·8	Potatoes	7·4	7·2
Herrings, tinned	2·7	—	Cabbage	4·9	4·8
Haricot Beans	2·6	3·3	All Eggs[2]	4·5	4·5
Potatoes	2·2	2·2	Cocoa	3·6	3·5
Rolled Oats	2·1	2·1	All Milk[1]	3·0	2·8
All Eggs[2]	1·3	1·3	Herrings, tinned	2·6	—
Meat	0·7	0·7	Swedes and Carrots	2·5	2·4
Lentils and Peas	0·6	0·6	Macaroni and		
Macaroni and			Semolina	2·3	2·2
Semolina	0·6	0·6	Syrup	1·4	1·4
Dried Fruit	0·4	0·6	Bacon	1·3	1·0
Syrup	0·4	0·4	Dried Fruit	0·7	1·0
Bacon	0·2	0·1	Margarine	0·7	0·7
Herrings, fresh	—	1·8	Cheese	0·4	0·6
Sausage Meat	—	0·2	Herrings, fresh	—	2·1
All other foods	0·3	0·3	Sausage Meat	—	0·5
			Cooking Apples	—	0·2
Total	100·0	100·0	Total	100·0	100·2

[1] Including dried Household milk.   [2] One in shell and 15 dried eggs.
[3] Lentils, peas, haricot beans.

Household milk can replace—or nearly replace—liquid full cream milk as regards its content of protein, calcium, iron, and vitamin B_1[1]; under these headings, therefore, all milk is shown together. But, as compared with full cream milk, Household milk is deficient in calorific value and in its content of vitamin A and vitamin C; hence for these items liquid milk is given separately. All vegetables in diet A —excluding potatoes—may be substituted for one another as far as calorific value and content of protein are concerned; cabbage, however, is a better source of calcium and iron than swedes and carrots, while carrots are much superior to all other vegetables in vitamin A potency. On the other hand, swedes and cabbage have about the same high net value of vitamin C potency, if we deduct 50 per cent for losses in cooking of swedes, and 75 per cent for those of cabbage.

Bread and flour are shown together in Tables V, VI, and VII, since, in proportion of about 3 to 4, they are perfect substitutes. Eggs in shell and dried eggs are also always given together, although

[1] Its content of vitamin B_1 is about 15 per cent below that of fresh full cream milk; but this is of minor importance, since diet A contains an abundancy of this vitamin.

TABLE VII

VITAMINS A, B$_1$, AND C IN 'HUMAN NEEDS' DIET A

Vitamin A: Per Cent of Total			Vitamin B$_1$: Per Cent of Total		
	April 1945	November 1945		April 1945	November 1945
Carrots	64·5	63·3	Bread and Flour	31·9	31·8
Margarine	13·0	12·7	Potatoes	18·1	18·0
Liquid Milk	8·7	8·5	All Milk[2]	12·1	11·3
Cabbage	5·1	5·0	Rolled Oats	10·6	10·6
All Eggs[1]	4·4	4·3	All Legumes[3]	8·5	9·5
Cheese	2·8	4·2	Carrots and Cabbage	5·1	5·1
Meat	1·0	1·0	Meat	4·6	4·6
Herrings, tinned	0·2	—	Bacon	4·6	3·4
Lentils and Peas	0·2	0·2	Macaroni and Semolina	1·6	1·6
Herrings, fresh	—	0·6	All Eggs[1]	1·6	1·6
All other foods	0·1	0·2	Swedes	0·8	0·8
			Sausage Meat	—	0·8
			All other foods	0·5	0·9
Total	100·0	100·0	Total	100·0	100·0

Vitamin C: Per Cent of Total

	April, 1945	November, 1945
Potatoes	46·4	46·4
Swedes and Cabbage	40·5	40·5
Liquid Milk	7·9	7·9
Carrots	3·9	3·9
Household Milk	1·1	0·7
Jam	0·2	0·2
Cooking Apples	—	0·4
Total	100·0	100·0

[1] One in shell and 15 dried eggs. [2] Including dried Household milk.
[3] Lentils, peas, haricot beans.

dried eggs are a somewhat poorer source of nutrients, in particular of the vitamins A and B$_1$. Yet, eggs in shell may be considered a luxury for a family with no infants, and we are here concerned essentially with the nutritional value of dried eggs.

Table V, VI, and VII, make impressively clear the importance of a properly 'mixed' diet; for only such a diet is likely to be a well-balanced one. For instance, a family that eats no carrots and substitutes for them, say, swedes, would thus forgo nearly two-thirds of the total content of vitamin A of the diet; or, if potatoes were largely replaced by bread and flour and few other vegetables eaten, the same proportion of vitamin C might be lost.

The relation between the cost of diet A and the nutritional intake obtained from it is pictured in some detail in Table VIII. It compares expenditure and the nutritional values obtained for it, for the several

TABLE VIII

RELATIVE OUTLAY ON, AND NUTRITIONAL INTAKE FROM, 'HUMAN NEEDS' DIET A

	Outlay	Calories	Protein[1]	Calcium	Iron	Vitamin A	Vitamin B₁	Vitamin C
April, 1945:								
Group (a)	55·0	48·0	31·3 (a) 12·8	27·6	52·6	21·7	32·0	1·3
Group (b)	16·3	8·1	12·7 (a)	41·7	2·5	8·7	10·2	7·9
Group (c)	15·5	38·1	36·7	21·5	31·6	—	50·0	46·4
Group (d)	9·3	1·3	2·1	8·5	7·4	69·6	5·9	44·4
Group (e) *excl. condiments*	3·0	4·5	4·4	0·7	5·9	—	1·9	—
Condiments	0·9	—	—	—	—	—	—	—
Total	100·0	100·0	100·0	100·0	100·0	100·0	100·0	100·0
November, 1945:								
Group (a)	50·8	46·2	24·9 (a) 14·0	25·9	50·8	22·5	31·1	0·9
Group (b)	16·3	8·1	12·9 (a)	41·5	2·5	8·5	10·2	7·9
Group (c)	17·0	38·1	37·4	21·4	31·0	—	49·8	46·4
Group (d)	6·3	1·3	2·1	8·5	7·2	68·3	5·9	44·4
Group (e) *excl. condiments*	8·7	6·3	4·2(a) 4·5	2·7	8·5	0·7	3·0	0·4
Condiments	0·9	—	—	—	—	—	—	—
Total	100·0	100·0	100·0	100·0	100·0	100·0	100·0	100·0

[1] An (a) after the figures in this column denotes protein derived from animal sources.

groups, in April and November, 1945. The substitution of un-rationed sources of animal protein—herrings and sausage meat—for the 'points' rationed tinned herrings, has reduced all through the values of group (a) in November and increased those of group (e). Apart from this the differences are slight, except for the relative outlay on groups (c) and (d), which is affected by the substantial changes in the prices of potatoes and of other vegetables.

In Table IX the figures of nutritional intake from diet A are given per 'man' per day. The upper part of Table IX is headed 'Ministry of Health Scale'. Actually, only the 'man' values used in this section of Table IX were obtained from data supplied by the Ministry of Health, and the individual values from which these totals were compiled will be found in Table X.

The nutritional intake figures are based on the data in Table IV, that is, on the White Paper on 'Nutritional Values of War-time Foods', which has now replaced the provisional data previously employed by the Ministry. In order to make it possible to compare the basic data of nutritional intake with those in the early articles of this series, when, owing to the absence of generally recognized simple scales of 'man' values and nutritional values, we compiled scales of our own which were bound to be much less precise than those now at our

TABLE IX

NUTRITIONAL REQUIREMENTS AND NUTRITIONAL INTAKE FROM 'HUMAN NEEDS' DIET A

	'Man' Value' of Family	Requirements[1] per Man	Intake per 'Man' per Day from Diet A	
			April, 1945	Nov., 1945
Ministry of Health Scale:[2]				
Calories	3·73	3000	3040	3040
Protein, animal	4·43	70 gm.	38 gm.	36 gm.
Protein, vegetable			49 gm.	50 gm.
Calcium	7·13	0.8 gm.	0·6 gm.	0·6 gm.
Iron	5·40	10 mgm.	12 mgm.	12 mgm.
Vitamin A	5·00	3000 I.U.	3760 I.U.	3830 I.U.
Vitamin B$_1$	4·68	0·9 mgm.	1·3 mgm.	1·3 mgm.
Vitamin C	5·00	30 mgm.	41 mgm.	41 mgm.
Institute of Statistics Scale:[3]				
Calories	3·75	3300	3300	3300
Protein, animal	3·75	50 gm.	51	51
Protein, vegetable		50 gm.	53	54

[1] Net values for the Ministry of Health scale, gross values for the Institute of Statistics scale.
[2] Food values based on the data in Table IV.
[3] Food values compiled from a pre-war scale of *gross* values.

TABLE X

INDIVIDUAL NUTRITIONAL REQUIREMENTS EXPRESSED IN 'MAN' VALUES

Age Group		Calories	Protein	Calcium	Iron	Vitamin A	Vitamin B$_1$	Vitamin C
Male	21 and over	1·00	1·00	1·00	1·00	1·00	1·00	1·00
Female	21 and over	0·83	0·86	1·00	1·00	1·00	0·83	1·00
Child	7–12	1·70	0·93	1·75	1·30	1·00	1·05	1·00
Child	3–7	0·50	0·71	1·63	0·80	1·00	0·75	1·00

disposal, we also continue this older set of data, under the heading 'Institute of Statistics Scale'. No further use, however, is made of these figures in this article and they are not referred to in any of the other Tables. It should be noted that the nutritional intake shown under the heading 'Institute of Statistics Scale' is expressed in gross values, while under the heading 'Ministry of Health Scale' it is given in net values.

On the whole, the nutritional intake from diet A is satisfactory. There is, in fact, a fair margin of safety for all the nutrients, with the exception of calcium, of which the diet only supplies 75 per cent of the optimum intake. With respect to this we can here only repeat what we have already pointed out in previous articles: first, that the deficiency of calcium intake is not a war-time phenomenon but was even more marked in the average pre-war family diet, owing to ignorance and bad dietary habits; and, secondly, that no general improvement in this respect is possible so long as milk and cheese remain scarce.

It may be thought that the 'surplus' amount obtained from diet A of most nutrients is rather large. Considering, however, that the family's food is distributed not by an expert dietitian but by a harassed housewife who tries to satisfy the various claims of each member of the family, such a surplus may be necessary if every member is to be reasonably assured of a sufficiency of nutriment. The fairly generous supply of vitamin B_1, results partly from the high content of this vitamin in war-time bread and flour, which is more than three times that of its pre-war content.[1]

In concluding, it is perhaps useful to underline the fact that this diet can only be bought and cooked by a family, and that no simple division by a constant would serve to calculate from it the minimum cost of a satisfactory diet for a single person, whose problems of catering and cooking are essentially different from those of the housewife with a family.[2] But our detailed analysis of food values shows not only that it is possible to provide for a family an inexpensive and yet well-balanced diet, but also indicates why inexpensive diets are so frequently anything but well balanced. A housewife may be a good cook and a careful housekeeper; in spite of this the family may be malnourished because of her ignorance of food values, or, indeed, because of the family dislike of certain essential foods.

---

[1] No calcium was added to the pre-war bread and flour, and its content of this mineral therefore only amounted to about 17 per cent of that of our present day bread and flour.

[2] Cf. T. Schulz, 'Human Needs', Cost of Living for a Single Person, Bulletin, Vol. 5, No. 9.

THE COST OF LIVING IN BRISTOL[1]

by G. H. Daniel

FROM BULLETIN, VOL. 3, No. 14 (OCTOBER 11, 1941)

FOR the purposes of this study, retail prices in Bristol were collected for August, 1939, and the first week of February, 1941. This information throws some light on the rise in prices of different commodities and different qualities of commodities, on changes in the variation of prices between separate districts of Bristol, and on the Ministry of Labour Cost of Living Index.

Prices were collected from representative chain and multiple stores and independent retailers in three large shopping centres which could be classed as (I) Middle Class, (II) Artisan, (III) Lower Working Class.[2] Data were also obtained from businesses such as the Co-operative Society with branches in many parts of the town and, altogether, prices were obtained for 235 commodities from sixty separate retailers, many of them with numerous branches or departments.

The commodities were chosen to represent each main head of household expenditure according to the Ministry of Labour, 1937, Budget Enquiry. Whenever possible, the price of a good quality and of the cheapest quality of each commodity was obtained, but only those commodities were taken which were susceptible to clear definition and available both in August, 1939, and in February, 1941, in the same qualities. Prices for August, 1939, were secured with the help of old order books, price lists and invoices. Shops which could not provide accurate prices for 1939 were excluded, but such cases were few. To allow for the effects of the purchase tax, prices were obtained inclusive and exclusive of tax and these were weighted according to estimates obtained from shopkeepers of the proportion of turnover on taxed and untaxed goods. In addition, numerous authorities were approached for estimates of the increase in cost of the main services.

[1] The present paper is based upon an investigation made on behalf of the National Institute for Economic and Social Research. The writer wishes to express his gratitude to the National Institute, to Professor Hamilton Whyte for the facilities placed at his disposal, and to members of the Oxford Institute of Statistics for their helpful suggestions. Thanks are also due to the retailers who very kindly co-operated with the inquiry.

[2] The shopping centres were: I. Whiteladies Road and Queen's Road; II. Stapleton Road; III. East Street and Bedminster Parade.

Price relatives were calculated relating February, 1941, to August, 1939, and the price relatives for the different shops within each district were arithmetically averaged for each commodity and each shopping centre.[1]

Increase in Price of Different Commodities

The increase in price of each commodity was obtained by taking the simple arithmetic mean of the relatives for the three shopping centres. The commodities under each head were combined with weights obtained from the Ministry of Labour's 1937–8 budgets of industrial households. Indices for the main groups are shown below.

TABLE I

PERCENTAGE INCREASE IN BRISTOL RETAIL PRICES, AUGUST, 1939, TO FEBRUARY, 1941

Cereals	11	Rent	0
Fats	23	Services	11
Sugar, jam, tea, condiments, etc.	28	Cleaning, medical, stationery	22
Meat	28	Fuel and light	30
Milk products and eggs	37	Drink and tobacco	45
Fruit and vegetables	70	Clothing	51
Fish	82	Furniture and household goods	80
All Food	35	*All Items*	29

Price increases have been more severe for body-building and protective foods than for carbohydrates and fats, and for clothing, furniture, and household goods than for rents and services.

Increase in Price of Different Qualities

The different trend of prices for high and low quality goods is shown in the next table, where the index for each group is simply the arithmetic mean of the indices for each article within the group. We have included, of course, only those qualities which remained unchanged during the period.[2]

For practically all of the groups below the cheaper qualities have risen more in price than the dearer qualities. Since, in addition, a great many of the cheapest pre-war varieties were reported to be

[1] In the present inquiry the average of ratios and not the ratio of averages is used throughout, that is, $\frac{1}{n} \sum \frac{P_1}{P_0}$ and not $\frac{\sum P_1}{\sum P_0}$. Since the latter is equal to $\frac{\sum \frac{P_1}{P_0} P_0}{\sum P_0}$ its use would result in the price changes for the dearer qualities or larger sizes of a commodity having a greater effect upon the average than those for other qualities or sizes.

[2] The following are examples of the two qualities chosen: home-produced and imported meat; tuberculin tested and pasteurized milk; full fruit standard and cheapest jam; King Edward and cheapest potatoes; roasting and boiling chickens and six guinea suits and fifty-shilling suits.

TABLE II

PERCENTAGE INCREASE IN PRICES OF DIFFERENT QUALITIES, AUGUST, 1939, TO
FEBRUARY, 1941

	Good Quality	Cheapest Quality				Good Quality	Cheapest Quality
Meat	18	25	Men's clothes		..	40	71
Groceries	16	26	Women's clothes		..	43	74
Cheese and milk ..	42	38	Shoes		..	34	42
Fruit and Vegetables	70	113	Materials		..	57	69
Fish and poultry ..	72	121	Household goods		..	41	56
Drink, tobacco, sweets	47	61	Furniture	..	..	69	85

unobtainable, the increases in price of the cheapest articles obtainable at the two dates, irrespective of quality, would be greater than those shown here. The different increases in price, according to quality, tends to ameliorate the rise in cost of living for the higher income groups and to sharpen it for the lower. Excluding the middle-class district (I) and taking the prices of the cheapest commodities wherever the figures were available, the increase in the Bristol cost of living, based on the 1937–8 budgets for industrial households, was found to be 32 per cent. Using the price data for the whole of Bristol and including the cheap and good qualities, the increase was 29 per cent. On the other hand, on a lower standard of living than the one represented by the 1937–8 budgets, proportionately more would be spent on cereals and rent, so that the difference between these figures might be somewhat less.

Variation in Prices between Districts

The prices charged in different districts of the city have apparently become more uniform during the first eighteen months of the war. The following table is based upon the prices of thirty-five foodstuffs which were available in the same qualities at both dates and in each of the three districts.[1] The first two rows were prepared by expressing each price as a percentage of the average price for all three districts and then averaging all the percentages for each separate district.

TABLE III

PRICE OF FOODSTUFFS IN DIFFERENT DISTRICTS

		Shopping Centre			Bristol
		I	II	III	Average
Prices expressed as percentages of average	Aug., 1939	103	102	94	100
prices in Bristol	Feb., 1941	101	99	100	100
Index of prices in Feb., 1941 (Aug., 1939 = 100) ..		150	149	163	153

[1] The foods include: 5 cereals, 10 groceries, 5 cuts of meat, 6 vegetables, 3 fruits, 4 varieties of fish, roasting chicken and rabbit.

The prices of these foodstuffs in 1939 were considerably higher in district I than in district III, but in 1941 the differences were negligible. Whereas before the war prices were lower in the poorer districts, to-day they appear to be practically the same in all areas, so that the rise in prices has been more severe in the lower working-class district III than in Bristol generally.

The greater uniformity between districts, combined with the sharper rise in price of cheaper qualities, has caused a marked concentration of prices above their averages. Thus, when the prices are all expressed as percentages of the average price for each commodity, we find that, in August, 1939, 64 per cent of all prices fell within 10 per cent of the average, while, in February, 1941, this proportion had risen to 86 per cent. The standard deviations of the distribution of these percentages were found to be 14·1 at the first date and 8·3 at the second. This increased uniformity is no doubt largely due to Government control and the tendency to charge maximum legal prices.

The Ministry of Labour Cost of Living Index

Through the kindness of the Divisional Controller, access was obtained to the prices of goods collected by the Ministry of Labour in Bristol. With this information an examination may be made of the Ministry's selection of shops in Bristol, its method of combining quotations and its choice of commodities.[1] This is done by comparing the rise in cost of living obtained when the present data and present selection of commodities and the average of price relatives are used with the rise in costs obtained when these factors are replaced, one at a time, with the methods employed in the official index.

Although the Ministry of Labour's Index is intended to refer, so it is stated, to 'the standard of living of the working-classes', several of the retailers supplying particulars of food to the Bristol Employment Exchange could be included under the present class I. Two of the five fishmongers, one of the five grocers, and one of the five greengrocers were actually situated in shopping centre I. Calculating the increase in the cost of food on the basis of the Ministry of Labour prices and our own figures and employing the same weights and selections of commodities, the Ministry's figures give 34·4 per cent and our own 34·0 per cent. Considering that only the Co-operative Society and one fishmonger were common to the two calculations,

[1] The effect of using weights based on 1904 and 1911 expenditures instead of on more recent data has been discussed by J. L. Nicholson (see pages 212–214).

this is a close agreement. It suggests that, as far as Bristol is concerned, the Ministry of Labour index covers the whole population rather than the working-class only.

The Ministry's method of dealing with the quotations received from different shops for the same commodities is to obtain the modal quotation for each district, average them arithmetically and take the ratio of these averages. In Bristol, five quotations are obtained for each commodity but, since there is quite a considerable variation, the price relatives obtained from the modes may be freakish. Calculating the official index by taking these modal prices on the one hand and by averaging the price relatives for each pair of quotations on the other, the increase in the cost of food was found to be 34·4 per cent and 31·9 per cent respectively. Such discrepancies may be expected to cancel out in national figures[1] but it can still be objected that the use of modes tends to make the index sluggish and that the ratio of averages may lead to inaccuracy if there happens to be correlation between price relatives and base year prices.[2]

To test the effect of the selection of commodities used in the official index, the following figures were calculated, using the present data and 1937–8 weights: firstly, including only those commodities represented in the official index and, secondly, using the more complete information of the present inquiry:

TABLE IV

PERCENTAGE INCREASE IN BRISTOL COST OF LIVING, AUGUST, 1939 TO FEBRUARY, 1941

	Commodities included by Ministry of Labour	All commodities included in present inquiry
Rent	0	0
Food	32	35
Clothes	55	51
Fuel and Light	34	30
Other Items	29	27
Total	29	29

Clothing, in the official index, is largely represented by a long list of materials, many of which are not commonly used at the present time and these were not included in our inquiry. Prices of materials have risen more than the prices of finished clothes (see Table II) and this, together with the exclusion from the Ministry's index of shoe repairs and repairs to clothing (which have increased by 15 per cent and 23 per cent respectively), tends to make the official figures

[1] For this and other reasons, the Ministry has never published indices for different districts.
[2] See footnote, p. 289.

for clothing too high. The difference between the figures for fuel and light is also accounted for by the exclusion from the Ministry's index of electricity, which has only increased by about 9 per cent. The effect of these over-estimates on the total increase, however, is partly counter-balanced by the under-estimate of the increase in food prices.

Finally, an impression of the total effect of the Ministry of Labour's method of combining quotations, selection of commodities and weighting can be gathered by estimating the increase in the Bristol cost of living as closely as possible according to the Ministry's method[1] and comparing the results with those of the present inquiry. The following table also shows the increases in prices for the whole country in the same period, as shown by the Ministry's published figures.

TABLE V

PERCENTAGE INCREASE IN COST OF LIVING, AUGUST, 1939, TO FEBRUARY, 1941

	Increase for Bristol Method used by Ministry of Labour	Present method	Increase for whole country (Min. of Labour)
Rent	0	0	1
Food	30	35	24
Clothes	58	51	65
Fuel and light ..	29	30	24
Other items	29	27	24
Total	28	29	27

Comparing these figures, it appears that prices in Bristol, especially of foodstuffs, have risen slightly more than in the country as a whole. Comparing the first two columns, it is seen that, despite the unsatisfactory method of averaging, the small number of commodities and the out-of-date system of weighting of the official index, the defects tend to cancel out and the agreement between the totals is remarkably close. Whether the official index will continue to give such a satisfactory approximation, particularly in view of government subsidies for certain foodstuffs, is another matter.

[1] Whereas the figure for food was estimated throughout according to the methods of the Ministry of Labour, it was not possible to do this as thoroughly for clothes and 'other items', and in all cases except food the data were derived from the shops used in the present investigation. The articles of clothing were confined to those for which information was collected in the present inquiry. For the miscellaneous group, where the weights are unknown, the 1937-8 weights were used.

TAXATION OF TOBACCO, BEER AND CINEMA ATTENDANCES

by J. Goldmann

From Bulletin, Vol. 5, No. 2 (January 30, 1943)

'THE success of a war-time budget must be judged not so much by the amount of revenue it raises as by the way in which it serves to concentrate the national effort on the war'. Among the principal changes which the last budget—thus commented upon by Sir Kingsley Wood[1]—brought about, were big increases in the taxes on tobacco, beer, and entertainment. Their declared object was to enable the Chancellor to 'help, through taxation,' his colleagues to keep demand and supply in better equilibrium. Since last April sufficient time has passed to justify an attempt to analyse how far and in what way the fiscal measures then adopted have achieved this aim.

1. The flat increase in the rate of customs duty on tobacco brought about a greater percentage increase in the duty for Empire tobacco than in the case of foreign tobacco; the weighted average increase was 53 per cent. The average rate of excise duty on beer is 40 per cent higher in the current financial year than the rate prevailing in 1941–42.[2] On the other hand, estimates of tax receipts in a full year in the 'Financial Statement' show a rise of 40·5 per cent for tobacco and of 29·5 per cent for beer. Thus the authorities allowed for a fall in consumption in both cases by about 8 per cent. This figure may be taken as an indication of the result that was expected from the operation of the price deterrent, that is, from an increase in the average price of tobacco by about 36 per cent and of beer by about 22 per cent.[3]

Consumption figures that have since been published give a different picture. During the six months, April to September, 1942, the output of beer, though lower than in the first quarter of 1942, was about at the level prevailing in the same period of the preceding year,

---

[1] Sir Kingsley Wood: *Times*, April 15th, and *Hansard*, April 14, 1942.

[2] In the last Budget excise duty on beer was raised by 45·5 per cent; as gravity was lowered in January, 1942, the average rate of duty, which depends on gravity, did not rise between the two financial years to the full extent of the increase in tax.

[3] Prices were only raised by the amount of the additional duty. Therefore, the percentage rise in prices is less than the percentage rise in duty.

and the same probably holds true of the amount of tobacco retained for home consumption (releases from bond minus drawbacks).[1] If the rising trend of consumption prevails in the current financial year, as it did in 1941–42, consumption in the full year may well be maintained—in spite of higher prices—at the 1941–42 level, instead of the expected fall by 8 per cent. As will be shown later, there are strong reasons for assuming that this will be the case, in view of the continuing rise in real income.

2. Similar computations for the entertainments duty are somewhat more difficult because consumption data are only available for cinema attendances, whereas figures of tax receipts refer to all entertainments. Since, however, nearly 90 per cent of the yield of entertainments duty comes from attendance at cinemas[2] the revenue from cinemas can be expected to vary in a way similar to the total revenue from entertainments duty.

In the 'Financial Statement' the yield of entertainments duty was estimated to rise by 87 per cent, against an average rise in duty on cinema seats of 95 per cent.[3] Unless considerable shifts between cinema attendances and other entertainments were anticipated, the conclusion may be drawn that the authorities expected a fall in cinema attendances of about 4 per cent consequent upon the increase in duty and the rise in exhibitors' charges which was then already under consideration.

What actually happened was again somewhat different from expectation. The combined effect of increases in tax and in exhibitors' charges to the public raised prices of cinema tickets by between 33 and 50 per cent; yet recent speeches by the chairmen of the more important cinema circuits suggest that attendances are still rising above the record level of 27 million attendances a week, reached in the past financial year.

3. The explanation of such unusual reactions of the consumer seems to lie in the fact that demand for mass luxuries is not so much determined by price as by income. Price rises may be accompanied by increased consumption if income is rising. It can be shown that in the period 1924–1938 there was a close correlation between the real

---

[1] Consumption in the first quarter of the current financial year was 5 per cent higher than in the same period of last year.

[2] Sir Kingsley Wood, Budget Speech, April 14, 1942.

[3] Tax was raised by 100 per cent on all seats except those at 7*d.* or less for which the rate was left unchanged. Such seats were estimated to account for about 5 per cent of the 1941–42 yield of entertainments duty from cinemas. (Namely, Sir Kingsley Wood, *Hansard*, June 4, 1942, column 811.)

wage-bill on the one hand and the consumption of tobacco or beer on the other. The relationship between the real wage-bill and tobacco consumption can be expressed by the equation:

$$y = 47 \cdot 1 + 0 \cdot 0647x + 2 \cdot 349t$$

where x is the wage-bill as computed by Professor Bowley,[1] in million £, deflated by the cost of living index, adjusted for the omission of services;[2] t is the number of years after 1931; and y is the amount of tobacco retained for home consumption (in million lbs.). The corresponding equation for beer is:

$$z = -23 \cdot 6 + 0 \cdot 02951x - 1 \cdot 055t$$

where z is the quantity of beer consumed (home production plus net imports, in million bulk barrels), while x and t have the same meaning as before.

Thus, over the period considered, a rise—or fall—in the real wage-bill by £10 million had a tendency to raise—or lower—tobacco consumption by about 0·65 million lbs. and beer consumption by about 0·3 million bulk barrels. Also, on account of long term changes in demand, consumption of tobacco tended to increase by 2·3 million lbs. a year and that of beer tended to fall by about 1·1 million bulk barrels. Both factors together, the course of the real wage-bill and the trend, account fairly well, as can be seen from the accompanying diagram, for observed changes in actual consumption; in other words, the values computed from the equations given above agree quite closely with observed values of consumption. The coefficient of multiple correlation, adjusted for the size of the sample and the number of variables, is 0·97 for tobacco and 0·91 for beer.[3] Moreover, there appears to be a lag of consumption behind income; the graph of consumption computed from the wage-bill, falls and rises earlier than the graph of actual consumption.

There were few price changes in the period under consideration.[4] In September, 1931, the beer duty was raised by slightly less than 1d. per pint on the average, with a similar increase in average prices and

[1] 'Studies in National Income', p. 58.

[2] A constant value was added to the official index throughout the period to allow for expenditure on services as ascertained in the Ministry of Labour Budget Enquiry, 1937–8.

[3] For the mean levels of income and consumption, the income elasticity of demand is 0·69 for tobacco and 1·98 for beer, which means that, at these levels, an increase (or decrease) in the wage-bill of 1 per cent tended to bring about an increase (or decrease) of 0·69 per cent in tobacco consumption and 1·98 per cent in beer consumption.

[4] Tobacco prices were slightly raised in 1927 and 1931. It appears that these changes were either too small to affect the consumer or that they were counteracted by shifts in demand to cheaper brands. The deviations between computed and actual consumption in 1927 and 1931 can be explained by the effect of the time lag. (See below, Section 4.)

it was lowered again in April, 1933, so as to permit a reduction in retail prices by 1*d*. Yet the effect of these price changes on consump-

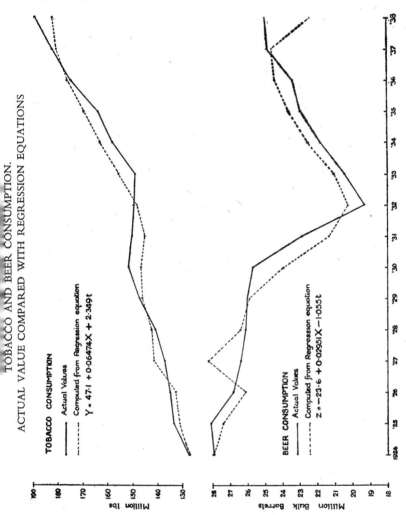

TOBACCO AND BEER CONSUMPTION.
ACTUAL VALUE COMPARED WITH REGRESSION EQUATIONS

TOBACCO CONSUMPTION
—— Actual Values
------- Computed from Regression equation
$Y = 47.1 + 0.06474X + 2.349t$

BEER CONSUMPTION
—— Actual Values
------- Computed from Regression equation
$Z = -23.6 + 0.02951X - 1.055t$

Million lbs.

Million Bulk Barrels.

tion was not very large. Beer consumption in 1932, the first full year after the rise, was only about 5 per cent below the level corresponding to trend and wage-bill (see diagram). In other words, in spite of the rise in prices, consumption was only 5 per cent lower than it would have otherwise been.[1] The remission of duty in 1933

[1] The increase in the retail price of beer in 1931 was estimated at 17 per cent in the *Brewers' Almanack*, 1938, p. 32, and at 8 per cent in G. B. Wilson, 'Alcohol and the Nation', p. 422.

U

and the consequent fall in price restored consumption to the level corresponding to trend and wage-bill. Throughout the period 1933–36 computed values are higher than actual values, probably because of the effect of the time lag; the upswing in the wage-bill, from which the computed values are obtained, started earlier than the upswing in consumption.[1]

4. If the deviations of computed from actual values are further analysed it is found that they are closely correlated with changes in the real wage-bill from one year to another. Whenever there is an increase in the real wage-bill as compared with the previous year, the computed value of consumption (which takes into account the level of the real wage-bill only in the current year) tends to be too high, and vice versa. This would agree with the assumption of a time lag between income and consumption. On the other hand, throughout the cycle 1930–38, these deviations are also correlated with changes in the relative prices of tobacco and beer as compared with prices of other goods (actual prices of tobacco and beer divided by the cost of living index). Whenever either of these goods is more expensive in terms of other goods, due for instance to the fact that its price remains constant while other prices fall, computed values of consumption again tend to be higher than actual values. It is not possible, therefore, to separate the effects of the time lag and of relative price changes, but the analysis reveals the fact that the combined result of both factors is small, compared with the effects of changes in the real wage-bill.

5. The result of the present inquiry may be summarized as follows:

(i) In the pre-war period there was a close correlation between the real wage-bill on the one hand and tobacco or beer consumption on the other, changes in income accounting for a very large part of the variations in consumption.

(ii) Changes in the prices of tobacco and beer, both absolute and relative, have a far smaller influence on the course of consumption than changes in real income.

(iii) In a period of rising income, indirect taxes are unlikely to bring about a lasting reduction in consumption.

---

[1] Lack of data makes the corresponding computation for cinema attendances impossible. But the figures relating to the yield of entertainment tax clearly indicate—after a rough elimination of the effects of changes in taxation—that a similar relationship exists between income and consumption as in the other two cases.

EXPENDITURE ON RENT

by J. Goldmann

FROM BULLETIN, VOL. 6, No. 11 (AUGUST 12, 1944)

RENT is still one of the largest single items in national expenditure. Yet, while total expenditure on rent and allied payments is known, no recent information is available as to its incidence on family incomes of different size. Generalizing from the few local enquiries that were made before the war, it is held that rent tends to form a declining proportion of total family expenditure as the latter increases. The problem is of considerable practical importance; an Inter-departmental Committee on Rent Control was set up in November, 1943, and it has been suggested that existing restrictions should be relaxed.[1] 'Not the least important of coming legislative measures', it has been said, 'is rent control.'[2] In these circumstances, it may be of interest to record the results of a survey which attempted to give a fairly comprehensive and up-to-date picture of the relation between rent and income at different income levels.

Structure of the Sample

The enquiry was carried out in May, 1944, by the British Institute of Public Opinion; the results are based on a national sample of 1,736 interviews. The regional distribution of interviews is proportionate to the regional distribution of the population; similarly, the socio-economic structure of the sample was controlled by assigning to each interviewer given numbers of working-class, lower middle-class, and upper middle-class families in proportions representative of the socio-economic structure in the respective regions. For the assessment of the social status of a contact, interviewers were instructed to use a combination of income and occupational characteristics; within the limits of their assignments, interviewers selected their contacts at random, either in the street or by house-to-house canvassing. In this way a representative sample was obtained within the limitations inherent in such a method of random selection.

---

[1] Recommendations by the National Federation of Property Owners, as reported in the *Times*, May 5, 1944; and suggestions by the Law Society, *Times*, June 23, 1944.
[2] *Sunday Times*, June 25, 1944.

For this survey, in which two other factual and some opinion questions were asked, altogether 2,057 persons were approached: 15 per cent refused to give an interview, a percentage which is usual in similar surveys even if they contain only questions on opinions. These refusals may, therefore, be held to be unrelated to the questions on income and rent.

Of the total number of 1,736 interviews, only those were analysed that had been given by householders or their wives, because it was held that other members of families could not be expected to give reliable information on family incomes. Moreover, their inclusion would have biased the sample in favour of families containing other adults apart from the householder and his wife, as such families would have had a larger chance of being selected.

Of the remaining 1,337 interviews it was found that 24·5 per cent related to families owning, or buying, their house. There are no official statistics to check this result, apart from the Ministry of Labour Working-Class Budget Enquiry, 1937–1938. In this enquiry, 18 per cent of the working-class households (industrial) and 4·5 per cent of the agricultural households were either owning or buying their home. In the present survey 14 per cent of the families classified as working-class were owning or buying their home. The agreement is quite good considering that the Ministry of Labour enquiry excluded some of the poorest working-class families, those on un-employment assistance.

Thus, we had 1,011 interviews from 'renting' families and 326 from 'house-owning' families: 88·5 per cent of the former, and 75·3 per cent of the latter, were found to be suitable for tabulation. The main reason for rejection was refusal to answer the income question. There were also some cases where information on rent was refused, and others, only 1 per cent, where families had houses rent free. A detailed analysis of refusals shows that they tended to be most frequent in the highest income groups, but, for the bulk of our data, it appears that the rate of refusals was so low that it is unlikely that information from these families, if it had been included, would have materially affected the results.

Results

The main results of the enquiry are given in the following Table. This shows for various levels of family income (net of income tax), (*a*) the percentage of families in the respective income group; (*b*) average rent paid by families renting their home; (*c*) the percentage of net family income spent on rent, and (*d*) the proportion of families in each income group who are owning or buying their home. Figures for rent include rates and water charges.

Expenditure on Rent, Rate and Water-Charges at Different Income-Levels

Net Family Income £ per week	Percentage of Families in Income Group	Average Rent Paid by Renting Families	Percentage of Net Family Income spent on Rent, etc.	Proportion of Families Renting their House in Income Groups
	Per Cent	sh.	Per cent	Per Cent
Up to 2	4·6	8·7	29·0	87
2 to 3	7·9	10·9	21·8	91
3 to 4	17·9	14·0	20·0	87
4 to 5	18·7	15·8	17·6	81
5 to 6	18·5	17·7	16·1	73
6 to 8	14·2	20·0	14·3	76
8 to 10	7·6	22·0	12·2	70
10 to 12	4 0	24·1	11·0	
12 to 15	3·1	25·7	9·5	} 51
Over 15	3·5	29·4	8·9	
	100%	Av. 16·6 sh.	Av. 15·6%	Av. 75·5%

The results may be summarized as follows. Absolute expenditure on rent rises with rising family income from 8*s.* 8½*d.* in the lowest income group (up to £2 per week) to 29*s.* 5*d.* in the highest income group (over £15 per week). For our sample, average rent is 16*s.* 7*d.*

Expenditure on rent as a percentage of family income falls with rising income. For the lowest group it is 29 per cent, while it is only 8·9 per cent for the highest group. For the sample as a whole, the percentage spent on rent is 15·6.

If rent is plotted against income, it will be found that the line connecting the two approximates a curve which is positively inclined for the range of observations and convex upwards (see Diagram). This would mean that the amount paid in rent rises with rising income, but at a diminishing rate.

The relationship between net income and rent is fairly regular. It can be expressed by the equation

$$Y = 5·97 + 2·34X - 0·06X^2$$

where X is average net family income in £ per week and Y average weekly expenditure, in shillings, on rent, rates, and water charges. The increase of rent per £1 of income is at first about 2*s.*, but diminishes fairly regularly as income increases. In the higher income ranges the increment of rent, corresponding to an increase of income of £1, is only about one shilling. The constant term of the equation

EXPENDITURE ON RENT, RATES, AND WATER CHARGES AT
DIFFERENT LEVELS OF NET FAMILY INCOME

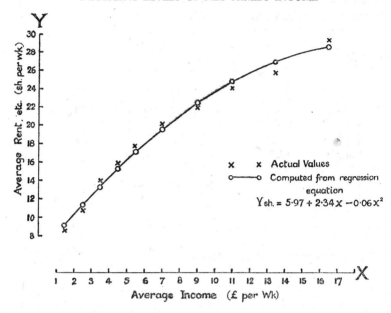

is positive, as is usually the case with *linear* income-outlay equations for necessaries, as distinct from luxuries.[1]

It thus appears from our data that the smaller the family income the smaller the share of that income available for food and other needs after rent has been paid. This observation is in agreement with the results of pre-war surveys, and it is interesting that war-time changes in the distribution of incomes have not basically changed the pre-war income-rent relationship. During the war the inequality of net incomes was somewhat reduced while rents remained fairly stable; but this reduction of the inequality of incomes was too slight appreciably to modify the regressive character of rent expenditure.

[1] The scatter of the observations about the regression curve would suggest that the dot representing the highest income group (over £15) is out of line as compared with the remainder. This is due to the fact that the conventional location of the midpoint of this open group places it too low on the income scale. If the open group had been left out altogether a better fit would have been obtained, although the constants of the regression equation would have been only slightly affected.

Allen and Bowley, in fitting a straight line to the results of a Budget enquiry carried out by the London School of Economics in 1932, obtained the regression equation $Y = 6.7 + 2.0X$, where Y is rent and rates, and X total family expenditure. See 'Family Expenditure', p. 32. (The constants given there have been transformed to give weekly rent expenditure in shillings; family expenditure is now given in £ per week).

It is obvious that a uniform increase in rents would constitute a greater burden to families with small incomes. This tendency is also strengthened by the fact that the proportion of families in each income group who are renting their homes falls as we move up the scale to higher income levels (see last column in the Table). For any income group as a whole, therefore, the effect of a rise in rents is the smaller, the higher the income of that group, because relatively less families are affected by such a rise.

The method of sample enquiry by interviews is still fairly new in the field of economic research and it will have to be shown that the results stand up to the usual tests before they will be readily accepted. There is some internal evidence in our figures of the stability of the sample in so far as the breakdown by income groups reveals a considerable internal consistency. But there is also some official information with which our findings can be compared.

According to the White Paper on National Income and Expenditure (Cmd. 6520) total personal expenditure on rent, rates, and water charges in 1943 was £510 mn.[1] If we assume that for owner-occupied dwellings the average of imputed rent, plus rates and water charges, is the same as the average rent, etc., for other dwellings, we may multiply the average rent paid per family in our sample by an estimate of the total number of families, and then bring the product on to an annual basis to make it comparable with the White Paper figure. (The Registrar-General estimated that the number of families would increase between 1931 and 1941 by 9 per cent and would reach 12·4 mn. Assuming the same rate of increase in the following three years we obtain an estimate of 12·8 mn. for 1944). Carrying out the operation we obtain for our sample a total expenditure on rent, etc., of £560 mn. Although the basis of comparison is a little uncertain, this figure is in fairly good agreement with the White Paper estimate of £510 mn.[2]

[1] This figure is stated to include an allowance in respect of buildings occupied by non-profit-making bodies, hotels, boarding houses, etc., but the expenditure in question is believed to be relatively quite small.

[2] The White Paper estimate of rent expenditure appears to include imputed rent. Another test can be applied by comparing the average rent, etc., paid by those sample families which were classified by the interviewers as working-class with the average expenditure on rent, etc., as ascertained by the Ministry of Labour budget enquiry of 1937–38. The discrepancy between the two figures is considerable, 14s. 8d. in our sample against 10s. 8d. in the Ministry of Labour enquiry, and cannot be explained entirely by a difference in coverage; on the other hand it is somewhat difficult to reconcile the latter figure with the White Paper estimate for the total of rent, etc., in 1938.

LABOUR COSTS IN HOUSING

by S. Moos

FROM BULLETIN, VOL. 5, No. 14 (OCTOBER, 1943)

AN enquiry into present-day building costs and their relation to pre-war and possible post-war costs is bound to be of a tentative nature. Too many changes have occurred with regard to material and labour used to make an accurate comparison possible, and the price indices of building materials and building labour which should measure changes over a period of time, have become less reliable by omitting certain war-time factors.

A few official data on the rise of building costs since the outbreak of war have been made available. Lord Portal, between March and June 1943, gave three estimates indicating an increase of 80 per cent,[1] 92 per cent, and 105 per cent. The latter figure, referring to housing, was given in a debate on training for the building industry,[2] Lord Portal pointing out that 'certain considerations arise during war-time which should not arise afterwards, but the figure (105 per cent) is approximately right'.

Some experts consider Lord Portal's figure rather an under-estimate.[3] They assess the war-time rise in costs at 110-120 per cent and consider a further increase of 30 per cent within a year possible. These estimates are rather surprising at first sight, when compared with the rise in the Board of Trade Index of Wholesale Prices for Building Materials (July, 1943) of 45 per cent and with the increase in builders' wages of some 31 per cent. The ratio of wages to materials used to be 40 : 60[4] before the war but was now said to be nearer 60 : 40.[5] If we assume a ratio of 45 : 55 as a probable figure,[6] total building costs on the basis of materials, prices and wage rates should therefore have risen by some 40 per cent.

In order to trace the sources of the discrepancy between price indices and newer estimates of building costs, let us first examine available

---

[1] Referring to December, 1942.   [2] On a motion by Lord Balfour of Burleigh.
[3] *The Builder*, July 16, 1943, and *Hansard*, July 23, 1943.
[4] By the B.I.N.C. and in Parliament by the Minister of Health and Minister of Works.
[5] By Mr. Hicks in House of Commons.
[6] Assuming an increase in the prices of building materials by 50–60 per cent, an increase in labour costs of 225–250 per cent would be necessary in order to reverse the ratio 40 : 60 into one of 60 : 40.

data on housing costs indicated by the following prices of cottages given recently.

Estimate of Housing Costs

	Highest	Lowest	Average (of highest and lowest)
	£	£	£
Tenders, Ministry of Health Plans[1]	937	747	842
+ lands, roads, sewers, etc. ..	50	100	75
Total	987	847	917
Tender, Ministry of Health Plans[2]			
Parlour	971	644	807
Non-parlour	868	646	757
+ lands, roads, sewers, etc. ..	33	53	43
Total	1004 901	697 699	850 800
Average Parlour and non-parlour	952	698	825
Tenders, Ministry of Works, non-parlour	807	635	721
Estimate 'A Planner'[3] ..			675

[1] *Hansard*, June 10, 1943.   [2] *Hansard*, July 22 and 23, 1943.   [3] *Times*, June 21, 1943.

The different estimates are neither strictly comparable with each other nor with pre-war costs, since the houses vary in size and in quality of materials and of construction. The Ministry of Health plans, for instance, provide more space and comfort than those of the Ministry of Works, and both categories show a reduction in the standard of many features as compared with pre-war conditions.

The approximate average pre-war cost of a house can be ascertained if we divide the costs of dwelling houses built by the number of building plans approved.[1] The figures for the first two quarters of 1939 are:

Pre-War Cost of New Dwelling Houses

	1st qr. 1939	2nd qr. 1939
Total cost of new dwelling houses (£000)	14,000	13,000
Number „ „ „	27,859	26,353
Cost per house (£)	501	488

These costs represent an average of all dwellings, the majority of which are working-class parlour and non-parlour houses, while the Ministry of Health tenders (above) refer to a limited group of houses only. But a comparison of the data gives a rise above pre-war costs of about 65 per cent.[2] 'A Planner' thinks that the £675 cottage may in peace-time have cost £400, an increase of some 69 per cent. Viscount Mersey[3] stated that an agricultural cottage which formerly cost £600 now costs £1,000, an increase of 67 per cent. Mr. L.

[1] By a selected group of 146 Local Authorities (Ministry of Labour Gazette).
[2] See first table.   [3] House of Lords, August 3, 1943.

Wallis[1] stated that a pre-war £750 house would at present cost £1,200, a rise of 60 per cent.

According to these data the war-time rise in costs appears to lie between 60 and 70 per cent. For a check on these estimates we may enquire into the development of the constituents of building costs, that is, wages, materials, overheads, and profits.

BUILDING LABOUR

With regard to labour costs we have to distinguish between the rise in the basic wage rate, changes in earnings, and changes in wage costs per unit of output.

Wage Rates

The basic rate of payment in the building and constructional trade is pegged to the cost of living index in a particular manner.[2] Whenever the average cost of living index for the preceding 12 months has changed by a complete $6\frac{1}{2}$ points, the standard rate (for Grade A towns 1s. 9d. per hour for craftsmen) is raised by $\frac{1}{2}d$. Since the outbreak of war wages are reviewed every four months.

Since the cost of living index underestimates the real changes in living costs and, in addition, builders' wages react so slowly on this modified index, the discrepancy will have to be balanced by supplementary payments (overtime, bonus) and no clear distinction between the two forms of payment can be made.

Basic wage rates had risen in July, 1943, by $21\frac{1}{2}$-29 per cent for craftsmen[3] and by 27-36 per cent for labourers (compared with 36 per cent for all other industries).

Earnings

Earnings in the Building and Contracting Industry are here given in comparison with October, 1938,[4] no rise in the wage-rates having taken place between October, 1938, and September, 1939. A comparison of changes in earnings and wage rates gives the following picture.

---

[1] President of the National Federation of Building Trades Employers on September 15, 1943.

[2] Wages in the London Area, before the outbreak of war, were 1s. 9d. for craftsmen and 1s. 3¾d. for builders' labourers. Wages in the building materials manufacturing industries are not linked to the cost of living index.

[3] Varying according to classification by districts. See Prof. A. L. Bowley, Prices, Wages and Earnings, London and Cambridge Economic Service, July, 1943.

[4] Ministry of Labour Enquiry.

Changes in Builder's Wages and Earnings

| | Increase in Earnings over 1938 | | | Increase in wage rates |
	All workers per cent	Youths per cent	Men per cent	All workers per cent
July, 1940	31·6	—	—	10·2
July, 1941	48·5	100·3	47·1	19·7
January, 1942 ..	27·7	75·0	27·5	21·8
July, 1942	54·6	105·8	54·5	24·9
January, 1943 ..	43·6	71·1	43·4	24·9
July, 1943	48·0[1]	—	—	31·2

[1] Mr. McCorquodale, Ministry of Labour (House of Commons, 23/7/43).

The 48 per cent increase in earnings compares with 63 per cent in all other industries covered by the enquiry. Only few juveniles seem to have flowed into the industry since the increase in their earnings hardly influences the percentage rise for all workers. A small number of women have been absorbed in the building and contracting trades, mainly in woodwork. On the whole, the earnings of adult male workers remained representative for the trade. The explanation for the discrepancy between wage-rates and earnings has therefore to be found in additional working hours and/or extra payments additional to the basic rates of wages.

From 6th November, 1942, except in cases of special urgency, excessive overtime (over 60 hours per week) was prohibited, overtime for juveniles restricted (note the decrease of earnings of youths in January, 1943, as compared with January, 1942) and Sunday work during November-February permitted on eight Sundays only. The data of earnings, however, suggest that in the cold winter of 1941–42 little overtime was worked, while the warm winter of 1942–43 was favourable for overtime. The guaranteed week providing for a full weekly wage in bad weather was in force on both dates, and, therefore, the difference between the increase in earnings and the increase in wage-rates (in January, 1943, compared with January, 1942) roughly indicate the magnitude of the share of overtime in the total increase of earnings, that is, 8–9 per cent. Overtime rates are $1\frac{1}{4}$ of the basic rate for the first two hours, $1\frac{1}{2}$ for the second two hours, and on Saturdays from 12 noon to 4 p.m. Double time is paid for any additional hours and Sunday work. The rate for overtime may thus average roughly 1·6 of the basic rate.

The war-time increase of 31 per cent in wage-rates compares with a 48 per cent increase in earnings. Of the difference of 17 points 8–9 can be explained by the increased rates for overtime and Sunday work, 5–6 for payments under the guaranteed week arrangement providing for the payment of wet time (indicated by the discrepancy between wage-rates and earnings in January, 1942) and $1\frac{1}{2}$ for holidays with pay,[1] leaving $1\frac{1}{4}$ due to the Payment by Results Scheme.

Payment by Results

This scheme, introduced by the Essential Works (Building and Civil Engineering) Order, 1941, was superimposed on the existing system of payment by hours. The Order established, with regard to brick-work, the number of bricks to be laid per hour before a bricklayer was entitled to a bonus. Contracting firms can adjust the basic output according to the job in hand.

It has been claimed that as a consequence of this order the efficiency of bricklayers decreased to such an extent that the increase in wages per unit of output is much higher than appears on the surface. Figures quoted suggesting that wages per unit of output have gone up by 100–200 per cent, seem worth closer examination.[2] In comparing the efficiency of bricklayers account has to be taken of the wide variations in the kind of building job to be done, in the size and quality of bricks used, in climatic conditions, in the time between ordering and arrival of materials and machinery, and finally in the composition of the labour force. The building industry operated in peace-time with some 200,000 unemployed so that mainly the physically fittest, aged 18 to 45, were continuously employed. Just these age groups have mostly been called up, and newcomers in the industry take a long time before they have acquired the considerable skill required from a builder's labourer. The Payment by Results scheme fixed a basic output per bricklayer per hour, varying from 24 bricks to 80 bricks according to the size of brick and the category of work to be done. The bonus to be paid above the basic output varies from 2s. 3d. per 100 bricks per bricklayer to 6s. 11d. The more frequent types of bricks, $4\frac{1}{2}$ in. and 9 in., pointed both sides, are scheduled at 30 and 42 bricks respectively (that is, 240 and 336 in an 8-hour day) and with bonuses of 5s. 6d. and 4s. (The bonus works out at about 1s. 8d. per hour.) A bricklayer's efficiency in peace-time has been estimated by an expert[3] as some 500 bricks in an 8-hour day,[4]

---

[1] For one week equalling £3. 16s.

[2] Mr. A. Hopkinson, Captain Gammans, and Mr. Higgs, in the House of Commons, and Letter to the *Times*, July 22, 1943, stated respectively that, a piece rate of 1·32d. per brick laid compares with 0·42d. before the war; 360 bricks, 9 in., pointed one side, in 8 hours compare with 700 bricks in $8\frac{1}{2}$ hours before the war and with 900 bricks in 10 hours before the last war; 4,000 bricks could be laid in a day under favourable circumstances ; 800–1,000 bricks could be laid in a day.

[3] H. A. Mackunin, *Builders' Estimates and Pricing Data*, 1936.

[4] With the help of a bricklayers' labourer.

representing an average of good and bad conditions. If we assume the output under favourable circumstances as being between 650 and 750, then the average of 500 suggests that some 250 to 350 bricks would be laid under less satisfactory conditions. The Payment by Results Scheme worked obviously on the hypothesis that the war-time deterioration in labour, management, material, and transport has to be allowed for, and that an incentive for higher output has to be given to the marginal worker.

The building labour force, totalling before the war some 1,300,000, has been weakened by the call-up of at least 500,000 of its young personnel to munition work and the services. Only part of them have been replaced, the inflow consisting of older men and of others not before engaged in the building industry. The number of crafts-men has been reduced by one-half to two-thirds and the average ratio of craftsman to labourer, varying in peace-time between 1 : 1, 1 : 2, and 2 : 3, has correspondingly deteriorated.

Cost per Unit of Output

Those labour costs resulting from the Payment by Results Scheme appear to be caused by this deterioration in the labour force, and the few data available suggest that the Scheme succeeded in its aim of raising the efficiency of building labour. (But it is not known if the relatively low level fixed for the basic output is the one best suited for achieving *maximum* efficiency.) Mr. Hicks stated

Cost of Bricklaying in a 10-hour Day

	Brickwork left rough			Brickwork pointed one side		
	4½ in.	9 in.	14 in.	4 in.	9 in.	14 in.
Bricklayers' actual output,[1] Bricks	650	780	870	560	700	790
Scheduled basic output[2] ..	400	500	600	340	450	550
Therefore bonus paid on: ..	250	280	270	220	250	240
Bonus per 100 bricks (sh.) ..	4/6	3/6	3/-	5/-	3/9	3/2
Total bonus	11/3	9/8	8/1	11/-	9/4	7/6
Basic wage 10-hour bricklayer, bricklayers' labourer and ganger[3]	33/5	33/5	33/5	33/5	33/5	33/5
+ 60 per cent additional over-time rate, for 2½ hours ..	5/-	5/-	5/-	5/-	5/-	5/-
Basic wage + overtime ..	38/5	38/5	38/5	38/5	38/5	38/5
Bonus as percentage of basic wage and overtime ..	29·5	25·0	21·0	28·5	24·5	19·5

[1] According to above sample.

[2] As provided in Payment by Results Scheme.

[3] A ganger supervising some 6 bricklayers and 3 labourers receives an additional pay of 1d.–3d. per hour. Therefore basic wage for bricklayer (2/1½): 21/3; for ½ bricklayer's labourer (1/8): 8/4; for 1/6 ganger (2/3½): 3/10; total 33/5.

in Parliament that according to an enquiry on 372 sites extending over three months and ending on April 30, 1943, the output of 9 in. brickwork left rough per bricklayer per hour was 78 bricks compared with 64 before the war. On the basis of this sample we can try to estimate the cost of the Bonus Scheme.

Bonus payments thus account for an addition of 20–30 per cent; if efficiency has increased (78 instead of 64 bricks per hour) by 22 per cent, the Payment by Results Scheme appears to be responsible for a relative rise in labour cost of probably 3 per cent and of not more than 8 per cent. Thus, the drop in efficiency due to war-time conditions has been mitigated, labour conditions have been improved and labour disputes evaded. Without the bonus system there would have been a greater urgency for an increase in basic wages which lagged behind the rising cost of living.

The Payment by Results Scheme should only be applied 'when practicable and desirable.'[1] Under the Scheme, until July, 1943, 8,500 sites had been scheduled, and in July, 1943, 235,000 operatives were employed on 2,600 sites. Work on non-scheduled sites does not fall under this official piece-rate scheme although other bonus arrangements may be made.[2] Therefore, out of the 800,000 or so building operatives a minority only has received the official bonus payments. If we take into account this fact as well as the close interconnection of bonus and basic wage as mentioned above, the share of the Scheme in total costs of building labour can hardly be more than $1\frac{1}{2}$–2 per cent.

This argument is based on bricklayer's output because an appproximate guess is possible from data given. The Payment by Results Order applies, however, to 12 other major operations in building, such as carpentry and joinery, painting, pipe-laying, etc. It has been assumed above that the principles of calculation applied to bricklaying are representative for other building operations included in the Scheme. This assumption would help to confirm the above explanation (p. 307) of the discrepancy between wage-rates and earnings for all building operations in housing.

Other changes introduced in war-time and traceable neither in wage-rates nor in earnings have raised the cost of building labour: the

[1] Mr. Hicks, House of Commons, July 23, 1943.
[2] Bonus schemes often form part of national agreements in individual industries, as in the Civil Engineering Industry. Allowance for this fact, difficult to assess, should be made in calculating the extra cost of the compulsory scheme.

obligation upon contractors to provide reasonable living and feeding facilities for the operatives, emergency medical services, recreational and transport facilities, and, in many cases, protective clothing and rubber boots. The costs of transferred labour have also to be counted in this category. Transferred workers receive a lodging allowance of 24s. a week, free travel home, cheap meals, regular leave, allowances for fare and travelling time, the home rate of wages in low-rated districts, and the craftsman's rate of wages if they are engaged as labourers.

Assuming that some 25–30 per cent of the total labour force consist of transferred labour, and some 10 per cent consist of craftsmen used as labourers and that allowances for travelling time and fares are paid to one-half of the labour force, some 20 per cent additional costs have to be taken into account.

Conclusion

To summarize, the costs of building labour per project expressed in terms of the *present* basic wage rate may have increased by 5 per cent by the Payment by Results Scheme (where applicable), 30 per cent by other war-time factors (overtime and Sunday work [8–10 per cent] and transferred labour[1] [20 per cent]), 10 per cent by new concessions to labour (holidays with pay, guaranteed week, new facilities). The wage-index calculated from the basic wage rate only cannot allow for this additional burden of some 45 per cent. Expressed in *pre-war* basic rates, which have risen by 31 per cent, these new charges account for 60 per cent. The total war-time increase in the costs of building labour is therefore as follows:

basic wage rates	..	..	..	31 per cent
additional changes	..	..	..	45 „ „
total increase (131 × 1·45)	..	..		76 per cent

Labour costs have further been increased in the transport of building materials. In order to save rubber tyres for road vehicles, building materials are nowadays largely carried by railway. The transport from the manufacturer to the site of building involves the additional processes of unloading from road vehicles to the railway carriage and vice versa.[2] Once sufficient labour and transport vehicles are

[1] A greater margin of error has to be allowed for this item which varies according to the quantity of local labour raised.
[2] The problem of higher freights resulting from this change in transport will be discussed in the second article.

again available an increase in the cost of building labour by some 40-45 per cent over *pre-war* may remain (of which 31 per cent are due to the basic wage rates, assuming the cost of living is stabilized on the present level and some 13 per cent to concessions to labour, provided they are maintained). The immediate post-war programme will certainly be burdened with higher costs.[1]

[1] After the last war, 715 houses were built in the first year and 30,000 in the second.

THE COST OF BUILDING MATERIALS

by S. Moos

FROM BULLETIN, VOL. 5, NO. 15 (OCTOBER, 1943)

IN investigating how far the Board of Trade Wholesale Index of building materials is representative for present-day developments, we have to examine the structure of this index and then test it against the changes in the relative importance as well as in the quality of the major building materials and in the costs of transport.

The Board of Trade Index

The Board of Trade Index, as reconstructed in 1935, is mostly based on weekly quotations from which a monthly average is derived.[1] While with other commodity groups the weights of individual items are based on the value of goods manufactured or produced within the U.K. as given in the Census of Production, 1930,[2] and the imports of corresponding goods, in the index for building materials the individual items are weighted in accordance to their importance for building purposes. The weights were arrived at by collecting information with regard to the principal classes of materials used in the construction and repair (a) of working-class dwellings and (b) of a superior type of stone-faced office building. By some unknown procedure, the provisional weights were combined with the Census of Production, 1930, figures and the final weights established (Paint 3, Iron and Steel 3, Timber 2, Bricks and other clay products (excluding tiles) 2, Cement, Sand and Lime 2, Slates and Tiles 1, Stone 1, Glass 1, Lead and Earthenware 1, Total 16).

As far as the weights are based on the Census figures, changes between 1930 and 1935 can be estimated from published data.

The consumption of timber[3] (including imports) in building has been estimated at £m. 40·1 for 1930 but no exact information has come forward. Nor are data on the value of paint used in the building industry available. The assignment of a weight of 3 to paint may be explained by the fact that the Board of Trade has included Repair

---

[1] The geometric mean is used in averaging the percentage price changes from the base year, a method which is said to reduce the influence of quotations which have become unrepresentative.
[2] Before 1935 the Census of 1906 formed this basis.
[3] Sawn softwoods, builders' woodwork, and plywood.

X   313

TABLE I

BUILDING MATERIALS IN THE CENSUS OF PRODUCTION, 1930, 1935

	Quantities		Value in £000			
	1930	1935	1930		1935	
				per cent		per cent
Building bricks (millions)	4,678	7,720	11,421	33.0	15,613	37·5
Tiles, Roofing (000 tons)	599[1]	823	2,040 ⎫		2,300 ⎫	
Tiles, Floors, Walls, and				10·7		11·8
Hearth (000 cwt.) ..	1,026	1,793	1,698 ⎭		2,654 ⎭	
Limestone[2]			2,587	7·5	2,329	5·6
Sandstone[2]			1,581	4·5	1,285	3·1
Cement[3] (000 tons) ..	5,002	6·214	7,764	22·4	9.260	22·1
Iron and Steel girders, beams, joists, pillars, etc. (000 tons)	357	513	2,902	8·4	3,639	8·7
Glass, Slate, and Sheet ..			4,727	13·5	4,666	11·2
Total of above items ..			34,720	100·0	41,746	100·0

[1] Equivalent to 528 million tiles.   [2] For use in building.
[3] For use in building and engineering.

work in the weights of the Index, and in the years preceding the war, repair accounted for some 25-30 per cent of total building work. However, the total value of repairs includes decorating, plumbing, heating, lighting, carpentry work, shop and office fittings, etc., and labour, so that paint still seems overweighted. On the other hand, various items in the sand and ballast group are not included in the Board of Trade Index.

As the B.O.T. Index is based on conditions existing in 1930, we would also have to allow for changes in technique and quality, for the relative development of prices of different materials, and for the changing character of building projects since that date.

A certain shift from one-family to large tenement houses can be observed, and dwelling houses play a smaller rôle in total building activity than before, their share falling from 63 per cent in 1930 to 57 per cent in the first half of 1939, while that of factories, shops, and offices increased, in the same period, from 13 per cent to 20 per cent.

TABLE II

BUILDING PLANS, IN £ MILL.

	Dwelling Houses		Factories and Workshops		Shops, Offices, Warehouses etc.		Churches, Schools, Public Buildings		Other Buildings, Additions, Alterations		Totals	
		%		%		%		%		%		%
1930	46·8	63	4·6	6	5·5	7	8·4	11	9·4	13	74·6	100
1935	78·4	68	7·7	7	7·9	7	9·0	8	11·3	10	114·3	100
1938	60·0	61	7·5	8	9·5	10	9·5	10	11·1	11	97·6	100
1 half 1939 ..	27·0	57	4·6	10	4·8	10	4·9	10	6·0	13	47·3	100
∴ 1939, theoretical	54·0		9·0		9·6		9·8		12·0		94 6	

Assuming the first half of 1939 to be representative for a full peace year, the value of building plans for new dwelling houses, between 1930 and 1939, rose by 15·4 per cent, but that for factories, shops, etc., by 84 per cent and the total value by 27 per cent. The important changes in building activity since 1930, the year on which the weights of the Board of Trade Index are based, continued up to the outbreak of war. Since then the character of building activity has been transformed, construction being concentrated on factories, hostels, barracks, airfields, shelters, etc. The output of bricks has shrunk to about one-fourth[1] of peace time, while the production of concrete has been extended. During and after the war, some building materials may be scarce and be substituted by others. Under present conditions, an accurate re-weighting of building materials in an index of prices seems extremely difficult. The weights will depend on the general building policy. Important issues such as pre-fabrication against traditional methods, flats versus houses, repair versus new houses, imported versus home-grown timber, etc., have first to be decided.

We can say, however, that a relative underweight of timber in the Index, if compared with steel, becomes significant when timber prices rise out of all proportion, as is the case at present. An increase in various building material prices of some 40–60 per cent compares with a 155 per cent rise in timber. The second largest price increase has taken place in ballast ('2 in. unscreened' having risen by 80 per cent and Thames ballast by 58 per cent) which is also insufficiently represented in the Index.

Bricks, Cement, and Timber

The Board of Trade Index suffers also from shortcomings in the price quotations used. Changes in the quality of the materials quoted cannot easily be allowed for, owing to the difficulty in estimating the degree to which inferior material[2] and substitutes for materials in short supply have been employed. Yet, a comparison of prices can only be of value in so far as the standard of quality is maintained. The extent of these shifts in quality may be gauged from the wide discrepancies in the estimates of price changes.

Estimates of the change in the price of bricks run from –2 per cent to as much as + 100 per cent. The differences in quotation are due to differences in the quality quoted, to the change in the type of brick

[1] To some 2,000,000,000. Mr. Hicks, in House of Commons, 23/7/43.
[2] The present scarcity of materials is an incentive for disposal of stocks which could not be sold on a normal market. During and after the last war, doors and windows were often made of green wood, and bricks were used which could not withstand the effect of frost.

used, to the inclusion or exclusion of freight to the place of delivery, and to the levy of 3s. per 1,000 bricks for the care and maintenance of 318 closed brick-works, a charge which is levied uniformly without regard to quality and may or may not be included in the quotation.

The war-time rise in the price of 1 ton of cement[1] has been given as 24 per cent (from 41s. to 51s.), as 41 per cent (from 41s. to 58s.) and as 50 per cent (from 42s. to 63s).[2]

The change in the prices of timber is difficult to estimate. The substitution of imported by home-grown timber involves not only a change in quality. While timber is imported according to specified grades in each particular species of wood, there is in home-grown timber no recognized grading, no special mark which would guarantee a certain quality. Although maximum prices are fixed by schedule, prices quoted seem to vary to such a degree, that no comparable figures can be given.

The maximum price schedule allows for special additions to be made of 10 per cent in case of selected lengths and 20 per cent for orders of less than £15 value for any one size and quality. In spite of official counter-measures there is always the possibility to split up large orders into £15 units. Often, lacking the sizes and grades wanted, more expensive wood has to be purchased. There is a further percentage increase on the maximum price of home-grown wood processed in this country, varying from 5 per cent to 50 per cent according to the location of the mill[3] and to other circumstances.[4] A 10 per cent addition is allowed if the material had previously beeen delivered to a depôt certified by the Ministry of Supply. It is thus not surprising that estimates with regard to the increase in timber prices (per standard), vary measurably, between 275 per cent (from £15. 10s. to £60); 140 per cent (from £20 to £48); 154 per cent (from £28 to £71); 205 per cent (from £18 to £55),[5] (pre-war compared with summer 1943).

The increase in the price of metal windows has been given as 75 per cent and as 25 per cent. In the first quotation, qualities which had

---

[1] The cost of which in building depends largely on the proportion of lime and cement to sand varying between 1 : 1 and 1 : 3.

[2] Estimates respectively by *The Builder*; Mr. Hicks, *Hansard*, 1943, p. 1330, and Mr. Quibell Brigg, *Hansard*, 1943, p. 1289.

[3] Town, country, or port-city mill.

[4] The Control of Timber Order, 1943, No. 192, differentiates between processed wood sold by a mill-owner and that sold by a retailer and between delivery to the buyer from the mill and delivery from a retailers' store.

[5] Estimates respectively by Mr. D. Quibell, House of Commons, 23/7/43; Mr. Hicks, House of Commons, 23/7/43; Softwood, planed boards, British Columbia Pine, *The Builder*, *Times*, 22/7/43, Letter to the Editor by the President of the Housebuilders' Association.

been widely used in peace but have meanwhile become scarce, were given their old pre-war weights, when the average price was compiled. The second quotation is based on a standard quality which has become representative for war-time building.

Two Estimates of Price Changes

Table III, giving prices of building materials as published weekly in *The Builder*, reflects the complications in comparing pre-war and present quotations.[1]

A comparison of the prices is misleading in so far as the quotations of 1939 refer to 'delivered to site' in the London Area, but are now partly given 'at works,' that is, excluding freight, partly to certain stations and partly 'to site'.

TABLE III

PRICES OF BUILDING MATERIALS (SOURCE, *The Builder*)[1]

		25/8/1939 delivered to the site	15/10/1943	Percentage Increase
		£ s. d.	£ s. d.	
Bricks, First Hard Stocks	.. per 1,000	4 15 0	4 13 0 (at works)	—2
Thames Ballast	.. „ yard	7 3	11 6 (Paddington)	58
Cement, in loads of 6 tons	.. „ ton	2 1 0	2 11 0 (London)	24
Slates, 20 in. × 10 in. ..	.. „ 1,000	20 15 0	30 5 0 „	46
Tiles, part machine made	.. „ 1,000	4 2 6	5 18 0 „	43
Softwood, Planed Boards, Brit. Columbia Pine ..	.. „ stnd.	28 0 0	71 0 0	155
Steel Joists, Girders, etc. ..	.. „ ton	16 0 0	24 0 0 „	50
White Lead Paint ..	.. „ cwt.	3 8 0	4 16 6	42
Sheet glass, 18 ozs. ..	.. „ ft. super	2¼	3¼	45

[1] Quoted by kind permission of *The Builder*.

This mode of calculation may be responsible for the fact that the rise in prices of several materials seems much lower in *The Builder* than in other sources. Iron rain-water goods are still quoted at pre-war prices. 2 in. Unscreened Ballast appears with an increase of some 60 per cent compared with 88 per cent in the *Architects' Journal*. The war-time levy of 3s. per 1,000 bricks is excluded. Owing to this omission and to the exclusion of transport costs, the quotation for bricks (first hard Stocks) has, in the course of the war, fallen by 2 per cent. The price for cement excludes the charge of 7s. for bags which in peace-time had been delivered free.

A comparatively good basis for comparison is given by the data

[1] It is this price list of *The Builder* from which the Board of Trade compiles its Index of Wholesale Prices of Building Materials. The following quotations in *The Builder* are used by the Board of Trade: timber, bricks, tiles, slates, cement, steel joists, bath stones, chalk, lime, ballast, glass, rain-water pipes, white lead paint.

published monthly in the *Architects' Journal*; they refer to materials delivered to site in the London Area if not otherwise stated. Table IV gives the development of prices, half-yearly since the outbreak of war. It can be seen that the different materials vary considerably with regard to the total increase and to the timing of price-rises. Of the materials quoted[1] the greatest rise has taken place in ballast and in sheet lead, 80 per cent and 65 per cent. Bricks have risen by only 29 per cent. Other materials are some 40–50 per cent higher than before the war. With the exception of white lead paint and stoneware drain-pipes, prices have moved only little since the second half of 1941.

If the Board of Trade weights are applied to the prices given in the *Architects' Journal*,[2] a war-time increase of some 53 per cent is arrived at, against 43 per cent as given by the Board of Trade for the second half of 1943.[3]

There are no Government fixed prices for bricks, tiles, lime, sand, and ballast.[4] The system of control of building materials[5] is based not on compulsory powers but on voluntary co-operation of the trade associations concerned.

Apart from the building materials listed above, the costs of specialists' work such as sanitary fittings, wall-tiling, ironmongery, and internal plumbing has to be considered. Enquiries with important firms gave the following results: Prices of Sanitary equipment have risen by some 50-to 55 per cent, of ironmongery 40 per cent, of wall-tiling for glazed tiles 75 per cent, for floor tiles 50 per cent, and of internal plumbing (including domestic and hot water) 45 per cent.[6] An average increase of some 50 per cent in the price of specialists' work seems therefore a good approximation.

Conclusion

Changes in the type and average distance of transport may be responsible for changes in cost out of proportion to the rise in freight rates. Overheads (which seem to run between 20 per cent and $33\frac{1}{2}$ per cent on wages, and 10 per cent to $12\frac{1}{2}$ per cent on materials) may

---

[1] Which do not include timber and glass.
[2] With the exception of timber and glass, taken from *The Builder*.
[3] In the 3rd quarter, 1943, the Board of Trade increase was 45 per cent.
[4] For paint, profit margins have been fixed at 1939 levels by the Central Price Regulation Committee.
[5] Most building materials are controlled by the Ministry of Works, although under different forms of control, some of them stricter than others. Timber and steel are the concern of the Ministry of Supply.
[6] Referring to working-class houses.

TABLE IV

WHOLESALE PRICES OF BUILDING MATERIALS, 1939–1943

(Source: *Architects' Journal*)

	Pre-War Price = 100			1 half 1940	2 half 1940	1 half 1941	2 half 1941	1 half 1942	2 half 1942	1 half 1943	3 quarter 1943
	£	s.	d.								
Portland Cement, per ton[1]	2	1	0	113·0	120·7	135·4	136·2	137·8	140·2	141·5	
2 in. unscreened ballast, per yard cube	1	5	9	117·5	131·8	154·4	166·0	171·0	171·0	179·7	
Fletton bricks (at station), per 1000	2	6	0	101·0	109·1	111·9	111·9	114·0	129·2	129·2	
Stoneware drain-pipes, 6 in. each[2]		2	0	109·4	112·5	118·8	120·4	128·1	137·5	138·6	
Roofing tiles, per 1000	4	15	0	109·3	126·5	120·0	130·0	130·0	142·5	144·0	
Steel joists, basic sections,[3] per ton	12	10	0	119·0	136·4	147·5	147·5	147·5	147·5	147·5	
Lime, grey stone, per ton[4]	2	2	0	115·9	121·0	131·0	134·7	135·3	135·3	143·5	
Sheet lead, 3½ lb. and over, per cwt.[5]	1	3	1	150·0	150·0	150·8	154·4	156·2	165·2	165·2	
Iron rain-water goods and soil pipes, 4 in. per yard		3	8¼	111·1	114·7	119·5	122·0	126·5	126·5	126·5	
Copper tubes, straight, 1½ in. each		3	6	125·3	125·5	127·7	127·7	129·8	129·8		
White lead paint, per cwt.	3	6	0	122·6	125·3	126·5	127·4	134·9	138·6		
Board of Trade Index of Building Materials	100·0			110·2	116·7	132·4	135·0	137·1	140·9	142·9	145·0

[1] Orders, 4 tons and over.
[2] Orders, 2 tons and over.
[3] Ex mills.
[4] 1 ton lots.
[5] Orders of 5 cwt. and over.

have risen out of proportion to prime costs in some cases. War Risk Insurance at 3 per cent on many material stocks must be counted. The effect of these and other small factors cannot be measured but allowance should be made for them. They are excluded from our final estimate of war-time changes in building costs which we can now summarize:

Building materials	..	..	..	..	..	55·0 per cent
Labour[1]	..	..	..	..	..	91·0 per cent
Wages and Materials (ratio 45 : 55)						72·0 per cent

[1] See 'Labour Costs in Housing', Bulletin, Vol. 5, No. 14.

The difference between this estimate and that of 60–70 per cent based on tenders for new dwellings in the previous article indicates the margin of error which may be due partly to an over-estimate of the costs of transferred labour, partly to the change in quality of buildings since the outbreak of war. If profit margins were higher than before the war, the increase in average costs of building would be over 75–80 per cent.

A permanent source of unnecessarily higher costs is to be found in existing Standard Building Bye Laws which do not allow for the progress, before and during the war, in building materials, and which retard the extension of dove-tail (pre-fabrication) building. The future trend of the cost of building materials cannot easily be assessed. The liquidation of private building activity during the war may have prevented a further rise in prices. But the absence of a stricter control of prices of building materials will make it more difficult to avoid sharp upward movements when private building is resumed.[1]

[1] During the building boom, 1920–21 building costs had risen to 300–350 per cent above pre-war before they fell to 60–80 per cent above the pre-war level. The average cost of a house (parlour and non-parlour) fell from £627–714 in 1921 to £310–429 in 1922. (Source: International Labour Office, *Housing Policy in Europe*).

Postscript: In October, 1945, building materials, according to the B.O.T. Index, had increased since August, 1939, by 51·6 per cent, wage-rates by 40 per cent; the Minister of Works stated, however, in the House of Commons, that the cost of a £1,200 house in November, 1945, corresponded to a £550 house before the War, that is an increase of 120 per cent compared with 72 per cent in July, 1943.

MEAT AND WHEAT

by J. Goldmann

FROM BULLETIN, VOL. 5, No. 5 (APRIL 3, 1943)

IT was announced recently that the first shipments of dried meat had arrived in this country and that it would take some time until supplies would be sufficient to allow distribution through retail shops as part of the meat ration. The prospect of dried meat becoming available for this purpose considerably affects the basis of the present meat policy, and it thus renews the interest in the standing war-time controversy of cattle-rearing versus wheat-farming.

1. During four years of war, about 7 million acres have been ploughed up. Since, however, part of this land has returned to temporary grasses, the net increase in tillage is smaller than 7 million acres, but to what extent is not known. The acreage under wheat had been brought up from 1·9 million acres in 1938 to 2·2 million acres by the Spring of 1942,[1] and subsequently Mr. Hudson asked for a further increase of 0·6 million acres. It follows that of the newly ploughed-up land only about 15 per cent went into wheat production, assuming that Mr. Hudson's request was fully complied with. Thus, the share of wheat in arable farming was, at best, kept constant during the war. There have been some increases in the area under potatoes, sugar beet, and vegetables, but the greater part of the new tillage is producing fodder crops.[2] In this way it became possible, in spite of the virtual cessation of imports of feeding-stuffs, to increase the cattle population above the pre-war level.[3]

2. It is not difficult to estimate—in terms of alternative uses—the cost to the war-economy of using the greater part of the additional acreage for the maintenance of the cattle population. Before the war, 7 to 8 million acres of arable land produced fodder crops (or temporary grasses). In view of the war-time increase, this figure may have risen to 11 to 12 million acres. Let us assume that the original policy of the Ministry of Agriculture of reducing the number

[1] See *The Times*, March 19, 1942.
[2] Dr. C. S. Orwin, *Manchester Guardian*, June 19, 1942.
[3] See *The Times*, August 17, 1942. There was a fall in the number of pigs, sheep, and poultry.

of cattle[1] had been carried out and that, for example, beef cattle production had been cut, say by a third, while dairy herds had been maintained. Since the share of beef cattle in the total cattle population is about 50 per cent, fodder consumption by all cattle would have been reduced by about one-sixth. Disregarding, for the moment, the claim of other live-stock on fodder supplies, it may be estimated that, under the assumption of the above cut, a sixth of the acreage under fodder, or about 2 million acres, would become available for other use.

The cut in home supplies of beef would be smaller than a third, since part of the supply of beef is derived from dairy herds. The net reduction may be taken as about 25 per cent of the home supply of beef[2] or about 130,000 tons a year. If the 2 million acres released from fodder production were put under wheat, milling barley, or rye, the gain in home-grown corn may be estimated—allowing for lower yields on marginal land—at about 1·5 million tons.

A fall in the fodder acreage would also affect the (already reduced) sheep population, but to a lesser extent, because sheep rely more on permanent grass land or rough grazing than cattle. In any case, even a 15 per cent cut in home-grown mutton supplies would only mean a loss of about 30,000 tons.

The net saving in shipping space may be smaller than the difference between the gain in corn (about 1·5 million tons) and the loss in meat (at most 160,000 tons), because of a possible increase in requirements of imported fertilizers which might occur if the cattle population were reduced; it is unlikely, however, that the net saving resulting from the assumed cut in the numbers of beef cattle by a third would be less than 1 million tons. (Supplies of milk would not be effected). Agricultural scientists and farmers differ as to the extent of the net saving that could be achieved, but Lord Cornwallis, Chairman of the Kent War Agricultural Committee, in a speech to the Farmers' Club, quoted and did not question a statement that 'it took 5 to 15 acres of crops fed to livestock to save as much shipping space as one acre under human food crops.'[3] This statement roughly confirms our estimate of a gain of 1·5 million tons of corn against

---

[1] 'The number of livestock would have to be adjusted so that a larger acreage of our land could directly grow human food.' Mr. Hudson, as quoted in *The Times*, March 6, 1941. Further: 'The Minister of Agriculture has now told the farmers that they must start to reduce the number of cattle on their farms as well as pigs and poultry.'

[2] Estimated from the average pre-war supply with an allowance for the reduction in yield of meat due to under-feeding, which was only partly offset by the increase in the number of cattle.

[3] *The Times*, October 7, 1942.

a loss of at most 160,000 tons of meat from the switch-over of a sixth of the acreage under fodder to corn crops. (The net saving should, perhaps, be reduced, by an allowance for additional import requirements of fertilizers.)

3. An independent check on the above estimate can be obtained by another method involving a few technical considerations.[1] Calves not intended for dairying, fattening, or breeding are usually slaughtered after one to two months and they yield about 100 lb. of veal. The average live weight of fat cattle is 11 cwt., yielding about 700 lb. of beef, a net increase of 600 lb., as compared with the yield of the calf.

The cost of fodder requirements can be estimated as follows: On the average the breeding of fat cattle takes two years, and the subsequently fattening process five months. During the breeding period, winter rations of fodder crops total 0·8 tons starch equivalent for the whole period. In addition, for summer feeding on the pastures one and a quarter to one and a half acres of grassland should be allowed per head. To maintain an annual output of one animal, two animals must be kept in the breeding stage in each year. This requires an annual production in fodder crops amounting to 0·8 tons starch equivalent, and the cultivation of 2·5 to 3 acres of grass land. The average yield of the main fodder crops is 1 ton starch equivalent per acre. It follows that 0·8 acres must be kept under fodder crops. The combined annual acreage requirements (feeding stuffs and grass), is, so far, 3·3 to 3·8 acres.

In addition, after about two years, the animal is fattened and consumes during the fattening period feeding stuffs of a starch equivalent of about 0·8 tons. This increases the acreage under fodder crops by another 0·8 acres, and brings the total acreage requirements to 4·1 to 4·6 acres. This is the acreage needed for an annual production of 600 lbs. of beef; or 15 to 17 acres to 1 ton of beef.

If the acreage producing one ton of beef were put under wheat, milling barley or rye, the yield in corn may be estimated at about 11 tons. Thus we obtain a similar ratio of meat to corn yields per acre as before.

4. Moreover, it will probably not be necessary to increase imports of meat to the extent calculated above. While the slaughtering-off is in progress the supply of home-grown meat would be greater than before and imports could even be reduced. This would not, however,

---

[1] Figures relating to beef and veal production given below are based on Watson and Moore, *Agriculture*.

necessitate a corresponding increase in the weight of meat imports at a later date, because then dried meat will be available in larger quantities. The deficiency in home-grown meat supplies, which will occur after the slaughtering-off process has been completed, will be covered by imports of dried meat weighing not much more than a third of the equivalent quantity of fresh or refrigerated meat.

5. A change in meat policy may also become necessary for another reason. Part of the land that has been brought into arable cultivation during the war is now sown to temporary grass to maintain soil fertility, and thus withdrawn from crops for human consumption. It has been stated by Mr. Hudson that in 1942 this factor went a considerable way towards nullifying, in respect of the net increase of tillage, the 800,000 scheduled acres of newly ploughed-up land. Other land, hitherto under grass, may be released in the process and become available for crops for human consumption. It is probable, however, that this land will be less suited for such crops and that their yield will be reduced. If this is so, more land will be required to produce the same supply of crops for direct consumption, and it will become even more urgent to reduce the area under fodder crops.

This factor will gain in importance during the next one or two seasons when large parts of the new tillage will return to temporary grasses. Then, the alternative to a reduction in the beef cattle population will not just mean foregoing economies in shipping which could be achieved by such a measure, but new demands on shipping space due to the reduction of home wheat supplies.

6. A reduction of the beef cattle population can only be effected through an adjustment of the present price structure for agricultural supplies. As long as it pays farmers to maintain their livestock, rather than to grow human food directly, they will do so and compulsory measures may prove abortive. The announcement of a long term purchasing policy with a price-differential favouring slaughterings in the nearest suitable period will help to overcome resistance to changes that have become necessary. On the other hand, price adjustments in themselves may be insufficient, in view of the strong influence of post-war considerations which may induce farmers to maintain their livestock, even if this should cause losses in the short run. Direct controls will, therefore, be required.

As prices of home-grown meat are considerably higher than prices of imported meat a temporary increase in the share of the former in total consumption would amount to an effective reduction in the existing meat ration, which is fixed by value. If a further cut in supplies of animal protein were inadvisable such a reduction could be avoided either by reducing the price of home-grown meat with an increase in the present subsidy, or by raising the money value of the meat ration. Both measures need only be temporary and could be cancelled when the slaughtering-off process is completed. If either of them were adopted, the additional saving in shipping space mentioned above (Section 4), would be somewhat reduced but the basic economy from the switch-over from beef production to direct human food would remain unaffected.

VI. INDUSTRIAL ORGANIZATION

CONCENTRATION IN THE 'NON-ESSENTIAL' INDUSTRIES

by T. Balogh and F. A. Burchardt

From Bulletin, Vol. 3, No. 4 (March 15, 1941)

THE measures announced by the President of the Board of Trade, which will concentrate production of 'non-essential commodities' in certain firms picked according to war needs, have been welcomed in principle by the industries concerned and by the public in general. They will permit a better use of labour and plant in these industries, thus freeing a large volume of both for the war sector, where they are urgently needed. The present position in which the cut in home consumption exhausted itself mainly by reducing the scale of operation of firms, instead of leading to the complete shutting of some, was not satisfactory. Costs rose as overheads had to be distributed over a smaller output, plant, and labour were not fully utilized, productivity declined. All this will be altered by the new policy.

It is reported that about one hundred industries, of which twenty are major ones, will be affected by the plan. In view of what the newspapers describe as the revolutionary nature of the measure, and in view of the differences in working conditions, organization, and location of the various industries, the Government's decision to take the industries, both employers and employees, into their full confidence seems to be a wise policy. The various industries are to work out their own plans for output concentration, and the discussions between the Board of Trade and industrial representatives are to begin this week and to be completed as speedily as possible. These preliminary talks should enable the Government to obtain an idea of the different conditions existing in the various industries and of the prevailing attitude of industrial circles towards a solution of the problem. It is realized that voluntary agreements may prove impossible and that the Government may have to enforce a scheme. For this eventuality and also as a criterion for judging the majority

326

decisions of voluntary agreements, the Government will have to work out certain guiding principles.

In fact, it will not be easy to persuade firms to disclose manufacturing secrets, customers' lists, etc., to their competitors, and it is doubtful whether private agreements can be arrived at about trade marks and goodwill. At any rate, private negotiations may entail delay. And delay retards the war efforts and may also, as the Cotton Board has pointed out, prejudice the position of many firms and the smooth introduction of the scheme. Further, if objective criteria such as demand for labour, safety of the area from air attack, profitability, etc., are to determine the 'nucleus firms' the less fortunate will be in a very poor bargaining position. As there is little doubt who they will be, it may be desirable to safeguard the weak firms against the demands of the better-off firms and also to decide whether or to what extent concentration of output should be permitted to promote concentration of ownership at onerous conditions for those taken over, which seems under the present plan inevitable. Quite apart from the fact that such development is not reversible and the Government has pledged itself to guarantee reinstatement after the war, industrial self-government taking the form of private monopolies does not, as demonstrated in the past, seem to produce the best solutions from the national point of view. Suitable interchange of managements, the reshaping of production technique, economy in replacements, is more difficult if the 'firm' even after energetic 'concentration' of production is retained as a unit. Thus, even though the proposed solution is an improvement on the actual position it falls short of the optimum possible.

The unscrambling of war-time arrangements, the restoration of goodwill and labour force to the closed-down firms, the protection of the weaker firms which the Government desires can be met in various ways. One solution, which may not appeal immediately to the industries concerned but has been mentioned in discussions about the reorganization of the industry, seems to offer definite advantage over more private arrangements. War-time Holding Companies unifying whole industries could be established. They could issue preference shares to all participating firms according to certain objective standards such as pre-war profits, capital, etc., and irrespective of whether they are to close down or not. All trading surplus, rent payments for buildings taken over by the Government, would be paid to the Holding Company, which would then distribute the revenue among the participating firms. Following the American example, controllers of these companies could be drawn from other industries *who have no private interests in the industry* and whose disinterestedness should command confidence. Such companies would be enabled:

(a) to appoint the best managers irrespective of their previous jobs;

(b) to rationalize production according to the most modern principles irrespective of the ownership of the plant, not only by concentrating production but also by transferring management, plant and labour as and when necessary;

(c) to accumulate and manage stock of commodities likely to become scarce, so as to minimize air-raid damage;

(d) to undertake such exports as deemed expedient irrespective of sterling cost.

It is more than probable that both the concentration of output, the growing scarcity of supplies and the safeguarding of the interest of all will demand simplification and standardization of products.

Independence of control of these factories will prevent them from degenerating into restrictive cartels and will safeguard the interests of the eliminated units, thus facilitating a return to peace conditions. In fact, the tighter State control is in war-time the more easy would seem to be a return to a freer economy afterwards.

The proposed reorganization could go a long way to achieve maximum technical efficiency and offer safeguards for the displaced firms, but can hardly do enough to reduce the hardship incurred by non-essential trades as a whole. It is significant that several of the major industries have at once raised the question of compensation. It is true, the new measures do not entail a further cut in production. They therefore do not increase the losses of industry. Indeed, if prices are maintained at the present level the mere concentration of output will increase the total surplus available for distribution.

Three ways of distributing the burden of concentration and restriction of production in non-essential trades are being discussed.

(a) To regard the existing cuts of production as a result of 'force majeure' and to distribute the extra profits of the 'nucleus firms' due to the transferred extra output according to certain standards among the displaced firms in each industry.

(b) To cover maintenance, current and capital obligations (partly or entirely) of the inactive firms by raising additional revenue by charging higher prices, that is by way of a levy.

(c) To provide for compensation out of State subsidies.

To judge from the official statement, the Board of Trade seems to favour the first method and has, at any rate, refused to grant compensation out of public funds. The extra earnings of the selected firms will obviously permit paying the displaced firms more than they have earned under spread-over conditions. They would thus indemnify the latter for losses due to concentration. That may or may not be sufficient to enable firms to meet fixed charges and maintenance costs.

Whether additional compensation should be given to enable all firms to cover these charges raises a different and wider question, namely, that of compensation for governmental restrictions of output. At the present scale of operations (and severer cuts may be inevitable) non-essential industries are incurring very serious losses, as the President of the Board of Trade stated. And the greatest conceivable increase in surplus (at given prices) may not be sufficient to cover minimum maintenance and fixed charges of the displaced firms. With or without concentration, these restrictions of production will either eliminate the weaker (marginal) firms[1] or compel them to amalgamate with their stronger competitors, unless the Government interferes with protective measures. Whether such a war-time purge of the non-essential trades is compatible with the Government's pledge to facilitate a return to the *status quo ante* and to maintain the independence of the individual units, has not yet been officially explained.

If compensation for loss of output were contemplated the worst means of raising compensation funds would be to levy them on the consumers by increased prices. The temptation for both the Government and the employers to compromise on this line is great, and Captain Lyttleton's speech left this question open. Yet, this solution should be firmly refused. For such an imposition of indirect taxes by private associations, where the rate of tax would be made largely dependent on the financial structure of the industry, would distribute the burden on the consumer in a haphazard way and may even drive production in undesirable directions. Moreover, the rise in prices will, through wage increases, further accentuate the vicious spiral. Finally, these levies are likely to become stumbling blocks in the demobilization period and will act as a lever for cartelization.

Should the Government be forced under pressure from the industries to grant them a measure of extra compensation for loss of output, straightforward subsidies would be the proper solution.

---

[1] The survival chances of the smaller firms might be greater under the present system than in the case of concentration which favours the large units.

Y

The reluctance of the Government to accept the principle of compensation for loss of output may be presumed to be based on these grounds:

1. That compensation in this case would create a precedent for claims of other firms, shops, and in fact income receivers in general hit by the war, and thus give rise to unforeseeable commitments.

2. That the country's finance could not afford additional payments for 'unproductive' purposes.

3. That it would lead to inflation.

Reason (1) may be regarded as a valid one; the validity of reasons (2) and (3), which are closely connected with one another, depends not on the payments made but on the way the payments are used.

Both the organizational and financial problem may not admit of a standard solution for all industries. But, if experimental plans are to be put in operation, it would appear desirable that at least in cases where no voluntary agreement has been reached, a scheme of War-time Holding Companies be given a trial, in order to compare the results of industrial self-government with that of rational State planning.

CONCENTRATION IN THE LEICESTER HOSIERY INDUSTRY[1]

by G. D. N. Worswick

FROM BULLETIN, VOL. 3, NO. 6 (APRIL 26, 1941)

PRINCIPLES OF TELESCOPING

THE principle of the concentration of production of non-essential goods into a reduced number of factories in order to release as much labour and factory space as possible for war-work has everywhere been accepted as necessary. But the method by which the telescoping is brought about is also of the profoundest importance. The Government scheme is nominally a war-time measure; nevertheless many of the changes it brings about will be permanent. It is vital, therefore, that the concentration process shall be one which not only benefits the community during the war, but also one which does not prejudice the future. During the war, sacrifices inevitably caused to particular interests should be distributed as evenly as possible, and so far as is consistent with the telescoping itself post-war interests should be protected.

In order to obtain an impression of how the scheme will work out in practice, a number of interviews was obtained with Hosiery manufacturers in Leicester in which they were asked to express their views of the Government scheme and to put forward any suggestions for its modification which they considered necessary.[2] The investigation was made easier by the fact that an *ad hoc* committee of small and medium manufacturers, representing over two hundred firms in and near Leicester, had recently been formed and it had already discussed many points and made certain specific requests

[1] The economic principles of concentration were amply discussed both in the BULLETIN and elsewhere when the scheme was introduced in March 1941. There were, however, many technical and organizational questions which arose in each particular industry. In order to throw some light on these problems a member of our staff paid a visit to Leicester to obtain the views of hosiery manufacturers on the concentration scheme and to form an impression of how it was working out in practice.—*The Editor.*

[2] The time available for this brief survey was extremely limited, and it was in no way comprehensive; in addition the answers of the Board of Trade to a number of important questions put by various firms had not been received and some of the problems raised in this article may, by the time of publication, have been solved in one way or another. I should like, at this point, to express my thanks to those manufacturers and others, who, at very short notice, did all they could to assist the investigation.

to the Board of Trade. As will be seen later, the hosiery industry has many problems peculiar to itself with regard to the concentration of production, but a description and analysis of these and other problems may suggest methods of telescoping which will have a more general application to other 'non-essential' industries. First of all it is necessary to outline the general procedure of concentration as it stands at present. A basic period—June to November 1940—has been taken, and every firm must calculate the value of its production of each of half-a-dozen different classes of hosiery, for both home civilian and Government order.[1] The Board of Trade indicates to the industry for each of the separate classes of hosiery how much of this production it considers 'redundant', and the production in future must be curtailed accordingly. For example, the 'redundancy' for outerwear, was, I was told, 60 per cent. For this class of good, therefore, a firm (A say) must calculate its production (in value terms) for the standard period; in future it may produce at a rate of 40 per cent of this figure. Furthermore, the number of machines must be so reduced as to produce this output on the basis of a 48-hour working week.[2] If, during the standard period a firm was using only 70 per cent of its machinery working on a 48-hour basis,[3] provided it is still producing the same line of good, in future it will need only 28 per cent of its machines, thus releasing 72 per cent of its plant. Suppose A wishes to qualify as a 'nucleus' firm, then it must find other firms B, C, D, etc., who will come into A's factory and produce on the remaining machinery their respective production quotas. Or, alternatively, A may shut down altogether, become an 'absorbed' firm and take over its quota to be produced by a 'nucleus' firm E. The financial arrangements are to be left to the firms to work out for themselves, subject to conditions laid down in the Government Explanatory Memorandum. In the main the idea of the official scheme has been to pool plant while preserving the identity of each selling organization. Clearly the success or failure of the plan depends on the ability or otherwise of A to produce B's product on A's machines or vice versa. And this is where the trouble begins, for according to the majority of the manufacturers interviewed, their sales, and thus their identity, depend on their continuing to knit a particular yarn according to a particular

[1] Exports are to be excluded from the concentration. If a firm were engaged 100 per cent on exports, it would presumably not be affected by the scheme, but this is a fictitious case.
[2] Where there has been no change in the quality of material the use of the *value* figure presents no difficulties; complications arise, however, when manufacturers have switched from one type to another or from wool to cotton.
[3] Actually it would probably have used all its machines, but on short time.

design, which was in turn dependent on the type of knitting frame used. To elucidate the point, it will be necessary to digress to pick out certain features of the organization of the hosiery industry in Leicester.

THE ORGANIZATION OF THE INDUSTRY

In the first place, hosiery is not homogeneous; it is, in fact, a very diversified product including all types of knitted goods. We have already mentioned the half-dozen main subdivisions, e.g., outerwear, underwear, hose, half-hose, etc. Within each subdivision there is wide variation according to the type of material used, wool, cotton, silk, rayon, etc., according to the weight of yarn, and also according to the type of knitting machine used. Army socks cannot be knitted in a frame which knits silk stockings, nor can a frame with 80 needles knit a design requiring 120 needles.

Secondly, there is a considerable variation in the size of firms, but, on the whole, the small unit employing less than 300 operatives predominates. For the whole country in 1935 these units produced over 50 per cent of total net output, and this figure is probably representative of the Leicester district. With regard to efficiency there seems to be a general opinion among independent observers in Leicester that the medium units are as efficient, if not more efficient, than the larger. The Census of Production 1935 shows a rise in net output per head as the size of establishment increases up to a maximum in firms employing 200—300 and 300—400 operatives. There is then a marked fall, until for establishments employing 750 and over the net output per head jumps suddenly to about 10 per cent above the earlier maximum. This apparent high efficiency may, however, be partly accounted for by the fact that some of the biggest firms are 'manufacturing wholesalers', i.e. wholesalers who manufacture some of the product bearing their name, but put out the remainder to smaller firms. Whenever trade declines, the 'manufacturing wholesaler' reduces the orders which he puts out and keeps his own manufacturing establishment running fully—thus obtaining a higher economic efficiency, but not necessarily implying a higher technical efficiency than the smaller units.

Thirdly, the methods of selling vary. We have mentioned the 'manufacturing wholesaler' who sells directly to the retailer. Some small firms sell to the manufacturing wholesaler, while others deal with ordinary wholesalers (who have no manufacturing business). Besides the well known trade names, many of the smaller firms depend for their sales on the individuality of their goods, which, as we have already seen, depends in turn to a considerable degree on their specific type of machinery.

Fourthly, there is a great number, probably the majority, of firms where the proprietor controls directly all sides of the business. He is works manager and accountant combined. These men have built up their businesses themselves, and the individuality of their goods depends on their personal supervision of production.

Finally, there are certain technical problems raised by the concentration. Factory space will be released, but, unless there is some guidance from the Government there is no guarantee that the shutdown factories will be the ones wanted by the Supply Departments, and if the latter continue to requisition according to their own needs, considerable confusion may arise when they want a factory housing a 'nucleus' firm. Most of the manufacturers interviewed were of the opinion that the Supply Departments had a definite preference for certain types of building, and it seems to me that it would be very helpful if the new Controller of Factories surveyed the factories and, without necessarily requisitioning at once, indicated those factories in which nucleus firms should not be established. The maintenance of idle machinery may also prove very difficult. Knitting frames are delicate and complicated and depreciate rapidly when not running. One firm stated that if their machines (knitting fine artificial silk hose and running twenty-four hours a day) were stopped for any length of time it would take months to restart them. Whenever possible, therefore, the most up-to-date machines should be kept in production.

TWO SOLUTIONS

In view of all this it can be seen at once that the problem of 'marrying' the firms into groups of from two to five or six in a particular building so that there is no change, beyond the reduction, in the styles produced, is extremely complicated. It resembles a jigsaw puzzle in which it is highly improbable that all the pieces fit together. There are two ways of approaching the problem. Firstly, if we assume that the Government's intention is to preserve, as far as possible, the complete identity of each existing firm, including its sales organization, then it is possible to state the conditions which appear to be necessary to bring this about. Secondly, we may consider a more radical solution, involving the disappearance of trade marks and the elimination, for the period of the war, of the identity of *all* firms, and the production of more or less standard lines in each class of hosiery. The former approach is that which receives more favour with the manufacturers, though the small and medium firms approved the latter scheme, provided it was applied to *all* firms.[1]

If 'identity' is to be preserved, then, in the view of all the small manufacturers interviewed, personal supervision of production must continue. Let us take an example: A is the 'nucleus' firm and B, C, D are the absorbed firms. Then B, C, D must be allowed to work in A's factory, buy their own materials, supervise the production processes and sell the goods in their own way. If A has not the specific machinery required, then, argued the small manufacturers, B should be allowed to bring his own machines in place of some of A's redundant machinery.[2] In such a case A, B, C and D would all be on an equal footing with regard to one another. As for overheads the majority agreed that all overheads should be pooled, including the cost of maintenance of the closed factories (any rental received from letting these factories being also pooled and subtracted from total overheads) and divided between A, B, C and D according to current production, past production, or any other criterion reached by agreement. Such agreement would also cover wages of operatives performing processes common to all; only one mechanic, for example, would be needed instead of the original four, to maintain machinery in one building. I came across only one case where an arrangement anything like the above had been arrived at. There were, however, several cases quoted where larger firms had offered to manufacture a smaller firm's quota at cost, without offering any arrangements for supervision of production or for pooling of overheads. The smaller producers disliked these offers which they felt would, in fact, destroy their identity, give away any secrets and leave them no chance of recovery after the war. There is, of course, no practical reason why the nucleus firm should always be the largest, but considerations of prestige militate against the absorption of larger firms by smaller ones. Many of the large firms owning several factories can, of course, form their own nucleus (almost certainly shifting some machinery) and the Explanatory Memorandum states that the Board of Trade may approve such arrangements.

Although the formula outlined above appears simple, concen-

[1] The attitude of the Board of Trade is not quite clear, for they emphasize the identity of firms; at the same time Sir Cecil Weir, when introducing the scheme to the hosiers, suggested, I was told, the disappearance of brands and trade marks.

[2] It should also be possible for each firm to carry with it some of its older workers.

tration is unlikely to take place unless there is a definite lead from the Government. The Explanatory Memorandum emphasizes heavily the advantages that nucleus firms will enjoy, with the consequence that no one wants to be absorbed. Already smaller firms are being bought out by larger ones, because they fear that they will go out of business anyway, despite any guarantees of post-war restoration. An emphasis on co-operation rather than absorption would remove many of these doubts.

This method is undoubtedly workable and would achieve the release of space and labour, with the least dislocation of normal trading practice. There is, however, no reduction in the selling organizations; in the hosiery trade the numbers engaged purely in selling and advertising are relatively small, but in other trades concentration of this sort would leave untapped a substantial reservoir of war workers. The method also neglects two important problems: the best use of machinery and labour conditions. Firm A with 100 per cent up-to-date machines has to reduce output to the same extent as firm B with many old-fashioned machines, and if B be larger than A it is unlikely that A will become the nucleus firm. Also if firms A, B, C and D were paying different wages before telescoping there may be difficulties after concentration. These problems can, in my opinion, only be completely solved by the elimination of all identities for the duration of the war. Certain war-time standard lines could be established.[1] All resources would be pooled and a controller for the industry could then pick the best factories and machines required to produce the necessary output, being advised by a committee representing the manufacturers large, medium and small, according to the numbers in each group. In this way, too, the standardization of wage rates, which, according to one trade journal is long overdue, could be achieved.[2]

Since this article was first written, the actual situation in Leicester has become a little clearer. At present the attitude of the small and medium manufacturers appears to be to await a further move from the Government, as they feel they are unlikely to be worse off under a compulsory scheme than if they attempted to concentrate themselves, or if they accepted the offers of larger firms. This develop-

---

[1] Despite the diversity of products at present, if sales were no longer dependent on fashion this would not be impossible. Already most manufacturers produce standard articles for the Forces.

[2] Wage rates in Leicester itself do not vary much, but there are considerable differences between wages in Leicester and in the surrounding districts, as also between Leicester and Lancashire.

ment strengthens the argument for standardization, for if the Government is obliged to use compulsion, it has the chance to introduce desirable changes which would not occur with voluntary arrangements.

The choice of method will probably differ between industry and industry according to the particular organization. In the latter case the Government will, to some degree, control the industry, but even in the former, if there is to be equality of sacrifice, the Government will have to supervise more closely than is indicated by the Explanatory Memorandum. Without Government protection, concentration will almost certainly hit the smaller units more heavily than the larger; to 'encourage individual firms to initiate the desired changes,' although in keeping with 'traditional British economic policy' is insufficient to achieve the best results unless more specific details are given as to the way in which these changes should be effected.

RATIONAL RETAILING IN WAR-TIME

by G. D. N. Worswick

FROM BULLETIN, VOL. 3, NO. 13 (SEPTEMBER 20, 1941)

THE drastic limitation of supplies of consumption goods, queues arising from haphazard distribution of these goods and the ever-increasing needs of the Supply Departments for men and women in the war industries, combine to make the issue of 'concentration' of the retail trade important and immediate. The advisory joint committee appointed by the Board of Trade at the end of May 'to examine present problems of retail trade in goods other than food, having regard to the immediate needs of the conduct of the war and to the position after the war', has recently concluded that four main problems have to be faced:

1. Goods (other than food) available for sale have been reduced by roughly 50 per cent, and the full effect has not been felt yet, owing to accumulated stocks which are now rapidly diminishing.
2. Price levels must be kept stable as much as possible.
3. The Government would not give compensation for loss of business to traders any more than to other sections of the community.
4. There must be a diversion of large numbers of retail workers to the Services and war industries.

So far, however, there has been no statement from the Committee or from the Government about the methods to achieve price stabilization and maximum release of labour. The object of this article is to examine the most important aspects of the problem, and to suggest certain lines of action which should be taken if the best results in terms of proper distribution and release of labour are to be obtained. The Board of Trade Committee is restricted in scope to the examination of trade in non-food goods; any rationalization of retail food distribution is to be left to the Ministry of Food. From a post-war point of view this dichotomy is unfortunate, since there are many shops which sell both food and non-food merchandise. It does not mean, however, that no rationalization of food distribution is intended or at any rate desired, as the recent abortive attempt to eliminate food shops with less than twenty-five registered customers showed.

The Reduction in Sales and the Release of Labour

In an earlier article we estimated that after removal of seasonal fluctuations the decline in the volume of sales of goods other than food, between the outbreak of war and the first quarter of 1941, was of the order of 40 per cent.[1] The same method of calculation which was used in that article shows a further decline in the volume of sales of clothing in the second quarter of 1941, and the July Retail Sales Index for clothing fell very sharply owing to the introduction of rationing. There was also a slight decline in the volume of household goods sold in the second quarter. Thus, in view of the depletion of stocks, the Retail Trade Committee's estimate of 50 per cent of the pre-war volume of sales of non-food merchandise can be reasonably used as a basis, and we may also assume at least a 10 per cent fall in the volume of food sales. In theory, to distribute 50 per cent of non-food goods and 90 per cent of the pre-war volume of food, 50 per cent of non-food retail proprietors, shop-assistants, salesmen, etc., and 90 per cent of the food workers would be required. Actually there might be a further saving if there were concentration in the most 'efficient' shops, but against this must be offset the additional work entailed in handling coupons, keeping Purchase Tax accounts, and so on. In any case, owing to the lack of recent statistical data, it is only possible to make the crudest estimates of the order of magnitude of the numbers likely to be made available for other work by concentration.

TABLE I

Numbers engaged in Retail Trade in 1931 inclusive of Unemployed
(thousands)

| | | Proprietors and Managers of Retail Businesses | | | | | Salesmen and Shop-assistants | | | |
		Food	Non-Food[1]	Mixed Business[2]	Food	Total	Non-Food[1]	Mixed Business[2]	Total
Males	.. ..	201	143	75	419	238	111	51	400
Females	..	57	49	44	150	113	191	90	394
Total	.. ..	258	192	119	569	351	302	141	794

[1] Coal, Tobacco, Ironmongery, Boots and Shoes, Textiles and other clothing, Stationery, Boots, etc., Furniture.

[2] The Census groups 'General and Mixed Businesses' and 'Other Businesses' are taken together under this heading.

Table I is compiled from the Occupational Analysis of the 1931 Census of Population, and shows the numbers who gave as occupa-

[1] 'Retail Trade during the War—Turnover and Population Movements,' BULLETIN, Vol. 3, No. 10, diagram, p. 210. The fall in real sales is greater than the fall in civilian consumption per head owing to the extensive mobilization.

tion the Retail Trade, whether they were employed or not. The Ministry of Labour does not give separate figures for unemployment in retail trade, only a wider group of 'Distributive Trades'. It does not involve any great error, however, if we apply the unemployment percentages of this group to the *employees* in the retail trade, and if we also assume the same increase in *employment* between 1931 and 1939 for the retail trade as occurred in the 'Distributive Trades' group of the Ministry of Labour. Thus, to obtain the numbers of workers *employed* in July 1939, the figures in the above table should be increased by 2 per cent for males, 7 per cent for females and 3 per cent for the total. We cannot apply these percentage additions to the figures for proprietors in Table I, for two reasons. Firstly, 11 per cent of employees were unemployed in the 'Distributive Trades' in 1931, and it is unlikely that as many proprietors were unemployed. So we subtract less than 11 per cent from the figures in Table I to get the active proprietors in 1931. On the other hand, we must not now add to the numbers of proprietors occupied in 1931 the full 16 per cent increase corresponding to the rise in employment of workers in the 'Distributive Trades', since some of this increase was due to an absorption of unemployed workers into existing shops and only part of it was brought about by the opening of new shops. Thus, to obtain the numbers of proprietors actually at work in July 1939, slightly higher percentages than for workers should be added to the corresponding figures in Table I, of the order (say) of 5 per cent for males, 10 per cent for females, and 6 per cent for the total.

Returning to the estimates of the reduction in the volume of sales and assuming that the numbers of employers and workers are reduced in the same proportion as the volume of sales (e.g. to sell half the goods of 1939 half the shops are used, each with the *same* turnover as 1939) we can see how many fewer workers and employers are required now than at the beginning of the war. For the group General Mixed and Other Business we shall assume a decline in volume of only 40 per cent as there may be some semi-food shops included in this group. The results are as Table II.

These figures must not be taken to give the release of labour to be expected from any future concentration, for various reasons. There has already been a substantial call-up of men, both employers and workers; this was probably offset in the early stages by a net inflow of women and young persons below military age, but now women workers are also being transferred into the Forces and war

TABLE II

Possible reduction in numbers of workers and employers below the level of 1939 to be obtained by
'concentrating' a reduced volume of sales[1] in a proportionately smaller number of shops (thousands)

		Proprietors and Managers of Retail Businesses				Salesmen and Shop-assistants			
		Food	Non-Food	Mixed Business	Total	Food	Non-Food	Mixed Business	Total
Males	..	21	75	32	128	24	56	20	100
Females	..	6	27	19	52	12	103	38	153
Total	..	27	102	51	180	36	159	58	253

[1] The reduced volumes are for food, non-food and 'other goods' respectively 90 per cent, 50 per cent and 60 per cent of pre-war figures.

industries. A considerable number of shops also have already been closed; Mr. Charles Madge states that 'of 19,000 shops in Glasgow at the beginning of 1939, 17 per cent have already been closed and the rate of closing is increasing rapidly.'[1] Between 40 and 50 per cent of the male employees are of military age, and 20 to 30 per cent of the employers, while about 30 per cent of the women employees have registered for National Service, and probably less than 10 per cent of women proprietors.[2] We have left out of account certain workers associated with retailing, roundsmen, van drivers and packing hands. Their numbers, however, are small, and already petrol rationing and calling-up have reduced deliveries to a very low level. A conservative conclusion from all this is that 'concentration' might release a further 75–100,000 proprietors and over 150,000 employees, while those remaining in the trade would not be more heavily worked than in 1939. These estimates, though extremely rough, give some idea of the size and importance of the problem.

Regional Distribution of Rationing

Any plan for 'concentration' must clearly take into account wartime movements of population; the 'degree' of concentration will be greater in the evacuation than in the reception areas. The first essential is therefore to base the distribution of supplies according to the population in each region. This at once raises two problems.

(1) Although there is already control of most foods by the Ministry of Food, there does not exist at present any organization to allocate non-food supplies to different districts in the same way. Of two drapers in Oxford, say, one may buy from a wholesaler in London, while another deals directly with a manufacturer in Lancashire. To meet this difficulty some form of co-operative whole-

[1] In an article entitled 'The Small Shop's Fate,' *Spectator*, August 15, 1941.
[2] These are estimates based on the age-groups in the 1931 Census.

sale buying organization for each big town or region seems essential.
Such a co-operative group of shopkeepers could be allocated a quota
of each type of goods, textiles, tobacco, etc., and then buy directly
from manufacturers, thus cutting out a considerable number of
middlemen.

(2) The problem of allocating regional quotas is complicated
by the fact that sales at present do not correspond only to the size
of population in any region, but also to the income level.

In the Bulletin article quoted above, we found no correlation
at all between changes in sales in various regions and changes in
population between 1938 and November 1940. Thus, we get from
a new angle an argument in favour of rationing of shop expenditure.
If this were introduced the allocation of supplies to different areas
would correspond almost exactly to the population;[1] only in so
far as a particularly poor area was unable to spend its complete
ration would there be an irregular accumulation of stocks. Such
rationing would also make it much easier to estimate the approximate
number of shops of each type which are required by a particular
area, and so enable a directive to be issued for the degree of concentration required in each district.

Thus it appears that co-operative wholesale buying by regions,
and rationing of expenditure, would both facilitate enormously
the task of distributing supplies equally and fairly over the whole
country. There still remains the task of deciding how many retail
outlets are required in each region and which shops must be shut.

A Plan for Concentration

For concentration in *industries* problems of location are not very
important. If there are several similar factories in one area, it does
not matter much from the point of view of production, selling or
labour, which particular factories are shut and which kept running.
In retail distribution, on the other hand, location is the principal
factor from all these points of view. The criterion of rational
retailing in war-time is simply to distribute a reduced quantity of
consumption goods evenly and fairly over the whole country,
with the minimum waste of man-power in the shops and of time
and energy on the part of the consumer. At present this waste on
both sides is only too apparent, and the suggestion of Captain
Waterhouse, in the House of Commons last April, that 'those who

[1] In fact, the allocation might be made in terms of total value, in order to allow for
regional differences in taste.

found it difficult to carry on might sell their stocks, and after investing the proceeds in Government securities, might find employment in other directions for the war period', was not very helpful simply because most shopkeepers hold on to the bitter end. And it is the financially weak, though not necessarily inefficient, small shops which go to the wall first.

There are, in fact, three very cogent arguments in favour of retaining the small individual shops which must be offset against the disadvantages, which will be considered later.

1. These shops are predominantly of the family type, and they are very numerous. To quote Mr. Madge: 'three-quarters of the Glasgow shops are single branch shops. In Slough more than half the shops had a floor space of 200 square feet or less, and some 80 per cent had two or less employees. An average of 1·6 members of the family work in the average shop. Half the shops had no employees outside the family, and 63 per cent of the families live in the same building as their shop.'[1] Many of the shopkeepers are older people and are least suitable for drafting into war industries. In so far as they live 'over the shop' the best *net* contribution to the national effort they are likely to be able to make is as fully occupied shop-keepers.

2. The use of small shops means the spreading of risk from bombing. In many towns the heaviest attacks have been concentrated at the business and shopping centres. The dispersion of stocks would clearly reduce the risk of loss (unless bombing became purely random).

3. The full use of small shops has many advantages for the consumer. Transport difficulties are considerable, and as more and more women are drafted into industry it is essential that the time necessary for shopping should be cut to a minimum.

There are, of course, many arguments against the use of the small shops—the larger ones are often more efficient; many consumers prefer to buy in big stores and would strongly resent being forced to shop at small local establishments; where, as in the case of clothing, for example, purchases only occur at rather infrequent intervals, the factor of proximity to the household becomes of little importance. In the case of food there are very few large individual central shops, the big firms having many branches which are situated in the local shopping areas. Except in certain evacuation areas, it is

[1] Ibid.

unlikely that the small reduction in the volume of food sales would allow of any 'concentration' at all.

The decline in the volume of sales of non-food goods is, however, already much greater than the fall in food sales and will be of the order of 50 per cent of the pre-war level. This is, of course, a national average for all non-food goods, and the actual percentage fall will vary between regions and between particular commodities. For the purpose of illustration, however, I propose to assume, first, that the 50 per cent cut applies uniformly over regions and different goods. In this hypothetical case, some such plan as the following might be considered. The shops should be broadly classified into small individual shops and large shops. As far as possible the small shops should be paired and the business of each pair taken over by one shop for the duration, while the other is closed. This pairing in unlikely to occur voluntarily, and the Board of Trade should give a lead, either by appointing regional and district officers to do the pairing, or else forming local committees of shopkeepers to work out the scheme themselves. For the bigger shops with several branches, they should each be obliged to halve the number of branches and the closing should be arranged between them so that there is the widest distribution of the shops remaining open. Big central stores could also, in many cases, be paired for the duration of the war. In this way the *structure* of the retail trade could be retained, which is of some political significance, as there is nothing worse for morale than the slow and painful elimination of shopkeepers, from the smallest upwards.

Compensation

The Board of Trade Committee has stated already that the Government cannot give compensation for loss of trade.[1] If there were rationing of expenditure, the arguments against compensation, based on the desire to avoid any aggravation of inflationary tendencies, would be no longer valid.

If, however, compensation is not paid by the Government, there must clearly be some agreement between the owners of paired shops. For the bigger shops the shareholders should simply divide the profit of the joint unit according to their number and holdings. For privately owned and small shops, however, the problem is more

[1] The Government state that they cannot compensate the retail trade any more than any other section of the community. It still remains true, however, that many war-time changes in all sections of the economy, e.g. concentration, would be rendered much easier if there were a comprehensive plan of compensation.

complicated. To divide proceeds equally would be unfair, since one man is doing the work of earning them while the other is not. On the other hand, to pay nothing, or only a subsistence income to the displaced shopkeeper, is also unfair. In some cases, it is true, he may be able to obtain work elsewhere, but this appears rather unlikely in general. Some compromise solution, such as the following, might be worth considering. Each owner should receive as a first call on profits the amount of profits he was earning *before* the merger. If total profits are insufficient they should be divided proportionately. It is to be expected, however, that the saving in overheads due to pairing will increase total profits above the sum of the separate pre-merger profits. The margin of current profits above this pre-merger sum might be divided into 75 per cent (say) for the working shopkeeper and 25 per cent for the one whose shop is closed.

Conclusion

These examples have been worked out, not as actual proposals, but as illustrations of a principle which might be applied. As we have already indicated, there must be elasticity in the 'degree' of concentration depending on the density of population and on the particular line of goods sold. In some cases, instead of a 'pair', there would be one shop closed in three, and so on.

Increasing standardization also simplifies some of the problems associated with the intricate task of concentrating distribution. The limitation of consumers' choice is one of the necessities of war, and if there were an increasing number of standard essential consumption goods of guaranteed quality obtainable everywhere, much of the reluctance of consumers to change shopping habits would disappear.

Nothing has been said, so far, about the second point made by the Board of Trade Committee, namely, that price levels should be kept stable. Unless there is limitation of expenditure, excessive demand will tend to raise prices, despite the Prices of Goods Act. On the costs side, there will clearly be some small reduction made possible by 'concentration', but it is not sufficient to tackle retail trade distribution alone. The wholesale side must also be concentrated, and the regional co-operative buying might achieve considerable reductions in cost.

z

CONCENTRATION—SUCCESS OR FAILURE?

by G. D. N. Worswick

FROM BULLETIN, VOL. 3, NO. 16 (NOVEMBER 22, 1941)

THE Explanatory Memorandum on the Concentration of Production, issued by the Board of Trade in March of this year, was
welcomed as one of the most imaginative steps in economic policy
taken by the Government since the war began. It was recently
announced that the programme of the concentration of industry,
as it was first planned, has been almost completed, with the important
exception of the woollen industry. It would therefore be appropriate
to summarize the achievements of the scheme, to criticize its defects
and to suggest alterations which might be applied to industries
already 'concentrated' or likely to be 'concentrated' in the future.
It must be said at the outset, however, that such an appraisal is
rendered extremely difficult, owing to the conflicting statements
from official sources about concentration which seem to bear little
relation to one another, and also to the fragmentary nature of the
statistical data which have been given from time to time.

On October 13th, 1941, the *Financial News* reported that 144,000
workers and 45 million square feet of factory space had been
released by concentration. Of the workers released only 103,000
had left their peace-time employment for war jobs. The total
release of labour is of the order of 26 per cent. of the estimated
employment in June 1941 in the industries coming under the concentration schedule. But it is not known how far these industries
had already contracted by March 1941, when concentration was
introduced, nor what is the proportion of present output to that of
March 1941, so that it is quite impossible to pass any judgment on
the bare figures, except to remark that in relation to the needs of
war industries, they appear very small.

The *Financial News* report goes on: 'it is officially emphasized,
however, that this bare statement is by no means the whole story.
The purpose of concentration was primarily the economical manufacture of the restricted volume of civil goods. The release of factory
space and labour is stated to have been merely incidental.' Turning
back to the Explanatory Memorandum, we find that it begins by

pointing out that contracting industries, if left to themselves, would probably spread over the whole industry the reduced volume of civilian output. 'A spread-over of this kind results in an uneconomical use of certain types of labour. It does not free the factory and storage space which will, in many cases, be needed for Government use. The effect of a diminished turnover on costs may . . . have serious repercussions. . . .' Later on a whole paragraph is devoted to the release of labour: 'The objectives are twofold: first to obtain labour required for war industries. . . .'

Clearly the release of labour and the economical manufacture of the reduced volume of output in 'nucleus' factories are two sides of the same coin; the more economical the manufacture, the greater the release of labour. Thus, one may reasonably infer that the change of emphasis to 'economical manufacture' and the relegation of the release of labour and factory space to the level of 'incidentals' implies that the scheme in the latter respect, and therefore as a whole, has not come up to official expectations. Furthermore the official expectations seem not to have been set at too ambitious a height: so many firms are 'nucleus' firms, so many are shut down, so many workers are released, that is all.

There still remain, however, certain highly important questions of economic organization which must be asked. Has the voluntary principle of concentration in fact shown the advantages claimed for it at the outset? Has there been justice between closed and nucleus firms? Has the *structure* of industries been modified, and in what ways? The answers to these and other questions can only be fully given by the Government officials concerned, but some light can be thrown on them by a consideration of the development of concentration in two industries, hosiery and cotton spinning. Some of the points raised have a general application and will enable us to suggest in conclusion what further steps seem necessary to achieve both efficient production and also fairness of treatment.

HOSIERY

Concentration in hosiery has been almost entirely on the voluntary basis called for in the Explanatory Memorandum, that is to say, groups of firms have agreed among themselves that one of them should be a nucleus firm and the others should be absorbed. The only part played by the Board of Trade was to indicate for each class of product the reduction in output which had to be made by all firms. Thus each firm had a certain quota of production for each type of good and these quotas had to be added, in what appears to have been a highly complicated way, in order to get 100 per cent. production for the nucleus firm. Nevertheless the very numerous firms managed to sort themselves out and, by September, the concentration process was more or less complete. Unfortunately, just as the industry was beginning to work normally on the new basis, special quotas were introduced for the manufacture of 'essential' clothing and the quotas for other clothing were reduced, with the result that the delicate balance of production quotas in the nucleus factories was upset and many of them were no longer able to produce at 100 per cent. for 48 hours a week. This is a fundamental objection to the principle of voluntary arrangements among individual firms, that any further contraction due to shortage of supplies completely upsets the previous equilibrium;[1] the voluntary system breaks down because it does not ensure 'the greatest possible degree of flexibility' claimed for it in the Explanatory Memorandum.

The voluntary basis was criticized from the beginning on the grounds that it would favour the big, financially powerful firms at the expense of the small units. In hosiery this was undoubtedly the case and the first month or two brought quite a number of outright purchases of small businesses by the large firms. This process was stopped, however, by the small firms themselves who organized an Association of Small and Medium Manufacturers, which arranged nucleus schemes *within* the association. These schemes, which were accepted by the Board of Trade after much negotiation, have been of three principal types:

1. The nucleus firm manufactures for the absorbed firm at cost. The absorbed firms retain their own selling departments.
2. The absorbed firms carry their own machinery into the nucleus factory and share the overheads with the nucleus firm.
3. A nucleus firm purchases the yarn 'quota' from the absorbed firm.

It will be noticed that in none of these types of concentration does the absorbed firm suffer a total loss of business. In the first two there is still a trading profit and in the third there is some return from the sale of the yarn 'quota'. In the particular case of hosiery, therefore, the small firms have saved themselves to some extent by

[1] An expansion due to an increased Government demand for a particular product is equally difficult within the framework of the voluntary system.

their own initiative, but in other industries it appears that they have borne the brunt of the inevitable contraction. It is also worth mentioning that the insistence of the Board of Trade on the concentration of like with like in respect of type of product tended to make the scheme less flexible. In one extreme instance there were only two firms producing a particular product and they were told that one must absorb the other; one was in Scotland, the other in the South of England! Furthermore the voluntary system means that the type of factory space released is purely haphazard.

COTTON SPINNING

Although the principle of voluntary formation of nucleus mills has been accepted in the cotton spinning industry, in fact the determination of nucleus mills was done by the Cotton Control. The reason was stated to be the acute shortage of cotton which made speed of concentration essential, and this throws a rather odd light on the choice of the voluntary system by the Government for the general scheme. The Explanatory Memorandum says: 'The Government have chosen this last means (the voluntary method) for several reasons. First, it promises speedy results.' In April 1941, some spinning firms were informed that they had been chosen as provisional nucleus mills and would continue to receive raw material licences, while others were told that they would receive no further licences at the end of the current or subsequent month. The Control seems to have chosen the nucleus mills according to their suitability for certain types of production and closed those mills in the areas where the demand for labour for war industry was greatest. Efficiency of the individual nucleus firm was not a major criterion, if it was ever considered.

As the concentration was compulsory, carried out by the Control, there should have been fairness between small, medium and large firms. It is difficult to speak with certainty, but there have been no complaints that the small firms have been especially badly treated. On the other hand, the difference between the financial prospects of nucleus and closed cotton firms is much sharper than in industries, such as hosiery, where the absorbed firms still carry on some business in goods manufactured in 'nucleus' factories. In cotton spinning the closed mills are out of business entirely, unless they can persuade a nucleus mill to hand over a share of its profits, an extremely unlikely occurrence since the closed mill has nothing to offer. To meet this problem the Cotton Board instituted a scheme for what was originally called compensation but is now called 'care and maintenance.' Nucleus mills pay a levy proportional to the number of spindles whether running or not, into a central fund, and closed mills receive a payment of £7,000 per year per 100,000 spindles to cover costs of maintaining the plant and premises in good condition and also of fire watching, etc.[1]

Purely from the point of view of maintenance the choice of the number of spindles as a basis for payment is open to criticism, for maintenance charges are not in any way proportional to the number of spindles in a particular factory. Spinners maintain that for a large mill with, say, over 100,000 spindles the maintenance allowance is too great, and therefore wasteful, since no benefit accrues to the spinner if he economizes on his allowance (if he does his payment for the next period is reduced). For small mills of, say, less than 50,000 spindles the allowance is insufficient. A more rational schedule of payments based on size of plant as well as number of spindles could be quite simply devised.

A more weighty objection to the present 'maintenance' system is that there is injustice between the shareholders of nucleus and closed mills. The former will receive the usual or even an increased dividend, while the latter receive nothing. Moreover closed firms may in no circumstances use money received from the maintenance fund for any payment of debt or in fact for any purpose other than maintenance of the factory. Firms, for example, who have in the last year or so borrowed money on debenture agreements and are now closed, are placed in a very serious position. The debenture agreements are still valid, annual payments must be made, but there are no trading profits from which to make the payments. So far all attempts by the closed firms to obtain a satisfactory solution of this problem, or even to have it considered by the authorities, have failed. No doubt the war effort does not suffer immediately because of such financial injustices, but in the long run the trail of wrecked businesses, and the subsequent buying up of closed firms by the more fortunate nucleus firms, may have serious repercussions. The Government states that it can give no compensation out of public funds for loss of business or goodwill. Whether or not this is the correct policy, it is no reason for leaving the inevitable sacrifices of the war to be borne haphazardly, especially when there is a simple

[1] The maintenance is paid for spindles already idle when concentration was introduced, provided the mill is 'maintained' according to the provisions of the scheme.

solution to hand. The profits of the whole 'concentrated' industry could be pooled, so that *all* shareholders would receive a reduced dividend, whether they held shares in 'nucleus' or closed mills. Such a pooling of profits would have to be carried out by the Cotton Board; it is no use asking nucleus firms voluntarily and individually to give up a share of their profits to any closed mill which might apply. If profit pooling were accompanied by technical pooling, then the concentration would be flexible and also enable maximum economies of manufacture to be achieved.

CONCLUSION

We may summarize the shortcomings of the scheme as it has developed so far:

1. The voluntary system is weighted against the small business.
2. Where the voluntary method has done the job, the resultant structure of the industry has become more inflexible.
3. Maximum efficiency cannot be a criterion of the 'nucleus' mills as determined by voluntary arrangements.
4. Where compulsion has been applied, there is injustice between nucleus and closed firms.
5. The lack of compensation, or devices to share the burden, is likely to have an undesirable effect on morale, and also it rules out the possibility of maximum efficiency.

As has already been indicated, in the case of cotton spinning profit sharing and technical pooling can still be applied with advantage, although any prolonged delay will make the task more difficult as more and more closed mills are bought up by running concerns. In particular the lack of pooling seems to be causing difficulty at present owing to an 'over-concentration' of the industry. In cases such as hosiery where the voluntary system has worked, pooling is more difficult; whether it should, nevertheless, be introduced depends on the expectation of a further reduction or possible increase in output.

It is impossible to devise a general plan to cover all industries, since each raises its own special problems, and there should be elasticity in any comprehensive scheme. For example, concentration of the retail trade might best be achieved by some compromise between full pooling and the voluntary method.[1] Here we must simply conclude that, on balance, the voluntary system has not

[1] See my article 'Rational Retailing in War-Time,' p. 338.

fulfilled the claims made for it, and that other methods, dealing with industries as a whole and not as a collection of individual units, should be tried. In particular compensation, or at any rate the spreading of losses over a whole industry, is an integral part of any satisfactory solution.

POSTSCRIPT [1]

The Board of Trade concentration scheme finally affected fifty industries.[2] Thirty of these came under the original scheme; the remaining twenty were brought in later. The policy of concentration was also applied by the Ministry of Food to certain of the industries under its control—the soft drinks industry and the biscuit trade, for example. In an article in the *Journal of the Institute of Bankers* (April 1945), Professor G. C. Allen stated that 'by the middle of 1943, when the policy had been substantially carried out, about 3,500 establishments had been closed, apart from those in the food and drink and brick trades to which a similar policy had been applied.' The then President of the Board of Trade, reviewing the progress of concentration in May 1943, said that 235,000 workers had been released for the services or for more essential work, and 61 million square feet of factory space had been made available for war production or for storage. About 75 per cent. of these savings had been realized from five industries: cloth,[3] hosiery, boots and shoes, carpets, and pottery.

Most of the schemes adopted were voluntary. In the cotton spinning industry (as mentioned in the article) the nucleus firms were chosen by the Cotton Control; and in two other industries (carpets and cutlery), where the producers failed to reach any agreement among themselves, the Board of Trade nominated the nucleus firms. In all other cases, however, voluntary methods seem to have prevailed. The usual procedure was for a group of firms to select one of their number to produce on behalf of the rest. The precise arrangements, of course, varied considerably; but usually the nucleus firm would either purchase outright the production quotas of the closed firms, or else manufacture for them at cost. In many cases the closed firms retained their own selling organizations,

---

[1] This postscript, outlining the further development of the concentration scheme after November 1941 was prepared in 1946 by Mr. David Henderson.
[2] For a list of these see the *Economist*, August 29, 1942. The list contains 51 industries, but it includes the brick industry, which did not come under the Board of Trade scheme but was under the control of the Ministry of Works.
[3] This presumably includes cotton, rayon, wool, and clothing.

and sometimes machinery was actually transferred from the premises of closed to those of nucleus firms.

There were, however, a few examples of the 'pooling' method— the creation of a company, in which all the firms in the industry hold shares, and which selects and operates the nucleus firms and distributes all profits among its members on an agreed basis. In the Leavers section of the lace industry, 'the [concentration] scheme was administered by a specially constituted company. Lace Productions Ltd., with capital contributed by all manufacturers in the section on the basis of £1 for each machine. The company had two main functions: first, it was the sole selling agency for the Leavers section on the manufacturers' side, all the nucleus firms being required to sell to it at cost prices . . . The second function was to provide for the care and maintenance of the laid-up machines. For this purpose a levy was imposed at 5 per cent. on the turnover of all member firms.'[1] In the curtain section of the same industry, 'the problem of wartime redundancy was met by the formation of a company, British Lace Furnishings Ltd. . . . . Of the 53 firms in the section when the company was formed, 49 became members by acquiring shares in proportion to their previous annual turnover . . . All the member firms with machines at work were operated as branches of B.L.F. The company bought all stocks of yarn in members' hands and it issued orders against this yarn either to the original owners or to the other branches. Like the Leavers scheme, that of the curtain section provided for the care and maintenance of all closed factories and standing machines, the cost being a first charge on the profits of the company.'[2] In the soft drinks industry, the manufacturers' War-Time Association (membership of which had been made compulsory by the Ministry of Food) took over the management of the industry. Brand-names and trade-marks were abolished, the products were rigorously standardized, and the profits of the Association were pooled and shared out among closed and operating firms.

These schemes appear to have been successful, and the pooling scheme had obvious advantages over the more usual group arrangements. In the first place, group arrangements were often inflexible, and readjustments—such as were actually needed under the 're-concentration' scheme in the summer of 1942—were difficult and complicated. Secondly, pooling schemes were likely to be more efficient: for example, when under individual or group agreements

[1] Cf. Mr. Well's paper in *Studies in Industrial Organization*, H. A. Silverman (Ed.), pp. 96–7.
[2] Ibid., pp. 97–8.

firms agreed to share factories, there was sometimes a transfer of machinery: a more comprehensive scheme might have avoided such expedients. Finally, pooling schemes ensured, more effectively than the looser agreements, that the closed firms would not be unfairly treated, and that the nucleus firms would not gain at their expense. Not all centralized compensation schemes (as the example of the cotton spinning industry shows) did this, and one centralized scheme (in the brick industry) was financed by the highly objectionable device of a price-increase.

At the same time, the group arrangements were not always unsatisfactory. In many industries (clothing was perhaps an example) there was probably no tendency for the smaller firms to suffer as a result of such agreements: and there is little evidence that the looser voluntary schemes led to serious inefficiencies.

Two of the criticisms in the article, in fact, need qualification. In the first place, while it is formally correct that: 'Maximum efficiency cannot be a criterion of "nucleus" mills as determined by voluntary arrangements', in practice this may not have amounted to very much. Productivity per man-hour in the nucleus factories would only be one of the many factors affecting the wider efficiency of the labour force as a whole. In so far as nucleus certificates were only issued when adequate labour supplies were in fact available, and not required for war work near at hand, the resulting set of working factories may not have differed widely from that which would have been chosen by a single concentrating authority. Moreover, since the pooling schemes were not, as was suggested by Messrs. Balogh and Burchardt (p. 328), controlled by Government nominees, but run by the industries concerned, the choice of running plants might also differ from the ideal required by the war effort: so that the criticism, in so far as it is valid, cannot be levelled at the group arrangement only. Secondly, there is no evidence, apart from the cotton industry instance quoted above, that 'where compulsion is applied, there is injustice between nucleus and closed firms.'

The conclusions drawn above need to be modified. A revised list is as follows:—

(1) The usual group arrangement was unfair to the smaller firms in some cases.

(2) When group arrangements prevailed, the resulting structure of the industry was often inflexible; any further readjustments were rendered extremely difficult, since they were likely to disturb the whole balance of such agreements.

(3) In certain cases, group arrangements appear to have been rather wasteful (e.g., when equipment was transferred from one firm to another), though this does not seem to have been very serious.

(4) The pooling method was superior to the looser scheme in all these respects: it was more flexible, since readjustments within the industry were far simpler than readjustments among a large number of groups; there was no danger that small firms or closed firms would be unfairly treated; and it was likely to be more efficient and economical. For these reasons, the Government might have suggested the pooling device as a model for many industries and encouraged such arrangements.

(5) Where the pooling method was adopted, the company set up to administer the affairs of the industry was controlled by the manufacturers concerned. It is arguable that the controllers of such companies should have been appointed by the Government from persons outside the industries.

(6) Arrangements for compensation were not always satisfactory —the cotton spinning and brick industries are the obvious examples. Once again, the surest way of securing fair treatment for closed firms was a pooling scheme, with the care and maintenance of closed plants a first charge on the profits of the company, and the distribution of the profits among all the constituent firms. In some cases, e.g., the leather goods trade, where the closed firms could not be used for alternative purposes, concentration probably caused appreciable losses. It can be argued that the Government should have provided compensation in such cases, and also (as in the case of carpets) where the industry was forced to cease production altogether.

UTILITY GOODS

by P. Ady

FROM BULLETIN, VOL. 4, No. 15 (OCTOBER 31, 1942)

THE official application of the term 'Utility' was given in April this year to 'articles produced in a limited range, clearly definable and of simple design': Utility clothing, footwear, crockery, pencils, mechanical lighters, and so on, are in varying quantities on the market, the Utility Clothing Scheme being the first of these to be mooted. The present situation is the third stage of development from the 'business as usual' days of the clothing industry in the early months of the war, a development systematically represented in the Tables appended.[1]

STAGE I

In the first few months of the war, control of textile manufacture was exercised only at the raw material stage, by the allocation of materials between various uses in the following order of priority: 1, military requirements; 2, exports; 3, home civilian needs. Government orders were met in full since they fell in the first category and so were the needs of the export trade, which was being encouraged, by bonuses, to expand; but wool allocations for home civilian needs were restricted. For cotton a loose system of priorities was introduced in February 1940. From April 1940, the Limitation of Supplies[2] Orders reinforced this restriction by limiting the sales of wholesalers and manufacturers of piece goods and made up-goods of cotton, rayon and linen. Sales were limited by quotas, expressed as percentages of quantities sold to retailers over earlier periods. Hosiery was included in the general Limitation of Supplies in June 1940 (quotas being expressed by percentages of values in earlier periods) and wool woven textiles in April 1941. Price control too, was effective only for raw materials, Home Trade Issue Prices being fixed by the appropriate Control, wool from the start, and cotton later, while rayon prices are now fixed by the trade. At the later stages of production the Prices of Goods Act was the sole check

---

[1] These are modifications of Tables published in the *Wool Digest* of June 1941. I am indebted to Dr. Blau of the International Wool Secretariat for permission to use them.
[2] This title was only given at a later date.

STAGES.	TABLE I, TO OCTOBER 31ST, 1941.		
	a: Quantitative Control a	b: Quality Control b	c: Price Control c
1 Raw Materials to *Manufacturer*	*Allocation* of raw materials ration for Home Civilian Trade by *Controls* (less rigid for cotton than for wool)		Fixing of Home Trade Issue Prices of raw wool, cotton, etc., by appropriate Control.
2 Cloth from Manufacturer to *Clothier* or *Wholesaler*			*All types of cloth.* Method of calculation of cost of production and profit margins fixed under agreement between *Textile Manufacturers Delegations & Central Price Regulation Committee.*
3 Cloth or clothing from Manufacturer, Wholesaler or Clothier to *Retailer*	Quantities of sales restricted on a percentage basis under Limitation of Supplies Orders		*All types of cloth.* Check—'Prices of Goods' Act, 1939.
4 Cloth or clothing from Retailer to *Consumer*	Against coupons under Consumer Rationing Orders, June 1941		*All types of clothing.* Check—'Prices of Goods' Act, 1939.
	TABLE II. NOVEMBER 1ST TO JUNE 1ST, 1942		
1 Raw Materials to *Manufacturer*	As Table I 1a. Special Quota for Utility Cloth separated from General Home Civilian Quota and graded up in a priority scheme		As Table I 1c.
2 Cloth from Manufacturer to *Clothier* or *Wholesaler*		Provisional emergency standards of minimum quality for *Utility Cloth* but in many cases defined only by price limit	*All types* as Table I 2c *Utility.* Over-riding maximum prices for Utility Cloth under Utility Cloth (Max. Prices) Order
3 Cloth or clothing from Manufacturer Wholesaler or Clothier to *Retailer*	As Table I 3a	Provisional emergency standards for Utility Cloth and directions for making-up Clothing	*All types* as Table I 3c *Utility.* Manufacturers', makers-up and Wholesalers' profit margins fixed, with over-riding maximum prices at each stage under Utility Apparel (Max. Prices) Orders
4 Cloth or clothing from retailer to *Consumer*	As Table I 4a		*All Types* as Table I 4c *Utility.* Retailers' profit margins fixed, with over-riding maximum price
	TABLE III. SINCE JUNE 1ST, 1942.		
1 Raw Materials to *Manufacturer*	Special Quota for Utility Cloth as Table II 1a Released by appropriate Control to manufacturer against presentation of sub-certificates up to total ration of Home Civilian Trade		As Table I 1c
2 Cloth from Manufacturer to *Clothier* or *Wholesaler*	Cloth supplied by manufacturer directly, or indirectly, through merchant, against clothing sub-certificate. These last are issued by clothier against 'key' certificate of estimated Utility cloth requirements. 'Key' certificates issued by Control under authorization of Board of Trade	Govt. guaranteed quality standards issued by B.S.I. C.C. 41, in many cases still defined only by price and type	From August 3rd *Non-utility*, Manufacturers' and makers-up prices fixed at level of June 30th, 1942 *Utility*, as Table II 2c
3 Cloth or clothing from Manufacturer, Clothier or Wholesaler to *Retailer*	Against coupons	Govt. guaranteed quality stds. C.C.41 *All types:* Rules simplifying styles Directions for making-up Utility	From August 3rd *Non-utility.* Wholesalers' profit margins fixed under General Approval & Cloth (Max. Prices & Charges) Order *Utility.* As Table II 3c Purchase Tax remitted
4 Cloth or clothing from retailer to *Consumer*	Against coupons as Table I 4a		From August 3rd *Non-Utility.* Retailers' profit margins fixed *Utility.* As Table II 4c

Most of the new provisions were promulgated before the beginning of June but did not take effect till then.

Quantitative Control

The Limitation of Supplies Orders were suspended completely from June 1st. From that date supplies were made to wholesalers, retailers and the public against the clothing coupons of the Consumers' Rationing Order. Clothiers, therefore, estimate their requirements on the orders they receive from the distributors, whose purchases have to be made both in ordinary and in coupon currency. Clothiers then supply the Clothing Control with these estimates of their needs in the next rationing period. From the estimates made in this way the Board of Trade decides the exact yardage of each type of Utility Cloth that each individual clothier may receive. The required output is not distributed evenly amongst the clothing manufacturers, but a certain number of them have been first selected as being peculiarly suited to undertaking such production most economically. The firms 'designated' in this way have been allotted 75 per cent. of the required Utility yardage. The Board of Trade informs the appropriate raw material Control of the quantities allotted to each 'designated' clothier and the Control issues to the latter 'key' certificates for each type of cloth they are permitted to buy. Against these 'key' certificates the designated clothiers are then permitted to issue sub-certificates to their suppliers, to the total mentioned on the 'key' certificate. These sub-certificates find their way either directly or through a merchant to a manufacturer, who passed them on to the Control, which releases to him the amount of raw material needed.

Clothiers, other than those designated, were not at first required to cease production, but were permitted to continue so long as they could obtain the necessary raw materials. 'Designation' was not therefore a form of concentration, but the latter has now been introduced in the clothing industry, superimposed upon the designation scheme and causing, therefore, some dislocation.

Quality Control

Issue of detailed Utility fabric specifications by the British Standards Institution began in June 1942, after consultation with the manufacturers, and to-day the list varies from the precise instructions for the manufacture of cotton fabrics to the old 'type and price' definitions which still govern the woollen industry. The Utility Mark and specification-number which all such fabric must bear has not the same precise quality significance in every case. Utility fabrics may be sold by the yard, but if worked up into clothing, in quantity, this must also bear the Identification Mark, but the same varying degrees of precision characterize instructions to makers-up.

The Board of Trade has, however, enlisted the aid of London's leading *couturières* in the designing of attractive Utility wear for women; from these patterns clothiers can now obtain, if they wish, templates at nominal prices, from which cloth can be cut in bulk for mass-production. Utility styles, like those of all types of clothing, have been simplified under the 'austerity' campaign launched this year. These Simplification of Styles Orders affect Utility Clothing, but are not part of the Scheme proper.

Price Control

The effects of increased supplies of Utility Clothing do not become discernible in the Ministry of Labour price index until September this year. By July, 1941, the clothing item had increased by 83 per cent over the level on September 1st, 1939; between May and August this year it became stable at 95 per cent, sinking to 91 per cent in September after the remission of Purchase Tax on Utility clothing. The full benefit of the tax remission does not accrue to the consumer, so some rearrangement of permitted costs and profit margins may have occurred, e.g. the ceiling prices of men's Utility suits have fallen from £4 17s. 0d. to £4 9s. 0d., a decrease of 10 per cent instead of the expected 25 per cent.

Whereas the Utility prices have remained stable since October, 1941, until this fall in August, the prices of non-Utility clothing continued to rise until the same month, when they came under more rigid control.[1]

The Utility Clothing Scheme, in its present form, attempts to achieve equality of sacrifice combined with the maximum utilization of resources. The first is an aim secured by the successful provision of adequate supplies of cheap clothing in which the ratio of real costs to prices is subject to a minimum standard. The second is a question of method: given that the community's needs are a certain list of articles in stated quantities (decided by the general

---

[1] Under the General Apparel and Cloth (Max. Prices and Charges) Order manufacturers' prices were fixed at the level of June 30. Wholesalers' profit margins were fixed at 30 per cent and retailers' at 37½ per cent.

THE ROLE OF COMPENSATION IN THE
WAR-ECONOMIC SYSTEM

by T. Balogh

From Bulletin, Vol. 3, No. 5 (April 5, 1941)

1. In an economic system in which production is carried on at the risk of individual entrepreneurs, income distribution, including loss of income, assures the adaption of production to changes in demand. Any serious interference with this mechanism, that is, with the positive and negative incentives through which equilibrium is secured, must retard the process of adaptation if an alternative mechanism is not set up to enforce it. Compensation payments would, in many instances, constitute such interference.

Compensation and Incentives

2. But the war necessitates a complete change in the task of the productive system. This change-over is supposed, in an individualist economy, to be included and accompanied by a rapid rise in profits and wages in the war-sector and corresponding bankruptcy and unemployment in the 'non-essential' sector. Both from the point of view of sheer technical efficiency and from a social and political point of view, such a course is impracticable. It will, in fact, not be possible to contract private demand *pari passu* with the expansion of Government demand.

The positive incentives which are supposed to induce a shift in production are thereby weakened as they work on the basis of *relative* profitability.[1] The increase in uninsurable risks has, moreover, reduced the sensitiveness of the reaction of entrepreneurs. If speculation was permitted it would result in withholding supplies in the war-sector and add to the spendable incomes of private people.

The 'negative incentives' for transfer of productive resources work equally badly as they are paralyzed through the inevitably inflationary policy of the Government. The fact that people have capital reserves has two adverse effects in this respect. Firstly, it enables them to maintain their consumption irrespective of taxation on *income* and

---

[1] If taxation could be raised sufficiently to preserve monetary equilibrium then the 'positive stimulus' of profits would be accordingly reduced.

irrespective of their contribution to the war effort. This frustrates endeavours to restrict consumption to a minimum. It also reduces the supply of man-power. Secondly, even if demand falls, firms intent on eventual survival will not close down, and they thus do not release the maximum volume of productive factors. They will try to maintain operations even at a loss, on the basis of their capital reserves. In point of fact, the inflationary background will probably permit them to charge prices at which profits will accrue in spite of the increased cost per unit.

3. An equally important argument against the maintenance of the individualist income distribution as the mechanism directing production and consumption, is its influence on morale. As long as changes in demand are relatively small and slow, the hardships caused might be tolerated on the plea of the efficiency of the system. But that plea cannot be sustained in war-time. The hardship caused would be quite exceptionally heavy. With increasing wealth the 'non-essential' sector in a community which can in an emergency be mobilized for war, expands. Moreover, it is in this sector that many of the small entrepreneurs and traders, who do not possess considerable reserves to weather the emergency, have in fact survived. No system which, in order to obtain a temporary redirection of the industrial effort, would inflict extreme and permanent injury on these people could be tolerated from the point of view of equity and thus of morale.[1]

These considerations show that an efficient organization of the economic system for the prosecution of the war can only be achieved by direct planning and controls. Conscious action must take the place of the indirect regulation of production by the interplay of demand and supply on the profit motive.

Allocation of Resources

4. Ideally speaking, direct allocation of productive factors and material both in the sphere of civilian consumption and of arms production should be substituted for 'economic incentives' as the regulator of economic activity. This would, theoretically, enable a complete separation between the physical and monetary aspect of productive activities. The normal economic incentive mechanism need, and should even then, not be wholly abandoned.

[1] Quite apart from the fact that it could not ensure a proper distribution of losses caused by enemy action, that is, uninsurable risks, losses which have nothing to do with the re-organization of production and whose equitable distribution would consequently not impair the war effort even in a truly 'market' country.

Once this is done the main argument against compensation for losses incidental to the war disappears. Compensation would then not retard the readjustment in the productive structure necessitated by the war. Indeed, it would be one of the methods by which the irksomeness of compulsion could be mitigated and the voluntary co-operation of all concerned could be obtained. It would be inappropriate in the extreme that direct planning should be accompanied by policies which would impede its working, cause grievances or kill all incentive implicit in some link between effort and remuneration. Compensation for losses caused by the war must therefore be conceived as part of the remuneration of the productive factors willing to co-operation in the war effort and must be made dependent on such co-operation.

5. In the financial sphere, policy, I think, should attempt so to regulate money incomes (either by a direct fixing of wages, salaries, etc., or by suitable compensation payments, including family allowances) as to enable people (*a*) to purchase their allotted real rations, (*b*) to maintain their financial obligations incurred prior to the outbreak of the war and thus avoid encroaching upon *current* productive effort, (*c*) to accumulate money capital reserves for lost or damaged goodwill or assets, to be used, after the war, according to a reconstruction plan assuring a stable economic development, (*d*) to maintain their relative—money—income and capital position subject only to *general* tax measures and qualified by (*e*) permitting them some—anticipated—satisfaction of additional money earnings for any extra effort or sacrifice they are asked to bear.

This policy aims at establishing a fixed pre-taxation status for every one willing to co-operate in the war effort.[1] No one would, in general, be worse off than before the war, in terms of his money obligations. He might be better off (on terms of money) if he contributes more to the war effort than before. Any change desired in relative pre-war incomes could then be brought about by a deliberate taxation of incomes or of property.

A policy fulfilling these aims would ensure (*a*) the principle of equity and (*b*) the willing co-operation of people free from the haunting fear of economic annihilation.[2] It would eliminate any

---

[1] A maximum limit will have to be fixed in practice.

[2] As long as complete direct control over consumption, and even more over production, has not been established it is important to differentiate between compensation payments:
    (*a*) in cases where it does not interfere with the incentive mechanism. In these cases—and all damage to houses inhabited by the owner, and destruction of earning capacity due to enemy action belong in this category—compensation could be paid even now;
    (*b*) where it infringes upon the incentive mechanism but where compulsion has been

resistance to transfer of resources. And it could be so organized as to facilitate the solution of the administrative problem of ensuring the maximum technical efficiency in the war effort.

Damages and Losses in War

6. The damages and losses can be divided into those caused: (1) by enemy action and (2) those caused by Government measures mobilizing productive factors. In each category there will be two sub-divisions: (a) losses of or damages to earning power and goodwill and (b) those to property (either used by the owner or yielding an income). From an administrative point of view there is a further important but rather different distinction between (i) property and goodwill which plays a part in the productive process and (ii) property which (such as houses) is used for, or yields income by, consumption.

Loss or Damage to Personal Earning Power

7. In general, I suggest that in case of loss or damage to personal earning power, the system adopted in the case of Civil Servants and University Teachers, as well as some other groups, should be extended and incomes should, either by direct State payment or by appropriate general wage and salary regulation, be brought up to pre-war level, subject possibly to a minimum so as to enable the poorest to obtain his rations (this might be done preferably by an appropriate fixing of minimum wages and grant of family allowances) and in practice also to a (generous) maximum.

Loss to Property and Goodwill

8. In case of damage to or loss of goodwill or assets the procedure ought to depend on whether the damage occurred to 'consumption' assets or to 'productive' assets.[1] In the former case *blocked credits or*

instituted to act as an efficient substitute. There is no objection to paying compensation (that is, soldiers' dependants; cut in non-esssential supplies; commandeering of property, etc.);

(c) where it interferes with the incentive mechanism but no compulsion has as yet been instituted (for example, the transfer of labour except in certain instances; and, up till recently, the task of closing down factories instead of running them short time). In these cases compensation or relief must not be so high as to weaken the effort of the individual to reintegrate himself into the war-sector. I venture to suggest, however, that this part-solution is both wasteful and harmful on morale. As long, moreover, as there is no rationing of consumption goods no free capital compensation can be granted and the income compensation will also be hampered by the fear of causing inflation.

[1] In certain cases the compensation—even in war—will take the form of physical replacement. These cases will presumably be exceptional.

blocked bonds (to be freed after the war) yielding a *free income* sufficient to replace the use of the lost asset (or its yield) would seem the appropriate form of compensation. The blocked capital grant should, however, be usable immediately for specified purposes, such as debt repayment.

The solution of the problem of compensation for damage to 'productive' goodwill or assets is bound up with the problem of efficient war-economic organization. The appropriate unit of war-economic organization are not single firms but industries (including distributive trades) as a whole. Once this principle is adopted both in the war and in the non-essential sector, the solution of the administrative problem of compensation is comparatively easy. The formation of war-time operating-holding companies which lease the plant, etc., of the constituent firms against some kind of participation in the surplus (including State subsidies, etc.) of the new company enables such payments to be made to the participating firms as would give them the desired level of income on a uniform basis. This procedure would incidentally secure a thorough and flexible rationalization of production which will not be achieved by private pooling arrangements as contemplated at present.

Conclusions

9. The arguments against such general solution of the problem of bearing losses and damage due to the war are firstly financial, secondly administrative. The financial arguments, 'we cannot afford it' or 'it would cause inflation', have been criticized as fallacious on several occasions in this BULLETIN. In a properly organized war economic system there is no problem of finance or inflation. The problem of National Debt ought to be easily tackled.

The second line of argument bases itself on the 'lack of suitable administrative man-power'. The critics of compensation and control schemes would be in a stronger position if the various Ministries had tried to make full use of the valuable administrative skill which is (or should be)[1] made unemployed by their policy of concentration and centralization.

It is not claimed that the solution outlined is easy to administer or that it solves all problems. But it has the merit of establishing a fair distribution of sacrifice, of providing a mechanism for an efficient use of productive factors and, last but not least, of avoiding prejudice to the methods of reconstruction.

---

[1] Especially in the food and distributive trades the system of spread-over is still rampant.

COMPENSATION IN PRACTICE

by T. Balogh

From Bulletin, Vol. 4, No. 12 (August 29, 1942)

THE practice of the Government in compensating the damage caused through Government (and not hostile) action has not been uniform.

A. In cases of *property* requisitioned the Compensation (Defence) Act, 1939, is the operative measure. The principle laid down in that Act is to pay the current price for the services of property taken over, disregarding, however, any *appreciation* in the value due to the emergency. This lopsided arrangement has been disregarded in several important instances.

(i) The Courtauld Combine award in compensation for the shares of the American Viscose Company is the most recent instance. The whole enterprise was apparently valued by Courtaulds at £32,000,000 exclusive of Goodwill and other intangible assets. The American Government apparently insisted on these shares being sold. They were accordingly vested in the Treasury and disposed of through a banking syndicate. The Treasury received, even at $4 to the £, the equivalent of £13,611,000 only, not less than £2,000,000 being absorbed by the marketing expenses and profits of the syndicate. An Arbitrator was appointed by Courtaulds and the Treasury in order to fix the amount of compensation to be paid to the Company. The Arbitrator fixed the award at £27,125,000 in cash, plus interest at 3 per cent from March 15, 1941, for 95 per cent of the Viscose shares.[1] The Treasury is therefore obliged to pay some £13,500,000 more to the Company than it received for the shares sold.

(ii) The compensation paid for vessels acquired under the Compensation (Defence) Act, 1939, was to have been based on their pre-war value in accordance with Section 4 (7) of the Act. Under Section 4 (I) -b of the Act it is provided, however, that compensation

---

[1] It does not seem probable that it represents the profit earning capacity of the Viscose Company over a period of years capitalized at the rate of interest now ruling for Government securities which will be substituted for it in the Company's assets. Whether the Company will be better off or worse off depends entirely on the success or otherwise of the Government's policy of maintaining sterling, and its management after the war of foreign trade and the balance of payments.

for vessels lost, not requisitioned, should be equal to the value of the ship immediately before the occurrence of the damage. The final financial settlement between the shipowner and the Government[1] provided not merely that the owners of all vessels (including requisitioned[2] vessels) lost should receive immediate cash payment equal to pre-war value of the ship lost,[3] but also that in addition and against the general principle, they should be credited with the subsequent increase in value in the Government Tonnage Replacement Account.[4] This is blocked and can only be used for the purpose of replacing vessels, including purchase of vessels from the Government. The Controller and Auditor General reports that this 'will result in payment to owners of large sums in excess of those provided for by Section 4 (7) of the Act'.[5] The new scheme[6] by which the Government sells vessels built on its own account to owners who lost vessels means that in this special case almost complete physical restoration is promised (some loss might be suffered by the owner if construction costs increased violently).

(iii) The Ministry of Food, when exercising their powers under the Defence Regulations by requisitioning very large quantities of foodstuffs did not proceed under Section 6 of the Compensation (Defence Act), 1939, either, which would have enjoined them to pay cost plus reasonable profit. According to the Controller and Auditor General[7] they fixed the terms of compensation on a flat rate basis negotiated with the Trade organizations concerned, with the advice of the Ministry's trade directors (in most cases interested in the Trade), and after consultation with the Treasury[8] on the basis of Section 15 of the Act. The Controller reports that he 'was not in a position to judge whether the prices fixed were in all cases reasonable'

[1] Cmd. 6218, Section 4.
[2] Vote of Credit Appropriation Account 1939, H.O.C., No. 72, 1941, p. 32, para. 76.
[3] This already is substantially more favourable to shipowners than the scheme laid down for owners of real property who receive blocked credits to be released at the will of the Treasury.
[4] There was to have been recourse to a Valuation Tribunal in case of disagreement. In actual fact no recourse has been made as insured or approved values were accepted by both parties. Civil Appropriation Accounts, 1940, p. xv, s. 3.
[5] Vote of Credit Appropriation Account, 1939, p. 32–3, p. 76.
[6] Vote of Credit Appropriation Account, op. cit., p 24 (56).
[7] According to Sir Henry French, the prices paid under Section 15 instead of Section 6, were 'probably on a higher scale than the most rigid interpretation of Section 6 would have resulted in'. (The Minutes of Evidence taken before the Committee of Public Accounts, 1941, p. 182, Question 1967).
[8] It was explained to the Committee that the average prices were such as to average out the price of commodities held in different stages of distribution. It seems, however, that in certain particular instances profits made by middlemen have been reimbursed by the State. Ibid., Question 1792.

although he had 'no reason to criticize them'. In some cases the Ministry went further, and made additional payments on the basis of equity.

(iv) A further exception from the strict application of the Act has been made in the case of railroads. The Companies receive payments slightly above pre-war profits, contrary to the strict words of the Compensation (Defence Act.)[1]

B. No compensation is being paid to *persons* whose earning power has been reduced by compulsory Government 'call-up' or 'directions' under the National Service or Emergency Powers (Defence) Acts. Here again there are some anomalous exceptions. Government and local Civil Servants receive at least their pre-war salary. Any difference between their war- and peace-time income is made up by the Government and local Authorities. The same is true of University dons and the employees of some private firms. Mr. Bevin encouraged the peace-time employers, even of people who were directed into (lower paid) war industrial jobs, to 'make up' the incomes of their erstwhile employees to the former level. In so far as such salaries are accepted as costs for purposes of Excess Profits Tax or of the Goods and Services (Control of Prices) Act or of Government contracts it is fair to say that compensation will be paid almost wholly by the Government itself or by a levy of indirect tax character on the consumer. In certain special cases, moreover, compensation is granted to people transferred from higher paid to usually lower paid jobs by way of permitting their new employers to continue to pay them their previous income and to charge higher prices (bricklayers working as labourers; certain cotton workers directed back from munitions). In some schemes the salaries of managers of closed-down factories can be continued (for example, cotton, brick, steel) and these payments can be charged to Care and Maintenance funds.

C. The most varied and thus anomalous position can be found in the case of *firms* whose earning power has been diminished or annihilated by Government measures. The principles here again is that no compensation should be granted by the Government. This was laid down by the Prime Minister in the House of Commons as early as September 5, 1940, when he announced the change in policy with respect to damage due to enemy action:

'Damage by enemy action stands on a different footing from any other kind of loss or damage, because the nation undertakes the task of defending the lives and property of its subjects and tax-payers

[1] Cf. M. Stewart, 'The New Railway Agreement', Bulletin, Vol. 3, No. 13.

against assaults from outside. Unless public opinion and the judgment of the House were prepared to separate damage resulting from the fire of the enemy from all those other forms of war loss, and unless the House was prepared to draw the distinction *very sharply* between war damage by bomb and shell and the other forms of loss which are incurred, we could not attempt to deal with this matter; *otherwise we should be opening up a field to which there would be no bounds'*. (My italics.)

In actual practice this principle has been violated in numerous cases and compensation was arranged for the loss of goodwill, either paid directly by the State or indirectly by the State, permitting the particular industry or trade to charge a certain amount on price to finance compensation, *that is*, extra-budgetary indirect taxation.

The main examples of such procedure can be found in the case of the Commodity Controls under the administration of the Ministries of Food[1] and Supply,[2] the late Petroleum Department,[3] the Mines Department[4] (now amalgamated into the Ministry of Fuel and Power), the Shipping Control exercised by the Ministry of War Transport,[5] and the Treasury.[6] The Ministry of Works and Planning has (lately) also joined this group by agreeing to the Brick Scheme,[7]

---

[1] Minutes of Evidence taken before the Committee of Public Accounts, pp. 196–7. 'Our broad aim would be to try to enable any butcher who has only a small number of registered customers to continue to exist'. Nor was a system of differential purchase prices or subsidies made use of in order to minimize the cost of the policy of maintaining traders. The subsidy to bakers has only recently been made discriminatory, even though large bakers were in no need for it.

The policy of maintaining retail outlets has been clearly reaffirmed by Sir Henry French ('Minutes of Evidence', Question 2131 to 2136). The Ministry 'have entered into arrangements for using, as if they were Ministry of Food Officers, the personnel of a particular trade, for instance, the Grain trade, the Milling industry, Oil Seed brokers, etc. Instead of our paying these individuals a salary, we pay into a pool a global figure resulting from a negotiated settlement covering the whole of the services that that trade is performing for the country and they divide that much money themselves (ibid., p. 124, Question 1981).

'The Grain trade themselves are forced, under our Agreement to weed out people who are unnecessary because, as the tonnage goes down, so their remuneration goes down' (Question 1983).

'In case of a Broker or business like the Grain trade, they have no risks to bear at all. They are merely acting under our instructions. Therefore we regard it as fundamental in our negotiations that a trade that is running no risks whatever should not be remunerated on pre-war level' (Question 1987).

[2] Timber and Cotton (as far as the Liverpool Cotton Exchange and the Care and Maintenance levy scheme is concerned).

[3] In the case of certain garages situated on the South Coast the Petroleum Department has, on the other hand, provided for compensation of the closed-down garages without arranging for pooling and thus utlizing the services of the closed-down plants.

[4] A levy was made to finance the maintenance of closed pits, later to help generally mines which suffered from the effect of the war.

[5] For example, The War-Risk Insurance Schemes.

[6] In cases of ship chartering and insurance.

[7] It is interesting to note that the Brick Committee quite openly advocates a Corporative Organization of the industry. The Ministry did not altogether accept the recommendation

havingrefused to entertain any compulsory poolingandcompensation scheme for the far more numerous and threatened building trades. The Board of Trade has been taking an intransigent line up till now with respect to retail trade[1] and unessential industry, but seems on the verge of reconsidering its attitude, having already permitted some exceptions. Under the Goods and Services (Price Control) Act, the view was taken that compensation must be arranged privately and the cost of compensation should not fall on the consumer. This latter proviso, however, has been violated in many cases and is yet another system of indirect extra-budgetary taxation.

Conclusion

This view shows that the policy of the Government has been illogical and varied from Department to Department. In fact, one may say that compulsory concentration was accomplished almost without exception, without compensation, and compensation was given in certain cases without insisting on concentration. The more powerful vested interests have got compensation, the less powerful have not. Where the individual citizen has been faced with com-pulsory measures of the Government the full rigour of the Compensa-tion (Defence) Act, 1939, was applied and the State benefited from any depreciation of the assets or services, whereas the individual citizen was not given the benefit from any appreciation, nor was he generally compensated for lost goodwill.[2] The usual explanation put forward [3] that compensation was not paid to traders but their 'services hired' for a fixed sum or a percentage payment on turnover

but it agreed to fix *minimum* prices for bricks apparently high enough to pay to closed firms part of their pre-war profits apart from care and maintenance. In so far as the Government is practically the sole buyer of bricks this means the acceptance of direct State-financed com-pensation for lost goodwill. In the case of some 800,000 building firms in dire straits this was flatly refused.

[1] In cotton and certain other industries, as explained in a statement on January 8, 1942, where concentration has taken place collectively, provision is made for a levy to be added to price and this price is admitted by the Price Regulation Committees under the Prices of Goods and other price-regulating Acts and Regulations issued under them. In certain other cases such as, for example, hosiery, it is understood that compensation payments by nucleus firms are regarded as profit sharing except in the case of certain special arrangements and/or if the manufacturer can prove serious hardship.

[2] Very much the same applies to the schemes as far as damages resulting from hostile action is concerned. There again the Administration tried to disregard any appreciation of the assets resulting from war and does not compensate for goodwill. Consequently there is a powerful motive for the damaged to press for repairs and the departments, not being able to compensate in many cases, permit rebuilding and repair to be carried out even though it may impinge directly on the war effort. This was especially the case with respect to retail trades and entertaining. As far as personal injury is concerned the Government instituted flat rate compensation irrespective of previous earning power and whenever such compensation was paid regrettable differences in the rates of pay have been permitted.

[3] For example, 'Vote of Credit Appropriation Account, 1939', pp. 25–57.

is beside the point. The services of those Trading Associations could have been obtained (for example, as in the case of Non-Ferrous Metal they were in fact so obtained) by making the traders Civil servants at a lesser cost. Most of the traders could, in any case, have easily been eliminated.

In the fourth year of the war it would seem to be difficult to introduce a new comprehensive compensation policy. In spite of these difficulties it is to be hoped, in view of the possible length of the war and the complete mobilization of all resources which it renders necessary, that the Government will try to assimilate the existing compensation schemes into a logical whole, granting *ex gratia* payments retrospectively to people who have suffered without having been compensated. It seems especially that measures should be taken: (1) to assimilate the war grants scheme paid to members of His Majesty's Forces on the basis of pre-war earning power, (2) the same thing should be done with pensions. The problem of shrinking industries, including retail trade, should be dealt with by financial pooling arrangements with sufficient subsidies to render this compensation policy feasible.

ECONOMIC INCENTIVE AND EFFICIENCY
IN WAR INDUSTRY

by J. Steindl

FROM BULLETIN, VOL. 3, NO. 8 (JUNE 7, 1941)

1. 'ECONOMIC incentive' has played a large rôle in recent discussion on the E.P.T. In view of the fact that the provision of the
supplies essential for the defence of this country is for the greater
part dependent on private contractors (though financially assisted by
the Government) economic incentive is, indeed, of great importance;
but its working depends on the way in which the services of private
contractors are remunerated.

There are several reasons why the remuneration in government
contracts should become a problem in time of war: (1) competition
between firms is, in many cases, almost eliminated; (2) there is need
for very urgent production; (3) it becomes very difficult to estimate
cost before production is finished.

2. Three broad types of remuneration are used in government
contracts:[1]

(1) *Fixed price contract.* Here, the price is agreed on before
the order is given, and the contractor bears the risk of subsequent
changes in cost; part of this risk, however, may be excluded by a
'variation clause' which may stipulate, for example, that the prices
vary in a certain way with subsequent changes in the wage rate or
material prices. The price is arrived at either by competitive tender
or by an estimate of the cost, based on technical costing or on experience with previous orders.

The fixed price contract is used extensively by the Ministry of
Works and Buildings; to some extent it is used by the Admiralty and
by the Air Ministry (Select Committee, 1940-41 (4), p. 25).

(2) *'Cost plus' contract.* Here, the Department agrees in principle
to bear the costs whatever they are, so that the contractor runs no

---

[1] Most of the factual material employed is taken from the Reports of the Select Committee on National Expenditure (quoted as Select Committee with the number of the Report
in brackets).

risk; the principle may be modified by imposition of a *maximum cost* and by the possibility of disallowing certain costs which were incurred unnecessarily. The profit or fee is stipulated either as a percentage on actual cost, or as a fixed sum.

'Cost plus' contracts were used by the War Office in the construction of militia camps (Select Committee, 1940(3)) at the beginning of the war and again later on, after the evacuation of France, in the construction of defence works (Select Committee, 1940-41 (4), p. 27). They are used by the Admiralty under the Emergency Repairs Agreement and by the Air Ministry under the McLintock Agreement for 'educational' orders on aircraft.

(3) *Target cost contract.* In this case a target cost is fixed before the work starts (actually it is often fixed much later); it is usually based on previous experience with similar work, and includes a fee. If the actual cost is below the target cost the contractor gets a certain percentage of the difference. If the actual cost is in excess of target cost, the difference is either borne wholly by the Department (in some cases only up to a maximum), or else a part of it is borne by the contractor; the contractor's share is, however, in practice reduced by detailed arrangements so much that it is fair to say that his risk is often limited.

Target price contracts were used by the War Office in the construction of camps; they are used by the Air Ministry in the construction of aerodromes and partly for the construction of planes under the McLintock Agreement. In combination with a maximum price the target cost is widely used by the Ministry of Supply.

It may be of interest to note that the target price system has found imitation also, in the Dominions. In Australia it is generally used in the 'Munitions Annexes,' which are financed and owned by the Commonwealth Government.

3. Under a fixed price contract the contractor bears the risk of the actual cost being higher than was expected at the time when the order was received. This risk will often be very great under war conditions: wage rates and raw material prices may change; efficiency of labour and quality of raw materials may vary strongly; temporary shortage of labour and material may cause idleness and therefore increase overheads; with new equipment, new methods of production, new design, etc., the ordinary routine on which calculation is based will be missing; equipment will be very intensively used, but probably not evenly, so that cost may fluctuate on this account.

The 'cost plus' contract obviously relieves the contractor of this risk. In its effects, however, the system has been unfortunate; it offers no incentive whatsoever to efficiency; under the peculiar type of 'cost plus percentage profit' system efficiency is, on the contrary, strongly discouraged, because profits increase with cost. That the system has, in fact, led to waste and inefficiency is shown by the Reports of the Select Committee. They show that most complaints of waste and inefficiency directed to the Committee were connected with work ordered on a cost plus basis (Select Committee, 1940-41 (4), p. 11). The most outstanding example of this are the militia camps. One of the features of the system is that it leads to Sunday work and over-time regardless of the effects on the efficiency of the workers, which are highly detrimental (Select Committee, 1940 (7), 1940—41 (3)).

The endeavours to remedy these serious defects and to offer some incentive to the contractor without throwing heavy risks on his shoulders led to the development of the target cost system. The main problem under this system is the fixing of the target price. If experience on the basis of previous orders makes it possible to fix the target cost at such a level that, with reasonable efficiency, the contractor can press the actual cost below target cost, then there will be incentive to efficiency. If, however, the target cost is so low that with reasonable effort there can be no saving on it, then the effects will be precisely the same as with the cost plus system.[1]

If cost is liable to unexpected variations *from one order to the next*, then the contractor does not know whether he will be able to earn a bonus or not; in this case the incentive will be considerably weakened or may become negligible. Alternatively, if the target price is fixed very high, the profits of the contractor would become unduly high.

The material of the Select Committee strongly confirms these expectations. In the case of camp construction, 'the cost of labour and materials varied so extensively' that 'the actual target price could not always be ascertained until the work was approaching com-pletion' (Select Committee, 1940 (3), p. 8). The final costs were largely in excess of original estimates (ibid.). In the case of

---

[1] It is assumed here that cost in excess of the target price is wholly borne by the department, which is the target principle in its original and purest form. In fact, often modified forms are adopted in which the contractors are liable to bear a share of the excess over target cost (which may be graduated up to 100 per cent), but to this extent the system approximates to the fixed price system, and the contractor is again bearing considerable risk.

In practice it is found that the provision of a 'penalty' for excess of cost over target price often means very little modification of the 'pure' target principle. In the contracts for the construction of aerodromes, for example, a penalty of 10 per cent for excess of cost over target cost is stipulated (Select Committee, 1940–41 (9), pp. 9–11). The Report, however, states that the sub-committee 'have not heard of any case where contractors have lost any part of their fee by way of penalty' (p. 11).

aerodromes (Select Committee, 1940-41 (9),) the target price is determined after work has been in progress, on the basis of wage rates, material prices, etc., in the first four weeks of the contract (ibid., pp. 8—9). But in practice 'the sub-committee have been surprised to learn that it is often the case that the target price is not finally settled for three months or more' (p. 10). The estimates, which were made before giving out the contracts, have been vastly exceeded by actual cost (p. 8). This clearly illustrates the difficulties of finding the target. The dangers of fixing target cost *after* work has begun are also indicated: 'An unscrupulous contractor employed on a contract of this type might deliberately buy at high rates during the first weeks' (ibid., p. 11).

There is reason to believe that the difficulties in fixing the target cost are not limited to the above examples. In the view of the Select Committee the system should be given up as far as possible in favour of fixed price contracts. But it seems doubtful whether this system can give a satisfactory solution either. Fixed prices mean a considerable risk to the contractor, and if he is prepared to take this risk at all he will do it only for correspondingly high profit. The assumption that with 'straight-run' production the risk of unexpected variation in cost is not great, is very doubtful under present circumstances. The proportion of skilled labour available, the quality of raw material, stoppages due to air raids, amount of overtime worked, etc., may vary considerably, especially over longer periods, and a reasonably quick adaptation of the fixed price to changed circumstances is not possible at present owing to the slow working of cost control. In its practical application the system is diluted by all kinds of clauses which protect the contractor against subsequent increases in cost (see Select Committee, 1940-41 (4), p. 30), for example, owing to war risks, overtime, difficulty of labour recruiting, etc. The problem in all these clauses is, of course, whether distinction can be made between changes in cost which are outside the reach of the contractor and those which he can control. This is by no means the case even in the common forms of the variation clause which allows for changes in price of raw materials. Cheap buying may well be within the control of the contractor, and the variation clause may sometimes make him pay unnecessarily high prices to related business interests.

Another difficulty is that fixed prices cannot be based on competitive tender, because competition does not work well under present circumstances, when most available firms are needed. The price has then to be found by post-costing or by technical costing, and a profit-margin has to be determined. Technical costing would have to take into account the special conditions in various firms, as costs vary strongly from firm to firm. As to post-costing, experience has shown that it works too slowly. Even if either of these methods works in some way, it does not, as the Select Committee thinks, provide a substitute for the missing competition. The main point about competition in ordinary peace-time tenders is that the inefficient contractor is excluded; no costing whatsoever will achieve this under present conditions, because, if the orders have to be placed and all equipment must be used, then willy-nilly the departments have to pay the inefficient producer a high enough price to cover his cost.

4. It may be concluded that in present circumstances the available types of remuneration do not work in a satisfactory way, and new types might not work much better. The reason is that some conditions which are indispensable for effective control of efficiency are not fulfilled under present circumstances.

(1) There is no automatic removal of incompetent managers, because competition is largely absent, and there is a tendency to protect the contractor against loss; efficiency, however, cannot be achieved by incentives alone, but only by incentives *and* elimination of incompetent managers (or selection of competent ones). The target principle would satisfy this condition if it were supplemented by the provision that the department can replace a manager who exceeds the target cost, if the reason for this excess-cost is not outside his control.

(2) A second condition for effective control of efficiency is the continuity of production; discontinuity of orders represents the most serious risk under present conditions. Only with planning of production for a sufficient time ahead can efficiency in the relevant sense be controlled. It must be noted that economy in real resources alone is relevant, and money costs are sometimes misleading: if production has to be stopped temporarily, the unemployment is pure waste. Another point is that a maximum efficiency in terms of cost can be aimed at only with given conditions of planned output, etc.; there are subsidiary 'aims', for example, speed, quality, etc., which must be settled in the plan.

(3) Under the present system 'the Departments have no power under their contracts to examine the current cost of production' (Select Committee, 1940-41 (3), p. 10). The post-costing has been a failure, because it reveals the waste of real resources only when it is too late to prevent it, and the delay involved in controlling cost

can be seen from the fact that the Select Committee 'has been unable to see the actual costs of almost any articles which have been delivered since the war began'[1] (ibid., p. 11). The Select Committee advocates, therefore, current control of cost.

(4) Efficiency can be controlled by comparison of *Process Costs* between factory and factory, and within each factory. Such a system was introduced in the last war, and is advocated by the Select Committee (1940-41 (4), p. 18). Manufacture of a shell, for example, is divided into subsequent 'processes', and the cost of each process is compared separately. The quality of raw material is taken into account as well as other particular circumstances which affect output; in this way it has tried to get results which are comparable between factories and to make it possible to control efficiency by finding out the weak spots quickly.

In present circumstances we cannot rely on the factors which are usually regarded as ensuring efficiency in times of peace. If efficiency of management is to be ensured there must be substitutes for the selecting forces of competition. Here, as in other fields, the suspended operation of the checks normally provided for by market forces must be replaced by direct controls if waste is to be avoided. If departments are empowered to control cost before the contract is finished, as the Select Committee recommended, interference with unrestricted freedom of management is inevitable. The position of the manager correspondingly approximates to that of an employee of the Government, in a similar way as the position of workers under the Essential Works Order also approximates to the position of Government employees.

The fact that a large amount of the equipment of war industries is financed and actually owned by the Government points in the same direction. It would be easier to bring this part of war industry under direct Government control, if it were not for the fact that part of it is 'mixed up' with and technically inseparable from private equipment. Direct control could be carried through—following other precedents—by requisitioning the privately-owned equipment, or else the Government could claim partnership in firms which are partly working with Government-owned equipment, and put a manager in with powers overriding those of the private manager. To render such arrangements effective will often require the use of new managers who are financially disinterested and independent.

The problem of offering an incentive to management could be

---

[1] I.e., after more than a year.

solved under these conditions. The target principle, for example, applied to 'process costs' would not be as hopelessly inadequate as it is now, because current cost control would make it possible to keep the 'target' up to date, and change it quickly with changing conditions; process costing would indicate the reasons for differences in cost in different units (plants), and make it possible to put the bonus for efficiency on a fair basis by eliminating changes in cost which are outside the control of the manager. Alternatives to the target principle could be found, but in any case the working of a bonus system would depend on current cost control and process costing.

THE PROBLEM OF PROFIT MARGINS

by M. Kalecki

FROM BULLETIN, VOL. 4, No. 5 (APRIL 4, 1942)

1. THE purpose of this note is to discuss the connection between the influence upon production of the Excess Profits Tax and the level of profit per unit of output (profit margins). The problem may be illustrated by two examples. Imagine a Government contract given on a fixed price basis to a firm which could do much to improve its organization of production. If the level of the price is such that with the present methods of production the firm is able to earn a total profit which is above or at the level of the 'standard profit' the incentive for reorganization is lacking because any additional profits which would be obtained by it would be taken away by 100 per cent Excess Profits Tax.

The second example is provided by conditions prevailing now in coal mining. It is alleged that collieries often work their worst seams because, with the existing level of costs and prices, they make in this way their standard profits and have the advantage of leaving the best seams for future exploitation. It is clear that thereby the coal output is reduced below the level which could be achieved with the same labour, and in addition there is a general deterioration of working conditions.

It is interesting to note that in both instances the Excess Profits Tax is not the only cause of ill effects. It should be remembered that even with the present Excess Profits Tax there is some inducement to make profits above the standard level; 20 per cent of 'excess profits' are repayable after the war and this item is not without some significance as a reserve; further, if the firm does not reach its standard profit in some year (which may easily happen even in armament industries owing to war damage), the deficiency is reimbursed out of its previous payments. The firms have thus an incentive to make excess profits, but a rather weak one. If appropriate labour were in ample supply the firms on war contracts would certainly increase output because taking in trained workers does not require any particular effort. But to reorganize production so as to obtain higher output with the same labour or to train workers is a different proposition which requires stronger incentives. The collieries would also increase their output to satisfy the existing demand if more miners were available (although even then they would still work the bad seams). The effects of the Excess Profits Tax upon production are thus due to some extent to shortage of labour. It is for this reason that a moderate reduction of the rate of Excess Profits Tax (say from 100 per cent to 75 per cent) would not make matters much better, because the incentive to increase output with the same labour would be still too weak.

However, the problem of incentives may be solved even with 100 per cent Excess Profits Tax by fixing appropriate profit margins per unit of output. If these are fixed so low that the firm cannot reach its standard profit unless it makes a reasonable effort for expanding output, Excess Profits Tax ceases to be a brake on production. The armament producer is compelled to reorganize production because otherwise he will get much less than his standard profit; the colliery must work its best seams just to earn its standard profit, etc. The producers move all the time within their standard profit. Excess Profits Tax does not come into the picture because excess profits do not accrue. In other words the Excess Profits Tax should be managed in such a way that it brings in as little revenue as possible. Its ideal is the same as that of a prohibitive customs duty.

2. I have dealt in another place[1] with the question of profit margins in Government contracts given on the basis of cost *plus* fixed profit margin per unit of output. My proposal there was, generally speaking, that profit margins should be fixed in such a way that the firm gets its standard profit upon reaching its 'target output' (fixed on the assumption of a reasonable efficiency of management) and thus proportionately less if the output is below the target level. (I allowed for complications arising out of the fact that a firm usually manufactures a variety of products. In the case when the factory is understaffed it was proposed that the 'target output' be estimated on the basis of full employment of the factory but after deduction of that number of vacancies communicated by the firm to agencies of the Ministry of Labour which the latter have been unable to fill).

It is easy to devise a similar scheme for contracts given on a fixed price basis (with a clause allowing for possible increases in prices of raw materials and wages). The price for goods concerned must be fixed at such a level that the 'target output' renders to the firm its 'standard profit'. Here, if the efficiency of the management is inadequate to reach the 'target output', not only is the actual output lower than the 'target output' but in addition the unit costs are

---

[1] Cf. 'Excess Profits Tax and Government Contracts'. (See p. 386).

higher than those on which was based the fixing of the contract price. Therefore, the firm which does not attain its 'target' is penalized here more severely than in the previously described case of a cost *plus* fixed profit margin contract. This should be, perhaps, counterbalanced by exempting from Excess Profits Tax the excess profits which the firm can make if it *exceeds* the target output.

3. So far we have applied our 'principle of low profit margins' only to Government contracts where profit margins or prices are fixed for each firm individually. We shall now consider the problem of incentives under Excess Profits Tax for marketable commodities where prices are not differentiated according to firms.

The problems arising in the industries concerned as a result of Excess Profits Tax are similar to those mentioned above in connection with coal mining. Firms will be inclined to use their most out-of-date equipment if they can make, in this way, their standard profit. In addition there will be no inducement for them to lower their costs by standardization of their products, etc., if the additional profits obtained as a result are taken away by Excess Profits Tax. Although the position in some of the industries is different from that in coal mining, because the main bottleneck is not labour but raw materials, there still exists the problem of economizing labour, either to release it for armament industries or to use it in the industries concerned to produce goods of more durable qualities.

Imagine now that the price is fixed at such a level that a medium cost producer gets his standard profit when working with reasonable efficiency. There arises then the following situation. The medium firms will tend to achieve a reasonable efficiency. The lowest cost producers may still afford some 'slacking'. Some high cost producers (although not necessarily an important part of them) may be unable to cover even their current costs. If these are deemed to be worth maintaining—either because medium and low cost producers are working up to capacity or for other reasons such as their geographical situation—subsidies may be paid.

A disadvantage of this solution is that the best establishments may still afford to work below their possible efficiency. If these, as is often the case, are large scale units they may be perhaps dealt with by direct control. In any case pegging of prices at such a level that the average producer is compelled to work with reasonable efficiency is a great improvement as compared with the situation which arises when prices are above that level.

The position in agriculture differs from other industries, in so far as the greater part of output is produced by small units, which are exempt from Excess Profits Tax because their profits are lower than £1,500 p.a. The policy of low profit margins if not accompanied by other devices, would be here double-edged. On the one hand it could increase the incentive to expand output for the large farms, on the other hand it could diminish it for the small ones.[1] In any case, higher prices of agricultural commodities by no means strengthen always the incentive for more intensive cultivation. The best solution would be to have a differential price policy for large and small farms.

4. The above analysis shows a new aspect of price control. This has usually been considered from the angle of the fight against inflation. As such it is efficient only when accompanied by rationing, because otherwise the discrepancy between demand for and supply of consumption goods reappears in the form of shortages and queues. We have seen that price control may perform a quite different task also, by restoring the production incentive under a regime of Excess Profits Tax.

[1] And possibly also for some marginal large producers.

EXCESS PROFITS TAX AND GOVERNMENT CONTRACTS

by M. Kalecki

FROM BULLETIN, VOL. 4, NO. 2 (JANUARY 31, 1942)

1. THE Excess Profits Tax is often considered a brake on the war effort because it deprives entrepreneurs of the profit incentive and thus prevents the full use of existing resources. We propose here to examine this problem for industries working on Government contracts and to show that the repercussions of 100 per cent Excess Profits Tax depend closely on the form of contract. It is in particular possible to construct such a form of contract that Excess Profits Tax would not hamper the expansion of output of the industries in question.

Imagine first that contracts are given on the basis of costs *plus* percentage profit margin. It is obvious that 100 per cent Excess Profit Tax by taking off the excess of total profits over the 'standard level' does not hamper production in this case for the simple reason that profits are here proportionate to *costs* and thus are no indicator of efficiency. Also, if Excess Profits Tax were abolished there would be, under this type of contract, no tendency to get out of a given plant the maximum output by a better organization, etc.; the entrepreneurs would merely strive even more than under Excess Profits Tax to increase the costs by, say, working as much overtime as possible, even though it may not increase but reduce the output per worker.

If the contract is on the basis of cost *plus* fixed profit margin per unit of output the total profit is proportionate to output and thus constitutes an incentive for its expansion. But the strength of the incentive is dependent on the level of the margin. If it is very high, the entrepreneur may not—even in the absence of Excess Profits Tax —strive very hard for better organization, etc., his profit being, anyhow, very 'comfortable'.[1] And clearly with 100 per cent Excess Profits Tax any efforts to increase output are of no interest to him. But if the profit margins are fixed sufficiently low so that only at a high degree of utilization of available resources the 'standard profit' (that is, the

---

[1] The position is here different from peace-time because of scarcity of labour. With ample supply of labour (and provided equipment is not fully used) the increase in output does not require a particular effort.

level of total profits the excess over which is taxed) is reached, even 100 per cent Excess Profits Tax will not hamper the entrepreneur's initiative; for he must then strive hard to increase the profit within the range not subject to Excess Profit Tax.

The position with a fixed price contract is similar. In this case the entrepreneur has a double incentive to increase the output per worker: to expand the output and to reduce costs. But if the margin of profit is wide he may, even in the absence of Excess Profits Tax, make no great efforts to reorganize production. This the more so that the reduction of costs may bring him additional profits only for the contract in question, while the next contract may be given to him on the basis of reduced costs. 100 per cent Excess Profits Tax will, of course, in this as in the previous case, wipe out any incentive for improvements of the methods of production. On the other hand, with a sufficiently low profit margin, even 100 per cent Excess Profits Tax will not disinterest the entrepreneur in such improvements.

2. We are now going to describe in some detail a form of contract which would reconcile incentive for an optimum use of available resources with 100 per cent Excess Profits Tax. Let us assume first for the sake of simplicity, that a factory is engaged only on production of one type of goods on contracts from one Government Department. Imagine now that contracts are given on the following conditions: (1) The actual costs of production are covered (not allowing, of course, for excessive repair and maintenance or unreasonably high managers' salaries). (2) The profit margin p is fixed at the level of the ratio of 'standard profit' as calculated for Excess Profits Tax and the maximum productive capacity M, or:

$$p = \frac{S}{M}$$

Thus, if the entrepreneur reaches the 'target output' M he earns his standard profit; if his rate of actual output is lower than M he gets proportionately less. In no case, therefore, is he subject to Excess Profits Tax and he has to strive to reach his 'target output' in order to earn his 'standard profit'.[1]

The concept of M requires, however, further elucidation. With a given crew, by M is meant here that output which would be achieved if each worker worked the optimum time, and if the organization of production (inclusive of the system of wage payment)

[1] Since firms working under this system will be unable to benefit from repayment of 20 per cent of Excess Profits Tax after the war, the 'standard profit' may be fixed a little more liberally, in particular where the pre-war profits were low (often the case with small firms).

costs, however, have been a serious problem throughout the war. The number of completed Ministry of Supply contracts awaiting costing at different dates was as follows:—

Completed Ministry of Supply Contracts Awaiting Costing

February, 1940	February, 1942	May 31st, 1942	May 29th, 1943
4,200	9,000	12,800	7,486[1]

[1] This reduction was achieved by using compromise settlements in a number of cases.

The consequence of this accumulation of arrears was that 'the limited staff of cost accountants available continued to be absorbed almost entirely on actual cost investigations, and for a long time the Ministry were unable to divert more than a small number to the important task of analysing the Department's records in such a way as to provide the data necessary for the determination of fair fixed prices for future orders.'[1] Arrears had begun to accumulate before the war broke out and it seems that until 1943 (no later data are yet available) the problem grew worse.

Current Costing can, under certain conditions, elicit sufficient information to permit moving contracts on to fixed prices. It also shows the *trend* of costs sufficiently early to prevent fixing prices consistently too high.

The Ministry of Supply used this method, which lessens the strain on the limited accounting staff, to a greater extent than other Departments. They did not, however, until 1943 make any use at all of the alternative of technical cost estimation. Indeed, in the memorandum to the Select Committee arguments are brought against using technical costing which appear weighty, until it is noticed that in 1942 the Ministry 'used a little less than two-thirds of one man's time' and in 1943 the time of only 9½ men on technical cost investigation. At the end of 1943 there were some 55 investigations being undertaken for the Ministry, practically all of a minor nature: in that year nearly 100,000 new contracts were placed.

Technical cost estimation was used before the war by the Admiralty and later by the Air Ministry as a means (*a*) of getting a sufficiently accurate estimate of what direct costs ought to be to allow the early movement of contracts on to fixed prices; and (*b*) of revealing at an early stage remediable inefficiencies in a particular firm. Both the Admiralty and the Ministry of Aircraft Production have used this method of costing widely during the war, checking it by selective

[1] Select Committee, Fourteenth Report, p. 39. Similar delays occurred in other fields. For example, the number of accounts outstanding for voyages which had been completed rose from 6,700 at March 31, 1943 to 8,000 at December 31, 1943 (Civil Appropriation Account, 1942).

post-costing. However, the personnel of the Technical Costs Section was too small to make the fullest use of this technique: in 1942 the staff was only 179, though it increased rapidly in 1943 to 277.

The odd situation mentioned above in which the evidence submitted by one Supply Department ignored completely the experience of other departments in the same field, does suggest that the co-ordination of contract policy was not very strong. The Select Committee, indeed, made this one of their major criticisms in 1943 and recommended that, not only should the Technical Costs section be strengthened and expanded, but there should be a special committee appointed to conduct a stocktaking review of the four years' experience of war contracts. Such a committee would consider 'methods of cost accounting, recording man-hours in jobs, etc., and for collating and interpreting such records.' The Treasury rejected the recommendation for immediate review by a special Committee. 'The Departments do not feel that at this stage of the war there is any necessity for, or can be any question of, a radical alteration of methods, and it is rather, in their view, a matter of reviewing procedure as will be necessary in the transition period.'[1]

IV. THE PROFIT RATE

'Profit is intended:—

(a) to give a return on the capital provided by the Company employed in the business, including money borrowed for the purpose of carrying on the business;

(b) to provide for the risk to the capital employed; this risk may be general and derive from the type of assets in which capital is invested, or particular and derive from the chance that a loss may be incurred in executing that particular contract;

(c) to give an incentive to the contractor to achieve maximum efficiency.

Provided that production is normally efficient, and that costs can be accepted as fair and reasonable, the general standard of profit approved for Government contracts in executing which the contractor is not at substantial risk, is $7\frac{1}{2}$ per cent on the capital employed in carrying them out.'[2]

This statement of principle refers mainly to fixed price contracts. For cost-plus contracts only item (a) has any application; there is no

---

[1] Twelfth Report from Select Committee: Session 1943–44, November 1944.
[2] Select Committee, Fourteenth Report, 1942–3, p. 101.

2 C*

risk to the capital employed; nor is there any incentive to increase efficiency. For maximum price contracts there is a negative incentive. But there is, in the opinion of the Select Committee, a definite tendency to set the maximum on the high or 'safe' side;[1] to the extent that this is the case the incentive is weaker and the risk is reduced at the same time. In theory, therefore, the profit should be just sufficient to cover the interest on the capital employed: 7½ per cent would seem more than adequate for this purpose.[2] Actual profit rates on costed contracts have been higher. In 1943, returns from 730 firms working on costed contracts for the Ministry of Supply over a period of 5 months showed a profit rate of 9·68 per cent on the capital employed of £240 million and a total cost of production of £350 million.[3] Much higher rates were earned on costed sub-contracts.[4] An analysis was made of some 3,300 trading results of Ministry of Supply sub-contractors, mainly for financial years ending in 1942 or 1943.[5] Less than 1,300 of these results relate to larger firms, with more than £50,000 capital employed. The profit rates of the larger firms are tabulated below.

Profit Rates Derived from 1,300 Trading Results of Sub-Contractors employing £50,000 Capital and over

Profit Rate	Per cent of Firms
Loss	2
0–15 per cent	25
15–30 per cent	35
30 per cent and over	38

No average profit rate for all the firms is given: but the Table shows that nearly three-quarters of the firms earned profits at a rate exceeding 15 per cent. Although the smaller firms showed a higher proportion of losses (9 per cent) they tended to obtain on the average an even higher rate of profit than the larger firms. In cases where the profits are very high the Ministry of Supply attempt to negotiate a retrospective price reduction; in general, however, they have to be

[1] Of a batch of 6,500 contracts examined by the Ministry of Supply 28 per cent were closed at the maximum price: the remaining 4,700 contracts were closed below the maximum, with a total 'saving' of 14 per cent of the value of the 4,700 contracts at maximum prices. Another sample was investigated by the Select Committee which produced a very significant result. 80 per cent of the firms in this sample fell into two clearly defined groups. One-third of this sub-group gave figures from 80–95 per cent of contracts closed *at* the maximum price: two-thirds, however, gave figures of 90–100 per cent closed below the maximum.

[2] Considerations of this kind were probably responsible for the reduction of the 'normal' profit rate from 10 per cent ruling at the outbreak of war to 7½ per cent.

[3] Minutes of Evidence taken before the Committee of Public Accounts, 1944, Appendix 15.

[4] Normally it is left to the main contractor to settle prices with sub-contractors, but in some cases the Ministry of Supply asked main contractors to include a costings clause in sub-contracts of £1,000 or over.

[5] Civil Appropriation Account (Class X) 1942, p. xxv.

content with a refund. Even new sub-contracts may be placed at the old price when it is known that a further refund will be necessary.[1]

In *fixed price* contracts all three principles of determining the profit rate come into play. The starting point is that the firm should, in general, earn $7\frac{1}{2}$ per cent on capital employed, but that higher rates should be allowed for where risk is abnormal, or where the firm is particularly efficient. The Ministry of Aircraft Production, for example, with Treasury approval, aim at allowing profits from 10 to 15 per cent on capital employed. The Public Accounts Committee were of the opinion that an actual level of 15 per cent would be out of proportion to the rate obtained under Treasury policy in costed contracts. Before discussing the actual profit rates obtained it will be convenient to set out the method of arriving at the fixed price, and some of the problems arising from it.

Profits are to be related to capital employed: however, what the Department is looking for is a profit 'mark-up' which, when added to cost, will give the price. No attempt is made, it would indeed be an impossible task, to isolate the capital employed on any single contract (unless the contract covers the entire output of the firm). In practice 'the rate of profit to be allowed on costs is obtained by dividing the appropriate profit return on capital by the ratio of the turnover[2] of the firm to the capital employed during the year or years in which the execution of the contract falls.'[3] Where part of the capital employed is provided by the Government (in 1943 about one-third for the major aircraft, aero-engine, propeller and turret firms) the remuneration on State capital is limited to a reward for management and a sum to cover the risk, if any, to the contractor in respect of the additional turnover. In normal cases one-eighth of the value of state assets is added to the value of the capital

---

[1] A minor undesirable consequence of this procedure is that the main contractors get a higher profit, as their costs include the unrevised sub-contract prices. A more weighty objection is that the Government appears to have acquiesced in a distinction between war contracts and 'non-war' contracts, by which prices of the latter are exempt from control. This distinction has no economic justification.

[2] Turnover is never precisely defined. On the basis of the figures quoted in the Table, see p. 401, it would appear reasonable to identify turnover with 'cost-of-sales', a term used elsewhere for the value of output at cost. Cost of sales *plus* profit gives turnover in the usual sense. In view of this unusual use of the term 'turnover' we refer to the profit 'mark-up' rather than profit margin.

[3] Select Committee, Fourteenth Report, 1942–3, p. 102. This statement which applies to M.A.P. contracts, appears slightly misleading. Since the essence of fixed price contracts is to settle them before production begins, or at an early stage, neither the total capital employed by the firm nor its total turnover for the period in which the contract falls can be known exactly, and presumably the ratio is based on estimates. This view seems to be confirmed by figures given in Appendix 15 to the Minutes of Evidence before the Committee of Public Accounts, 1944.

knowledge that a rebate may be requested can only reduce the incentive to efficiency. Moreover, the Departments themselves may become less insistent in pressing down prices, or in encouraging main contractors to 'squeeze' sub-contractors, if they know that mistakes can be partially rectified by later negotiations for rebates. It would have been, and would still be, for example, far more important in the case of sub-contracts, in which the excessive profits largely arise, if the efforts of the Department had been devoted to reorganizing the placing of sub-contracts through Regional Boards, instead of to the collection of refunds.

It is interesting, in the light of the above discussion, to look at the few data available about the results of the fixed price policy. Before the war and in its early stages it does not seem always to have been very successful. The best known example is that disclosed by a cost investigation conducted in 1941 into the fixed price contracts for 32 warships placed between 1936 and 1939, representing about a quarter of the ships ordered in the period.[1] The results were as follows:—

Profit on Cost (Hull and Machinery)	Number of Cases
Less than 10 per cent	4
Between 10 and 20 per cent	5
„ 20 „ 30 „	9
„ 30 „ 40 „	7
„ 40 „ 50 „	2
„ 50 „ 60 „	1
„ 60 „ 70 „	1
„ 70 „ 80 „	2
Over 80 per cent	1

No weighted average for all these contracts, whose total cost, including profit, was some £90 million, is given, but the unweighted average of the above figure gives a profit rate of 35 per cent *on cost*. No data are yet published to indicate the profit rates in subsequent periods.

The most comprehensive data concerning fixed-price contracts have been given in Appendix 15 of the 1944 Report from the Committee of Public Accounts. They cover some 20 firms comprising all the principal contractors engaged almost exclusively on direct contracts with the Ministry of Aircraft Production.

The 'prevailing profit rate' is the rate of profit which the Department allows for in fixing the price. The 'emergent profit' is the actual profit earned.

It will be noted that the prevailing profit rates on both the com-

[1] Report from the Committee of Public Accounts, 1943, pp. 7–8.

Capital, Costs, and Profits of 20 Principal Aircraft Contractors
Profit Percentage on Cost of Sales

	1941	1942	1943
Cost of Sales	£150,000,000	£209,000,000	£250,000,000
Prevailing Profit Rates	4·41%	3·76%	3·4%
Emergent Profit Rate ..	6·38%	5·60%	—

Profit Percentage on Capital Employed
(Capital computed substantially on E.P.T. basis)

	1941	1942	1943
Total Capital	£62,700,000	£76,000,000	£86,000,000
Companies' Capital	£50,000,000	£54,000,000	£56,000,000
Government Capital	£12,700,000	£22,000,000	£30,000,000
Profit at prevailing rate as percentage of total capital ..	10·55%	10·32%	9·88%
Emergent profit as percentage of total capital	15·26%	15·37%	—
Profit at prevailing rate on Companies' capital as Percentage of that capital	12·82%	13·77%	14·23%
Emergent profit on Companies' capital as percentage of that capital	18·51%	20·40%	—
Profit at prevailing rate on Government capital as percentage of that capital	1·65%	1·90%	1·78%
Emergent profit on Government capital as percentage of that capital	2·50%	3·11%	

panies' capital and Government capital were slightly rising: but with the increase in the relative importance of the latter the over-all rate was falling. The prevailing rate on *cost*, however, was steadily falling.[1] The emergent rate on cost also fell from 1941 to 1942 but was in both years about 50 per cent higher than the prevailing rate. It was suggested to the Public Accounts Committee that the difference between the emergent profit and the prevailing rate is an indication of the success of the fixed price policy and shows the extent to which the firms, by their own efforts, beat the price. Such a conclusion, however, is not valid. The attitude of the Department in fixing a price should surely be to set it in such a way that only if the firm strives for maximum efficiency will it be able to earn the 'prevailing' rate: for the special efficiency bonuses for particular firms have already been included in the prevailing rate. Thus, the continued gap between 'emergent' and 'prevailing' rates measures the failure of the Department to keep pace with the downward movement of costs.

[1] In 1939, 1940 and 1941 profit rates on 'sales' in major American Aircraft contracts were respectively 16·1, 23·6 and 27·0. *Office of Price Administration, War Profit Studies No. 2.*

DUAL CAPACITY

by G. D. N. Worswick

FROM BULLETIN, VOL. 5, NO. 5 (APRIL 3, 1943)

THE problem of 'dual capacity', the appointment of business men to responsible posts in Government Departments, particularly where the activities of these Departments affect the industries in which the business men were concerned before the war, has remained one of the open questions of war economic policy. In each of its Reports since the outbreak of war, the Public Accounts Committee has been particularly concerned with two aspects of this problem: (1) the source of remuneration of the officials, and (2) whether the Treasury and the Departments continue to be satisfied that the public interest is fully safeguarded under the existing arrangements. One may obtain a general outline of the policies of Departments run by business men from the industries concerned, especially the Raw Material Controls and the various divisions of the Ministry of Food. But while one can then analyse critically the policies pursued, it is very difficult to say definitely how far these policies would have differed, either for better or for worse, if the Controls, etc., had been staffed in another way, as for example in the last war, when business men were in charge of one another's industries and not their own.[1] In this article we outline the position in this country, in the light of the latest Report and Minutes of Evidence of the Public Accounts Committee (Second Report and Proceedings of the Committee: ordered to be printed November 10, 1942. In what follows we shall refer simply to the Report, giving the paragraph, or the Minutes, giving the question number). We shall then summarize the contents and conclusions of a Report of the United States Senate Special Committee, on the 'charge by Robert R. Guthrie in connection with the Administration by dollar-a-year men of the conversion programme . . .' which deals with the 'dual capacity' problem in the United States war economy.

The Present Position in Britain

In this country '. . . temporary civil servants can be divided into three main categories in that respect (their remuneration): those who come and are paid

These officials had, of course, advisory panels of men drawn from the trades concerned.

404

entirely by the Government (in this case the Ministry of Supply), but who, no doubt, have relations with their firms in that they have understandings that when the work is finished they will go back to the firms; the second category are paid a Civil Service remuneration, and we are aware that in those cases a balance representing the difference between their Civil Service pay and their old pay is made up to them by their firms; there is a third category who receive no pay whatever from the Ministry, but who receive, presumably, either the same remuneration as they had before from their company or something less.' (Answer to question 7793, Minutes.)

The number of persons in the third category seems to be very large:

'. . . in the Ministry of Supply there are hundreds of persons not connected with the iron and steel trade but connected with other trades who are giving whole-time service to the Ministry of Supply, and whose remuneration is derived from their previous firms.' (Answer to question 8270, Minutes.)

In the Iron and Steel Control in 1942, 65 per cent of persons who might be in a position to commit the Ministry of Supply are paid individually by their firms (7779, 7780, Minutes). The issue of 'dual capacity' is therefore one which affects profoundly the war economy. Steps are taken by the Departments to ensure that all temporary civil servants are fully aware of their position:

'The routine is that when a person is appointed to the staff, whether as a temporary or as a permanent civil servant, his attention is drawn to the staff rules, of which he receives a copy, and certain paragraphs of which lay down the doctrine, as we understand it, about dual capacity. In particular, when appointments of controllers of raw materials commodities are made, to which I think special reference was made last time this question was discussed, they receive a letter of appointment from the Minister, and in that letter reference is made to this question, so that they can be under no misapprehension; in addition, on the first occasion in which they come to headquarters, a member of the Raw Materials Department takes them over the ground, so that in that way we think we have covered the position fairly adequately, if I may say so.' (7771, Minutes.)

It would appear from the above quotations, therefore, that a temporary civil servant may continue to be paid by his firm, while in his official capacity he may influence policy with regard to an industry which, in turn, will affect his firm. There are, however, special checks with regard to contracts.

'they are under a series of very special obligations to keep us informed as to what their trade interests are, and they are kept from dealing with contractual matters in the Ministry in a sphere which is their own in outside industry.' (7803, Minutes.)

In view of the 'not unnatural public apprehension that the people concerned have more of a weather eye to their relationship to their own organizations than they have to the Government Department to which they are giving such excellent service,' (7800, Minutes), it may be asked why such persons are not made whole-time employees of the nation and paid accordingly. This is the more pertinent because it is not difficult to see that many such persons are indirectly paid by the Treasury; for where the firm is paying E.P.T., the E.P.T. paid will be less by the amount of the salary[1] of the person loaned to a Government Department.[2] If the Government paid this salary directly, its balance between revenue and expenditure would remain precisely the same. Thus, this first argument that '. . . we should simply not have been able to give those people the remuneration necessary to give them the standard of living to which they had been formerly accustomed' (7794, Minutes) seems not to be valid.[2] The second argument is more cogent. The salaries of the business men appointed as temporary officials are, in general, very much higher than those of Civil Servants of equivalent rank and 'if those gentlemen who at present are paid by outside firms were to be paid directly out of Government funds at the rate of remuneration which they received as business men before they came into the Government service, that might have some reaction on Civil Service salaries' (7804, Minutes). This does not, however, prevent the Departments paying the appropriate Civil Service salary, even if this rate is supplemented from outside. When the 'dual capacity' problem in the Ministry of Works and Planning received wide-spread publicity in 1942, the then Minister arranged for the business men concerned to become direct servants of the Ministry, but the Treasury did not feel 'that there was any necessity to make that rule a general rule' (9029, Minutes). The justification of this varied and

[1] Subject to certain qualifications with regard to the shareholdings of directors. See Bayley and Taylor, *Excess Profits Tax*, p. 47 ff.

[2] That the Government seems, paradoxically, not to be much concerned with this argument is suggested by the following interchange between Sir Irving Albery and the Ministry of Supply official giving evidence (7791–2, Minutes). '. . . Would it be in many cases a fact, or, rather, would one be justified in suggesting in many cases where firms are making big profits and paying Excess Profit Tax, that in fact the Government is to a large extent indirectly paying the salaries or remuneration of these persons?—That gets one into metaphysical reasoning into which I could not possibly attempt to follow you, Sir.'

'Would you not admit that it is possible?—I would rather state it otherwise, if I might, and say that we in the Ministry are indebted to very many firms all over the country for the loan to us of persons who are working night and day and giving us complete satisfaction.'

[3] This principle, moreover, was not admitted in the case of the members of the armed Forces or those who were conscripted for industrial work.

empirical policy was summed up by the Treasury official, in evidence
to the Committee:

> 'The real question is not who pays, and how much is paid, but the real
> question is whether the person still remains connected with the business in the
> sense that he expects to return to it afterwards; and, of course, he does; and nothing
> overcomes that real fact except that we have confidence, and I believe the public
> as a whole have confidence, that while these gentlemen are in the service of the
> Government, they will serve the Government faithfully and steadfastly' (9030,
> Minutes.)

> 'Frankly, I do not think the public interest requires very greatly to be safe-
> guarded in this matter, as long as we get hold of the right kind of people, as
> we do.' (9020, Minutes.)

As regards the issue of salaries alone, this attitude may be reasonable,[1] but on the second, and more general issue, the Treasury and
the Departments tend themselves to become interested parties and
to act in a 'dual capacity' in so far as they are responsible for the
arrangements. The persistence of the Public Accounts Committee
in examining the question of 'dual capacity', and its reiteration in the
latest Report that 'such arrangements will continue to require the
most careful attention by all' is evidence, apart from outside criticism,
that the public is still apprehensive.

An Instance of Dual Capacity in U.S.A.

In this country, as we have mentioned, there has been no authori-
tative investigation of the working of 'dual capacity' as such.
A similar problem was created, however, in the United States
with the appointment of 'dollar-a-year' men to the Administration.
On March 14, 1942, Mr. R. Guthrie made a statement to the
press that his efforts to achieve maximum conversion of the consumer's durable goods industries to war production had not been
supported by his superiors, and on the same day he resigned his
position as Chief of the Textile, Clothing and Leather Goods
Branch of the War Production Board, as did his deputy and executive assistant. Mr. Donald Nelson thereupon asked for an inquiry
by the Senate Special Committee to Investigate the National
Defence Programme (Truman Committee). In the following
paragraphs we summarize the contents and conclusion of the resulting Report. (Senate, 77th Congress, 2nd Session Report 480,
Part 8, June 14th, 1942.)

After Pearl Harbour it became apparent that production of non-
essential civilian goods which consumed 'critical' materials had to

---

[1] But compare the American experience mentioned below.

give way to war production. Such conversion to war production could be accomplished either by voluntary action on the part of industry or by controls exercised by the Government. Primary responsibility for formulating policies regarding the conversion of civilian industry was placed in the Division of Industry Operations, headed by James S. Knowlson. The responsibility was shared by the Bureau of Industry Branches, one of the several bureaux within this Division. Investigation disclosed that widely divergent philosophies existed among officials of the War Production Board as to how the various orders should be used in achieving an effective conversion programme. One philosophy exemplified by Mr. Robert P. Nathan, Chairman of the Planning Committee, held that curtailment of civilian production should be ruthlessly accomplished. In a memorandum dated March 16, 1942, Mr. Nathan stated to the chairman of the War Production Board:

'. . . Complete cessation of durable goods for consumers involves insignificant hardship relative to defeat at the hands of the enemy. Normal production of the durable goods industries must be ruthlessly ceased. The industries will not engage in an all-out conversion until they are absolutely closed. Where a modest output is absolutely essential, then this output should be confined to the smaller plants in the industry . . .'

The other philosophy exemplified by Mr. James S. Knowlson, held that civilian production should be curtailed gradually.

'I believe that the best policy to be followed is that of curtailing production by means of conservation and limitation orders and at the same time crowding war production in factories and progressively forcing conversion without breaking up more than necessary valuable organizations which have taken years to build.'

The philosophy of ruthless curtailment of non-essential civilian production was supported by the Labor Division and the Division of Civilian Supply of the War Production Board. Mr. Guthrie charged that, prior to his resignation on March 14, 1942, civilian production by the consumers' durable goods industries of such items as refrigerators, washing machines, juke boxes, metal furniture, bicycles, electric ranges, and other products with a high metal content was allowed to continue practically unabated. The Report draws attention to the period of inaction between January 5 and March 17, and mentions that a new drive to curtail civilian production followed immediately after Mr. Guthrie's resignation. The charges are then examined in detail, and it appears that in many cases of delay in issuing curtailment orders, and of resistance to curtailment of civilian production, the responsible officials were dollar-a-year men from the industries affected.

After the cases were examined the Committee stated its conclusions. They pointed out that the nature of the request to investigate the cases received from Mr. Nelson made it necessary for them to speak frankly. They criticized especially Mr. Reed, chief of the Bureau of Industry Branches: 'In so far as Mr. Guthrie is critical of Mr. Reed and certain other dollar-a-year men, and of the slowness with which curtailment orders were issued by the Bureau of Industry Branches, the Committee believes that Mr. Guthrie was correct.' The Committee went on to discuss the general issue of dual capacity in the following terms:

'In his testimony before the Committee, Mr. Knowlson expressed the opinion that the employment of dollar-a-year men was a matter of personal integrity of the individual. The Committee does not wholly concur in this conclusion. It believes that the Guthrie case points to the conclusion that certain dollar-a-year men within the Bureau of Industry Branches are unable to divorce themselves from their subconscious gravitation to their own industries. The Committee feels that the evidence introduced in this case confirms its conclusions in its Reports of January 5, 1942. "... The Committee believes that most dollar-a-year and 'without compensation' men are honest and conscientious, and that they would not intentionally favour big business. However, it is not their intentional acts that the Committee fears, but their subconscious tendency, without which they could hardly be human, to judge all matters before them in the light of their past experience and conviction."'

The policy of the War Production Board with regard to 'dual capacity' was set out in administrative order No. 4, Section 2, which provided that: 'No person so engaged (on a dollar-a-year basis) shall make determinations directly affecting the affairs of the firm or company in which he is employed.' The Committee took the view that, in the light of the foregoing facts, this provision should be amended by striking out the words 'firm' and 'company' and substituting the word 'industry'. They stressed that this proposed amendment was in no way as 'a reflection on the integrity of any dollar-a-year men'.

The Committee finally drew attention to the 'paradoxical situation of the Division of Civilian Supply which speaks for the consumer and which would therefore be expected to argue for a larger supply of civilian commodities, but instead was advocating an all-out war effort. The Labor Division, which again might be expected to oppose drastic curtailment in view of the great dislocations in employment, has also been a constant advocate of an accelerated

all-out conversion. On the other hand, the Bureau of Industry
Branches, prior to Mr. Guthrie's resignation and the concerted efforts
of Robert R. Nathan and Mr. Knowlson, consistently advocated a
policy of temporising, moderation and delay.' The Committee
pointed out that 'the Labor Division is largely staffed by persons
from the Labor Movement who are on regular Governmental
salaries, the civilian supply division largely by paid personnel, a
majority being recruited from old line Government agencies, as
contrasted with the Division of Industry operations and its Bureau
of Industry Branches which are largely staffed by dollar-a-year
men from industry.'

Conclusion

How far a parallel may be drawn between the United States
experience and our own is difficult to say. In the British case, for
instance, the 'dual capacity' problem goes somewhat deeper, in
that whole Trade Associations become intimately linked with the
Executive. This structure, according to industries, of part of the
Government Control may indeed go some way towards explaining
the slowness in establishing the Regional Boards, so strongly
advocated by the Select Committee on National Expenditure from
time to time during the last three years. But, despite this and other
differences, the American experience undoubtedly gives support
to the attitude of the Public Accounts Committee in demanding the
most careful attention to the question. Recent official statements in
this country have stressed that the war may be long, and, in addition,
that Government Control must be retained for a considerable
period after the war. With the mobilization of man-power already
at a very high level, further increases in war output can only be
achieved by administrative changes within the Government
economic machinery itself. An exhaustive examination of the
question of 'dual capacity' is, perhaps, one of the most important
preludes to such reorganization.